Templey

COGNITION AND THE
DEVELOPMENT OF LANGUAGE

Cognition and the Development of Language

Editor

JOHN R. HAYES

Carnegie-Mellon University
Pittsburgh, Pennsylvania

Contributors for this Volume

ROGER BROWN, Harvard University
HERBERT H. CLARK, Stanford University
MARGARET DONALDSON, University of Edinburgh
SUSAN ERVIN-TRIPP, University of California, Berkeley
CAMILLE HANLON, Connecticut College
JOHN R. HAYES, Carnegie-Mellon University
CARLOTA S. SMITH, University of Texas
ROGER J. WALES, University of Edinburgh
WILLIAM C. WATT, Carnegie-Mellon University
THOMAS G. BEVER, The Rockefeller University

The fourth of an annual series of symposia
in the area of cognition under the
sponsorship of Carnegie-Mellon University

JOHN WILEY & SONS, INC.
New York   London   Sydney   Toronto

For Barbara

PREFACE

Since 1965, Carnegie-Mellon University has sponsored an annual symposium on topics in the general area of cognition. The first symposium was concerned with problem solving; the second, with concept formation; and the third, with judgment. The fourth symposium – the subject of the present volume – dealt with developmental linguistics, or, more specifically, with the processes by which children acquire language.

The symposium was held on April 11th and 12th, 1968, at Carnegie-Mellon University. Roger Brown was the first speaker of the symposium, presenting the Brown and Hanlon paper on the morning of the 11th. Susan Tripp's presentation completed the morning session. Carlota Smith presented the first paper in the afternoon. She was followed by John Hayes, who read the Hayes and Clark paper. Allen Newell's discussion of these two papers completed the afternoon session. The symposium then adjourned to take up animated conversation during cocktails, dinner, and the remainder of the evening. On the morning of the 12th, Margaret Donaldson presented the Donaldson and Wales paper. Thomas Bever was the final speaker of the morning session. The afternoon session began with Herbert Clark's discussion of the papers presented during the morning. The remainder of this final session of the symposium was devoted to a lively general discussion in which Roger Brown, Herbert Clark, Thomas Bever, William Watt, Allen Newell, Margaret Donaldson, and many others were actively engaged.

The simple recounting of the schedule of events doesn't fully convey the large amount of interaction which actually took place at the symposium. To do so would require us to report a myriad of incidentals such as the questions from the audience which each speaker had to field, the cross-examination of the discussants by the nettled subjects of the discussion, the exchanges over donuts during the coffee break and over Scotch at the cocktail hour, etc. Rather than attempting this task, we will simply assert that the symposium was a time of intense interaction among all of the participants.

The present volume is an outgrowth of the symposium, but it is not a simple reporting of the papers which were presented before the symposium audience. While some of the papers that follow (e.g. Brown and Hanlon, Hayes and Clark) were read in April, 1968 in essentially their present form, others reflect considerable development since that time. Both Tripp's paper and Bever's paper are considerably evolved from the papers which these authors delivered at the symposium. Watt's two papers were not presented at the symposium at all.

vii

Rather, they report post-symposium reflections or issues which the symposium raised. We are confident that the interchange of opinion at the symposium played a role in shaping these post-symposium developments.

This volume, then, is not a collection of papers prepared independently. Rather it is the product of authors who have interacted on the issues discussed here and have been stimulated by their colleagues to modify or to elaborate their points of view.

The introduction was prepared for the convenience of the general reader who wants an introduction to the problem area of the symposium. It includes an elementary discussion of some relevant concepts in modern linguistic theory and the problems involved in applying these concepts to the study of language development. The specialist in the area should start with Chapter 1.

The publication of this volume has been made possible by grants from the Carnegie Corporation and the National Science Foundation.

Special thanks are due a number of individuals whose help has been invaluable. Foremost of these is Mrs. Betty H. Boal, who handled the enormous mass of administrative and secretarial detail involved in conducting the symposium and in preparing this volume with ease and dispatch, and who absorbed much of the worry that would otherwise have been my lot. Herbert and Eve Clark were extremely generous with both time and energy in helping to plan and carry out the symposium. Without them, it would have been very different and much less successful. Sincere thanks are also due Garlie A. Forehand, Roger Brown, and David McNeil for their helpful advice in planning the Conference, and to all of my friends and colleagues who have helped me in this venture.

John R. Hayes

CONTENTS

COGNITION AND THE
DEVELOPMENT OF LANGUAGE

John R. Hayes

Carnegie-Mellon University

COGNITION AND THE DEVELOPMENT
OF LANGUAGE

In this volume, we see the three major traditions in cognitive psychology converging in the effort to understand the development of language. Donaldson and Wales approach the subject with a "Piagetian" orientation, while Hayes and Clark reflect the influence of the information processing point of view. The majority of the papers, however, represent a third tradition — the tradition of modern psycholinguistics. In this introductory article, we have concerned ourselves entirely with the third tradition, because only in this area are the issues either too technical or too recent in origin to have come to the attention of the general reader.

By modern linguistics, we refer to the impressive development in the psychological study of language which have been inspired by the recent advances in the theory of grammar. These new theories have caused excitement among psycholinguists because they have provided new models for language processing, rationalized new experiments, and instilled new hope that difficult old problems might soon be solved.

At the time of the conference (spring 1968), the new grammatical theories had their first impact in psycholinguistics. Some very encouraging first results were obtained and the relevance of grammatical structures to psycholinguistic processes was clearly established (11). It began to appear, however, that the relationships between grammar and psycholinguistics were not as simple as had at first been hoped. Some experiments failed to give the expected results (12, 10, 15, 4, 1), and others gave results which clearly contradicted theoretical predictions (9). Furthermore, penetrating criticisms (8, 2, 3) shook the faith of many psycholinguistists that they really knew how to use the results of the grammarians in making predictions about human language use. This was the situation of theoretical uncertainty which prevailed as our symposium convened.

The purpose of this introductory chapter is to provide the general reader with some background in current psycholinguistic issues. In particular, we will discuss the following points.

1. The modern theories of grammar.
2. The application of these theories in psycholinguistics.

3. The criticisms which have been made of these applications.
The reader who is already familiar with these matters should pass directly to
Chapter 2.

In the modern view, a grammar is a set of rules which serves two functions.
First, it differentiates grammatical sentences from ungrammatical strings of words.
Second, it identifies grammatical relations among the various parts of the sentence.
For example, it identifies such relations as subject of, verb, and direct object of.

There are many different forms which such a set of rules might take. The
form most favored by modern linguists is "generative grammar", so called because
each consists of sets of rules which "generate" sentences in the same way that the
axioms of geometry "generate" theorems. The set of rules in Fig. 1 provides an
example of a grammar which generates a set of English sentences from an initial
symbol "S."

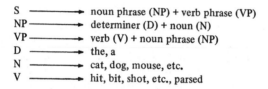

```
S  ───────────▶  noun phrase (NP) + verb phrase (VP)
NP ───────────▶  determiner (D) + noun (N)
VP ───────────▶  verb (V) + noun phrase (NP)
D  ───────────▶  the, a
N  ───────────▶  cat, dog, mouse, etc.
V  ───────────▶  hit, bit, shot, etc., parsed
```

Fig. 1

Rules of this sort are sometimes called "rewrite" rules because they are read "S
may be rewritten as noun phrase plus verb phrase," and so on.

The tree diagram in Fig. 2 shows how the rules may be applied in succession
to generate an English sentence. The part of the diagram above the dashed line is
called the "phrase marker" of the sentence. The lowest line of the phrase marker,
just above the output sentence, is called the "terminal string."

In a generative grammar, the phrase marker provides a complete description
of the grammatical relations among the parts of the sentence. We can determine,
for example, whether a noun is the subject, the direct object, or the indirect
object of a sentence simply by knowing where it fits in the phrase marker.

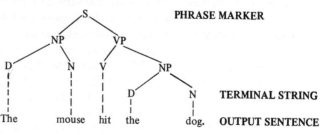

Fig. 2

The important thing about a generative grammar, though, is not its generative form but rather the fact that it is perfectly explicit. Such grammars, unlike traditional grammars, spell out *all* of the rules for deciding whether a sentence is grammatical or not. Nothing is left to the reader's linguistic intuition.

The rules which we illustrated above are of the type called "phrase structure" rules. Chomsky (7) argues that phrase structure rules are not sufficient in themselves to yield an adequate grammar. He claims that a grammar must also contain rules of another type called "transformation" rules.

A transformation rule is a rule which takes the terminal string of a phrase marker and modifies it to produce a new string. Fig. 3 shows in simplified form how a passive transformation rule might modify the terminal string in Figure 2 to yield a passive sentence.

$$D_1 + N_1 + V + D_2 + N_2 \qquad D_2 + N_2 + was + V + by + D_1 + N_1$$

The dog was hit by the mouse.

Fig. 3

Chomsky argues for the inclusion of transformation rules in the grammar because they simplify the description of some common grammatical relations. Consider the four sentences shown in Fig. 4.

S.A.A.D.	The mouse hit the dog.
(Simple Active Affirmative Declarative)	
Passive	The dog was hit by the mouse.
Negative	The mouse did not hit the dog.
Question	Did the mouse hit the dog?

Fig. 4

Clearly these sentences are closely related. If the grammar contained only phrase structure rules, the four sentences would have very different-appearing phrase markers and these would in no way reveal this close relationship. If the grammar contained transformation rules as well, however, all four sentences could be derived (by the application of active, passive, negative, or interrogative transformations) from the *same* underlying phrase marker, such as the one shown in Figure 1. The identical phrase marker would represent the core of sameness among these sentences, and the different transformations which modify it could represent the differences.

Chomsky describes the transformation rules as belonging to the "surface structure" of the grammar because they determine immediately-apparent details such as the word order of the spoken sentence. The phrase structure rules, on the other hand, belong to the "deep structure" because they reflect underlying structural properties. In the example above, we saw that the phase markers reflected underlying similarities among sentences which were superficially quite different. In ambiguous sentences, on the other hand, the phrase markers will reflect underlying differences between sentences which appear superficially identical. The simplified phrase markers in Fig. 5 reveal the structural differences in the two sentences which have the form "They are playing cards."

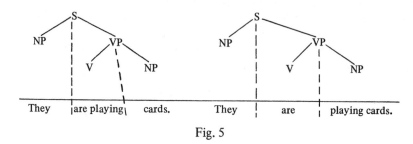

Fig. 5

Important in the discussions to follow is the distinction that modern linguists stress between the concepts of competence and performance. This distinction has been introduced in an effort to clarify the relation between linguistic data and linguistic theory. Unfortunately, it has not been interpreted consistently throughout the literature. Fodor and Garrett (8) point out that there are at least two common interpretations, which we will call Competence/Performance I and Competence/Performance II.

Competence/Performance I is the distinction between the observed linguistic data (a finite set of spoken sentences, grammatical judgments, etc.) and a grammar, inferred from the data, which describes the speaker's ability to generate an infinite number of sentences and to make an infinite number of judgments of the kinds observed. The focus here is on the distinction between that which is observed and the underlying ability or competence which is inferred from the observed data. It is important because the linguist wishes to make it clear that his interest is not in the sample of sentences which he happened to observe but rather in the underlying competence which he infers.

Competence/Performance II is the distinction between an inferred grammar that describes the speaker's "best judgment" on grammatical matters and an inferred performance mechanism that actually produces speech. It is assumed that the performance mechanism will occasionally produce sentences that are ungrammatical in the speaker's best judgment. The focus here is on the difference between the (by definition) error-free grammar and the fallible output mechanism. The distinction is an important one because the linguist wishes to absolve himself of the responsibility of accounting for "errors" which may have been introduced by the performance mechanism and not by the grammar. If limitations of memory or of the ability to articulate rapidly produce errors in speaking, the task of accounting for them seems to fall more naturally to the psychologist than to the linguist.

Competence/Performance II is an extremely tricky distinction and the reader should be wary of it. The problem is that, while it looks like a definition, it in fact implies a theory of the relation between the grammar and the output mechanism. In particular, it implies that sentences are generated by the grammar and transmitted by unspecified (and possibly noisy) processes to the Performance mechanism. Since the theory is a very reasonable one, it can easily pass unnoticed. As Fodor and Garrett (8) warn us, however, it is not the only possible theory, and it may very well be false.

GRAMMAR AS A MODEL OF HUMAN LANGUAGE PROCESSES

Impressed by the success of the new grammatical theories, psycholinguists were anxious to borrow what they could from the grammarians for application to their own problems. So, with an eye to sharing the scientific wealth, psycholinguists launched a vigorous experimental program to find psychological correlates for such grammatical structures as transformations and phrase markers.

One major hypothesis underlies most of these investigations, namely, that the sequence of rules used in the grammatical derivation of a sentence — that is, the derivational history of the sentence — corresponds step by step to the sequence of psychological processes that are executed when a person processes the sentence. In the remainder of this article, we will call this the "correspondence hypothesis."

Brown (5) put forward a form of the correspondence hypothesis in connection with his research on the language of young children. He proposed that the phrase structure grammars which describe the speech of his young subjects be viewed as models for the mechanism which the subjects actually use to generate sentences.

The best evidence for the correspondence hypothesis comes not from studies of phrase structure rules but rather from studies of transformations. The experiment of Miller, McKean, and Slobin on transformations (13) illustrates one rather direct approach to the correspondence problem. Subjects were given two lists of sentences. The second list consisted of grammatical transformations of the sentences in the first list but arranged in different order from those in the first list. The subject's task was to match the sentences with their transformations as fast as he could. In some conditions only one transformation was required. For example, to get from "Joe hit the ball" to "The ball was hit by Joe" requires only the passive transformation. Other conditions required two transformations.

For example, to get from "Joe hit the ball" to "The ball was not hit by Joe" requires both passive and negative transformations. Examples in which no transformations were required were included to provide baseline data. The measure of performance was the time required to match all of the sentences minus the baseline time.

The rationale of the experiment was this: according to the correspondence hypothesis, a longer grammatical derivation implies a longer sequence of psychological processes. A longer sequence of psychological processes, in turn, requires more time. Thus, matching sentences which are two transformations apart should take more time than matching sentences which are one transformation apart.

The results were quite encouraging for the correspondence hypothesis, as Fig. 6 shows.

	Seconds Longer Than Base Search Time
SAAD ⟷ Negative	1.1
SAAD ⟷ Passive	1.4
Passive ⟷ Passive, Negative	1.7
Negative ⟷ Passive, Negative	1.9
SAAD ⟷ Passive, Negative	2.7
Negative ⟷ Passive	3.5

Fig. 6

The double arrow indicates that the results are averaged over both directions of the transformation e.g. passive to negative and negative to passive. Other experiments have confirmed these results in their essential features (12).

Another approach to the correspondence problem is illustrated in the extremely clever experiment of Savin and Perchonoch (14). This experiment tested two hypotheses simultaneously. First it tested the correspondence hypothesis in the following form: Remembering a transformation of many steps requires more memory slots than remembering a transformation of few steps. Second, it tested Savin and Perchonoch's hypothesis that sentences are stored as an underlying SAAD sentence plus transformations. Thus, "The ball was not hit by Joe" would be stored as "Joe hit the ball" plus "negative" plus "passive."

The subject's task in the experiment was to listen to a short sentence followed by a list of unrelated words, and then immediately to repeat as much as he could of what he had just heard. The subjects almost always correctly remembered the sentence and some but not all of the unrelated words. The number of unrelated words remembered, then, was a good measure of how much memory was occupied by the sentence.

There again the results were quite encouraging for the correspondence hypothesis. Subjects remembered an average of 5.27 unrelated words when the sentence was an S.A.A.D. They remembered between 4.30 and 4.78 unrelated words when the sentence required one additional transformation, and they remembered between 3.48 and 4.02 unrelated words when the sentence required two additional transformations.

The two experiments which we have described in detail represent a large number of such studies which have given predominantly positive results. As a whole they have made quite a strong case for the correspondence hypothesis.

CRITICISMS AND SECOND THOUGHTS

Despite the rosy picture painted in the last section, there are some very serious reasons for questioning the truth of the correspondence hypothesis. Fodor and Garrett (8) have listed several of these reasons in their critical review. First and most important is the fact that a number of experiments have given negative results. Two such experiments were the study performed by Mehler (10) and the study performed by Miller and McKean (12). Both experiments concerned verbal auxiliaries like "Joe warned the boy," "Joe had warned the boy," ". . . was warning . . . ," ". . . had been warning . . . ." The Mehler study concerned the speed with which the auxiliaries could be learned and the Miller and McKean study employed the matching procedure described in the last section. Neither experiment showed any effect of derivational complexity.

An experiment which yielded both positive and negative results was performed by Bever, Fodor, Garrett, and Mehler (1). These authors used the Savin and Perchonock techniques described in the last section to measure the amount of memory required to store various sentences. They found the same effect of derivational complexity as did Savin and Perchanock for passives, negatives, questions, etc., but found no such effect for other grammatical relations; for example, "John phoned up the girl" (simple) versus "John phoned the girl up" (more complex).

An experiment which gave results contradicting the predictions of the correspondence hypothesis was performed by Fodor, Jenkins, and Saporta (9). These authors studied the tachistoscopic recognition of sentences which varied in derivational complexity and found clear evidence that more complex sentences were sometimes easier to recognize than less complex ones.

Other reasons mentioned by Fodor and Garrett for doubting the correspondence hypothesis have to do with the nature of the experiments which yielded the positive results. First, these studies have been concerned with a very narrow range of grammatical relations (passives, negatives, questions, emphatics, etc.) Second, the studies have often confounded derivational complexity with other variables such as length and meaning. For example, "John was hit by Joe" is derivationally more complex than "Joe hit John," but it is also longer.

Fodor and Garrett do not claim to have disproved the correspondence hypothesis. They have made a sufficiently strong case, however, to force us to realize that the hypothesis is by no means proved and that the accumulating evidence may eventually prove it false.

We should note at this point that these criticisms of the correspondence hypothesis do not apply to the grammar. If the evidence were to force us to modify or to reject the correspondence hypothesis, it would in no way commit us to a parallel modification or rejection of the grammar. Since grammar is intended as a formal representation of the speaker's linguistic competence, the grammar's merit is judged by its simplicity and its accuracy — that is, by its ability to differentiate correctly the grammatical from the ungrammatical. If it happens also to serve as a model of the psychological processes involved in language processing, then the psychologist can count himself undeservedly fortunate. If it is not a good psychological model, we must not be too surprised, for that is not what it was intended to be.

In this brief review, we have been able to give the reader only the sketchiest account of modern grammar and of the developments in psycholinguistics related to it. For the reader who desires more detailed background information we can only recommended more competent sources such as Chomsky's *Syntactic Structures* (6), the first two very readable chapters of his *Aspects of the Theory of Syntax* (7), and review articles such as that of Miller (11) and that of Fodor and Garrett (8).

A final note on notation: In some of the articles which follow, an asterisk or a question mark placed before a sentence indicates that the sentence is either ungrammatical or that the sentence is of questionable grammaticalness. In the list of sentences below, the asterisk indicates that a. is ungrammatical and the question mark indicates that c. may be grammatical or not (depending on the number of Thomas's being discussed.)

      a.   * Himself spoke to Thomas.

      b.   Himself spoke to himself.

      c.   ? Thomas spoke to Thomas.

REFERENCES

1. Bever, T. G., Fodor, J. A., Garrett, M., and Mehler, J. Transformational operations and stimulus complexity. Unpublished, M.I.T., 1966.

2. Bever, T. G., Fodor, J. A., and Weksel, W. On the acquisiton of syntax: a critique of "contextual generalizations." *Psychological Review,* 1965, 72, 467-482.

3. Bever, T. G., Fodor, J. A., and Weksel, W. Is linguistics empirical? *Psychological Review,* 1965, 72, 493-500.

4. Bever, T. G., and Mehler, J. The coding hypothesis and short-term memory. Unpublished, M.I.T., 1966.

5. Brown, R. *Social Psychology.* New York: Free Press, 1965.

6. Chomsky, N. *Syntactic Structures.* The Hague: Mouton, 1967.

7. Chomsky, N. *Aspects of the Theory of Syntax.* Cambridge: M.I.T., 1965.

8. Fodor, J. A., and Garrett, M. Some reflections on competence and performance. In J. Lyons and R. J. Wales (Eds.), *Psycholinguistic Papers: The Proceedings of the 1966 Edinburg Conference,* 1966, Edinburgh: Edinburgh University Press.

9. Fodor, J. A., Jenkins, J. and Saporta, S. Some tests on implications from transformational grammar. Unpublished, Center for Advanced Study, Palo Alto, California.

10. Mehler, J. Some effects of grammatical transformations on the recall of English sentences. *Journal of Verbal Learning and Verbal Behavior,* 1963, 2, 346-351.

11. Miller, G. A. Some psychological studies of grammar. *American Psychologist,* 1962, 17, 748-762.

12. Miller, G. A. and McKean, K. A chronometric study of some relations between sentences. *Quarterly Journal of Experimental Psychology,* 1964, 16, 297-308.

13. Miller, G. A., McKean, K. and Slobin, D. The exploration of transformations by sentence matching. In G. A. Miller, Some psychological studies of grammar. *American Psychologist,* 1962, 17, 748-762.

14. Savin, H. and Perchonock, E. Grammatical Structure and the immediate recall of English sentences. *Journal of Verbal Learning and Verbal Behavior,* 1965, 4, 348-353.

15. Slobin, D. Grammatical transformations in childhood and adulthood. Unpublished doctoral dissertation, Harvard University, 1963.

CHAPTER 1

Roger Brown and Camille Hanlon *

Harvard University

DERIVATIONAL COMPLEXITY AND ORDER OF ACQUISITION IN CHILD SPEECH †

Fodor and Garrett (1966) have made a useful retrospective analysis of the experiments done in the past five years to test the "psychological reality" of transformational grammar. It seems to them that investigators in this tradition have been testing the proposition that the complexity of derivation of a sentence, measured by the number of optional transformational rules applied, corresponds with the psychological complexity of processing the sentence. The idea that derivational complexity ought to correspond with psychological complexity derives, Fodor and Garrett suggest, from a notion that the grammar of a language might function as an actual component of the psychological programs involved in understanding sentences. The grammar could be a literal component if, at one implausible extreme, a listener assigned a structural description to a received sentence by synthesizing all possible sentences up to the point (some months later) at which he generated a match. The grammar could also be a literal component if, somewhat more plausibly, a received sentence were assigned a structure through the rewriting of less general symbols into more general ones utilizing a set of reversed phrase structure rules in reverse order.

The early experiments on the psychological reality of transformational grammer seemed to provide impressive evidence for a rather direct relation between derivational and psychological complexity. Later on, the grammer moved from beneath these early experiments, changing the character of the derivational complexities involved and calling attention to the fact that changes of meaning were also involved. In the early experiments, complexity was often confounded with sentence length, frequency, and naturalness as well as with meaning; replications controlling for one or more of these variables have generally yielded results in which the importance of derivational complexity seems much reduced.

* *Camille Hanlon is now at Connecticut College.*

† *For the 1968 Carnegie – Mellon Symposium on Cognitive Psychology; this investigation was supported by PHS, Grant HD-02908 from the National Institute of Child Health and Development.*

The early experiments stayed nervously close to a small family of sentences: the simple, active, affirmative, declarative (SAAD), the negative (N), the question (Q), the passive (P), and such compounds of these as passive-negative (PN), negative question (NQ) and so on. Later experiments broadened the range of sentences studied and, at the same time, complicated the idea of derivational complexity. When separable verbs in transformed position (*Put your coat on*) are compared with separable verbs in non-transformed position (*Put on your coat*), we have a difference of one optional, singulary, meaning-preserving transformation. When the negative (*I don't see it*) is compared with a corresponding SAAD (*I see it*), we have a difference in the morphemes generated by the phrase structure rules as well as a difference of obligatory transformations (T*do*) and optional transformations (T*not*). When verbal auxiliaries of varying complexity are compared (for example, *He was going* and *He would have been going*) we have, among other things, a difference in the number of times a particular obligatory transformation must be applied in a single derivation. The only cases in which an increase in derivational complexity is at all reliably associated with an increase in psychological difficulty seem to be those in which meaning is also changed.

The earliest experiments in the tradition (those George Miller did with McKean and Slobin, 1962) undertook to assess complexity by measuring the time required to transform sentences of one type into sentences of another type. Later on, other indices of psychological complexity were utilized: time to understand a sentence well enough to judge it true or false; and ability accurately to recall sentences in a free-recall situation and in a single-sentence, immediate-recall situation with buffer material added to make it possible to measure the storage space required for the sentence. For this range of tasks, it is not surprising that a difference of derivational complexity, even when it is of a single fixed type, does not show a stable relationship to psychological complexity. With respect to an SAAD and its corresponding negative (N) and passive (P), for instance, it takes more time to transform from SAAD to P than from SAAD to N, but the N takes longer to comprehend than does the P.

Fodor and Garrett draw the one general conclusion that it is now possible to draw from this literature: derivational complexity, in the sense of the number of rules applied in deriving a sentence, does not correspond in any simple way to the psychological complexity involved in understanding and retaining the sentence. Fodor and Garrett also accept the one clear implication of their conclusion: transformational grammars are not actual components of the routines by which sentences are processed; the relation between the formalization of the native speaker's presumed competence (the grammar) and his psycholinguistic performances must be less direct than had been imagined. The Fodor and Garrett conclusions are the ones the experimental literature now justifies, but these conclusions are probably not the last or the most interesting statements that will be made about these results. The complex pattern of evidence that now speaks wholly negatively may find an affirmative voice in the future.

In this chapter we propose to ask whether derivational complexity is related to the order in which constructions emerge in child speech. In view of the outcome of the experimental literature on adult processing of sentences, it is necessary to say why any relation of the kind described should be expected in child speech.

We shall, in the first place, limit ourselves to relations of derivational complexity of the type we call "cumulative". When the derivation of a sentence "Y" follows all the rules applied in the derivation of a sentence "X" plus at least one rule not applied in X, then Y has greater cumulative derivational complexity than X $(X < Y)$. The negative passive sentence in English has greater cumulative derivational complexity than both its negative active counterpart and its affirmative passive counterpart. However, the negative passive does not have a similar status with respect to the *yes-no* question, even though more rules are applied in deriving the former than in deriving the latter. The crucial point is that the negative-passive utilizes some rules not utilized in the question, but the question also utilizes at least one rule not utilized in the negative-passive.

Some of the experimenters who have studied adult processing of sentences have explicitly limited their predictions to the cumulative case (for example, Savin and Perchonock, 1965), but others have simply calculated derivational complexity in terms of the number of rules applied, without requiring the rules to stand in a cumulative relation. The difference is, of course, that when psychological complexity is predicted to follow derivational complexity calculated simply in terms of the number of rules, an assumption is made that any one rule equals any other in adding a constant increment of psychological complexity. This assumption is rather improbable, even when the only consideration is the fact that one rule may employ just one of the elementary transformations (deletion, substitution, adjunction, and permutation), while another rule employs several. When psychological complexity is predicted from *cumulative* derivational complexity, there is no assumption that one rule equals another. The suggestion is simply that, when the derivation of one sentence involves everything that the derivation of another involves, plus something more, than the something-more sentence will be more complex psychologically.

But why should derivations, which are more like proofs in geometry than like programs for speaking or understanding, have anything to do with the order in which children begin to understand and speak sentences of various kinds? A generative grammar is intended to represent the linguistic knowledge of the native speaker even though it does not represent the *manner* in which such knowledge is brought to bear in speaking and understanding. The native speaker's feeling for the way that a sentence splits into a hierarchy of sub-wholes is represented by the phrase-structure rules, which also represent his feeling for such relations in a sentence as subject-predicate and verb-object. Transformational rules represent the native speaker's sense that large sets of sentences are related to one another in such a way that, for each member of one set, there is a specific counterpart in the other set. One sometimes has the feeling, as generative grammars undergo their own historical transformations, that the powerful systematic requirements of the whole structure are moving the formalization a long way from "untrained" intuition. Still, through 1965 at least (Chomsky, 1965; Katz and Postal, 1964; Klima, 1964), the main lines of M.I.T. intuition are similar to our own.

Since a grammar formalizes adult knowledge, it is reasonable to hypothesize that the child's knowledge of the structure of his language grows from derivationally less complex grammar to derivationally more complex grammar. The hypothesis is reasonable, but not necessarily true. To test it, we should have good experimental techniques for inquiring about the young child's knowledge of the structure of sentences. Since we do not have such techniques, we propose to infer — with much uncertainty — the points at which grammatical knowledge emerges, from the study of naturally-occurring linguistic interaction between child and mother. We propose to treat the child's production of a construction, in quantity and over a good part of its proper range, together with evidence that he understands the construction when others use it, as *signs* that he has the grammatical knowledge represented formally by the derivation of the construction in the adult grammar. It seems possible to us that the order of emergence of such knowledge would reflect derivational complexity even when the *speed* and *accuracy* with which such knowledge is employed in understanding and retaining sentences does not.

Probably the derivation is no nearer to being a description of performance for the child than it is for the adult. There may be numerous kinds of strategies of speaking and understanding which, from the first, make the relation between grammar and performance an indirect one. We do not mean to suggest otherwise, but rather to suggest that when performance over a range of sentences and situations attains a near-adult level of excellence, the performance may be taken as a sign of the acquisition of knowledge. Between knowledge and the grammar there may be a fairly direct relation.

There is reason to think that for some of the sentence types on which we shall report, it is particularly reasonable to treat performance as a sign of the acquisition of structural knowledge. The total set comprises *yes-no* questions (Q), negatives (N), truncated predicates (Tr), truncated questions (Tr Q), negative questions (NQ), truncated negatives (Tr N), and truncated negative questions (TrNQ). Although there are some knotty derivational problems (discussed at a later point), the sentences in this set may be partially ordered in terms of cumulative derivational complexity. The most complex in the set are the truncated negative questions, which are such negative tags as: *The old man drives well, doesn't he?* One of the more complex types is the truncated question, which is an affirmative tag like: *The old man doesn't drive well, does he?* With respect to these tags in particular, the inference from performance to structural knowledge seems strong.

INTRODUCTION TO TAG QUESTIONS

When he was four years and seven months old, the boy we call Adam produced 32 tags in a two-hour sample of conversation. Included among them were the following sentences.

Ursula's my sister, isn't she?

I made a mistake, didn't I?

Me and Diandros are working, aren't we?

He can't beat me, can he?

He doesn't know what to do, does he?

The truncated questions at the ends of these all seem to have the same semantic; they are requests for confirmation. There is one minor variation. The negative questions appended to affirmative propositions convey a presumption that the answer will be affirmative and, in fact, the most common answers to these were *Yes* and *That's right*. The affirmative questions appended to negative propositions convey a presumption that the answer will be negative, and *No* was the most common answer.

There are simpler mechanisms than the tag question for requesting confirmation. English speakers can use *huh*? or *right*?, and the children we have studied used these forms much earlier than they used the tags. In some languages even the mature tags are, like *huh*?, forms that do not vary with the structure of the sentences to which they are appended; the Germans can always ask *nicht wahr*? and the French *n'est-ce pas*? We would suppose that forms like these could be learned as fixed routines, but mature English tags cannot be. Adam requests confirmation with *isn't she*?, *didn't I*?, *does he*?, *aren't you*? and in many other ways. This variation of form occurs with no appreciable variation of semantic, but it is not a free variation; the form of the tag is fixed by the structure of the declarative.

Suppose Adam gave us the sentence *Me and Diandros are working*, without the question, and, on a different occasion, as an independent utterance, the question *Aren't we*? and we wondered how much the child knew of the structure of these sentences. Did he know that the subject of the first was *Me and Diandros* and that this subject was plural in number? Did he know that his second sentence could be derived from a declarative counterpart

(*We aren't*) by interchanging the subject and the first member of the auxiliary (plus *n't*)? Did he know, that this second sentence could be derived from an affirmative counterpart (*Are we?*) by adjunction of the negative morpheme? In the record itself there would be nothing to go on but the fact that the sentences were produced. Even if there had been time to prepare experimental tests to inquire about Adam's knowledge, it is doubtful that such tests could have been invented. Suppose that we imagine the situation changed to the actual case in which the two sentences were produced as one, as the tag question *Me and Diandros are working, aren't we?* The fact of such production now offers fairly powerful evidence of grammatical knowledge.

The negative truncated question in the tag is a complex derivative of the antecedent declarative. It may be said loosely that the question is derived by the following processes: pronominalization, negation, interrogation, and truncation. Still speaking loosely, the processes go like this. As it is the subject that must be pronominalized, the child must know that *Me and Diandros* constitutes the subject. This is the kind of knowledge one would represent in the tree structure of the sentence by showing that *Me and Diandros* constitutes an "NP" directly dominated by "S." Clearly, the subject of a sentence cannot, in the few examples from Adam — let alone in English generally — be identified with any surface feature of the sentence such as the first word in the sentence or the first noun. To select the correct pronoun *we*, it is necessary to know that the subject is plural and inclusive of the speaker. In other cases it would be necessary to know the gender of the subject. From *Me and Diandros are working*, by the process of pronominalization alone, the sentence *We are working* is obtained, and that is still a long way from the ultimate tag form.

Negation can be roughly said to adjoin *n't* to the first member of the auxiliary. To do that Adam must have had the auxiliary properly bracketed and labeled. In deriving *didn't I?* from *I made a mistake*, Adam seems to have known something like the fact that the first member of the auxiliary is the morpheme "Past," which requires *do* support in the absence of any other auxiliary. By adding negation to pronominalization, we arrive at *We aren't working*.

Interrogation interchanges the first member of the auxiliary plus *n't* with the subject, yielding *Aren't we working?* Predicate truncation deletes all of the predicate except the first member of the auxiliary plus *n't*, and so at length we obtain the truncated negative question *Aren't we?* This loose derivation is summarized as follows.

Sentence	*Grammatical Change*
Me and Diandros are working.	Pronominalization
We are working.	Negation
We aren't working.	Interrogation
Aren't we working?	Truncation
Aren't we?	

The structure of English sentences is so obvious to the native speaker that he can scarcely realize how difficult it would be to derive truncated questions from declaratives without knowledge of sentence structure. Consider the following numerical parallel in which the string of digits following the comma can be derived from the string before the comma by using a constant function.

321118596,6210

95617,5227

22421391 28746,6224

34229997,____?

Is there anyone who feels able to complete the last utterance? The rules are as follows.

1. Consider the subject to be the first set of digits summing to 5 or more. To pronominalize, if the subject is exactly 5, double it. If more than 5, triple it. Place after the comma and follow it with the rest of the antecedent string.

2. The first member of the auxiliary is the first set of numbers following the subject that sums to 3 or more. To adjoin the negative, insert the number "2" after the first member of the auxiliary.

3. The interrogative is created by interchanging the subject and the first member of the auxiliary together with the negative "2." If the first member of the auxiliary sums to exactly 3, double it (for *do* support).

4. Truncate the predicate by deleting the string after the subject.

So the step-by-step derivation of the last tag goes like this.

Sentence	Grammatical Change
34229997	Pronominalization
21229997	Negation
212229997	Interrogation
222219997	Truncation
22221	

It is difficult to see how Adam could produce the variety of tags that he does if he did not have all the structural knowledge described, which is a large part of the knowledge formally represented in the derivation of tags. To be sure, one could argue that, since the form of the truncated question is fixed by the form of the declarative, Adam could have learned all his 32 sentences in the one sample as fixed routines. However, the unlikeliness of this possibility becomes increasingly evident as more and more tags are studied, practically all of which are one-time occurrences.

For both negative and affirmative tags, the fact of production is strong evidence of grammatical knowledge. For the other kinds of sentences to be considered, one cannot feel as sure that correct production and evidence of comprehension are signs that the child has all the knowledge represented by the derivations in the adult grammar. The evidence is unevenly strong across sentence types and situations. A truncated negative declarative (TrN) like I *can't* produced in response to a parental sentence like *You can lift it* strongly suggests knowledge of the negation and truncation rules as well as correct bracketing of the verbal auxiliary. With respect to *yes-no* questions (Q), one can get fairly convincing evidence of comprehension, since these sentences are produced by others and tend to elicit responses from the child. For a full discussion of all the evidence, readers should consult the full grammatical discussions prepared by the project. In this paper we propose to simply present production figures for sentence types, since that is the aspect of the evidence that is easily made public. For all the sentence types, there is evidence of comprehension which appears in advance of production.

SENTENCE DERIVATIONS AND THE ORDER OF COMPLEXITY

We will start with an overview of the loose grammatical conception guiding the study, and then introduce formal rules as refinements of this conception.

An Overview

The kinds of sentences to be considered are as follows.

1. Simple, active, affirmative, declarative (SAAD). For example, *We had a ball.*
2. Simple, active, affirmative, interrogative (Q). For example, *Did we have a ball?*
3. Simple, active, negative, declarative (N). For example, *We didn't have a ball.*
4. Simple, active, affirmative, declarative, truncated (Tr). For example, *We did.*
5. Simple, active, negative, interrogative (NQ). For example, *Didn't we have a ball?*
6. Simple, active, affirmative, interrogative, truncated (Tr Q). For example, *Did we?* (Also used as affirmative tag.)

7. Simple, active, negative, declarative, truncated (TrN). For example, *We didn't*.

8. Simple, active, negative, interrogative, truncated (TrNQ). For example, *Didn't we?* (Also used as negative tag.)

Examining the above scheme a reader may wonder why we did not rotate sentence types in all the slots, including, for instance, passives as well as actives and complex sentences as well as simple ones. In the case of passives, the answer is that well-formed passives, not truncated but complete with agents, had only just begun to appear at the point where our records presently terminate — about age five. In the case of complex sentences, which include the various kinds of embeddings and conjoinings, the problems of analysis and interpretation are so complicated as to call for an independent study.

The cumulative derivational complexity of the seven types of sentences named and exemplified above works out roughly like this.

SAAD $<$ Q $<$ NQ,TrQ,TrNQ	4 predictions
SAAD $<$ N $<$ NQ,TrN,TrNQ	4 predictions
SAAD $<$ Tr $<$ TrQ,TrN,TrNQ	4 predictions
SAAD $<$ NQ $<$ TrNQ	2 predictions
SAAD $<$ TrQ $<$ TrNQ	2 predictions
SAAD $<$ TrN $<$ TrNQ	2 predictions
SADD $<$ TrNQ	1 prediction

The notation "A $<$ B" means that A is less derivationally complex than B. Sentence symbols separated by commas (for example, NQ,TrQ,TrNQ) are not ordered relative to one another in this writing. In the listing above, each independent prediction is listed only once; since we have Q $<$ NQ in the first line, we do not repeat it in the fourth. It should be noted that the sentence types are not completely ordered in terms of derivational complexity; we do not have an order for the pairs Q and N, Q and Tr, N and Tr; Q and TrN, N and TrQ, Tr and NQ; and NQ and TrQ, NQ and TrN, TrQ and TrN. If the facts of partial ordering are kept in mind, then the following representation of the overall order is helpful.

Q NQ

SAAD N TrQ TrNQ

Tr TrN

Why should the complexity order be as we have represented it? SAAD sentences are not, of course, uniform in the number of rules applied in their derivations; there may be from one to four auxilaries, and the more there are, the more often the obligatory affixation transformation must be applied. Likewise, a noun phrase may have one or several determiners, and predetermi- ners as well; an SAAD may have none, one, or many adverbials; an SAAD may involve complex selection rules and transformations to accomplish number agreement and it may not. However, for each SAAD there is a Q counterpart which employs all the rules of the SAAD plus the rule that transposes subject and elements of the auxiliary. Similarly, for each SAAD there is a negative counterpart which applies the rules of the SAAD; the rule that accomplishes preverbal placement of the negative morpheme; and sometimes also the rule contracting the negative. Finally, for each SAAD there is a truncated counterpart which may apply all the rules of the SAAD — if it is derived from a specific full declarative — plus the rule which cuts the predicate back to the first member of the auxiliary. It can then be said that Q, N, and Tr, though not in that order, are all more complex than SAAD. Thus, the increments of derivational complexity are clearly not uniform. The added rules are all different, and negatives often involve contraction when the other types do not. In addition, there is a difference of meaning between SAAD and either N or Q but not between SAAD and Tr. The deep structures of N and Q contain morphemes missing from otherwise corresponding SAAD sentences.

This is perhaps the right point at which to call attention to an important difference between the naturalistic study of child speech and the experimental studies mentioned at the start of this paper. In an experimental study of derivational complexity, sentences that are exact counterparts of one another can be compared; for example, *The boy hit the ball*; *Did the boy hit the ball?*; *The boy didn't hit the ball*; etc. To simplify our above description of the sentence types that concern us, we carried a single example *We had a ball* across all types. In fact, however, only one of these sentences actually came within the empirical compass of the study; the little girl we call Sarah did produce the tag *We had a ball, didn't we?* It is not possible to study exact counterpart sentences in a naturalistic study in the way that one can in an experiment. We shall be comparing frequencies of sentences of any one type (for example, negatives) with frequencies of entirely different specific sentences of other types. We must, therefore, make the large assumption that the population of sentences of one type (such as negatives), with respect to all grammatical features except those defining the type, is of the same average complexity as the population of sentences of each other type.

The sentence types N, Q, and Tr are more complex than SAAD sentences because each of the first three types adds at least one new rule, not only to particular sentences, but also to the grammar as a whole. The rules are Tnot, Tq, and Ttr. According to our rough general conception, the remaining differences of complexity arise from the application of additional rules in particular derivations but not from the addition of new rules to the grammar. We think of NQ, TrQ, and TrN as combinations of two rules employed one at a time in N, Q, and Tr. We think of TrNQ as a triadic combination from the same set. There is then a qualitative difference between the predictions of the first level (comparing Q, N, and Tr with SAAD) and those of the later levels, and it will be interesting to see if this qualitative line can be seen in the data. In addition, some of the comparisons of the later levels, like some of those on the first level, involve semantic changes (for example, Q and NQ), whereas others do not (Q and TrQ).

Formal Rules and Problems

In general, our discussion of rules follows the assumptions of the transformational generative grammar of 1965 and draws upon such works as those at Chomsky, 1965; Katz and Postal, 1964; and Klima, 1964. We are working at the level of what might be called the second generation version of transformational grammar, which differs from the first generation version (Chomsky, 1957) in many respects; in the 1965 version rules of semantic interpretation are conceived to apply only to underlying P-markers (deep structures) and transformations are written so as not to change meaning; selection restrictions are represented by the expansion of complex symbols and the use of syntactic features; and so forth. Of course, the grammatical frontier has moved on since 1965. A lag of about five years seems always to exist between linguistics and psycholinguistics. In so laborious an undertaking as the longitudinal study of child speech it is inevitable.

Unfortunately, there is considerable disagreement even among transformationalists publishing around 1965 and, still more unluckily, nowhere in the writings of this period can we find a consistent and fully satisfactory set of rules covering the range of constructions with which we are concerned. We therefore offer, in Table 1.1, a set of imperfect rules based on what we have learned from what has been written and on what we have been able to work out on our own.

The rules of Table 1.1 do not constitute a full set of rules required to derive the types of sentences with which we are concerned, and the sample derivations of Tables 1.2, 1.3, and 1.4 are not complete derivations, but only the steps utilizing the rules of Table 1.1 We have not included any phrase structure rules, any of the steps in complex symbol expansion, or any morphophonemic rules. We have not included such transformational rules as accomplish number agreement in predicate nominatives, and NP movement for separable verbs, since these involve

TABLE 1.1   Transformational Rules for Negation, Interrogation,
Truncation, and Tagging

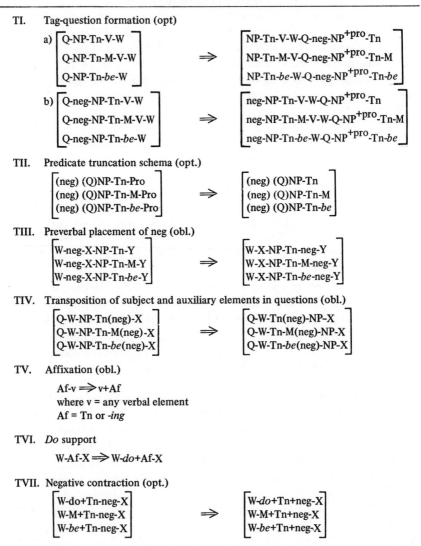

TI.   Tag-question formation (opt)

a) $\begin{bmatrix} \text{Q-NP-Tn-V-W} \\ \text{Q-NP-Tn-M-V-W} \\ \text{Q-NP-Tn-}be\text{-W} \end{bmatrix} \Rightarrow \begin{bmatrix} \text{NP-Tn-V-W-Q-neg-NP}^{+pro}\text{-Tn} \\ \text{NP-Tn-M-V-Q-neg-NP}^{+pro}\text{-Tn-M} \\ \text{NP-Tn-}be\text{-W-Q-neg-NP}^{+pro}\text{-Tn-}be \end{bmatrix}$

b) $\begin{bmatrix} \text{Q-neg-NP-Tn-V-W} \\ \text{Q-neg-NP-Tn-M-V-W} \\ \text{Q-neg-NP-Tn-}be\text{-W} \end{bmatrix} \Rightarrow \begin{bmatrix} \text{neg-NP-Tn-V-W-Q-NP}^{+pro}\text{-Tn} \\ \text{neg-NP-Tn-M-V-W-Q-NP}^{+pro}\text{-Tn-M} \\ \text{neg-NP-Tn-}be\text{-W-Q-NP}^{+pro}\text{-Tn-}be \end{bmatrix}$

TII.   Predicate truncation schema (opt.)

$\begin{bmatrix} \text{(neg) (Q)NP-Tn-Pro} \\ \text{(neg) (Q)NP-Tn-M-Pro} \\ \text{(neg) (Q)NP-Tn-}be\text{-Pro} \end{bmatrix} \Rightarrow \begin{bmatrix} \text{(neg) (Q)NP-Tn} \\ \text{(neg) (Q)NP-Tn-M} \\ \text{(neg) (Q)NP-Tn-}be \end{bmatrix}$

TIII.   Preverbal placement of neg (obl.)

$\begin{bmatrix} \text{W-neg-X-NP-Tn-Y} \\ \text{W-neg-X-NP-Tn-M-Y} \\ \text{W-neg-X-NP-Tn-}be\text{-Y} \end{bmatrix} \Rightarrow \begin{bmatrix} \text{W-X-NP-Tn-neg-Y} \\ \text{W-X-NP-Tn-M-neg-Y} \\ \text{W-X-NP-Tn-}be\text{-neg-Y} \end{bmatrix}$

TIV.   Transposition of subject and auxiliary elements in questions (obl.)

$\begin{bmatrix} \text{Q-W-NP-Tn(neg)-X} \\ \text{Q-W-NP-Tn-M(neg)-X} \\ \text{Q-W-NP-Tn-}be\text{(neg)-X} \end{bmatrix} \Rightarrow \begin{bmatrix} \text{Q-W-Tn(neg)-NP-X} \\ \text{Q-W-Tn-M(neg)-NP-X} \\ \text{Q-W-Tn-}be\text{(neg)-NP-X} \end{bmatrix}$

TV.   Affixation (obl.)

Af-v $\Rightarrow$ v+Af
where v = any verbal element
Af = Tn or *-ing*

TVI.   *Do* support

W-Af-X $\Rightarrow$ W-*do*+Af-X

TVII.   Negative contraction (opt.)

$\begin{bmatrix} \text{W-do+Tn-neg-X} \\ \text{W-M+Tn-neg-X} \\ \text{W-}be\text{+Tn-neg-X} \end{bmatrix} \Rightarrow \begin{bmatrix} \text{W-}do\text{+Tn+neg-X} \\ \text{W-M+Tn+neg-X} \\ \text{W-}be\text{+Tn+neg-X} \end{bmatrix}$

grammatical features expected to vary from sentence to sentence but not to differentiate among the types involved in our analysis. For the most part, Table 1.1 lists just those transformational rules that account for differences of derivational complexity among sentence types. The single exception is the pair of rules, TV "affixation" and TVI "*do* support." The second of these rules is not applied in the derivation of SAAD sentences, but is applied in Q, N, and Tr sentences whenever the only auxiliary is "tense." So TVI is a rule that is added to the child's grammar with Q, N, and Tr. Nevertheless, it does not strictly operate so as to make one sentence more complex, cumulatively, than another, because whenever it is not applied, TV must be. One or the other rule is obligatory in every sentence, but SAAD sentences use only TV. We have included TVI because, through its association with the more complex sentences, it has a certain interest for us. Inclusion of TVI makes it desirable also to include TV, so that the derivations of Tables 1.2, 1.3, and 1.4 may all be complete at the same level and so that we shall not mistake the application of TVI, in all sentences except the SAAD, for a strict increment to cumulative complexity.

Looking first at the derivations of Table 1.2, we see that Q, N, and Tr all differ from SAAD in that they use TVI "do support" where SAAD uses TV "affixation." The sentences Q, N, and Tr also all differ from SAAD in that each applies a single additional rule. The respective rules are: TIV "transposition of subject and auxiliary elements" for Q; TIII "preverbal placement of neg" for N; and TII "predicate truncation" for Tr. The N sentence, in addition, applies TVII "negative contraction." Finally, Q and N differ from SAAD in their deep structures by virtue of the fact that they include, respectively, the morphemes "Q" and "neg." It is because these morphemes are in the deep structures that the rules TIV and TIII are obligatory (obl.) rather than optional (opt.) as they were in Chomsky's 1957 treatment.

It is worth pausing at this point to notice some profound similarities linking Q, N, and Tr. If you examine the rules TII, TIII, and TIV, you will see that they all rely on the same organization of the auxiliary. All three rules organize the first member of the auxiliary as "tense" (Tn) alone or as "tense" and "modal" (M) or as "tense" and "*be*" (either as copula or auxiliary). TIV transposes this element; TIII places "neg" just after this element; and TII deletes the predicate just back to this element. Closely related to the organization of the auxiliary is the addition of the rule for "Do support", which is applied in just those cases where the auxiliary element consists of "tense" (Tn) alone. We might expect the learning of Q, N, and Tr to occur at about the same time, since a large part of the structure involved is common to all three. We shall see that that is the case. It also seems to be the case that other sentences that utilize this organization of the auxiliary (*wh* questions and emphatics, for instance) appear at about the same time.

TABLE 1.2 Derivations of SAAD, Q, N, and Tr

String (*We had a ball*)	Rule
we-Pas-have-a-ball	TV
we-have+Pas-a-ball	morpho-phonemics
we-had-a-ball	
String (*Did we have a ball?*)	**Rule**
Q-we-Pas-have-a-ball	TIV
Q-Pas-we-have-a-ball	TVI
Q-do+Pas-we-have-a-ball	morpho-phonemics
did-we-have-a-ball- ?	
String (*We didn't have a ball*)	**Rule**
neg-we-Pas-have-a-ball	TIII
we-Pas-neg-have-a-ball	TVI
we-do+Pas-neg-have-a-ball	TVII
we-do+Pas+neg-have-a-ball	morpho-phonemics
we-didn't-have-a-ball	
String (*We did*)	**Rule**
we-Pas-Pro	TII
we-Pas	TVI
we-do+Pas	morpho-phonemics
we-did	

The rule for predicate truncation, TII, involves various problems, the solution of which is beyond us. In our overview we spoke of predicate truncations (or ellipses) as if they were derived from specific sentences containing complete predicates. This is certainly the impression one gets from the study of such sentences in actual discourse. In a typical sort of exchange, a parent says *Eat your peas* and the child responds *I will*. One is inclined to derive *I will* from *I will (eat my peas)*, since that is certainly what the truncation means. To do so, however, involves violating what Katz and Postal call the requirement of "unique recoverability." From *I will* and a truncation rule one cannot recover the source *I will eat my peas*. It is perhaps possible to satisfy unique recoverability by deriving *I will*, not from a specific full predicate, but from a dummy predicate like *I will do something*. We have suggested such a solution in TII by using "PRO" to stand for such a dummy predicate. However, TII involves, in detail, problems we have not solved. For instance, one might hear an exchange like this. Parent: *It is a dog*; child: *It is*. The dummy in this case would have to stand for an NP, and so TII as written, with a single symbol "PRO," does not attain unique recoverability. For these reasons we have called TII a "schema" rather than a "rule." By this we mean to say that while it represents certain aspects of the facts it is not a genuine algorithm as presently formulated. There are additional problems with this rule that arise in connection with tags.

Table 1.3 presents sample derivations for the paired operations NQ, TrN, and TrQ. Let us defer for two paragraphs the special problems created by tags. We see that the first sentence (NQ) involves all the rules involved in N (III, VI, and VII) plus one that is not (IV), and also all the rules involved in Q (IV and VI) plus two that are not (III and VII). The second sentence (TrN) includes all the rules of Tr (II and VI) plus two others (III and VII), as well as all the rules of N (III, VI, and VII) plus one other (II). The third sentence (TrQ not a tag) includes the rules of Tr (II and VI) plus one other (IV), and the rules of Q (IV and VI) plus one other (II). All of this confirms our overview.

In two minor respects the derivations of Table 1.3 raise problems. The semantic of a NQ like *Didn't we have a ball?* does not really seem to include a negative meaning as the morpheme "neg" suggests it does. It seems to us that we use negative questions when the probabilities of *yes* and *no* answers are not equal, when the presumption is that the answer will be *yes*. The meaning of these questions does not then seem to be a compound of the meanings associated with the morphemes "neg" and "Q" though that is what the underlying string suggests. The second problem is one in connection with adult speech only. The rules of Table 1.1 will generate a negative question with a contraction, such as *Didn't we have a ball?*, but will not generate an uncontracted NQ, *Did we not have a ball?* However, while adults would judge this latter sentence to be grammatical, the uncontracted NQ is not found at all in the speech of the children we have studied.

Finally, there is the derivation of the tags themselves, the affirmative tag in Table 1.3 and the negative in Table 1.4. Our TI "Tag Question Formation" is modeled after a rule of Klima's (1964). The rule works like this. The tag question is derived by optional transformation from underlying phrase markers which either contain "Q" alone or else both "Q" and "neg." In the former case, TI leaves the first proposition affirmative but adds "neg" to the question and so the tag question becomes a negative one. In the latter case TI retains "neg" for the first proposition but the tag question itself is affirmative. By these means Klima represents the fact that when the first proposition is affirmative (*We had a ball*), the question must be negative (*didn't we?*), whereas when the

TABLE 1.3 Derivation of Paired Operations from the Set:
Interrogation, Negation, Truncation, and Tag

String (*Didn't we have a ball?*)	Rule
neg-Q-we-Pas-have-a-ball	TIII
Q-we-Pas-neg-have-a-ball	TIV
Q-Pas-neg-we-have-a-ball	TVI
Q-do+Pas-neg-we-have-a-ball	TVII
Q-do+Pas+neg-we-have-a-ball	morpho-phonemics
didn't-we-have-a-ball-?	

String (*We didn't*)	Rule
neg-we-Pas-Pro	TII
neg-we-Pas	TIII
we-Pas-neg	TVI
we-do+Pas-neg	TVII
we-do+Pas+neg	morpho-phonemics
we-didn't	

String (*Did we?*). Not a tag.	Rule
Q-we-Pas-Pro	TII
Q-we-Pas	TIV
Q-Pas-we	TVI
Q-do+Pas-we	morpho-phonemics
did-we- ?	

String (*We didn't have a ball, did we?*) Tag.	Rule
Q-neg-we-Pas-have-a-ball	TI
neg-we-Pas-have-a-ball-Q-we-Pas	TIII
we-Pas-neg-have-a-ball-Q-we-Pas	TIV
we-Pas-neg-have-a-ball-Q-Pas-we	TVI
we-do+Pas-neg-have-a-ball-Q-Pas-we	TVI
we-do+Pas-neg-have-a-ball-Q-do+Pas-we	TVII
we-do+Pas+neg-have-a-ball-Q-do+Pas-we	morpho-phonemics
we-didn't-have-a-ball-did-we-?	

TABLE 1.4 Derivation of Triples from the Set: Interrogation,
Negation, Truncation, and Tag

String (*Didn't we?*) Not a tag.	Rule
Q-neg-we-Pas-Pro	TII
Q-neg-we-Pas	TIII
Q-we-Pas-neg	TIV
Q-Pas-neg-we	TVI
Q-do+Pas-neg-we	TVII
Q-do+Pas+neg-we	morpho-phonemics
didn't-we- ?	

String (*We had a ball, didn't we?*) Tag.	Rule
Q-we-Pas-have-a-ball	TI
we-Pas-have-a-ball-Q-neg-we-Pas	TIII
we-Pas-have-a-ball-Q-we-Pas-neg	TIV
we-Pas-have-a-ball-Q-Pas-neg-we	TV
we-have+Pas-a-ball-Q-Pas-neg-we	TVI
we-have+Pas-a-ball-Q-do+Pas-neg-we	TVII
we-have+Pas-a-ball-Q-do+Pas+neg-we	morpho-phonemics
we-had-a-ball-didn't-we- ?	

first proposition is negative (*We didn't have a ball*), the question must be affirmative (*did we?*). These first aspects of Klima's rule also say, in effect, that the tag question *We had a ball, didn't we?* is equivalent in meaning to the simple *yes-no* question *Did we have a ball?*, since both have an underlying phrase marker containing "Q" but not "neg." That seems to us an incorrect claim, since the simple *yes-no* question does not presuppose the answer *yes* as does the NQ. Klima's rule, similarly, says that the tag question *We didn't have a ball, did we?* is equivalent in meaning to the NQ *Didn't we have a ball?*, since both have "neg" and "Q" in the underlying phrase marker. This claim, too, seems to be incorrect, since the affirmative tag presupposes the answer *no*, whereas the NQ presupposes *yes*.

To continue with Rule T1, it provides a basis for pronominalization by adding the marker "+pro" to the subject NP. Morpho-phonemic rules would complete the job of pronominalization. In the children's tags we find that pronominalization is not an essential or even usual aspect of tag formation. It often happens, as in *We had a ball, didn't we?*, that the subject NP of the first proposition is already a pronoun. The rule could be easily modified to make pronominalization optional.

Rule T1 does not truncate the predicate in the underlying phrase-marker but rather repeats it, just through the first auxiliary. Roughly speaking, it changes *We had a ball* into *We had a ball we did*. Consequently, when tags are derived using Rule T1, no use at all is made of Rule TII "Predicate truncation", and so the tags in Tables 1.3 and 1.4 are not combinations, respectively, of Tr and Q (Table 1.3) and Tr, Q, and N (Table 1.4). That, however, is the way we represented them in our advance overview.

The problem is complicated further by the fact that we do have, from the children, instances of TrQ not used as a tag (Table 1.3) and also of TrNQ not used as a tag (Table 1.4). They arise in interchanges like the following.

Mother: *We had a ball.*   Child: *Did we?*

Mother: *We didn't have a ball.*   Child: *Didn't we?*

Notice that a sentence corresponding to the first proposition of a tag is here produced *by another speaker*. Notice, further, that the questions, sounding like echoes, match the antecedent sentences in that an affirmative antecedent elicits an affirmative question and a negative antecedent elicits a negative question. When antecedent and echo are bound together in a tag question, there is an affirmative-negative or negative-affirmative switch. So these echo instances of TrQ and TrNQ do not seem to be the same as proper tags. The echoes are what the tags were represented to be in the overview — combinations of the basic operations Tr, Q, and N.

There is, we think, some possibility that tags should be represented in the way that echoes are, as combinations including truncation. Our Rule T1, modelled after Klima's, is, we have seen, faulty in semantic respects. Furthermore, the effect that Rule T1 accomplishes by repeating the underlying predicate through the first auxiliary is essentially the same as the effect accomplished in TII by truncating the predicate back to the first auxiliary. Since a rule like TII is, in any case, needed for truncations that are not tags, we would have a simple grammar if we could derive both kinds of sentences with TII. The problem is, how to do it? Presumably we would have to consider the tag to be just the final appended question, *did we* or *didn't we*, and not the complete sentences, *We didn't have a ball, did we?* and *We had a ball, didn't we?* There is something to be said for this approach, since in actual discourse the child sometimes breaks the two sentences with an utterance-final intonation. There are even interruptions like the following.

> Child: *We had a ball.*
>
> Child: *Didn't we?*
>
> Mother: *Yep.*

However, if the tag is identified with the question alone, then the perfectly regular affirmative-negative and negative-affirmative switches fall outside the scope of a sentence-generating grammar. It is possible that the switches should fall outside the grammar, that they might better be captured by a rule of discourse. We are just not sure.

What difference do the formal rules make in the ordering of the constructions (presented in the overview) for cumulative derivational complexity? If we substitute the echo forms of TrQ and TrNO for those called tags in the overview, then the ordering there is still exactly correct. Recall that Tr Q and TrNQ have the following relations (across all the lines in which they appear).

$$\text{SAAD,Tr,Q} < \text{TrQ} < \text{TrNQ}$$

$$\text{SAAD,TrQ,N,TrQ} < \text{TrNQ}$$

These relations are preserved by the derivations of Tables 1.2, 1.3 and 1.4. TrQ involves all the rules of Tr (II and VI) plus one more (IV), as well as the rules of Q (IV and VI) plus one more (II). TrNQ involves the rules of Tr (II and VI) plus one peculiar to Q (IV) plus two peculiar to N (III and VII).

How is the situation changed with respect to tags which, using Rule T1, are not TrQ and TrNQ but rather TgQ and TgNQ? There is no change at all unless a relation involves both a Tr and either TgQ or TgNQ. The following, for example, still hold.

$$\text{Q} < \text{TgQ, TgNQ}$$

$$\text{N} < \text{TgQ, TgNQ}$$

$$\text{NQ} < \text{TgNQ}$$

$$\text{TgQ} < \text{TgNQ}$$

All of these (and others) hold because when tags are derived with TI rather than with the truncation rule TII, the derivations are in other respects the same. Tags derived with TI still use the Q and the N operations. Consequently TgQ and TgNQ relate to SAAD, Q, N, NQ, and one another exactly as TrQ and TrNQ do. Changes in ordering are limited to the following relations.

> Tr cannot be ordered relative to TgQ and TgNQ.
>
> TrN cannot be ordered relative to TgNQ.

These three pairs cannot be ordered within a pair because each member involves something the other does not — either Tr or Tg. Of the original 19 predictions, then, we lose 3. If these 3 should nevertheless be confirmed for tags, that might be taken as evidence that the tags should, after all, not be derived with Rule TI but rather with the truncation rule (TII).

RESULTS

The data come from our longitudinal study of the development of grammar during the preschool years in three children whom we call Adam, Eve, and Sarah. For this study we have transcribed at least two hours of conversation each month between mother and child at home; often we have transcribed more conversation and also done small experiments on one or another aspect of the child's sentence comprehension or production. The principal goal of the study is to describe the growth of grammatical knowledge in the form of a succession of generative grammars.

The developmental period on which our work has focused is defined in terms of a range of values on mean utterance length, which is quite a good index of development for the first few years after the child begins to speak. The period begins when the mean value is 1.75 morphemes and the longest utterance is 5 morphemes; it ends when the mean is 4.00 and the longest utterance 13 morphemes. Grammars are being written for 5 points (designated I, II, III, IV, and V) which are evenly spaced across the total interval. At each point we draw a sample of 700 utterances from each child and the grammars are written from these samples. The first versions of Grammars I, II, III, and V, but not yet of IV, have been written for all three children. For special studies of negatives, wh questions, inflections, forms coding aspects of time, and so forth, we and our associates have used more of the data than is included in I-V. This paper reports another such study.

The main data to be reported are frequencies of the constructions with which we are concerned at levels I through V. We have not counted SAAD sentences because simple forms of these are present in good quantity from I on. For negatives (N) and questions (Q) we have simply taken the figures from the 700-utterance grammar samples. For the remaining constructions (Tr, TrN, TrQ, NQ, and TrNQ), it is necessary to take larger samples for the reason that the base output rates for these are much lower than for N and Q in adult speech as well as in child speech. Samples of 700 utterances would yield rather unreliable figures. The size of the samples for the less frequent constructions is 2100 utterances. We simply added on to the basic 700-utterance grammar samples, the next 1400 utterances. For Eve at IV and V this procedure ran into difficulty; Eve developed very much more rapidly than Adam and Sarah and her IV and V were so close together that we were able to obtain for IV only about 1500 utterances. The difficulty at V is that Eve left the study just after V (the family moved to Saskatchewan) and so her sample V consists of just the basic 700 utterances. Eve's withdrawal introduces another asymmetry into the report of the data. The transcriptions for Adam and Sarah go right on after V and so we have reported for them on a 2100-utterance sample taken 7 months after V; there is no such sample for Eve. We did not bother to count N and Q in this last sample since these constructions had long been fully productive at that point.

The figures in Tables 1.5, 1.6, and 1.7 tell the story rather well; SAAD sentences were present from I; N, Q, and Tr develop for all the children between III and V; TrQ, TrN, and NQ tend to develop at least as late as N, Q, and Tr, but there is quite a bit of variation from child to child; and TrNQ is at least as late as V in all.

TABLE 1.5 Occurrences Across Time of Seven Sentence Types in Adam

	N^a	Q^a	Tr^b	TrN^b	TrQ^b	NQ^b	$TrNQ^b$
I.	0	0	0	0	0	0	0
II.	1	0	2^e	0	0	0	0
III.	$\boxed{13}^c$	12^d	0	2^f	0	0	0
IV.	19	11^d	4	0	0	0	0
V.	31	$\boxed{25}$	$\boxed{11}$	$\boxed{16}$	5	0	0
Seven months later.			8	8	0	2	$\boxed{10}$

[a]Based on 700 utterances per sample.

[b]Based on 2100 utterances per sample.

[c]The box indicates the first occurrence of 6 or more.

[d]All questions beginning *D'you want*.

[e]Both are *I did* and are used inappropriately.

[f]Both are *I can't*.

TABLE 1.6 Occurrences Across Time of Seven Sentence Types in Sarah

	N^a	Q^a	Tr^b	TrN^b	TrQ^b	NQ^b	$TrNQ^b$
I.	0	1	1	0	0	0	0
II.	[7]^c	0	5	[8]	0	0	0
III.	26	1	[18]	8	1	0	0
IV.	28	[11]	21	12	4	0	0
V.	33	28	30	16	[6]	4	[7]
Seven months later.		29	18	12	3	9	

[a]Based on 700 utterances per sample.
[b]Based on 2100 utterances per sample.
[c]The box indicates the first occurrence of 6 or more.

TABLE 1.7 Occurrences Across Time of Seven Sentence Types in Eve

	N^a	Q^a	Tr^b	TrN^b	TrQ^b	NQ^b	$TrNQ^b$
I.	0	0	0	0	0	0	0
II.	0	0	0	0	0	0	0
III.	[13]^c	0	0	0	0	0	0
IV.	25	2	2	0	0	0	0
V.	35	[27]	[9]	3	0	0	0

[a]Based on 700 utterances per sample.

[b]Based on approximately 2100 utterances per sample except for IV which is based on 1500 and V which is based on 700.

[c]The box indicates the first occurrence of 6 or more.

The benchmarks, I to V, fall at the same points for all the children in terms of mean length of utterance, but not in terms of chronological age. Sarah was somewhat older than Adam at each point and much older than Eve. A comparison of Sarah's table (1.6) with those of Adam and Eve shows that in respect to the sentence types with which we are concerned, she was ahead of the others relative to the mean length of utterance. From writing the grammars we have learned that the children at a given Roman numeral level will be much alike in terms of those features of grammar that increase utterance length when they are learned – such as obligatory inflections and determiners. In other dimensions we have found that Sarah's age tells and that she knows more, relative to the length of her sentences, then do the other children.

Table 1.8 supplements the partial data of Tables 1.5, 1.6, and 1.7 with complete counts of Tr, TrN, TrQ, NQ, and TrNQ in all samples for Adam from III on. Table 1.8 confirms the impression created by the partial data of Table 1.5 that Tr and TrN occur in quantity before the other constructions, that TrQ follows next but is particularly variable in frequency, and that NQ and TrNQ do not occur at all until near the end of the 18-month period. In the last two samples the TrNQ tags jump from a long-term zero frequency level first to 16 instances and then to 32. These last output rates are 4 to 8 times adult rates. The children have often shown this kind of brief infatuation with a construction when it was first learned; the frequency typically falls back within a few weeks to a level approximately that of adult speech.

We should like to submit our predictions concerning derivational complexity and order of acquisition to a more explicit test than simple inspection of the data, but to do that we require a criterion of acquisition. If the criterion becomes complicated, as it sometimes does in the grammars, the possibility of the reader inspecting the evidence becomes remote. The best we can do, therefore, is to adopt a largely arbitrary but not unreasonable criterion and check the data against that. We have counted the sentence types in question in 1400 utterance samples drawn from the three mothers, at times just prior to II and III. We find that the lowest output rate of any of these sentence types in any of the mothers is 6 in 2100 utterances. So we have adopted the value "6" as our threshold of emergence; the first child sample in which a sentence type attains that value or higher is considered to be the sample of emergence. From what we have learned in writing the grammars, this value places the emergence points about right. In general, the children were giving evidence of understanding the constructions by that point and, in general, after that point they steadily produced the construction.

There is one case in which we are sure that the frequency criterion is misleading, and in this case we have deserted the criterion. The exception appears in Table 1.5. Adam used 12 well-formed *yes-no* questions in III and 11 in IV, but we have identified V as the sample of emergence. The reason is that all of Adam's well-formed questions in the period from III through IV began with the fixed form *D'you want*. There were no instances at all of such closely related forms as *Did you want, Does he want, D'you see*, and the like. For these and other reasons we do not, in the grammar for III, generate Adam's questions with rules like the rules of the adult grammar. There are other occurrences of sentences which we do not, for one reason or another, take to be adequate evidence that the child knows the underlying structure but in these other cases the frequency does not attain the criterion value of 6.

TABLE 1.8 Occurrences in All Samples for Eighteen Months of Five
Sentence Types in Adam

Sample	Tr	TrN	TrQ	NQ	TrNQ	Sample	Tr	TrN	TrQ	NQ	TrNQ
19	0	0	0	0	0	35	7	12	0	0	0
20	1	0	0	0	0	36	2	4	1	0	0
21	3	1	0	0	0	37	4	2	3	0	0
22	0	1	0	0	0	38	4	5	0	0	0
23	1	1	0	0	0	39	7	3	3	0	0
24	1	0	0	0	0	40	4	6	2	0	0
25	0	0	0	0	0	41	4	2	1	0	0
26	3	0	0	0	0	42	2	2	3	0	1
27	2	2	0	0	0	43	5	1	2	0	0
28	2	1	0	0	0	44	5	2	1	0	0
29	4	4	2	0	0	45	3	3	0	0	6
30	2	1	0	0	0	46	3	1	0	1	1
31	1	2	2	0	0	47	2	4	0	1	3
32	0	2	1	0	0	48	2	4	1	0	3
33	4	6	4	0	0	49	1	3	1	0	16
34	8	8	0	0	0	50	5	1	0	5	32

Using our criterion for emergence, we have checked the 19 predictions based on the order of derivational complexity presented in the overview, an order that does not distinguish between TrQ and TgQ, or TrNQ and TgNQ. The results appear in Table 1.9. For Adam, 16 predictions are confirmed; 2 are disconfirmed; and 1 is not settled either way by the data. For Sarah, the respective results are 15, 2, and 2. For Eve, they are 16 confirmed and 3 unsettled. In arriving at these figures, we have assumed that any sentence type which had not attained criterion in the data presented did attain criterion at some point later than the times represented in the data. The prediction that constructions would emerge in the order of derivational complexity described in the overview is supported by the results.

What of the distinction between TrQ and TgQ; TrNQ and TgNQ? As we have seen, there are a few cases in which we can define an order of cumulative derivational complexity for TrQ and TrNQ where we have no basis for defining such an order for the tags. The cases (marked with an asterisk in Table 1.9) are these:

$$Tr < TrQ$$
$$Tr < TrNQ$$
$$TrN < TrNQ$$

The first difficulty with this fine-grained analysis is that there are no more than three or four cases of TrNQ in either Adam or Sarah. It is only TgNQ that attains criterion. As it happens, TgNQ appears later than Tr and TrN in all cases. This may mean that TgNQ is cumulatively more complex than Tr and TrN and should, in fact, be derived with the aid of Rule TII "Predicate truncation." Alternatively, however, it may simple mean that the tags are more complex than Tr and TrN in ways we have not considered. The comparison would have been stronger if we had had a basis for predicting that TgQ would occur before Tr and TrN, while TrQ should appear after them. In fact, however, we simply had no basis for odering TgQ and Tr; and TgQ and TrN. Since, however, the cases labeled TrNQ in Table 1.9 are in fact almost all cases of TgNQ, confirmations should be counted somewhat differently than was done for the first row of "Totals" in Table 1.9. The relations between TgNQ and Tr and TrN are not in fact predicted by cumulative complexity, and so their confirmation should not be counted in favor of the hypothesis. The number of confirmations is appropriately reduced in the second line of totals.

With respect to TrQ and TgQ, there is a single prediction that applies to one and not the other. TrQ should be later than Tr, but for TgQ there is no basis for a prediction. When TrQ and TgQ are separately examined, the prediction is confirmed for both, and so we are where we were with TrNQ and TgNQ; the result may mean that TgQ should be derived with the aid of Rule TII

Derivational Complexity and Order of Acquisition in Child Speech

TABLE 1.9 Predictions Confirmed (+), Disconfirmed (-), and Unsettled (?)
for Derivational Complexity and Order of Acquisition

	Adam			Sarah			Eve		
	+	?	-	+	?	-	+	?	-
SAAD $<$ Q	√			√			√		
Q $<$ TrQ	√			√			√		
Q $<$ NQ	√			√			√		
Q $<$ TrNQ	√			√			√		
SAAD $<$ N	√			√			√		
N $<$ TrN	√				√		√		
N $<$ NQ	√			√			√		
N $<$ TrNQ	√			√			√		
SAAD $<$ Tr	√			√			√		
Tr $<$ TrQ*	√			√			√		
Tr $<$ TrN		√				√	√		
Tr $<$ TrNQ*	√			√			√		
SAAD $<$ TrQ	√			√			√		
TrQ $<$ TrNQ		√			√			√	
SAAD $<$ TrN	√			√			√		
TrN $<$ TrNQ*	√			√				√	
SAAD $<$ NQ	√			√			√		
NQ $<$ TrNQ		√				√		√	
SAAD $<$ TrNQ	√			√			√		
Totals[a]	16	1	2	15	2	2	16	3	0
Totals[b]	13	1	2	12	2	2	14	2	0

[a]Appropriate totals if doubtful cases are TrQ and TrNQ.

[b]Appropriate totals if doubtful cases are TgQ and TgNQ.

*Prediction not made for tags (TgQ or TgNQ).

"Predicate truncation" or it may simply mean that TgQ is, in other ways, more complex than Tr. While a certain number of clear instances of both TrQ and TgQ can be identified, there are also many cases in which the identification is not clear. Therefore we have simply added them together in Table 1.9. If we think of the instances of TrQ then the first set of totals is the correct one. If we think of the instances as TgQ then the number of confirmations must be reduced by the number of pairs for which there is no prediction in the case of TgQ. This has been done and is reflected in the second set of totals.

In connection with TgQ there is a point of incidental interest. Both Adam and Sarah made an interesting kind of error in their early use of TgQ; they failed to make the affirmative-negative switch and so, in effect, overgeneralized TgQ. They produced, for instance: *He'll catch cold, will he? But it's all over, is it? This is Boston, is it?* The reciprocal error, which would overgeneralize the negative question, never occurred. There were no instances of sentences such as this: *We didn't have a ball, didn't we?* What should cause this asymmetry? It could, of course, simply result from a difference of derivational complexity. TrNQ is more complex than TrQ. Our guess, however, is that another factor is important.

The children produced TgNQ fairly often and TrNQ not at all, whereas they produced (correctly) both TrQ and TgQ. Probably this difference reflects a difference in adult speech. Probably there are fewer occasions calling for the negative echo question (TrNQ) such as *Didn't we?* then there are occasions calling for the affirmative echo question (TrQ) *Did we?* The affirmative echo question does not involve the negative-affirmative switch of the affirmative tag. Since TrQ and TgQ are, except for their relation to an antecedent, identical, it is to be expected that they would interfere with one another. Furthermore, clear cases of TrQ tend to appear before clear cases of TgQ, in Adam and Sarah. In Sarah's data, for instance, TrQ sentences begin 20 weeks before TgQ sentences. It seems likely, then, that the child confuses affirmative tags when they first appear with echo questions and so uses affirmative tags for a time, without observing the negative-affirmative switch.

SENTENCE LENGTH, FREQUENCY, AND SEMANTIC

What factors other than derivational complexity could account for the order of emergence of SAAD, Q, N, Tr, TrN, TrQ, and TrNQ? Length and frequency are not cognitive variables, but we cannot be sure that they will, on that account, fail to influence results obtained by cognitive psychologists. In experimental studies of sentence comprehension and recall, sentence length has often been confounded with complexity, the two increasing together.

For example, Savin and Perchonock (1965), in their study of immediate recall, made 17 predictions on the basis of cumulative derivational complexity; 13 of these 17 would also be made if one simply used sentence length as an index of complexity. For the *wh* question in their experiment, Savin and Perchonock decide that there are no predictions from cumulative complexity, but they fail to note that sentence length makes 10 predictions in this case, of which 9 are confirmed.

Sutherland (1966) and others have suggested that complexity is also likely to be confounded with frequency in such favorite sets of sentences as SAAD, Q, N, P (passives), NQ, NP, and NPQ. Since no one seems to have cited any actual counts of sentence types, we may as well do so. We have made many such counts in our study for the speech parents use to children. In a sample of 700 sentences, the number of SAAD sentences will run between one and two hundred; Q and N will both be something like one half to one quarter as frequent as SAAD; of passives, negative questions, negative passives, and the like there will typically be between none and half a dozen. Of course we do not know how representative such counts are of adult speech generally, but in parent-to-child speech, at any rate, complexity is confounded with frequency in the kinds of sentences that have been most often used in experiments.

Are length and frequency confounded with complexity in the sentences we have studied? Consider length in the following sample set.

SAAD.	*We had a ball.*	(4 words)
Q.	*Did we have a ball?*	(5 words)
N.	*We didn't have a ball.*	(6 words)
Tr.	*We did.*	(2 words)
TrN.	*We didn't.*	(3 words)
TrQ.	*Did we?*	(2 words)
TgQ.	*We didn't have a ball, did we?*	(8 words)
NQ.	*Didn't we have a ball?*	(6 words)
TrNQ.	*Didn't we?*	(3 words)
TgNQ.	*We had a ball, didn't we?*	(7 words)

Of the 19 predictions from derivational complexity that apply when we have TrQ and TrNQ, rather than complete tags, 7 would go the same way if sentence length were used as an index of complexity, but 12 would go differently. Of the 16 predictions from derivational complexity that apply when we have the tags TgQ and TgNQ, sentence length predicts the same way in 11 cases and differently in 5. So, in our sentences, length and derivational complexity are partially but not completely confounded. Examining the outcomes of the 12 predictions for which length and complexity predict differently (when we have Tr and TrQ) across the 3 children, we find that complexity is correct in 31 instances. The outcome is unsettled in 4 instances and length is correct just once. The results are about the same with tags included. So it does look as if sentence length will not explain the order of emergence, even though sentence length is a variable that increases with age. One of the reasons this family of constructions caught our eye in the first place was that we were surprised to find such short utterances as tags and truncations developing quite late in the child's speech.

Frequency turns out to be a more serious variable than length. In order to see whether differential construction frequencies in parental speech could affect order of emergence in child speech, we wanted a count of parental frequencies that antedated emergence and was relatively free of influence from the children. So we used two samples of 700 utterances each taken immediately prior to II and III. At III the children were not regularly producing any of the constructions except the SAAD sentences. We counted the 8 major constructions in the two samples for each of the three mothers and used just those sentences of the mother that were neither imitations nor expansions of sentences produced by the children.

As in all counts we have made for parental speech, the frequency profiles of the three mothers were highly correlated. Of the results we will report the average value per 700 utterances, across mothers and samples, for each main sentence type. They are:

	Q(53)	TrQ(2)	
SAAD(139)	N(56)	TrN(2)	TrNQ(4)
	Tr(13)	NQ(4)	

Clearly, frequency and derivational complexity are closely related.

The apparently quite general correlation between grammatical complexity and frequency has a certain independent interest. It is not, to begin with, simply an artifact of a system of sentence classification. Potentially there are as many different sentences of one type as of any other type. Any SAAD is susceptible of, for instance, negation, truncation, interrogation, and tagging. Apparently, however, there are many more occasions calling for declaration than for interrogation, for affirmation than for negation, and relatively few occasions calling for truncation and requests for confirmation. One is reminded of Zipf's (1949) empirical law relating word length inversely to word frequency, and also of his general idea that the relation exists because of a Principle of Least Effort that causes our frequently used tools to be kept simple and close to hand. The derivationally simple sentence types seem to be those we most often need, and the derivationally complex types those we need less often. If psychological complexity is related to derivational complexity, then it may not be inappropriate to invoke a Principle of Least Effort.

Of the 19 main predictions made by derivational complexity, 17 are also made by frequency, and the two predictions on which complexity and frequency do not agree are based on very small frequency differences in our counts. It is possible, then, that the order in which the child's knowledge of the sentences develops is determined by the frequency with which parents model the sentences.

We have often found before that parental frequencies predict the order in which constructions will "emerge," in terms of some frequency criterion, in successive samples of child speech. In the early months of our study we had to consider seriously a really radical alternative to the notion that frequent modelling of a sentence type facilitates learning its structure. Suppose the children had known everything from the beginning but emitted constructions according to a frequency profile like that of the parents. The chance that any particular construction would attain an arbitrary frequency criterion in an early sample would be greater for frequent constructions than for infrequent constructions. So what looked like a pattern of successive "emergences" might simply be a kind of sampling phenomenon. Up to a point that is true. But when you have more than two years of zero frequency for something like the negative and affirmative tags, you can be confident, when they eventually appear, that something new has been learned. You can be particularly confident when you see the sudden overproduction we have seen in Adam's sample #50. So we think that at least we no longer need seriously to consider the possibility that the children were learning nothing new, but we must still consider the possibility that modelling frequency affects the order of learning.

In addition to the differences of length and frequency among sentence types, there are semantic differences. Interrogatives, negatives, and tags all differ from SAAD sentences in the meanings they communicate. Is it perhaps the meanings that account for the order of emergence? As it happens, the children have primitive ways of asking questions, negating, and requesting confirmation, and the primitive forms are present even in I and II. The primitive negative is created by preposing a negative word, *no* or *not*, to a sentence: *No want, Not Sarah's*, and the like. Primitive *yes-no* questions are created by using a rising interrogative intonation for any sentence or sentence fragment. Primitive requests for confirmation are chiefly *huh*? and *right*? Of course, the mature grammatical forms provide for semantic refinements that the primitive forms miss; the difference, for instance, between *Do you see him*? and *Will you see him*? Still, it cannot be the basic semantics of interrogation, negation, and confirmation that defer the acquisition of the mature grammatical structures. The basic meanings have been expressed from the beginning of our records. What has happened developmentally is that immature means of expression have been displaced by mature means.

We must now distinguish between two sorts of order of emergence in child speech. The first sort is an order among constructions that are all mature adult forms. This is the sort of order with which the present paper has been concerned. We have asked whether the order of emergence of some eight types of well-formed adult sentences reflects the derivational complexity of the types in terms of the adult grammar, and found that it does. The second sort of order concerns constructions which are equivalent semantically but which exist in one or more immature or childish forms as well as, eventually, the adult form. This kind of sequence exists for questions, negatives, and tags and for many other constructions. The children we have studied asked *wh* questions with preposed question word, but without interposing subject and auxiliary, long before they made *wh* questions in which they did both. They said *Why you went* and *What he's doing* before they said *Why did you go?* and *What is he doing?* The children combined negation and indeterminates to form sentences like *I didn't see something* and *It don't have some tapioca in it* before they learned to make indeterminates into indefinites in negative sentences and so to say *I didn't see anything* and *It don't have any tapioca in it*.

With respect to the sort of sequence that moves from immature to mature constructions, it is possible to ask again about the role of derivational complexity. However, the immature forms are not generated by adult grammar; they are ungrammatical from the adult point of view. Consequently, the notion of cumulative derivational complexity with which we have thus far operated has no application to the second sort of sequence. The relevant standard of complexity is not the adult grammar but the child's own grammar. What kinds of changes must be made in his system if it is to generate mature negatives, tags, *wh* questions, indefinites, and the like? Additional rules may be required; old rules may lose some of their generality; and rules of an entirely new type may be introduced. This is going to be a long and complicated story and we are not ready in this paper to try to tell it.

There is another interesting question about the progression from immature to mature forms. What causes it to occur at all? Why should the child relinquish old ways? Is it because they are ineffective? Does the necessity of communicating exercise a selection pressure in favor of adult forms? Or are the old ways given up simply because parents express disapproval of them and approval of more mature forms? Is there a pressure toward maturity exerted by contingent approval? Our records offer some information on these questions and we turn to that now.

COMMUNICATION PRESSURE AND CONTINGENT APPROVAL

The data to be reported in this section flatly contradict what most parents say about their own child-training practices. That may mean that parents do not act as they think they act. It may also mean that the parent-child interaction in our records is simply not representative; it is probably not representative of parents generally, and perhaps not even representative of the parents of Adam, Eve, and Sarah. May not the presence of a psychologist and a tape recorder have altered usual practices? It certainly may have. However, one should not assume that it must have. A single investigator stayed with each child over the course of the study, in one case for three years. The investigator became a family friend and interaction with him and in his presence seems completely without self-consciousness after the first couple of weeks.

Communication Pressure

Do ill-formed constructions in child speech give way to well-formed constructions because there is a selection pressure in communication which favors the latter? Child utterances often seem to function as instrumental acts designed to accomplish effects in other persons. Surely the well-formed utterance, since it would be correctly interpreted, is a superior tool to the ill-formed utterance, which must often be misunderstood or simply not comprehended. The protocols we have permit a rough test of this proposition with respect to some of the constructions that interest us.

Yes-no questions, *wh* questions, negatives, and tags all occur in child speech in primitive of ill-formed versions before they occur as well-formed constructions. The ill-formed constructions start well in advance of the well-formed versions. Some of the primitive forms are eventually entirely displaced by mature forms (negatives and *wh* questions). Some primitive forms, the *yes-no* question that does not interpose subject and auxiliary and the *huh*? tag, are acceptable alternatives in adult speech, and these are not displaced entirely but rather simply make room for mature forms. In all cases it is possible to find samples in which primitive and mature forms are both present in quantity. What we want to know is whether there is a difference in the quality of response from adult interlocutors to the two kinds of form.

To test the proposition we used (except in the case of tags) two of the samples, corresponding to grammars, for each construction. For *yes-no* questions, we used samples III and V; for *wh* questions, and also for negatives, samples III and IV. The samples were selected so as to maximize the numbers of both primitive and well-formed constructions of the type in question for all three children. They represent times when the construction was undergoing change and the child was vacillating between primitive and well-formed versions, times when communication pressure should have operated if it ever does. Tags had to be treated somewhat differently from the other constructions. There were, in Eve's records, no well-formed tags at all; in Sarah's they start at V; and in Adam's they do not start until after V. Consequently, the study of responses to tags, primitive and well-formed, is limited to Sarah and Adam and is based on just those 2-hour samples from each child which contained the largest numbers of tags: Adam's sample 50 and Sarah's samples 100-103.

Interlocutor responses to child utterances were classified in the following terms. *Yes-no* questions, *wh* questions, and tags all request answers and such answers are one sort of comprehending response. Sometimes a response does not directly answer a question, but nevertheless clearly shows comprehension and represents a reasonable sort of continuation; for instance, in response to *Where Christmas cookies?* we have *We ate them all*. These two kinds of response to questions are grouped together in Table 1.10 as "Sequiturs" or clearly relevant and comprehending reactions. "Non Sequiturs" in Table 1.10 represent the conjunction of several different sorts of reactions. Sometimes the interlocutor queries all or some part of the child's question; for instance, in response to *Where my spoon?* we have *Your spoon?* Sometimes the interlocutor responds with a new topic or seeming irrelevancy; for instance, in response to *Where ice cream?* we find *And the potatoes*. Sometimes a response reveals an actual misunderstanding of the child's question; *What time it is?* elicited *Uh, huh, it tells what time it is*. Sometimes there was simply no response at all to a question. Sometimes there was a response of doubtful classification. Non Sequiturs, then, are made up of "queries" plus "irrelevancies" plus "misunderstandings" plus "no responses" plus "doubtfuls." The sequiturs and non sequiturs of Table 1.10 do not always sum to 100% because there was a residual category which seemed not to belong with either of the others, a category of "repeats." Repeats of ill-formed utterances usually contained corrections and so could be instructive; repeats of well-formed utterances would not be corrections. Interlocutor responses to negatives were categorized in the same way as responses to questions, with a single exception. Negatives do not request answers in the way that questions do. Sequiturs are all simply continuations strongly suggesting comprehension of the child's utterance.

Table 1.10 presents the percentages of sequiturs and non sequiturs in response to primitive and well-formed constructions of each type for each child. The mean percentages of sequitur responses to primitive and well-formed constructions are exactly the same (45%). The mean percentage of non sequitur responses is slightly, but not significantly, higher to primitive constructions than to well-formed constructions; 47% in the former case and 42% in the latter. The obtained difference on Non Sequiturs should be

TABLE 1.10 Sequiturs and Non Sequiturs Following Primitive and Well-Formed Constructions

	Yes-No (III and V)		Wh (III and IV)		Tags (Adam 50; Sarah 100-103)		Negatives (III and IV)		Means	
	Primitive	Well-formed	Primitive	Well-formed	Primitive	Well-formed	Primitive	Well-formed	Primitive	Well-formed
Sequiturs	.70	.83	.44	.45			.70	.31	.61	.53 Eve
Non Sequiturs	.18	.13	.37	.18			.20	.49	.25	.27
Sequiturs	.48	.46	.45	.37	.54	.56	.00	.24	.31	.36 Adam
Non Sequiturs	.50	.43	.50	.52	.42	.44	.86	.52	.62	.49
Sequiturs	.47	.52	.38	.52	.52	.36	.33	.41	.42	.45 Sarah
Non Sequiturs	.53	.47	.62	.43	.48	.57	.56	.51	.55	.50
									.45	.45 Means
									.47	.42

interpreted in the light of the fact that a great many of the non sequiturs were "no responses," and it is not clear that these should all be considered unsatisfactory responses. In some cases the child was talking fast and scarcely seemed to expect or leave time for an answer. When non sequiturs were counted more narrowly — as instances of genuine misunderstanding — we found precisely one instance (the example given earlier) for all children and all constructions. In general, the results provide no support for the notion that there is a communication pressure favoring mature constructions.

When coding the transcriptions for communication pressure, one forms the impression that the primitive forms were understood perfectly well by adult interlocutors, who, indeed, did not notice anything primitive or ill-formed about the constructions. Rising intonation is a fairly good sign of a *yes-no* question, as is the preposed *wh* word of a *wh* question, and *no* or *not* for the negative, and *huh*? for the tag. The operations the child fails to perform on these utterances are in fact redundant as far as the meaning of the construction is concerned.

It is possible, of course, that communication pressure plays an important role in speech progression at other seasons of development and with other constructions. It may, for instance, be the force that causes the child to relinquish holophrases in favor of sentences. Unfortunately, there is a kind of paradoxical difficulty in the way of demonstrating such an effect with nonexperimental data. In order to prove that a child learns new means of expression because he has messages to communicate that cannot be handled with the means at his command, the investigator must be able to detect such uncommunicated messages. The investigator is not, however, the only person trying to "read" the child and probably not the most expert person; the child's parents or siblings are likely to be the experts. Therefore, it is usually the case that any message the investigator can make out, the family can also make out, and so the child will in fact already be communicating any idea that we can be sure he has. In naturalistic studies we usually have to admit that we did not know a child possessed a given refinement of meaning until he started to produce the construction expressing that refinement.

Contingent Approval

It might be supposed that syntactically correct utterances come to prevail over those that are incorrect, through the operation of positive reinforcement and punishment on the part of adults. A positive reinforcer is generally defined as any event which, being made contingent upon the emission of an antecedent response, increases the frequency of that response. In this sense, reinforcers can never be specified before one has observed their effect. Whether or not an event is a reinforcer waits upon information as to whether or not it has, in fact, reinforced.

The definition of *punishment,* in Skinner's sense, begins with the notion of a "negative reinforcer." An event subsequent to a response is a negative reinforcer of that response when the *withdrawal* of the event, being made contingent on the emission of the response, causes the response to increase in frequency. Shock is often a negative reinforcer. Punishment, finally, involves the *presentation* of a negative reinforcer, and while punishment does not seem to extinguish a response, it does depress the frequency of its performance.

Strictly speaking, there is no way to disconfirm the following proposition: "Syntactically correct utterances become more frequent because of reinforcement and less frequent because of punishment." To disconfirm it, one would have to show that there is no event (or better, no way of conceiving events) which increases the frequency of syntactically correct utterances when its presentation is made contingent on such utterances, and also no event which increases frequency when its withdrawal is made so contingent. Because events subsequent to child speech are indefinitely various (or better, susceptible of being conceived in indefinitely various ways) one can never be sure that there is no event which functions as a reinforcer or punishment.

In practice, of course, we know that certain events are likely to be reinforcers or punishments for a given response because we have seen that they have this effect on many other responses. Money is supposed to be such a conditioned "generalized reinforcer" and social approval is supposed to be another. In *Science and Human Behavior* (1953, p. 78), Skinner wrote: "Another person is likely to reinforce only that part of one's behavior of which he approves, and any sign of his *approval,* therefore, becomes reinforcing in its own right. Behavior which evokes a smile or the verbal response 'That's right' or 'Good' or any other commendation is strengthened. We use this generalized reinforcer to establish and shape the behavior of others, particularly in education. For example, we teach both children and adults to speak correctly by saying 'That's right' when appropriate behavior is emitted." By extension, it seems reasonable to think that signs of disapproval would be generalized punishments. The proposition "Syntactically correct utterances come to prevail over syntactically incorrect utterances through the selective administration of signs of approval and disapproval" is a testable one.

The proposition cannot possibly be true for the natural case of parents and children at home unless parental approval and disapproval are in fact appropriately contingent on syntactical correctness. If the reactions *are* appropriately contingent, then they may or may not have the effects proposed. In our materials parental reactions do not even meet the minimal circumstance of appropriate contingency and so the proposition may be discarded without testing its further implications.

The demonstration goes like this. In order to investigate contingencies at different levels of child proficiency, we worked with samples II and V. We first listed all of those exchanges in which a parent responded with such signs of approval as *That's right, Correct, Very good,* and *Yes,* and such signs of disapproval as *That's wrong* or *That's not right* or *No.* We could not, in this analysis, limit ourselves to approval and disapproval following the constructions on which we have focused in this paper (questions, negatives, tags, etc.) because such exchanges were too infrequent.

The general plan, of course, was to contrast the syntactic correctness of the population of utterances followed by a sign of approval with the population followed by a sign of disapproval. There are some problems about scoring the syntactical correctness of a child's utterance. When an utterance consists of only one word it has no syntax and so cannot be either correct or incorrect. All such were disregarded. Child utterances, like adult utterances, can be well-formed even though they are not complete subject-predicate sentences, so we do not want to measure them against some notion of the grammatically complete sentence. The indices we used are not responsive to all aspects of syntax but they are responsive to those that can be confidently scored for spontaneous speech. An error was scored whenever some grammatical marker that was obligatory in terms of the surrounding context of the utterance was missing. For instance, *He not walking* contains an error because *is* is missing. An error was also scored whenever the form of a morpheme required by the context was erroneous; for instance, *Her curl my hair* or *I throwed it*, or *I don't want something.* Finally an error was scored whenever morphemes were not in the correct order: *What he's doing.*

The results are summarized in Table 1.11 as a set of frequency tables for which an utterance was simply counted correct or incorrect — whatever the degree of incorrectness. Another analysis scores degrees of correctness and uses mean scores. In neither case is there even a shred of evidence that approval and disapproval are contingent on syntactic correctness.

What circumstances do govern statements of approval and disapproval from parents? Surely they are not emitted without reference to the child's speech. Table 1.12 provides a few examples which suggest the answer. Approval and disapproval are not primarily linked with the grammatical form of the utterance. They are rather linked to the truth value of the proposition, which the adult fits to the child's generally incomplete and often deformed sentence. And so, though Eve makes a grammatical error when she expresses the proposition that her mother is a girl with the utterance *He a girl,* the proposition itself is true and since it is the proposition rather than the grammar that governs response, the response is approving. By contrast, when Sarah points and says *There's the animal farmhouse*, her syntax is impeccable but the proposition is false, and so the reaction is disapproving.

The truth value of a presumed proposition is the most important determinant of approval and disapproval, but it is not the only determinant. When Eve says something that may be approximated as *What the guy idea*, she says something that can be neither true nor false; it is a kind of exclamation. The exclamation is identifiable as a poor performance of a familiar routine, and mother elects to disapprove phonological aspects of the performance and to model an improved version. While there are several bases for approval and disapproval, they are almost always semantic or phonological. Explicit approval or disapproval of either syntax or morphology is extremely rare in our records and so seems not to be the force propelling the child from immature to mature forms.

TABLE 1.11 Relations between Syntactic Correctness of Antecedent Child's Utterance and Approving or Disapproving Parental Response[a]

	Sarah			Adam			Eve	
	Correct	Incorrect		Correct	Incorrect		Correct	Incorrect
App.	4	9	App.	4	3	App.	6	19
Dis.	4	6	Dis.	2	0	Dis.	3	5

(a) At II

	Sarah			Adam			Eve	
	Correct	Incorrect		Correct	Incorrect		Correct	Incorrect
App.	23	4	App.	13	6	App.	33	29
Dis.	12	2	Dis.	7	1	Dis.	12	15

(b) At V

[a]Only 1 of 6 in right direction. Remaining 1 is not significant.

TABLE 1.12 Examples of Utterances Approved and Disapproved

Approval

Adam.	*Draw a boot paper.*	**Adam's Mother.**	*That's right. Draw a boot on paper.*
Eve.	*Mama isn't boy, he a girl.*	**Eve's Mother.**	*That's right.*
Sarah.	*Her curl my hair.*	**Sarah's Mother.**	*Um hmm.*

Disapproval

Adam.	*And Walt Disney comes on Tuesday.*	**Adam's Mother.**	*No, he does not.*
Eve.	*What the guy idea.*	**Eve's Mother.**	*No, that's not right. Wise idea.*
Sarah.	*There's the animal farmhouse.*	**Sarah's Mother.**	*No, that's a lighthouse.*

Conclusions

What is the significance for child speech of the two sorts of sequence and what is the significance of the negative findings with respect to communication pressure and contingent approval? The fact that some constructions appear in one or more "ungrammatical" forms before they appear in adult form shows that children are learning rules and not simply utterances. A sentence like *I don't see something* has the same force on the syntactic level as *I goed* on the morphological. Both suggest the generalization of rules to cases that ought to be exceptions.

I see smoke.	*It is snowing.*
I don't see smoke.	*It snowed.*
I see something.	*I am going.*
I don't see something.	*I goed.*

The fact that some ungrammatical or immature forms have been used by all the children that have been studied shows that children are alike in the innate knowledge, language-processing routines, preferences and assumptions they bring to the problem of language acquisition. One such preference seems to be for a small number of rules of maximal generality (McNeill, in press).

The combination of negatives and indeterminate pronouns (for example, *I don't hear someone*) treats these pronouns as other pronouns and, indeed, noun phrases generally, are so treated. The failure to make the affirmative-negative switch on tags, resulting in such sentences as *We can play, can we?* treats the tag question as if it were an echo question given in response to another speaker's production of the first proposition. It is even conceivable that children say *What he wants?* and *Why you went?* because they are trying to use a single rule for *wh* questions and embedded *wh* clauses as in: *We know what he wants* and *We know why you went.*

The immature rules for interrogation and negation may arise as McNeill (in press) has suggested because they are much closer to the base structure than are the transformed adult forms. The transformations are certainly language-specific and so must be learned. The base structure has a better chance of being universal and innate.

If the negative results for communication pressure and contingent approval are representative of parental practice, then these cannot be the forces causing the child to relinquish immature forms and adopt adult forms. In our data the two principles of response (or rule) selection fail to meet the first requirement one can set; they are not contingent in the way that they are required to be. We suspect that the only force toward grammaticality operating on the child is the occasional mismatch between his theory of the structure of the language and the data he receives. Piaget's terms, "assimilation" (the present theory), "accommodation" (the impact of the data), and "disequilibrium" (the mismatch), were created to deal with a similar lack of extrinsic motivation in the child for progressing toward operativity. Of course this formulation leaves most questions unanswered. For instance, why do data have an impact at some times and at other times no effect at all?

The fact that there is a sequence, among well-formed constructions, from those that are derivationally simple, in terms of the adult grammar, toward those that are derivationally complex, suggests that the adult grammar does, at least roughly, represent what it is that the child is learning. Of course we do not yet know how general the sequence is. It seems to be the case (when a lot of underbrush is hacked away) that control of the base structure precedes control of transformational knowledge and that simple sentences precede conjoinings and embeddings (as these were understood in the linguistics of 1965). On the other hand, in many points of detail, we do not find a progression from derivational simplicity to complexity. For instance, noun phrases with separable verbs occur in transformed position well before they occur in untransformed position.

Finally, there is the relation between parental frequency and order of emergence among well-formed constructions. Our guess is that this is an inci-

dental consequence of the relation between frequency and complexity and
that frequency, above some minimum level, does not determine the order in
which structural knowledge emerges. What would happen if the parents of a
child produced tags at a much higher rate than is normal? We have some basis
for a guess.

The parents of Adam, Eve, and Sarah did produce certain *wh* questions at
a very high rate in a period when the children did not understand the structure
of *wh* questions. What happened then? The children learned to produce the
two most frequently repeated *wh* questions, *What's that?* and *What doing?*, on
roughly appropriate occasions. Their performance had the kind of rigidity that
we have learned to recognize as a sign of incomprehension of structure; they
did not produce, as their parents of course did, such structurally close variants
as *What are those?* and *Who's that?* and *What is he doing?* When, much later,
the children began to produce all manner of *wh* questions in the preposed form
(such as *What he wants*), it was interesting to note that *What's that?* and *What
are you doing?* were not at first reconstrued in terms of the new analysis. If
the children had generated the sentences in terms of their new rules, they ought
to have said *What that is?* and *What you are doing?* but instead they, at first,
persisted with the old forms. One of us (Brown) found himself doing a comparable thing when he studied Japanese at Berlitz. Early in his lessons he learned,
and made heavy use of, the form *korewa* meaning "this-one-here." Quite a bit
later he learned about the particle *wa* (roughly nominative, but see McNeill, in
press, for complications) which was added to nouns and pronouns. He did not,
however, reanalyze *korewa* into *kore* and *wa*, but continued to think of it as
a single word, until one day he heard *kore-no* (genitive) and then *kore-o* (accusative) and thought "Why it's *kore-wa*!"

We suggest that any form that is produced with very high frequency by
parents will be somehow represented in the child's performance even if its
structure is far beyond him. He will find a way to render a version of it and
will also form a notion of the circumstances in which it is used. The construction will become lodged in his speech as an unassimilated fragment. Extensive
use of such an unanalyzed or mistakenly analyzed fragment probably protects it,
for a time, from reanalysis when the structure relevant to it is finally learned.
Such, we suspect, are the effects of frequency.

In closing, we would like to express the distaste experimentalists must
feel for the assumptions, compromises, and qualifications involved in the use of
naturalistic data. We find that naturalistic studies build an appetite for experiment — for controls, complete data, large samples, and statistical analysis. But
we also find the reverse. The two kinds of research are complementary activities
and complementary forms of evidence. In experimental work one uses the
ingenuity he has on advance planning for data collection, whereas in naturalistic
work little ingenuity goes into the data collection and all that is available goes

into data analysis. The history of psychology generally and of psycholinguistics in particular shows that careful experimental work provides no sure path to the truth. Neither does naturalism. There are rich opportunities for error in either method. But on the whole, the opportunities arise at different points, and when the methods are used in combination, the truth has a chance to appear.

REFERENCES

Chomsky, N. *Aspects of the Theory of Syntax.* Cambridge, Mass.: M.I.T. Press, 1965.

Chomsky, N. *Syntactic Structures.* The Hague: Mouton, 1957.

Fodor, J. and Garrett, M. "Some reflections on competence and performance." In J. Lyons and R.J. Wales (Eds.), *Psycholinguistics Papers.* Edinburgh: University Press, 1966.

Katz, J.J. and Postal, P.M. *An Integrated Theory of Linguistic Descriptions.* Cambridge, Mass.: M.I.T. Press, 1964.

Klima, E.S. "Negation in English." In J.A. Fodor and J.J. Katz (Eds.), *The Structure of Language.* Englewood Cliffs, N.J.: Prentice-Hall, 1964.

McNeill, D. "The development of language." In P.A. Mussen (Ed.), *Carmichael's Manual of Child Psychology* (in press).

Savin, H.B. and Perchonock, Ellen. "Grammatical structure and the immediate recall of English sentences." *Journal of Verbal Learning and Verbal Behavior,* **4,** 348-353, 1965.

Skinner, B.F. *Science and Human Behavior.* New York: Macmillan, 1953.

Sutherland, N.S. Discussion of Fodor, J. and Garrett, M. "Some reflections on competence and performance." In J. Lyons and R.J. Wales (Eds.), *Psycholinguistics Papers.* Edinburgh: University Press, 1966.

Zipf, G.K. *Human Behavior and the Principle of Least Effort.* Cambridge, Mass.: Addison-Wesley, 1949.

CHAPTER 2

W. C. Watt

Carnegie-Mellon University

COMMENTS ON THE
BROWN AND HANLON PAPER*

The foregoing chapter by Brown and Hanlon needs no "comment" in the usual sense of exegesis, since it unfolds with the complete clarity that we have come to expect of its senior author. The inquiry is straightforward, it is well-aimed at answering an important question, and the conclusion that the authors base on their data is quite warranted. Indeed, the paper under review seems destined to take its place in the small canon of permanent contributions to the burgeoning literature of developmental psycholinguistics. The few objections I have to minor points here and there in their presentation seem almost unmannerly next to the value of their work; and I have listed these objections, or sometimes just emendations, as "Marginalia", meaning literally that they are little more than suggested corrections in proof.

On the other hand, while Brown and Hanlon's structure is solidly built, it rests on uncertain foundations. The theoretical framework in linguistic psychology that should support experimental conclusions and whose basic insights should provide the assumptions on which investigation proceeds, is just now in the process of being partly dismantled, and it is difficult even to ascertain which parts are in place and which have been carted away. Compounding the difficulty, the old explanations and hypotheses which have been forced aside by new empirical findings have yielded, not to new explanations and hypotheses, but to qualifications of the old ones. Thus the broader implications of Brown and Hanlon's work are not easy to gauge.

It seemed to me imperative to bring into the open the most crucial of the untested hypotheses underlying current work in psycholinguistics (whether or not developmental), and to subject these hypotheses to scrutiny in light of the continuing revaluation of fundamental concepts. In addition to the marginalia

*This work was supported by the Advanced Research Projects Agency of the Office of the Secretary of Defense under Contract SD-146.

55

mentioned above, there seemed to me to be a need for a separate note with a somewhat broader outlook, and I have presented my comments accordingly. The marginalia are given first; the broader comments appear as Chapter 5, "On Two Hypotheses Concerning Psycholinguistics."

MARGINALIA

There are four minor points of difference with Brown and Hanlon; I discuss them below in no particular order.

1. The first minor defect found occasionally in the Brown and Hanlon paper is unconsidered phraseology. An example of this is their remark (p. 11) to the effect that transformations can change meaning, as against the generally accepted view to the contrary (which they do not dispute). A more serious example is found on p. 19, where the authors define their notion of "cumulative derivational complexity," q.v.; of course it can never be the case that any sentence "Y" applies "all the rules" applied in the derivation of a sentence "X," unless "Y" actually *contains* "X," since some of the rules that yield "X" are morphophonemic and depend, therefore, partly on the specific form of "X" itself. Thus "all" must mean "all except morphophonemic," at the least.

Parenthetically, their definition of cumulative complexity is further compromised, it seems to me, by their apparent belief (pp. 19 and 22) that the more complex "Y" must, in addition, have a base which differs from the base of "X" *only* in that "Y" may contain morphemes (e.g., "Q" or "Neg") that are absent from "X"). They state, for example (p. 22), that ". . . Q and N differ from SAAD in their deep structures by virtue of the fact that they include, respectively, the morphemes 'Q' and 'neg.'" This version of cumulative complexity is untenable, I think, on deeper examination of the way in which SAAD are specified. That is, the SAAD must have morphemes in their bases that the corresponding Q and Neg sentences do not have. Brown and Hanlon (in company with some linguists writing on this issue) appear to assume that SAAD sentences, to contrast them with just Q and Neg sentences, are simply those which result when no Q or Neg morpheme triggers an obligatory Q or Neg transformation; that is, the SAAD are the "faute d'autre" sentences of English. But this ignores the fact that SAAD sentences are not just non-questions, but declarations; they are not just non-negatives, but affirmatives. To illustrate this with a related point, it is certainly not the case that a sentence must have *either* "Q" or "Imp" (imperative), since some sentences have both: "Will you pass the ketchup, please?". Thus, whether these signals of sentential mood (question, imperative, affirmative, and so on) are conveyed by segmental morphemes or by features (+Decl, -Decl, and so on), the fact remains that the SAAD sentences ought to contain elements in their bases that the corresponding Q and Neg sentences do not contain. The definition of "cumulative complexity" should be revised accordingly, in the obvious way.

2. The authors mention, in passing, an aspect of the much-vexed question of whether or not a discourse grammar is required to supplement the sentence grammar; I do not think that their position on this question is justified by the evidence they cite. The evidence has to do with "interrupted utterances" like Speaker A's in the dialog below:

> A: "We had a ball. . ."
> B: "Yep."
> A: ". . .didn't we?"

Brown and Hanlon remark of such sequences (p. 28), that A's utterance may be "outside the grammar" and ". . .might better be captured by a rule of discourse." Two comments are germane to this assertion:

(a) Interrupted sentences are the very hallmark of human converse, and do not, just by the fact of their interruption, call for a discourse-grammar, any more than the fact of incompletion ("Listen, pal, how would you like a. . .") calls for a grammar of truncation. As long as one speaker (A) controls the entire utterance, that utterance can be viewed as proceeding from that speaker's competence (in the conventional use of that term), no matter what any other speakers are doing. Even when one sentence is produced jointly by more than one speaker (such as Donald Duck's nephews) it is not necessarily true that rules of discourse are needed to account for such sentences, since each successive speaker can be viewed as having generated the whole sentence, though performing only part of it. (If each had not generated the whole sentence, he could not perform the right part at the right time.)

(b) Of course it might still be claimed that the production of the *entire* discourse (A's interrupted sentence *and* B's interruption of it) requires a discourse grammar, since "We had a ball . . ." "Yep" ". . .didn't we?" is a well-formed discourse but not a well-formed sentence. This issue (which is not the one raised by Brown and Hanlon) is, taken in isolation, factitious, since it is quite hopeless to describe, with any grammar, what can be a well-formed discourse *of the type under discussion*. For example, I see no way to admit the discourse just quoted while excluding "We had a ball. . ." "Ahi lassa!" ". . .didn't we?"; but if this last is a "discourse," then any English sentence interrupted by *anything* is a "discourse," and so no grammar is possible for such "discourses." If, on the other hand, these "discourses" are restricted to the cases where (interrupted-sequence + interruption) is of some prescribed form, then apparently the interrupted-sequence must not be an interrupted sentence like the one Brown and Hanlon cite; and the dialog then becomes a sequence of sentences, akin to a sequence of question-answer pairs. While it might seem that such sequences are the paradigm case of sentential sequences in need of a discourse-grammar, precisely this claim has been denied by Katz and Fodor (1964, p. 491, n.), a denial which has yet to be overturned. (Although for partial counterevidence see Watt, 1968a, pp. 118-121.) Thus, even on this plausible ground, affirmations of the need for a discourse grammar could not, unless supported, be taken seriously.

In fact, more generally, the question of whether or not a distinct discourse grammar is required has been largely misconstrued. The question should not be limited to the issue of how to generate grossly well-formed sentence sequences (and no grossly malformed sequences, these being rejected only if they contain one or more malformed constituent sentences); even a crude sentence grammar might acquire this ability just by being redesigned to generate some internal sentence breaks, each break representing, essentially, a variety of asyndetic conjunction. The question becomes truly significant only when it involves the issue of how to generate all and only those sentence sequences (with or without internal sentence breaks) that are also well-formed discourses — well-formed paragraphs, for example. But of these two issues the latter—which may or may not concern only "performative" matters, conventionally speaking—is obviously superordinate to the former; and so, in the final analysis, the question of the degree to which there is need for a distinct discourse grammar demands resolution of this more difficult issue.

3. The authors' general remarks include a note on one minor phenomenon — the rarity in children's speech of truncated negative questions like "Didn't we?" — for which they provide an explanation and on which they base the explanation of another phenomenon. Neither explanation is persuasive to me, and perhaps it is worthwhile to show why.

The authors first note that, as against the complete absence from their subjects' speech of the *truncated* negative questions ("Didn't we?"), *tag* negative questions ("We did, *didn't we?*") are found "fairly often;" and they note (p.36) that this situation with the negatives is quite unlike that with the affirmatives, since their subjects produced truncated *affirmative* questions ("Did we?") and *tag* affirmative questions ("We didn't, *did we?*") in equal abundance. Having noted the phenomenon, Brown and Hanlon propose an explanation for it; they suggest that the children fail to use (to acquire the use of) the "We didn't?" sentences because they scarcely ever *hear* them: there are "fewer occasions" for their use on their elders' part than there are for the use of "We did?" sentences (ibid). The authors offer no evidence in support of this assertion, and I am bound to own that, to me, it is implausible. The truncated questions are used to 'echo' prior statements, having the function (informally stated) of asking for confirmation or reassertion, as in the following dialog. A: "We didn't put any oysters in the oyster stew." B: "Didn't we?" Thus the claim that there is less occasion for negative truncated questions than for affirmative ones is, in essence, equivalent to either of these two claims: (a) negative statements are about as common as affirmative statements, but negative statements are scarcely ever "echoed" with a request for confirmation; or (b) negative statements may be as often "echoed," but they are themselves exceedingly rare, with concomitant rarity of the "echoes." Claim (a) is backed by no evidence that I know of, and has no plausibility in the absence of such evidence; I would provisionally reject it. But claim (b) can be rejected on the authors' own statement (p. 37) that negative statements, in the speech of the children's elders (their parents), were from "...one half to one quarter as frequent as SAAD," comprising from 25 to 100 of a sample of 700 sentences. Thus, presumably, negative statements are *not* so rare as to cause the complete absence of the "echo" negative questions dependent on them. Hence, in sum, the authors' explanation of the rarity of the "Didn't we?" sentences is unpersuasive. I have no alternative explanation to offer for the phenomenon in question, which in fact seems a little mysterious, unless of course it is a mere statistical accident, the "Didn't we?" questions being absent from the speech-sample used, but not absent (only uncommon) in the child's speech as a whole. The statistical accident, then, would spring from two facts of children's speech: first, the relative rarity with which statements (negative *or* affirmative) are echoed; and second, the relative rarity of negative statements as against affirmative ones. Whether or not this explanation holds water cannot be ascertained from the paper under review, since the authors do not present in full their statistical findings on sentence-occurrence. (The explanation is, possibly, contested by the authors' remark that affirmative echoes occur "fairly often"; this would depend on *how* often.) I think I should note, in addition, that my own judgments in this matter may be warped to a degree by the fact that in my Philadelphia dialect the common "echo questions" are not "Did we?" and "Didn't we?", but rather "We did?" and "We didn't?". But even if this last observation should hold for all dialects, it would not, of course, account for the phenomenon in question; it would just make it all the more mysterious, since Brown and Hanlon's children would then be using echo-sentences they could scarcely have heard at all.

The rarity of the "Didn't we?" type of echo-question is used, in turn, to explain a second phenomenon, a pattern of mistakes in the speech of the authors' subjects. The children do form incorrect *affirmative* tags (*"We have a ball, do we?") but they never form incorrect *negative* tags (*"We don't have a ball, don't we?"). The authors explain this fact in this way: the incorrect tags

have the forms of *correct* "statement + echo" dialogs, and children who controlled the use of "Do we?" as an 'echo' to, for example, "We have a ball,"
might be expected to make the mistake of using "Do we?" as a 'tag' to the same
sentence. The tag-question would then have the form of a "statement + echo"
produced by one speaker instead of by two. (It might be pertinent to recall
Weir's observation [1962] that a child's monologs may contain dialogs, including
[p. 91] question-and-answer sequences, which are conducted with himself as
interlocutor.) But, since the children do not control the negative echo, they
would not (on this reasoning) be moved to form incorrect negative tag-questions
along the same lines, since the basis of such malformations would be missing.

Now, unless the absence of "Don't we?" is only a statistical accident, this
is of course a possible explanation; but it is not the only one. One could,
alternatively, assume that in using "We have a ball, do we?" children are only
misusing the common sarcastic or disputative sentence of exactly that form.
For, of course, these affirmative sentences are *not* always malformed; as dispu-
tations, they are quite grammatical. But, explaining the children's failure to
misuse them, the *negative* counterparts ("We don't have a ball, don't we?") are
ungrammatical with or without disputative meaning, and hence are presumably
absent from the elders' speech, on which a child's mistake could be based. Now,
misusing the affirmative disputative sentences would entail the children's
ignoring the fact that, in disputative use, these sentences have a quite distinctive
("sarcastic") intonation pattern; and it might be contended that the children
would not do this, since they acquire command over intonations rather early
(Weir, 1966, pp. 156-158). However there seems to be no evidence that
children control (or comprehend) the *sarcastic* intonations early, and, pending
discovery of such evidence, my proposed explanation remains a plausible alternative. It is not *more* plausible than Brown and Hanlon's explanation; but it does
at least accommodate the (otherwise coincidental) fact that the affirmative
malformations, but not the negative ones, are properly formed under the disputative interpretation. Of course it would be disproven if it were to be shown
that parents are never disputatious.

4. The authors express willingness (pp. 38f) to invoke a Zipfian "Principle
of Least Effort" to account for the putative fact that, in English, frequency of
a sentence type (such as SAAD) varies as the inverse of derivational complexity.
They say:

> The derivationally simple sentence types seem to be those we most often need,
> and the derivationally complex types those we need less often. *If psychological
> complexity is related to derivational complexity* (italics supplied), then it may
> not be inappropriate to invoke a Principle of Least Effort.

In other words, what the authors seem to be suggesting is that when a sentence
type (SAAD) is used very often its derivations in time become simplified, so

that in the end the most used have been the most simplified, and it becomes
fitting to extend the "Least Effort" principle in (partial) answer to the ontologi-
cal question: why do the sentences of English have the derivations that they do,
instead of some other derivations?

Three comments seem germane to this important proposal:

(a) The *basis* for any general "Least Effort" principle of the kind proposed must
be twofold: (1) it is really true that the "derivationally simple sentence types
seem to be those we most often need. . ."; and (2) the phrase ". . .most often
need. . ." reflects a preponderance of need that is significant and that, presumably,
is unconsciously "felt" by speakers.

As to (1), this claim is put into doubt by the fact that there are common cases
in English of two meanings very similar and therefore presumably not in grossly
unequal demand, but one of which is represented by an SAAD and the other
by a sentence of *complex* derivation. For example, two sentences can differ in
that one has a definite subject, the other an indefinite one; the former sentence
is an SAAD ("The typewriter's on the table"), while the latter is of more complex derivation ("There's a typewriter on the table"). Other cases of two
sentence types (neither an SAAD) in which the more derivationally complex
sentence "X" is more (not less) frequent than "Y," are these: ("X." "Shelley
has been read by *everyone*." "Y." "Shelley, *everyone* has read.") and ("X."
"There's a typewriter on the table." "Y." "On the table there's a typewriter.")
In addition, we note that the category "SAAD" is quite undefined, and that the
set of sentences which at first glance might seem to be legitimate SAAD and
therefore to have closely-related bases, in fact includes pseudo-SAAD that have
no such relation at all. Thus, for example, "The hammer hit the nail" appears
to be an SAAD, but it is probably only a variant of "Δ hit the nail with the
hammer," having essentially the base of the latter sentence, which (Lakoff, 1968,
esp. pp. 23-29) is representable as "Δ used the hammar to hit the nail." So
"The hammer hit the nail" is not an SAAD, really, and neither are some other
apparent members of this set. But to cut away the set's membership is to reduce
the frequency with which the set's members occur; the SAAD are less frequent
than at first appears. From all of these considerations it follows that, although
SAAD are derivationally simple and are also relatively common, it very much
remains to be proven that there is any general connection between frequency-of-
use and derivational simplicity.

As to claim (2), this assertion is scarcely so burdened with plausibility as
to be accepted as a basic assumption, yet neither is it supported by any empirical
findings. True, this particular claim of preponderant frequency is not among
those that Chomsky once punctured (1957, pp. 16-17), but it seems no less
doubtful. Everyone knows that there are genuine rarities among linguistic

forms — such as "waste not, want not" — and such *extreme* rarities we might
expect to be felt as such, in some sense, by speakers. (They are unproductive,
are foregrounded, are perhaps delivered with peculiar intonation, and the like.)
But apothegms are a far cry from sentence-types used scores of times a day by
the average speaker, as must be the case, for all but the veriest recluse, with
such common sentence types as questions and negatives. In other words it is
hard to believe that questions are enough rarer than declaratives to be "felt" as
such by speakers; but if they are not so "felt," *in some sense*, there is no warrant
for supposing that they are less subject to "Least Effort" simplifying pressures.

(b). However, the correlation between frequency and derivational complexity, while probably too weak to sustain a *universal* "Least Effort Principle"
(hereafter, LEP), might still serve to uphold a more local such principle, if
"felt preponderance" could be lent some slight credence; the most frequent
sentence type *is* the one most simply derived, and LEP might offer a more
acceptable explanation of this relationship than would mere accident. Let us,
then, restricting ourselves to the SAAD itself, try to determine whether it is
reasonable to say that an LEP contributed significantly to the present-day
derivational complexity of the SAAD.

Brown and Hanlon's claim amounts to this: an LEP operated at some
time in the past so as to make the English SAAD more simply derived; that is,
in their usage, more simply derived from its deep structure. This means than
an LEP has operated so as to make the SAAD (and its derived constituent
structure) more *like* its deep structure, in some significant respect; for as a
sentence diverges increasingly from its deep structure it requires a more complex derivation to achieve the divergence. For the purposes of the present discussion we will, like Brown and Hanlon, restrict our attention to the so-called
"simplex" sentences whose deep structures were distinguished by Chomsky
(1965, p. 17 and elsewhere) as "base phrase-markers," or simply, as we will use
the term here, "bases." Now, any active (SAAD) sentence with a passive
counterpart contains exactly the same words as the corresponding passive
(except the constants—like "by"—of the passive transform), and so it cannot
be that LEP has operated so as to make the lexical constituents of the SAAD
more like those of the base than are those of the passive. In the *Aspects* version
of the grammar the bases of questions, negatives, and passives contain different
segmental morphemes by which transformations will subsequently be triggered;
but LEP cannot have brought the named sentence types closer to the base by
eliminating these morphemes, since the effect of such removal would simply be
the excision from the language of questions, negatives, and passives. Thus LEP
cannot have operated so as to delete (or add) either lexical or non-lexical constituents. The only reasonable expectation of an LEP, it would seem, is that
LEP has changed the *order* of elements, in either base or SAAD, so as to make

the two orders less distant. This change in order—shifting our attention to
non-simplex sentences for a moment—cannot have been one which affected only
the order in which noun and modifying adjective occur, or some similar relation,
since this change would affect all sentence types equally, bringing all closer to
the base, thus failing to single out the SAAD as closest. Ignoring one or two
minor leads, we see that the only *significant* way in which the SAAD could have
been brought closer to the base is that the order of the SAAD's main elements
(subject, verb, and object) must have been changed so as to accord more closely
with the order of those elements in the base; or that the order in the base must
have rearranged so as to accord more closely with that in the SAAD; or a combination of both movements. Such a change would typically not affect all other
sentence types equally, especially not those (question, negative, and passive)
whose frequencies (with Brown and Hanlon) are competitive with that of the
SAAD, since generally (and notably in the three sentence types just named) the
effect of transformations, in contributing to the composition of these other
sentences, is to reorder elements of the base, so that if the SAAD represented
the *minimal* reordering, in the language in question, a necessary consequence
would be that these other reorderings would force the other transforms further
than the SAAD from the base.

There are languages that have interrogative sentences which consist of
"interrogative particle" + SAAD, and which are therefore, presumably, as close
to their base (the base augmented by a 'Q' particle) as the SAAD are to *their*
base; Hopi is such a language (Whorf, 1956, p. 117). But then Hopi might be
put down as "exceptional," as just making LEP "general" rather than "universal."
Let us adopt that position here, for the time being, in order to give LEP as much
rope as possible. For the same reason we will also accept the *Aspects* (Chomsky,
1965) notion of base—the notion "base phrase-marker" mentioned just
above—since in this formulation SAAD and base are characteristically quite
similar, thus offering LEP whatever support could be offered by similarity alone.
Hereafter, though, in the interests of clarity, we will refer to "the" base only
if we mean the base considered without regard to how it may have been augmented by the morphemes ("triggers") that distinguish paradigms and that often
subsequently trigger transformations; thus we will say that in English the SAAD
and the negative are not equidistant from "the" base. The SAAD and the negative have different bases, but their bases differ only in that the negative contains
a negative morpheme, or "trigger," while the SAAD contains either an affirmative morpheme or, conventionally, no morpheme of this category at all. When
in discussion of a particular sentence type we refer to "*its*" base, we will mean
its base as distinctively augmented.

The test of the effect of LEP has boiled down to this, then: taking
S(ubject), V(erb), and O(bject) as the basic constitutents of both base and SAAD,

we will seek to discover whether there has been any change in the order of those
elements (such as from SOV to VSO) in either base or SAAD; and, if so, if that
change was such as to bring base and SAAD closer together; and, if so, if that
decrease in distance seems reasonably attributable to the ministrations of an
LEP. "Distance" and "decrease in distance" we will measure in what I think is
the obvious way: we will determine, of any two forms, how many context-
sensitive rules are required, at the minimum, to derive either from the other,
and this number will be assigned that pair of terms as their index of distance.
Thus, SVO has a distance of 0 from SVO, a distance of 1 from SOV, a distance
of 2 from OSV, and a distance of 3 (the maximum) from OVS. A reduction in
distance will be reflected as a decrease in these indices of distance. If an SVO
base was formerly associated with an OSV SAAD (a distance of 2), and is now
associated with an SOV SAAD (a distance of 1), the achieved change in distance
is obtained by subtracting the old distance from the new; that is, the change is
-1. (This information is presented in tabular form below, in Table 2.1 and 2.2.)

The order of the elements in the present-day English SAAD is of course a
given; it is SVO. The order of those elements in the *Aspects* base is, on the other
hand, a hypothesis having (deeply) to do with the form of the SAAD, with the
structure of the grammar as a whole, and with properties of pertinent linguistic
universals. In constructing a grammar for English with a given base one may,
roughly speaking, rely on all of these criteria (to the extent that they are mutually compatible), or else, rejecting the third ("universal") criterion, one might try
to set up a base founded on principles inherent in English alone; thus, briefly,
one may use purely "local" criteria or else rely more on "universal" criteria.

Taking up the "universal" basis first, we begin by observing that if the
"universal" base is to have a consistently close relationship to the SAAD of each
language having the "universal" base, then that closeness could be assured only
if the languages of the world were remarkably similar with respect to their SAAD.
But they *are* remarkably similar. Greenberg has shown (1961, p. 77) that in the
overwhelming majority of languages the SAAD is such that the subject precedes
the object; in fact, Greenberg (ibid., p. 105, n. 5) could discover only three
exceptions to this fundamental S. . .O order. Thus the "universally"-founded
base should also, to correspond correctly to the general SAAD, have the order
S. . .O. Then, of the six possible combinations of S, V, and O, the only candi-
dates for "universal base" are SVO, SOV, and VSO, since VOS, OSV, and OVS
are disallowed. Of these possible combinations, still according to Greenberg,
SVO is the most common SAAD, followed by SOV; not only is VSO much
rarer, but also (ibid., p. 79) whenever a language has a VSO SAAD it has in
addition an SVO Active Affirmative Declarative. Thus VSO has an inferior status with respect to the other two forms. We note the probable reason for this:
assuming a tendency in every language for the SAAD to have a derived consti-

tuent structure in which V(erb) and O(bject) are dominated by the constituent "V(erb) P(hrase)"—assuming this, we observe that such a domination by VP is possible only in the forms SVO and SOV, since, of the three possible forms, only these two preserve the verb phrase in its unbroken state, whether VO or OV. In VSO the V is separated from the O; and when V and O are separated in this way they can no longer, in a conventional phrase structure, be dominated by VP (or by any other node that does not also dominate SS), since there is no structure of the following sort.

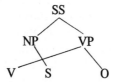

In VSO, there *is* no verb phrase. We see then that SVO and SOV are the only two combinations of S, V, and O that obey both of these criteria: (1) S and O are to occur in that order, and (2) V and O are jointly to be dominated by the node VP. Thus a language's SAAD will tend strongly to be SOV (German and Latin) or SVO (English and French); and insofar as the base and the SAAD are to be similar, the "universal" base has the form $S \begin{Bmatrix} VO \\ OV \end{Bmatrix}$.

This is not really the place to justify further the "universal" base, but at least passing reference must be made to two pivotal points mentioned above. The first of these is the question of why the S. . .O order is so widespread in the SAAD of the world's languages. The answer is that there is reasonable consensus (Jakobson, 1961, p. 269; Chomsky, 1965, pp. 11, 225) that "iconic" factors are involved here (where "iconic" is a rather undefined term meant to designate the extent to which we mirror our perceptions in our sentences). Here of course the presumption is that our attention tends to be seized first by the "subject" of an action being perceived and being put into language—and only secondarily by the "object," if any, or perhaps (as construed above, this comes to the same thing) only secondarily by what (in the VP) is to be predicated of the subject. Thus, as Jakobson puts it (op cit., pp. 268-270), all orders other than $S \begin{Bmatrix} VO \\ OV \end{Bmatrix}$ are generally felt to be departures from the ("iconic") norm.

This brings us to the second pivotal point, the question of why it is taken for granted that the quasi-universal SAAD ought to imply a similar quasi-universal base. The reason is that both base and SAAD are, at their respective levels, the maximally "neutral" forms and the maximally "unmarked" forms. In this sense we say of the English passive, or of the primitive 'VP+NP' inversions like "and so say all of us," that they have "shifted" the "basic" order of elements. (For a discussion of other "marked" and "unmarked" sentence types, see Clark and Clark, 1968). This sense of the SAAD as representing the "neutral" base is to some extent borne out by psychological experiments (Mehler, 1963) which seem to show that speakers of English mistakenly remember passives as actives much more readily than actives as passives, and that in respect to the active the passive shares this "recessive" character with negative and interrogative sentences. The interpretation proposed for this result (Mehler, ibid.; Miller, 1962) was that sentences are remembered as "Base + Transformations", and that the transformations are often forgotten, leaving just the base, which, if retransformed into a sentence (offered by a subject to the experimenter), would be the SAAD. Of course this interpretation was based on the then-current model of grammar, in which negativization was simply an optional transformation. In the more recent model (Chomsky, 1965), negativization is *primarily* a negative particle in the base, and *then* an obligatory transformation triggered by that particle; but in an interpretation based on this recension we could still say that such elements as the negative particle, which are optional in the base, tend to be forgotten more readily than the simple base, and so the Miller-Mehler explanation retains plausibility. (For difficulties with Miller-Mehler, see Fodor and Garrett [1966, 1967]; for difficulties with Fodor and Garrett, see Watt [1969].) Thus it is reasonable to say that there is some psychological warrant for thinking that the English SAAD is virtually "a pronunciation of the base", hence some psychological reason—in addition to other reasons—for saying that in English the form of the SAAD is, independently, a strong clue to the form of the base. It might, in fact, seem plausible that in *any* language the SAAD ought to offer such a clue; but here a cautionary note is needed. A language may, rarely, have a sentence type that is closer to the putative base than its SAAD is, and in any such language the "proximity hypothesis" would predict that speakers should mistakenly remember the further sentence type as the closer (since they are essentially misremembering the base itself), and so their response-bias would be away from the SAAD rather than toward it. In such a case the hypothesized base could, perhaps, be unseated by psycholinguistic testing that showed that the bias was not as predicted.

In any case, without taking these brief comments any further, we see the reasonableness of the assertion that, at least in English, the SAAD is closer to its base than is any other sentence type to *its* base. (It should perhaps be remarked, lastly, that other sorts of evidence, of the kind cited in Chomsky, 1957, pp. 79-81, seem compatible with the present reasoning.)

Granting the "universal" base to be S $\left\{ \begin{matrix} OV \\ VO \end{matrix} \right\}$, and taking as a given the present-day SAAD's form, SVO, let us see what effect LEP can have had in making the English SAAD the sentence that is closest to the base. First of all we note that on the simplest view the fact that the English SAAD is SVO implies that the current English base is SVO too; but for the moment we will not draw this conclusion. Let us say only that the English base is now, and has been in the past, either SOV or SVO, having had, possibly, a form in the past different from the one it has at present.

Now we consider just two stages of the language: T_n, the stage, including the present, at which the language is as it is now, and T_f, the most recent former stage at which, in the respect under examination, the language was different. We have observed that it is possible that LEP operated so as to narrow the distance between the base and the SAAD by altering the base or the SAAD or both. Let us first consider, illustratively, a case where the SAAD was changed in the direction of the base, the latter remaining constant. Let us say that the base at T_f was SVO. The SAAD at T_n is also SVO (this will remain a given throughout this discussion). If the SAAD at T_f was SVO too (like the Base at T_f and like the SAAD at T_n), then no change has taken place; none was necessary; and LEP could not have operated. The old SVO SAAD and the new SVO SAAD had the same distance from the old SVO base; this distance, measured by context-sensitive rules in the manner presented above, was 0.

We now widen our scope to include the full set of combinatorily-possible SAAD, as shown in Table 2.1, where it appears, at first glance at least, that LEP could have operated in any one of five cases so as to reduce base-SAAD distance.

TABLE 2.1

		T_f				T_n		Change in Distance
	Base	SAAD	Base-SAAD Distance	Base	SAAD	Base-SAAD Distance		T_f-T_n
(i)	SVO	SVO	0	SVO	SVO	0		0
(ii)	SVO	SOV	1	SVO	SVO	0		-1
(iii)	SVO	VSO	1	SVO	SVO	0		-1
(iv)	SVO	VOS	2	SVO	SVO	0		-2
(v)	SVO	OSV	2	SVO	SVO	0		-2
(vi)	SVO	OVS	3	SVO	SVO	0		-3

In extending these comparisons so as to cover other kinds of base and of SAAD, we may properly disregard the outlandish SAAD (OVS,OSV,VOS) given in the complete range of Table 2.1; and we have already shown reason for holding that the plausible English bases are SVO and SOV. (Either base might, more abstractly, be derived from the proto-base S $\left\{ \begin{matrix} VO \\ OV \end{matrix} \right\}$.) Excluding all of the impossible cases, then, the remaining possible effects of LEP can now be given, in Table 2.2.

TABLE 2.2

	T_f				T_n			Change in Distance
	Base	SAAD	Base-SAAD Distance	Base	SAAD	Base-SAAD Distance		T_f-T_n
(vii)	SVO	SVO	0	SOV	SVO	1		+1
(viii)	SVO	SOV	1	SOV	SVO	1		0
(ix)	SVO	VSO	1	SVO	SVO	0		-1
(x)	SVO	VSO	1	SOV	SVO	1		0
(xi)	SOV	SVO	1	SOV	SVO	1		0
(xii)	SOV	SVO	1	SVO	SVO	0		-1
(xiii)	SOV	SOV	0	SOV	SVO	1		+1
(xiv)	SOV	SOV	0	SVO	SVO	0		0
(xv)	SOV	VSO	2	SOV	SVO	1		-1
(xvi)	SOV	VSO	2	SVO	SVO	0		-2

From Table 2.1 we have already struck from serious consideration all of the outlandish cases, leaving just (i) and (ii) from that table. And, even though Table 2.2 contains no outlandish examples, we can still strike two more cases from it, namely (vii) and (xiii), since in both of these cases the base-SAAD distance *increased*, hardly the possible effect of a Least Effort Principle (though a *Greatest* Effort Principle might have applied). This leaves us, after eliminating the preposterous and/or counter-LEP examples, ten cases; but then from these we must subtract in turn all cases where LEP can only have operated vacuously, if at all: the cases where the change in base-SAAD distance was nil. This criterion eliminates (i), (viii), (x), (xi), and (xiv); so that finally we are left with only five cases—(ii), (ix), (xii), (xv), and (xvi)—in which, if they represented actual events in the history of Englsih, LEP could have operated. However, three of these cases—(ix), (xv), and (xvi)—represent events in the history of English which are known not to have taken place, for at the most recent time when it was other than SVO the SAAD was, not VSO, but SOV (Mossé, 1952, p. 129 ff.).

This leaves us, finally, with the two cases (ii) and (xii); for convenience, we repeat these two in Table 2.3.

TABLE 2.3

	T_f				T_n			Change in Distance
	Base	SAAD	Base-SAAD Distance	Base	SAAD	Base-SAAD Distance		T_f-T_n
(ii)	SVO	SOV	1	SVO	SVO	0		-1
(xii)	SOV	SVO	1	SVO	SVO	0		-1

 Cases (ii) and (xii) are of course quite similar; they differ only in that (ii) implies that when the base is SVO, then the SAAD must follow suit, while (xii) implies that when the *SAAD* is SVO then the *base* must follow suit.

 We now consider these two cases. We first make the hypothesis, really no more than a rather obvious observation, that when at any time a language's base is differently-ordered from its SAAD, in some "case," that "case" is scarcely maintaining that the base is just an abstract version of the SAAD, and must be maintaining, instead, that either (a) that particular base is an absolute universal, or (b) the language is in a state of transition and the SAAD has temporarily outstripped the base, or vice versa. Thus, in (ii), where base is SVO and SAAD is SOV, either SVO is an absolute universal (and SOV is not a possible base in any language), or else base and SAAD used both to be SVO (and the SAAD changed to SOV) or used both to be SOV (and the base changed to SVO). To take these possibilities up in order, if SVO is the base in every language, then it is the base in German, another language with an SOV SAAD; but then if in English this variety of base/SAAD disparity led to a change in the SAAD to SVO, agreeing with the base, and if this change was forced by LEP, why did not LEP force the same change in German? Surely we cannot grant psychological reality to a Least Effort Principle that operates among some language-populations but not among others; this would reduce to "All speakers use the least effort, but some use less least effort than others." And so, if (ii) happened because of disagreement with a universal base, the change cannot be attributed to a plausible LEP. We now take up the second possibility, that both base and SAAD had been SVO, but before T_f the SAAD had changed to SOV, leaving behind a laggard base. We note first of all that to admit such an event as possible is to torpedo LEP, since any such change increases the Base-SAAD distance by one, which (unless the SAAD underwent a great decline in frequency prior to the distance-increase) means that LEP is sometimes directly countered. But,

ignoring this issue for the time being, let us ask if, in any case, some prior event
like that just described as setting the stage for (ii) actually happened in the history of English. That is, did English have, before it had its present SVO SAAD,
an SOV SAAD, and before that SOV SAAD, an SVO SAAD? The answer, on
the available evidence, is "No"; before English had its present SVO SAAD it
had an SOV SAAD (we will return to this point in a moment), and had had this
SOV SAAD for many centuries. Thus this interpretation of (ii) loses credibility
because the "transitional" stage of English that it postulates is very low in credibility. Let us, lastly, take up the third possibility, that (ii) describes a transitional stage of the language, but one in which, after a time when both base and
SAAD were SOV, the base has become SVO. Now, while we cannot really *prove*
that a language's base cannot move from under its SAAD, increasing the distance
separating them, on the other hand such an event in linguistic history has no
warrant either in theory or in empirical fact (whatever such fact might be).
Thus this interpretation of (ii), while not strictly disprovable, is deserving of
little credence. (And note that, like the second interpretation, it also destroys
LEP.) But if all three of these interpretations can be cast out, then case (ii) has
no plausible Interpretation, and so case (ii) itself may be cast out.

  We now turn to case (xii). Because case (xii) is, under one interpretation,
superficially plausible, its various *im*plausible interpretations need not detain us.
Under its two more plausible interpretations, then, case (xii) implies either that
from a previous time when both base and SAAD were SVO, the base has changed
to SOV at T_f—changing back to SVO at T_n—or else that from a previous time
when both base and SAAD were SOV, the SAAD at T_f has changed to SVO, the
base catching up at T_n. Put this way, as can be seen, the first interpretation is
in fact quite preposterous—and it explains no observable fact of language
change—but on the other hand, the second interpretation actually appears to
describe an event in the history of English. For it is well known that, while in
Old English the SAAD had the basic form SOV, in Middle English the SAAD
became SVO, as at present. This is precisely the change that is reflected by
Closs (1965) in what are (essentially) base-formation rules for Old and Middle
English; compare her rules 4.3 (p. 407) and 5.3 (p. 410) for a representation of
this change. Here, then, we have exactly the change in the SAAD—from SOV
to SVO—that might explain the state of affairs at T_f in (xii), since we might with
some reason hypothesize that in Old English both SAAD and base had been
SOV, but that at the beginning of Middle English—T_f—the SAAD, but not yet
the base, had already changed over to SVO. Thus (xii) was, exactly, preceded
by (xiii), where T_n of (xiii) is the same as T_f of (xii).

  This leads us, however, to ask why it was that the base did not, immediately, follow suit, so that there would have been no observable stage like T_f at all;

that is, we ask how can speakers (or their language, early Middle English) have changed the SAAD to SVO without at the same time changing the base?

There is, in fact, good reason for thinking that just the stage represented by T_f in (xii) *would* come about, persisting for something like a linguistic generation. In particular, there is reason to expect that the first generation of speakers to change to an SVO SAAD—those who had begun speaking with an SOV SAAD—would not alter the deeper structures of their mental grammars, and so their SOV bases would remain undisturbed. (Of course neither their alteration nor their failure to alter were at all conscious acts, though we might suppose many to have been aware of the novelty of the SVO SAAD.) Thus the stage T_f of (xii) catches English at just the point where SVO is now the predominant SAAD, but where no generation of speakers who *began* with an SVO SAAD has yet come of age. This is not a trivial observation, since, as has been widely acknowledged, a language changes in part because of what children make of the language in the process of learning it. This has been recognized at least since Hockett (1950), and has achieved a more rigorous formulation in Halle (1962). Crediting Meillet with having adumbrated this notion some years before, Halle (p. 65) asserts that an adult's grammar (in his case, an adult's phonological component) may be innovative in an inefficient way that violates the criterion of "simplicity" of grammars, whereas children, to learn such a language from the start, may be expected to construct for that language the simplest possible grammar; hence, by implication, a grammar simpler than their elders'. Then Halle's notion of a child's (unconsciously) constructing a better grammar for a newly-altered language is precisely the notion that can explain case (xii), if (xii) actually happened: a generation of adults innovated an SVO SAAD but, being "maximally conservative" in Halle's phrase (ibid.) they did not alter the structure of the base—whence the status of English at T_f. What makes the essential difference by T_n is that in the interim at least one generation has come of age that has learned the new SVO SAAD from the start, integrating it into a better (simpler) grammar, one with an SVO base. (A grammar with both SAAD and base SVO is simpler by virtue of dispensing with the transformation—really just the CS rule OV → VO—that was necessary during the "interim" period.)

Complicating this picture, but at the same time making this interpretation of (xii) even more plausible, in a way, is the fact that, as might be expected, the change of the SAAD from SOV to SVO did not happen all at once, or simultaneously among all speakers (or among all English dialects), or—importantly—even among all SAAD. Ignoring the dialectal differences, the changeover seems to have begun around 1300 (I cannot agree with Closs, 1965, p. 408, that the change was complete by 1200), and at first to have affected the nominal objects unequally, shifting full-fledged noun phrases to

SVO somewhat faster than the pronouns were shifted. Thus, while Mossé (1952) says of this period that "the *usual* order (italics supplied) puts the object after the verb," he cautions that the OV order was fading only gradually. For full-fledged nouns the change seems to have been consolidated by about 1350, but with OV examples still cropping up a bit later; with pronouns the change was probably consolidated not long afterward, perhaps before 1400. Giving age 14 as that at which speakers reach linguistic majority, this would mean that even if the changeover had happened all at once, the base changeover should have been delayed by about 14 years; as it is, given the vagueness of the dates and the diffuseness of the change, it is hard to say whether the children would be constructing a simpler grammar, in founding it on an SVO base, when most SAAD with nouns were SVO, or when most SAAD, including those whose O(bjects) were pronouns, were SVO. But in any event it seems clear that the thesis that at the beginning of Middle English the SAAD preceded the base in becoming SVO, is quite plausible, and is virtually a necessary consequence if Halle's hypotheses are expanded into *general* hypotheses that hold also for syntax. Thus case (xii) has a great deal of plausibility indeed, as describing the latter stage of a diachronic change (in the base subcomponent) that took place at around 1400. It remains to be seen whether or not the plausibility of (xii) serves to uphold LEP.

In fact, the plausibility of (xii) appears to *disconfirm* Brown and Hanlon's proposed LEP. We have built up a case for the plausibility of (xii) on an interpretation underwhich the state of affairs at the onset of (xii)—Base SOV and SAAD SVO—was brought about by a change in the SAAD from its previous SOV, and so was brought about, as was mentioned above, precisely by an event corresponding to case (xiii). Thus (xii) is really only plausible if (xiii) is plausible. But (xiii), as is shown in Table 2, *increases* the base-SAAD distance by 1, which if the SAAD maintained its frequency runs directly counter to LEP. Thus the plausibility of (xii), necessary to uphold LEP, is contingent on the plausibility of (xiii), which serves to reject LEP.

It might at first seem that Halle's simplicity hypotheses, as expanded, are also directly undercut by (xiii), but they are not; and the fact that they are not is sufficient to dispel any hope that LEP can be saved by being merged with, reformulated as, or made a corollary to the expanded simplicity hypotheses. LEP claims that a sentence's relative frequency determines its relative distance from the base, and that distance can increase only if the frequency *de*creases; thus, according to LEP, (xiii) reflects a significant decline in the frequency of the English SAAD, or at least reflects the fact that the SAAD's frequency was surpassed by that of some other sentence type. One could conceivably argue that the coming to prominence of some new sentence type might influence the *base* in some way; but is it at all credible, finally, that the Middle English SAAD changed its form because it declined in relative frequency? Thus even without considering whether such a decline actually took place, (xiii) renders LEP implausible. But the simplicity hypotheses do not make any claim that is undercut by (xiii), since they make no claim about the forms of sentences or about the forces that influence those forms. All that the simplicity hypotheses apply to, in the present instance, is the restoration of the grammar, as altered by (xiii), to the simplicity gained in (xii). Nor do the simplicity hypotheses entail any claim about the *frequency* of the SAAD toward which (in my tentative proposal) the base has moved. Thus, the expanded simplicity hypotheses and LEP part company over the central issue of whether or not sentential frequency determines grammatical complexity, and they cannot be reconciled save by gutting LEP of its main feature.

On the other hand it might still be claimed, as was suggested above, that frequency does play a role here and there, although ample evidence has been adduced to show that LEP's role must be, at the most, very fitful. It would certainly be interesting to know whether an absolutely "performative" aspect like sentential frequency could influence the form of the mental grammar, however negatively; but at present it seems fair to say that LEP remains undemonstrated.

The same comment, with little qualification in favor of LEP, holds for any still weaker versions of LEP that might be put forward. (Of course these would not resemble the strong version put forward by Brown and Hanlon, and I do not mean to impute such notions to those authors.) But any such weaker version, as far as I can see, must be so weak as to explain nothing that is not already, necessarily, explained by a stronger theory. Any theory of syntactic LEP, then, lacks independent confirmation, and is constrained to account for the fact that LEP is so unreliable.

We have, in explaining why it is that in English base and SAAD are so similar in form, rejected LEP; but in so doing we have not taken a fresh look at the phenomenon we began with—the fact that the SAAD is both the most frequent sentence-type and, undeniably, the closest to the base. (We have already shown that it is not *generally* true that frequency varies as the inverse of proximity to the base; but this demonstration does not apply directly to the SAAD, since these sentences do display the correlation, and we are obliged to show whether this restricted correlation is the result of accident or, rather, obeys some principle.) Let us return, very briefly, to this question. We have shown that it cannot be that the frequency of the SAAD draws them closer to the base: could it be that their proximity determines their frequency? Manifestly not, for any such "Principle" would have it that speakers use more SAAD because the SAAD are simplest, rather than because speakers have more need of declaratives than of questions, or of actives than of passives; that is, this

"Principle" would hold that speakers take no interest in what they are saying. Even where the speaker chooses between two paraphrastic sentences, as between SAAD and the corresponding passive, there seems no reason to suppose that the SAAD predominate (Svartvik, 1966) just because they are simpler, since adopting this position would entail claiming that the passive does not differ from the SAAD in any way (*other than derivational complexity*) that could influence the choice between SAAD and passive. But this entailed claim is false; among both psychologists (Osgood, 1954, p. 170; Clark, 1965; Johnson-Laird, 1968) and linguists (Jespersen, 1933, pp. 120-123; Svartvik, op.cit.; Halliday, 1967, pp. 213, 215-218), it is well known that the passive performs the essential function of allowing inversion of the underlying subject and object while preserving, on the surface, the usual SVO declarative order. There has even been some study of why these inversions are sometimes favored (Firbas, 1964, and other works there referenced; Halliday, op.cit.). Thus speakers are not free—or not often free—to choose the SAAD just on the grounds of their simpler derivation—and so we are still barred from concluding that the SAAD's simplicity plays any significant role in conditioning their frequency.

It would seem, then, that the SAAD's simplicity and frequency are not connected either as cause and effect or vice versa. In fact, their relationship appears to be this: they are both effects of the same cause, namely, the fundamental nature of the order-of-elements, SVO in English, that is reflected in the base and in the SAAD and—explaining the SAAD's high frequency—in the usage of speakers. Given the present dearth of information on the subject, the "fundamental nature" just cited must be purely hypothetical; but defenses of this hypothesis, in effect, may be found in Jakobson, op.cit.

In brief, then, my suggested replacement for LEP, in explanation of Brown and Hanlon's observed phenomenon, is this: there is a fundamental tendency to put subject and object in that order, with, in modern English, the verb in between; for this reason, and also because this tendency is very widespread, the base in English orders the major elements S,V,O; and for this reason also, the maximally neutral sentence type, the SAAD, has the order S,V,O; thus the SAAD is closest to, hence most simply derived from, the base. For the same reason, people tend to use the order S,V,O—and hence, the SAAD—as their basic sentence, barring cause to do the contrary, which cause is exceptional rather than dominant. (Alternatively, one could say that in English, the basic criteria of ordering on the surface concern topics and foci; that the English SAAD has the basic order topic, verb, focus; that in English the surface topic is most often the basal subject; that in the SAAD the topic is made the surface subject, thus making the surface subject of the SAAD identical with the basal subject;

and, finally, that the surface object, the focus, is identical in the SAAD to the basal object.)

In conclusion, LEP appears to have made no significant contribution to the present-day derivational simplicity of the SAAD, and so LEP cannot explain the simplicity/frequency correlation observed to obtain for sentences of this type. We have not touched directly on the other sentence types for which this correlation was also claimed to obtain; but since LEP has failed to account for the most basic sentence type it promises little in explication of the others. For such an explication various hypotheses come to mind, consistent with the explication for the SAAD offered above; but speculation along these lines seems particularly unprofitable in the absence of broader confirmation of these correlations, and so for the time being the matter may be laid to rest.

(c) We have not quite cut the jugular of the "Least Effort" principle, however, for there is one case, different from the two already considered, in which a *reverse* LEP (where simplicity influences frequency) probably does play a role. This case involves the sentential paradigms containing only sentences which are paraphrastic *and* which have the same order of major lexical constituents, such as the following examples.

(a) "Henry wanted to present the best paper at the Conference in order to win the Pulitzer Prize in linguistics."

(b) "Henry's purpose in wanting to present the best paper at the Conference was to win the Pulitzer Prize in linguistics."

(c) "Henry wanted to present the best paper at the Conference because he wanted to win the Pulitzer Prize in linguistics."

(d) "Henry's wanting to present the best paper at the Conference was due to his wanting to win the Pulitzer Prize in linguistics."

Ignoring minor differences irrelevant to the main issue, sentences (a) through (d), and many others, are paraphrastic *and* have the same order of major lexical constituents; thus, from the point of view of motivating a reason for transforming them from the underlying base, they are equal. No "iconic" factors, then, interfere with the judgment that their differences are arbitrary, or "stylistic"— unless a "Least Effort" principle applies. As I have in effect argued elsewhere (Watt, 1968*b*), it seems reasonable to assume that a reverse "Least Effort" principle does apply here. Sentences (a) and (c) are more simply derived than (b) or (d), and they seem also to be likelier than the other two—in short, more frequently used. Thus it may well be that *when everything else is equal,* a "Least Effort" principle can apply after all.

This concludes my brief list of points in which I differ with Brown and Hanlon on general issues. I have not in this short review attempted to treat every case in which their grammatical explanations are at variance with presently accepted doctrine or with my own opinions; their divergences in such matters generally make no real difference, and as they themselves point out the body of accepted linguistic opinion is constantly shifting, so that belaboring these questions, where grammar itself is not at issue, is scarcely worthwhile.

Lastly, as I noted at the beginning, the few criticisms I have made of some aspects of their report do not directly involve the validity of their chief conclusion or the value of their work as a whole; these are beyond serious challenge.

REFERENCES

Chomsky, N. *Syntactic Structures.* The Hague: Mouton and Co., 1957.

Chomsky, N. *Aspects of the Theory of Syntax.* Cambridge: M.I.T., 1965.

Clark, H.H. Some structural properties of simple active and passive sentences. *Journal of Verbal Learning and Verbal Behavior,* 1965, 4, 365-370.

Clark, H.H., and Clark, E.V. Semantic distinctions and memory for complex sentences. *Quarterly Journal of Experimental Psychology,* 1968, **20,** 129-138.

Closs, E. Diachronic syntax and generative grammar. *Language,* 1965, **41,** 402-415.

Firbas, J. From comparative word-order studies. *Brno Studies in English,* 1964, **4.** 111-126.

Fodor, J., and Garrett, M. Some reflections on competence and performance. In Lyons, J., and Wales, R.J. (Eds.) *Psycholinguistics Papers.* Edinburgh: University of Edinburgh, 1966.

Fodor, J., and Garrett, M. Some syntactic determinants of sentential complexity. *Perception and Psychophysics,* 1967, 4, 304-306.

Greenberg, J.H. Some universals of grammar with particular reference to the order of meaningful elements. In Greenberg, J.H. (Ed.), *Universals of Language.* Cambridge: M.I.T., 1961.

Halle, M. Phonology in generative grammar. *Word,* 1962, 18, 54-72.

Halliday, M.A.K. Notes on transitivity and theme in English, part 2. *Journal of Linguistics,* 1967, **3,** 199-244.

Hockett, C.F. Age-grading and linguistic continuity. *Language,* 1950, **26,** 449-457.

Jakobson, R. Implications of language universals for linguistics. In Greenberg, J.H. (Ed.), *Universals of Language.* Cambridge: M.I.T., 1961.

Jespersen, O. *Essentials of English Grammar.* University, Ala.: University of Alabama, 1966. (Original edition, 1933.)

Johnson-Laird, P.N. The choice of the passive voice in a communicative task. *British Journal of Psychology,* 1968, **59,** 7-15.

Katz, J.J., and Fodor, J.A. The structure of a semantic theory. In Fodor, J.A., and Katz, J.J. (Eds.), *The Structure of Language.* Englewood Cliffs, N.J.: Prentice-Hall, 1964.

Lakoff, G. Instrumental adverbs and the concept of deep structure. *Foundations of Language,* 1968, **4,** 4-29.

Mehler, J. Some effects of grammatical transformation on the recall of English sentences. *Journal of Verbal Learning and Verbal Behavior,* 1963, **2,** 346-351.

Miller, G.A. Some psychological studies of grammar. *American Psychologist,* 1962, 17, 748-762.

Mossé, F. *A Handbook of Middle English,* tr. J.A. Walker. Baltimore: The Johns Hopkins Press, 1952.

Osgood, C.E. Effects of motivational states upon decoding and encoding. In Osgood,
    C.E., and Sebeok, T.A. (Eds.) *Psycholinguistics*. Bloomington: Indiana University,
    1954, 2nd Edition 1965.

Svartvik, J. *On Voice in the English Verb*. The Hague: Mouton and Co., 1966.

Watt, W.C. English reduplication. *Journal of English Linguistics*, 1968a, 2, 96-129.

Watt, W.C. Habitability. *American Documentation*, 1968b, 19, 338-351.

Watt, W.C. On two hypotheses concerning psycholinguistics. In this volume, 1969.

Weir, R.H. *Language in the Crib*. The Hague: Mouton and Co., 1962.

Weir, R.H. Some questions on the child's learning of phonology. In Smith, F., and
    Miller, G.A. (Eds.), *The Genesis of Language*. Cambridge: M.I.T., 1966.

Whorf, B.L. Some verbal categories of Hopi. In Carroll, J.B. (Ed.), *Language Thought and
    Reality: Selected Writings of Benjamin Lee Whorf*. Cambridge: M.I.T., 1956.

CHAPTER 3   *Susan Ervin-Tripp*

University of California, Berkeley

DISCOURSE AGREEMENT: HOW CHILDREN ANSWER QUESTIONS*

Wick Miller and I began the research of which this is a part in 1959 and 1960. This work grew out of the insights into English syntax which *Syntactic Structures* (Chomsky, 1957) had suggested. We had the idea that the structural features described there had important implications for language development, and that for the first time the methods of descriptive linguistics should be rigorously applied to yield successive synchronic descriptions of the grammars of individual children. These would be treated not as deviants from the adult system but as systems with internal consistencies to be discovered. Further, the work of Jean Berko (1958) indicated that for many features of grammar systematic testing might be feasible. Our design, therefore, included both a series of text-eliciting sessions from a small group of children over a period of a year and a half, and a monthly testing session with two dozen children including the intensive sample. The starting ages ranged from 1.11 to 2.5. Because we were more interested in internal patterning than in norms, differing outset ages seemed unimportant.

I need hardly point out that within a few years we learned that Roger Brown 1964 and Martin Braine 1963 had undertaken similar studies at the same time, and that in the ensuing years as the results of more studies have been published we have come to ask more of data on child language than could be yielded by the methods we used at the time. In particular, we all wish we knew more about children's processing of input. The data I am describing here are our closest approach to comprehension research in that study.

This work was originally done with support from grant M3813 from the National Institutes of Mental Health. The current analysis was supported by the Institute for Human Learning and University of California Research Committee. I am much indebted to my colleague, Wick Miller, for designing the tests reported here and collecting the early small-group data, and for relevant analyses in his manuscript for our forthcoming book on the small-group material. Susan Curtiss did the astute coding of the raw data, which were concorded under a program developed by Sydney Lamb and Laura Gould.

79

These data consist primarily of monthly interviews with standardized questions about a picture book, for 24 children starting at about 2.6 - 3.1, and continuing to 3.3 - 4.2. There were two forms of the questions, so that the identical questions were re-asked at two-month intervals, but generally similar questions occurred on both forms. Of course, the story was extremely well-learned by the time the children were tested at later sessions. For five of the children, the collection of free response texts prior to testing provides evidence on stages prior to the testing, which began rather late, we found, in the development of discourse agreement. The children were found through the list of applicants for the University Child Study Center, consisting primarily of children of University personnel and families living near the University.

REQUIREMENTS OF ANSWERS

At first glance, it seems far easier to answer a question than to ask one. The surface structure is shorter, ellipsis allows the use of short phrase responses, and the hearer can frequently rely on relatively minimal cues in the question in finding a short, highly probable response. But this simplicity is deceptive, as we can see from the fact that questions and responses tend to develop contemporaneously. One could consider five features of the question-answering process, but in the following discussion we shall primarily be concerned only with those two which concern the grammatical relations of question and answer. The importance of the structure of answers goes beyond a mere concern with syntax in children; the discourse agreement of question and answer is but one example of the dense internal grammatical relations tying utterances in conversations, and we can consider the child's learning of the question-answer relation to be but one, perhaps the first, of the sequential conversational rules he will learn, and continue to learn in adult life.

Below are some features of answers that we could consider.

(a) The child must learn to discriminate questions from other forms of speech in others, since questions require a different response from him than do other sentence types.

(b) Some semantic interpretation is made of a question, unless it is merely a routine. In addition, a pragmatic interpretation may be required.

(c) The hearer must have an information-search method for locating an answer. On this point, I shall have no more to say.

(d) Among all possible answers to questions, some are appropriate from the standpoint of grammatical category. During the period of development examined here, there is a striking convergence in the direction of restricted distribution of response types for question types. This we will call category agreement.

(e) There is a strong tendency in adult speech for tense and aspect of question and answer to match. The match appears to be semantic rather than strictly a surface match of tense and aspect, however. In addition, ellipsis may mask agreement by permitting an unmarked verb or no verb at all. For these reasons the data on verb agreement are not as satisfactory as the material on category agreement. In this article the primary focus will be on the last two forms of agreement.

RECOGNIZING QUESTIONS

The recently examined texts (Slobin, 1968; Drach, 1968; Kobashigawa, 1968; Pfuderer, 1968) of speech to children by adults and other children indicate that such speech is rich in questions, very repetitive, and consists of short utterances with few errors and false starts. The high percentage of questions suggests that there is in fact a kind of prodding for feedback from the caretakers of the children that could very well help children discriminate questions, since we can expect (though this needs to be verified) that there is higher repetition when nonresponse or inappropriate responses occur. Kobashigawa found that in the text he examined, 15 percent of the statements, and 25 percent of the questions, compared to 60 percent of the imperatives, were repeated.

Brown (1968) has suggested four frames in input sequences which could give a child instruction in the formation of Wh-questions. A fifth frame would give a supplied answer as well as ask a question, teaching a child a direct relation between a question form and the expected reply — such as **Mother:** "Where's the ball? Here's the ball!" If the game is very repetitive, these expected replies may lead to rote routines, so that we find "What happened?" typically brings a reply like "Fall," or "Fall down." The genesis of this connection can be easily surmised.

I am hesitant to suggest that input prompts or training frames are necessary in the input to children; even the new evidence that supposedly appropriate input is more prevalent and the speech addressed to children less "degenerate," ungrammatical, and complex than has sometimes been supposed, is simply speculative in its implications and we sorely need experiments on this point. The age for studying the initial discrimination of questions must be from the very onset of speech, at least well before 1; 9, when we found such discrimination already well established in our youngest subject.

SEMANTIC INTERPRETATION OF QUESTIONS

Do you want some MILK?
Are you SLEEPY?
Where's DADDY?
What's THAT?

In making a semantic interpretation of questions, a hearer may rely on
non-linguistic cues or on single words in the question, without fully processing
the grammatical structure of the question. Systematic exploration with younger
children should therefore include aberrant sentences, such as Carlota Smith reports in this volume, to locate the semantic information. For instance, at the
stage when children typically give locative answers, a question consisting merely
of a noun or of a nonsense word plus noun might produce a locative response.

Later there is the complication that items that are realized syntactically
as interrogatives may be interpreted as requests, requiring an action on the part
of the hearer.

Why don't we bring out the swing?	Yes. Yes I do.	Laura 2.10
Why don't we sit up here on the chaise lounge?	Me too.	Carol 2.10
Why don't you put it in the wastebasket?	Throw away?	Sally 2.00
Whyncha come down here and read the carrot seed book, OK?	I read it. [riyd]	Carol 2.10

The children regularly interpreted "why not" sentences at this age as requests,
and if there was no way to perform the response, they did not reply.

In addition, they commonly learned to produce requests of the syntactic
question form, as in "Could you give me a cookie?" before they productively
employed "could" or "would" elsewhere. In other words, these were stock
forms preceding an imperative just as "please" might.

Beyond the period under study, there is a further ambiguity arising from
the neutralization of information requests with other requests; for example, "Do
you know where Sproul Hall is?" cannot receive a merely affirmative answer, any
more than the "could you + predicate" form can.

Any account of how children process questions must, to be complete, at
some point consider their ability to distinguish the information or action required
of them by alter, complicated as the input may be by the pragmatic neutraliza-
tions of polite discourse.

While most previous work on answers to questions has been semantic in
focus, my attention in this paper is on what our data can best indicate: formal

agreement. We did not have the kind of probing interview that could tell us enough about semantic interpretations.

CATEGORY AGREEMENT

We assume that the development of the semantic features of children's lexicons will be such that the following stages, at least, will be found in answers to questions.

(a) A stage in which replies to Wh-questions could be interpreted as associative responses to stressed words in the questions, plus a few answer routines that are rote learned. Syntactically, we would expect such responses to look like samples of free speech. An ideal experiment would contrast questions, including cue words, with statements, including the same cue words in similar situations, so that the only difference would be the Wh-word and its syntactic consequences. We do not have such ideal data, and in the free texts, one sees that questions are often asked in just those situations most likely to produce categorially appropriate answers.

(b) A stage at which some Wh-words, but not all, have acquired semantic (and syntactic) features. Thus at this point, *what* has the marker [+NP] or possibly [+NP, -an]; *where*, [Adv,+loc]; *who*, [+NP, + an], and so on. We have pointed out above that we wish to avoid, for inadequacy of data, issues of semantic interpretation, but feature-marking does inevitably raise the question of the semantic nature of the features.

At this stage, we assume that lexical entries not in the dictionary will be assigned the features of some form to which they are assimilated, normally another Wh-form already in the lexicon of the child. Why one rather than another form is the one to which assimilation occurs may depend on the context in ways to be examined.

(c) All common Wh-forms have distinctive semantic features, though they may not yet fully correspond to adult features.

Early Texts

By the time the text collection began, from 1; 9-2; 5 with five children, all five had clearly mastered locative features of *where*, and the nominal, non-animate marker for *what*. Four of the five controlled the possessive, + animate, + NP marking for *whose* by 2; 3, and four controlled + animate as a feature of responses to *who*, at the outset of text collection. In the large group study also, *what* and *where* were always appropriately answered.

It is obvious that the capacity to reply within these categories must be related to the development of these units within the phrase structure of the children's grammars, so it comes as no surprise that among the earliest structural units to be found in multi-word sentences in our study were NP, N [+an, +poss] , (distributed __N), and locative phrase.

If we examine the *production* of questions in this early set of texts, we find that *what* and *where* questions are both earliest to appear and most frequent throughout. Other categories of questions did not appear until the middle or end of text collection in some cases, allowing some comparison between the age at which replies are given and the age at which questions are generated. We found delays, in some cases of several months, between good evidence of giving replies to questions and of productive use, at least in the small texts we have. So did Brown (1968).

The use of *who* raised interesting questions at this stage. It was used relatively late by some of the children in their own questions, and the first questions were fixed forms like "Who's that?"

The items in Table 3.1 give a complete set of replies to "who" questions and a partial set for "what . . . doing." In order to compare the structure of replies with free utterances, a procedure for drawing control utterances was used. From the concordance for each sample, a sentence was drawn, using a word from the reply, or one structurally like it, if none existed in the child's text, and the nearest utterance which was not itself a reply, an imitation, or part of a build-up or breakdown set was selected.

It is immediately apparent that Carol reacted to the "who" questions distinctively, whether or not she offered a reply. Her utterances were markedly shorter and simpler than those in free speech. They included replies which more appropriately could have been offered to *what, where,* or *what-do* questions. But they also included more simple NP-hum replies than occurred either in free speech or in her replies to the *what-doing* questions below in Table 1.

Laura, at 2.7, gave almost all location answers for *what-doing* questions, suggesting that she did not discriminate them from the *where* questions with which they were intermingled in the text.

Since a whole VP might be an appropriate reply to such a question, it is relevant to consider what the VP is for the child who is answering. We still see in the control sentences instances like "socks on" and "Bonnie bath," in which particle or object can serve as predicate. Thus it is unclear, in the replies of Sally and Carol, whether they hear the questions as a *where* or *what* question, or whether they give noun and location replies as accurate versions of their VP. We

TABLE 3.1 Replies and Control Free Utterances

Child	Reply	Control[a]
Carol at 2.6		
1. Who is this?	Dolly.	On this *doll* here.
2. Now Papa Small comes home. And who is coming to meet Papa?	Papa getting home.	This is *Papa* Small there.
3. Who's holding onto the toast?	Who's? [imitative]	*What's* that?
4. Now who is this apple for?	Carol's apple.	No. This Joe's *apple.*
5. Who's watching Daddy?	Hm?	
6. Who's watching Daddy?	Shaving.	Joe *sleep.*
7. Who's that?	Paul.	This one help *Paul* there.
8. Who's cooking lunch?	Hm?	
9. Who's eating?	Meat. [F. cutting meat]	Joe take a *nap.*
10. Who is doing the dishes?	Hm?	
11. Who's watching Mama?	(No reply)	
12. Who took Suzy to bed?	Baby wake up.	*Baby* got a toast already.
13. Who took Suzy to bed just now?	Baby wake up. Baby went to bed.	*Wake* up now. Oh, where *go?*
14. Who took Suzy to bed?	Take Suzy bed.	I *take* the bandage off.
15. Yea, who took her to bed?	Mother took her bed.	I want to *take* out there.
16. Hm?	Baby.	That *baby?*
17. Who came in the room just now?	Hm? [baby]	
18. Who's here?	Baby wake up.	Wanta *walk*ey

TABLE 3.1 Replies and Control Free Utterances (cont.)

Child	Reply	Control[a]
19. Who's combing your hair?	Mommy comb hair (of) Carol.	And *cross* a street.
20. Who's watching Daddy?	Huh? Oh, that's baby.	*Baby* out.
21. Who's that?	That baby.	Baby.
22. Who put it in? Who put the car in?	In that hole.	This is *horse*.
23. Who put the car in that hole?	Choochoo-train get that, that choochoo-train go in there.	There's a green *truck*.
Carol at 2.5 – 2.6		
24. You know what the father's doing?	Apple in it. [cutting oranges]	See Santa Claus eating the *apple?*
25. What's the girl doing?	That putting cereal in.	Want *put* a dress in.
26. What's the boy doing now?	He take a bath. And boats.	Want that *take* off there?
27. What's Tommy doing?	Socks in. [putting on socks]	*Socks* on.
28. What's Tommy doing?	Putting shoes.	*Put* it on there.
29. What're they doing now?	Car. [going away]	Joe *cake.*
30. Now what are they doing?	Picnic. [having one]	I want *panties* out.
31. What's Papa Small doing?	Papa looking at baby there.	This is *Papa* Small there.
32. What's George doing here?	Pipe. [smoking]	Where's the *pillow?*
33. What's he doing with his hand?	Bye-bye. [waving]	Dog don't say *bye-bye.*

TABLE 3.1 Replies and Control Free Utterances (cont.)

Child	Reply	Control[a]
34. What's Paul doing?	Huh? Over there.	Baby got teeth hurt *there.*
35. What's the boy doing now?	In the bath.	There go a *bed.*
36. What are you doing?	Fold diaper.	*Fix* on.
37. What are you doing?	Tearing off.	*Tear* up.
38. What are you doing with those pieces of Kleenex?	In there. In there. [in playpen]	Take shower in *there.*
39. What are you doing with the blocks?	Floor. Floor.	Mommy sit down on *floor.* [imperative]
40. What are you doing with the blocks?	Have them.	*Have* these Cindy. [blocks] [imperative]
41. What are you doing with those two lemons?	In there.	Miller sit *there.* *[imperative]*
42. What are you doing?	Joe bath.	Bonnie *bath.*
43. What are you doing?	Juice (for) you.	Here is a *lemon.*
44. What are you doing?	Cooking dinner yum yum yum.	Joe *eat.*
Laura 2.7		
45. What's Papa doing?	He's there.	*There's* Polly.
46. What's baby doing?	There's Mama.	*Mama* sweep floor.
47. What's Papa doing	There's Papa.	That *Papa.*
48. What's Polly doing with the baby?	Baby-toy. [in carriage]	This is Joe's other *toy.*
49. What's Paul doing?	Right there.	*There's* Polly.

TABLE 3.1 Replies and Control Free Utterances (cont.)

Child	Reply	Control[a]
50. What's he doing?	Bye-bye Papa. [waving]	*Wash*ing.
51. What's Papa doing?	Papa face. [shaving]	This is a shoe feet *hand.*
52. What's Polly doing?	Baby-toy.	Baby in baby-*toy.*
53. What's Papa doing?	In car. [going away]	In *car.*

[a] Control utterances were selected by choosing the lexical "center" of the reply, and locating in a concordance a contemporaneous free utterance that was neither a reply, an imitation, or part of a build-up sequence by the child. If no other utterance with the same words met these constraints, another word with similar syntactic features was chosen. Underlined forms are the search items.

would particularly expect such replies if the verb vocabulary required were too difficult, or if the verb were of a dummy type, as in "take a bath" and "have a picnic," in which the "do," or "have" is (like "faire"), a mere carrier of whatever action is suitable for that object. Thus for a child perhaps it is appropriate to "do" a pipe or a bye-bye.

In general, it appeared that the first question responses were for *Yes-no,* next *what,* and next *where* or *what-do,* in the small-group texts.

Large-Group Questions

The materials for the large group study consisted of a book of pictures (Charlip, 1957). The children were shown the book at their first visit for this test. They had already been tested on earlier occasions for plural and possessive morphology, so they knew the setting and examiner. Each session included thirty questions, structured to sample a range of the question forms of English. The test was designed by Wick Miller, my collaborator. It had two forms, so that identical items were elicited every two months, and in many cases grammatically matched items every month.

Before we embark on the details for each category, an overview can be seen in Table 3.2. The Ns in this table vary from case to case because the number of simultaneous mastery instances varies and occasionally the evidence was too ambiguous to include. The judgment of "mastery" will be clear in the

TABLE 3.2 Difficulty of Response Categories

Category	Category Acquired Earlier					
Acquired Later	Why	Who-S	How	Where from	When	Who-O
Why	xx	5	3	4	1	2
Who-S	6	xx	4	3	3	2
How	12	12	xx	8	3	2
Where-from	14	11	10	xx	6	7
When	19	16	13	12	xx	8
Who-O	15	13	11	13	9	xx
Number mastering by 3.1	18	19	12	12	11	11
Number mastering by 3.4	22	20	16	13	17	12

discussion to follow. Usually the first of successive appropriate replies was counted, allowing one "performance" error if it followed more than two successes.

From Table 3.2 it can be seen that the order of acquisition is roughly as follows: why, who-subject < how, where-from < when, who-object. However, there is so much variability in this order for different children, and so few questions in each category, that we must be doubtful of the statistical reliability of the order. Even at the extremes, there were three children who responded to time questions before who-subject questions with categorially appropriate replies, and also one who had explanations later than temporal replies. Since we do not know of work even proposing an order from better data, this provides at least a first glimpse of relative difficulty.

Who

There were four questions relevant to "who": "Who is feeding him?" "Who is petting him?" "Who is he feeding?" "Who is he petting?" In each case a man, boy, and deer were pictured. First, we want to know if "who" is heard as [+an] , and the "feeding" questions allow us to answer this question to some degree, though not perfectly because the structure of a "what" question would be slightly different. Inanimate things, such as food, were given as replies sporadically, but very seldom, so we can conclude, as the small group data indicate, that semantic markers for [+an] are already present by the time testing began.

Of greater interest in this time period is the distinction between who-subject and who-object. About a fourth of the children select the object rather than the subject at around 3.1, when this error is still most prevalent, but this is rare after this point and has disappeared by 3.9. On the contrary, in the questions about the object, the children give appropriate responses all of the time by 3.0, if they reply. *After 3.0 an upsurge of errors begins,* the proportion giving *subject* replies to object questions being very high around 3.10.

Two explanations, which cannot be checked from these data, come to mind. One is that the children have come to respond to the fact that distributionally subjects tend to be animate, objects inanimate. Therefore, as a quick processing strategy they interpret "who" as a subject indicator, so that they are right more often than not for the Who-S sentences but wrong for Who-O. If this is the case, the children who give these responses would never make the reverse error. If one allows for matching at different testing sessions, this prediction does not seem to hold up, though the test cases are few. Thus a child giving an object reply to a subject question at 3.4 did the reverse at 3.7. Of course, one might argue these are merely distractable children, and a richer intra-session set of data must be collected.

Another possibility is that the older children have come to mark Who [+hum], and for this reason give "boy" or "man" as replies to all the "who" questions. Whatever the explanation is, it is also necessary to note that at the earlier stage, that is, before 3.1, most of the children could already make the correct reply to both types of questions, and thus the listing of Who-O in Table 2 of late acquisition is misleading. Whatever their sentence-processing strategy was at that time, they could interpret the inversion already.

Why

1. Is the wagon getting an ice cream cone? Why? (For example: Because it doesn't have a mouth. It doesn't have hands. Tom don't want to give his to the wagon)
2. What is the deer drinking? Why? (He's thirsty. He's hungry. He likes it. He wants some)
3. Why is the deer eating? (He's hungry. He wants to eat. He's spoiled)
4. Why did the man go in the house? (Because it was starting to rain. They might get all wet.)

5. Is the boy going to get wet? Why? (Cause I don't want him to. He's in the house. Because the house isn't raining. The windows are closed. They both hide)

From the beginning of the interviews, the majority of children could give relevant answers to "why" questions, either related logically, or using the structural signals appropriate to such replies, or both. From the beginning, then continuing until a peak at 3.2, we find that "Why is the deer drinking?" and "Why is the deer eating?" are also given nominal answers, that is, they are heard as "what" questions. Though the majority of these replies were concentrated at early ages and in children who had not yet given any indication of mastery of any but a possibly primitive kind of reply to this question, it did occur spasmodically later as a performance error, as did Y/N replies.

Among the most common forms of reply given in the early protocols were "because" alone, and "because he is," "because he isn't," "because he did," and so on. These answers sometimes follow other types of response developmentally for the same item, as in the following set for alternate months between 2.9 and 3.9 for number 4: "the rain, cause it rained, cause is raining, cause he did, because, because dint want to get wet with his clothes."

The most interesting feature of these "why" answers is that for a while they also become common replies to "when" and "how" questions as well, suggesting their centrality in the schema of appropriate replies to adult questions. In the case of "when" and "how" questions, these replies become dominant over nominal and locative replies after 3.1. In the case of "how" questions, and to some extent of "when" questions, "because" answers took over; a child who gave one gave several, so the replies (with a few exceptions for "when" items) didn't seem to be spasmodic "performance" errors but rather to represent the stable answer for that kind of question at that stage. Perhaps parallel to the famous "why" asking stage in children, there is a "because" stage in which many replies take the form of giving logical motivational and causal links.

How

There are four "how" questions:

1. How is the deer going to eat? (For example: From the dish. With his mouth. Better.)
2. How did he get there? [deer in forest] (The forest just opened up. He walked by the tree. He hurried. He went around the corner. He just sloped in the rain. He climbed the trees. He flied. The man opened the door to the forest.)

    3. How did he get there? [bird in tree] (He flied. He opened it [tree].
Just fly and go crash. He just swam, he just crawled there. Maybe swim in there
and turned around and made his nest and sat down laid his eggs. Real faster.)
    4. How did the man get into the house? (He walked. That way.)

    There were several stages in the development of these answers, starting with
a period when locative answers were very common, followed by an increase in
nominals to a peak period at 3.1, and then an increase in "because" replies until
they are nearly equal to categorially "appropriate" replies at 3.6.

    Locatives such as "Her get in the forest. A tree." were usually replies to
the second and third question, the nominals to the first. From this, and the
other questions about food, one has the impression that children usually interpret anything containing "eat" as being a "what" question not unreasonable
in the light of the usual questions they hear in everyday life. With the exception
of one child, the "because" replies were for the last three questions, rather than
the first.

    One interpretation of a rise in certain kinds of response confusion might be
that the children learn the questions and come to anticipate them. If so, the
presence of similar questions should increase the likelihood of interference.

    However, we have both a "how" and a "why" question (on two different
forms) about the deer's eating, but no "what" question, yet it is strikingly the
"what" form that is taken over. There is no "why" for how-2 or how-3, but
the "because" replies are just as common as for how-4, which is followed by a
"why" question. Thus it does not seem plausible that the response contamination
is due to some kind of associative learning with responses confused. Rather, the
semantic probabilities and structure of the question itself seem to select the
kind of response given.

    What kind of answers do we find for "how" questions, which are gram-
matically heterogeneous in adult speech, including full clauses, prepositional
phrases with "by," "from," or "with," and phrases containing gerunds? The
first is both the earliest and most common form. In this respect it does not
parallel the replies for "why" questions, which usually gave an explanation with
a formal marker. The prepositional forms tended to appear in few children who
used the same phrase repeatedly as a fixed reply to a given question. Gerund
forms tended to be late, as one might expect, though the earliest was given at
2.10.

    Where-from appeared in only one question — "where did the bird fly from?"
In the picture, the bird is flying with his tail toward a tree and the house on
which he had been standing on the previous page, and facing the sun.

    From the beginning the majority of children can correctly decode "from"
and give the answer "tree" or "house." A common early response is also one
which equates the question to "Where did the bird fly?" and ignores the

"from" — reporting "In the sky" or "To the sun" as an answer. Also, in a few cases, the "from" is reported correctly, but the meaning of direction toward is given to it, as in "From the sun." The locational answers diminish, suggesting that the children have learned at least a directionality feature for "from."

The learning of this particular item seems to be unusually wide in its variability. There were six children who already controlled it on first testing, but five and possibly six did not answer it appropriately by the end of the year of testing or more. Such might be expected of grammatico-semantic items that are not of any great difficulty cognitively, but are sufficiently uncommon or of uneven distribution in usage so that accidents of training are strongly reflected in individual differences. The question "where from" does not occur in the texts we have of children's speech, and even the preposition itself is rare — one of the children, who had not learned the appropriate answer by 3.10, did not himself ever use the word "from."

When

The temporal questions are the most interesting of the categories, both because a sense of time is acquired late and can be seen in development in this age range, and because of the wide diversity in answer types. Richard Cromer (1968), in research on the cognitive development of time concepts, points out that many do not develop until after age four, no matter how often they are represented in the mother's speech.

We are, of course, principally concerned with the emergence of temporal answers, whether or not semantically appropriate, that indicate the discrimination of time questions from other categories of questions. The questions themselves could be appropriately answered with "soon" or a when clause, as seen below.

1. When will the deer eat?
2. When will the deer drink?
3. When will the sailboat come?
4. When did the sailboard come?

As might be expected, the favorite replies in the early months were nominal for the first two questions and locative for the last two. These outnumbered temporal replies until after age three. Around this point, causal explanations come to the fore, just as they do for "how" questions, and continue to appear with some frequency until three and a half, even though in the majority of replies temporal categories were used.

There are three common kinds of response to the question in the general range of temporal replies. One type is rote learned and semantically irrelevant, such as "December, 8:30." The rote learning of these replies can be seen quite early sometimes; my two-year-old says "one o'clock" for all the time items on this test as of today.

The adverb-using children (seven), who used forms like "no," "soon," and "December" before using adverbial clauses, were generally laconic for this question. They averaged five nonresponses and even for nontemporal replies usually used one to three words, like "Supper," "Some water," and "With his mouth." The clause-using children (seven) were much less laconic, having less than two nonresponses, and averaging more than three words per utterance for nontemporal replies, such as "He has to drink," "Cause it did come," and "Deer wants to eat the food." When they learn a temporal response, we can have such complex replies from this group as "In 15 minutes, when we turn the page." In addition, the clause-using children began giving time responses both earlier relative to other answers and younger in absolute terms (median age 2.11 vs. 3.3).

The difference between "When will . . ." and "When did . . ." is recognized by very few children, so that there is at this age little point in examining past temporal markers, though it may be that the problem is a result of the kind of items used. Many of the children even at the end give explicitly future time markers for "When did . . .", such as "In a minute," "Soon," "And right after this page" — even though the sailboat is visible at the time. We can summarize our results on order by indicating that:

1. From the earliest stages of our data, children understood that "what" questions required NP. Possibly the fact that answers were [-an] was an accident of the kind of questions asked. No situations were created in which an animate and an inanimate object were both available as possible answers, such as to "What did he see?" "Where" was understood as Adv [+loc] or Adv [direction towards] shortly afterwards. These also were among the earliest and most frequent questions asked by the children.

2. Verb questions received verb replies at about the same time as the acquisition of the locatives. Earlier answers tended to be locative or nominal.

3. "Whose" as NP [+an, + poss] was relatively early, though whether it antedated "who" is not sure.

4. "Who" was not marked [+an] at the time answers to "what" were already appropriate, and "who" frequently elicited [-an] or [+ loc] replies as though the question were understood as a "what" or "where" question. The distinction of subject and object may have developed before the period of the large group study, but later appears to be complicated by other factors. It might be that "who" was then assumed to be the subject because of the high probability of animate subjects, or it may be that "who" received a restriction to [+hum] at about this time.

5. The directionality signalled by prepositions was learned at widely vary-ing times, suggesting that the acquisition depended on idiosyncratic features of the child's environment.

6. There was a period after three when causal explanations were offered not only for "why" questions but commonly for "how" and "when" questions as well.

7. "When" was generally the latest form for the children to recognize, and by the end of the period under study a *past* time identifier "When did . . . ." was still not part of their system. Those who learned time categories earlier were somewhat more talkative in response to the "when" question from the start, and framed their replies in terms of relative events rather than absolute time words or adverbs.

It was a striking property of the distribution of response categories for questions (see Table 3.3) that at no time were there random responses. Response acquisition does not seem to be simply a narrowing to match question and reply. The child's productive grammar is undergoing concurrent development, so that not all output categories are equally available to him. If one examines replies before a category is used appropriately, one sees that the replies are not like random utterances (see Table 3.1), being shorter and structurally like replies to some other question. They do not usually include imperatives and questions.

Can one predict what the answer will be categorically, before the stage of category matching or mastery of the Wh-word? We have anticipated that one strategy might be to answer as though the question word were one already known to the child, that is, to use familiar response categories. But it is not the case that at the same stage the answers to all "when" questions look alike categorically. There are some further factors at work.

I shall try to represent these factors in a very simple fashion by giving a series of strategies that might account for most responses of most children and require minimum knowledge of the idiosyncrasies of each child. The results look like this those below.

1. *If you recognize a familiar question word, give an appropriate reply.* Now, of course, children don't necessarily give only appropriate replies after the "mastery" age is reached, and indeed, the following strategies appear to apply to "errors" after this point as well as to earlier replies.

2. *If there is a transitive verb, respond with the object of that verb.* This strategy appeared throughout the range of ages in the large group, and accounted for two thirds of the replies to "how" and "when" questions and 84 percent of the replies to "why" questions that contained transitive verbs. The chief defect was that the cause strategy sometimes influenced even transitive verbs. If rules were different for each child we might be able to weight in terms of such per-vasive response preferences.

TABLE 3.3 Confusion Matrix with Ages Pooled

Output Answer	Who-S	Who-O	Input Question Why	When	How
Who S	87.3%	17.6%			
			.8%	–	0.8%
Who O	9.8	77.9			
What O	2.0	3.7	4.8	17.4%	9.0
Where	–	–	0.3	14.8	5.2
Why	–	0.8	90.9	10.9	23.9
When	–	–	0.3	53.2	1.5
How	0.8	–	0.2	1.1	58.7
Y/N	–	–	2.7	2.5	0.8
Number of replies classifiable	245	244	662	357	465

3. *If you are over three, and there is an animate subject and intransitive verb, give a causal explanation.* This accounts for 84 percent of the "how" questions, but no "when" questions meeting the specifications were asked.

4. *For the remaining intransitive verbs, give a location or direction if it is missing.* This rule accounted for three quarters of the cases.

The relatively low percentage of the success of these strategies as general characterizations – ranging from 67 to 84 percent prediction, and post hoc at that – arises principally from two error sources. One is absolute age placement, whereas the point at which "why" answers become prevalent varies. Secondly, the rules were necessarily simplified to be the same for all children, and of course if we had more evidence on acquisition histories we could see temporary strategies or response perseveration occurring. For example, one child, who has been answering "where" questions with locatives, now frequently answers them, as well as many "when" questions, with "At noon," especially if there is a verb other than "is." This preference for particular new answers would, of course, appear as error in these predictions, as do causal replies which some children give even for transitive verbs or inanimate subjects.

The strategies can be summarized as giving NP for transitive verbs, causal accounts for intransitives with animate subjects, and locative adverbials for other intransitives if place is not mentioned. In each case the category can, of course, only be employed if this type of reply is already in the child's repertoire. I am assuming that up to a certain point, when a new entry is made in the child's lexicon, he does not distinguish the "new" Wh-words from others already familiar. He evidently makes little use of the phonetic qualities of the words (though how much remains to be discovered) and infers semantic features from the rest of the sentence, especially the transitivity of the verb, animateness of subject, and presence of locative information.

How could a child acquire such strategies? One possibility is that transitive verb questions tend to be "what" questions, animate subjects "why" questions, and intransitives locative questions. As a quick test of this hypothesis I examined two sets of data, one, the concorded questions from Wick Miller's efforts to elicit speech from children in our small group texts, and the other, mother-child interaction in a study in Oakland, California by Claudia Mitchell. As one can readily imagine, it was overwhelmingly the case that questions containing a transitive verb and no object following were "what" questions. It was also the case, though the number of instances was small, that intransitive verbs with inanimate subjects and no location offered were usually location questions, such as "Where did it go?"

The distribution of question types for animate subjects with intransitive verbs was sufficiently complex to make one suppose that the strategy for question answering could not come from such a source as the question itself. Another possibility, of course, is that it comes from the child's sentence-processing strategies of a more general type. For example, it is very likely the case that children who hear transitive verbs routinely process any noun immediately following as an object; that they in some sense "expect" an object, and, lacking one, might offer one as a response to a question, given that they can perceive that a question is asked. The notion that an SVO strategy occurs at a certain point has also been offered by Bever (as in this volume) to account for errors in comprehending passive sentences.

The intransitive verb + locative strategy may be related to the fact that "come" and "go", the intransitives used here, have a very high frequency of locative or particle complements.

What I am suggesting, then, is that these interpretation strategies may arise, not merely from experience with questions and the contextual distribution of the familiar Wh-forms, but more broadly from the high-frequency sequences in speech that lead to certain quick ways of processing sentences. How one accounts for the clear ability of children to go beyond these strategies later on and avoid errors that they would produce is another problem.

AUXILIARY AGREEMENT

The second major form of discourse agreement with which we were concerned in this test was the development of similarity of tense and aspect in question and answer. In general, the constraints are more semantic than formal, but in adult speech there is often identity of auxiliary features. The most conspicuous case where exact identity is required is in answer ellipsis in yes/no questions, which we did not examine here, since most said merely "Yes" or "No." In the "what-do" questions, however, we do have some evidence of agreement for past, "future" ("going to" or "will"), and progressive aspect.

At the time testing began, there were very few nonverb answers to "what-do" questions, so that we have to go back to the small group texts, as in Table 1, for evidence as to the order of development in verb questions.

Stage 1. No recognition of the verb category. In the earliest stage, names, descriptive replies, and locatives were common. Many answers were imitations of parts of the question. Like the answers to other Wh-questions prior to marking of the Wh-word, the responses do look like replies, but are categories already within the familiar response types recognized the child.

Stage 2. Unmarked verbs. When verbs were first used in replies, they were often unmarked for tense or aspect, and lacked modals. For this reason, it was sometimes unclear whether the child merely failed to understand the auxiliary features of the question, or whether he both failed to understand and could not produce. In the case of the past tense, there were instances where the semantic content indicated that the child was talking about the past but not marking it grammatically.

Stage 3. Ellipsis. In this phase children give unmarked forms when also appropriate in adult speech, as in future tenses.

Stage 4. Occasional full forms. These forms indicate competence in their use, including full forms with subject.

What-doing

1. What is the bird doing? [flying above the hills] (Form A)
2. What is the boy doing? [petting the deer]
3. What is the deer doing? [drinking water from the river]
4. What is the bird doing? [flying towards the sun] (Form B)

Most of the children already gave the −*ing* suffix with replies, that is, were at stage 3 at the time testing began (Table 3.4). This suffix is an early form of verb indicator, and we regularly found it as the earliest auxiliary form in the texts of the small group, several months prior to the past tense. Semantically, it does not necessarily mark activity vs. states as in adult English, since we find it with stative verbs like "have." However, it appears in complementary distribution with modals from the beginning, suggesting that it does carry aspectual significance contrasting with that realized by the modals, which at the beginning include "wanna," "gonna," "can," and "will," and the negatives "can't" and "won't."

The productive use of the suffix in sentences follows its use in answering questions, according to our small-group texts. Naturally, the first occurrence is usually without the presence of BE, which constitutes a later development. Phonetically, the early forms of −*ing* seem like the −*ie* suffix in some children, and frequently one cannot distinguish "sleepy" from "sleeping" for many months. There is sometimes also an ambiguity in cases when a transitive suffix −*it* is in use, since the −*ing* and the −*it* may be phonetically identical. For this reason, replies to questions are diagnostically useful.

At the time that inflections are coming in, there was free variation between the past and the −*ing* forms. In this case, we might expect to find occurrences of −*ing* responses to "what did" questions, and vice versa. This proved to be the case.

In response to "What is the bird doing?" we find:

It flied out.	3.0
It flied in the house.	3.1
Flew away.	2.10
Flew into the sun.	3.6
Bird flies.	2.6
He looks like made.	3.10
Bird goes in water.	3.3
He's got wings.	3.1

All of the children who occasionally gave past tense replies to *what-doing* questions did the reverse too at the same time period or later. We could not check the present nonprogressive contrast since there were no appropriate questions.

TABLE 3.4 Confusion Matrix for Auxiliaries, first 4 Tests*

Output	Past	−Ing	Going to	Will
		Input categories		
Past	34.9%	1.0%	2.5%	0.8%
−Ing	9.2	83.1	13.2	10.6
Going to	−	0.5	31.4	9.7
Will	−	−	1.6	20.4
Unmarked Verb	23.6	3.9	37.2	46.8
Subject + Unmarked V	19.5	5.3	5.8	6.2
Adjective	2.0	−	−	−
Descriptive Other	8.2	3.9	8.3	5.3
Present V	2.5	2.4	−	−
Total Coded Responses	195	207	121	113

*First four test sessions, usually four successive months. Onset ages varied from 2.6 to 3.1. Number of children was 24, but nonresponses account for variable totals.

What Will Do

1. What will the boy do? [pick up dish]
2. What will the deer do? [eat]
3. What will the deer do? [go into the forest]

Before the children correctly interpreted the semantic features of "will," they commonly reacted to the question as referring to the present, and their replies were very commonly marked with −*ing*. Eight children gave so many −*ing* replies to these questions in the early months that one could interpret this either as their standard answer, or, at least, as in free variation with the unmarked verb. Nine other children gave −*ing* responses more spasmodically in the early months.

The presence of elliptical responses in the form of unmarked verbs or verb phrases caused an analytic difficulty for this and the other future question. These responses are, of course, acceptable by adult standards. However, they undoubtedly included a number of instances in which the child could not be regarded as, in any sense, "deleting" tense, since other contemporaneous responses are regularly unmarked for tense. In general, elliptical responses decreased in frequency with age, suggesting that they were not truncations grammatically but primitive forms.

By the time the children interpreted "will" as referring to intention, they also distinguished "will" from "going to." Although the requirements of adult grammar are, it seems to me, only that a semantic match be made, 23 out of the 24 children gave distinctive replies to these two questions. Most of the children regularly gave the same form back in their reply, suggesting that even if the two questions are synonymous, the children recall and use the surface structure in answering. For several children, "will" answers were given only to the "will" question, but most had a few crossovers.

What Going To Do

It is not clear how early children can interpret these questions, which included a few examples in our small-group texts:

What are you gonna do with the sand?	On here.	Charles 3.1
What are you going to do with Liz?	I go put her in bed.	Laura 2.9
What are you going to do with your plane?	Have it.	Henry 2.8
What are you going to do with them?	Take a piece off it.	Sally 2.2

These few examples — the question was rarely asked — indicate approximately similar distributions to those of the later materials tested; that is, a locative, truncated unmarked forms, and a full reply.

1. What is the man going to do? [feed the deer]
2. What is the boy going to do? [go into the house] (Form A)
3. What is the boy going to do? [go into the house] (Form B)

In the large group testing, responses to "will" and to "going to" developed at about the same rate, though full, non-elliptical answers appeared slightly earlier for "will" questions.

A common kind of reply to this question, and also a common one to the "will" question, was *X is going + locative*. There are, of course, two difficulties here. One is that we do in fact use V —ing in the context of future events, such as "I'm going to the Post Office tomorrow." However, the incidence of this response was much higher when the main verb was "go," which unfortunately was the case for two of the "going to" and one of the "will" questions. Because of the pictures used, the result was semantically ambiguous, since it could have indicated either present or future action, and therefore we cannot know how the child interpreted the question.

The fact that the *going* frequency is higher, V —ing in the case of other verbs suggests a selective factor against repetition of "go." Slobin and Welsh (1968) noted that in one child whose imitations were studied intensively there was a deletion of repeated verbs, though not of repeated nouns, suggesting a kind of editing of input, or else an output rule which does not permit identical verbs in series. Such an interpretation assumes that the child hears the two "go" forms as the same. Children's difficulties in repeating sentences like "They do do it" suggest that they have difficulty in cases where the realization of main verb and an auxiliary are the same. In the case of "going to," this difficulty should not exist if a child treats "gonna" as a single morpheme. An example with both forms occurs in a child who gave the following:

2.6	He's not going up in the clouds.
2.7	Go inside the house, go inside the house.
2.8	Go in his house.
2.9	He's going in the house now.
2.10	The boy's going in the clouds.
2.11	Gonna feed him. He's going in his house.
3.0	He's gonna get wet.
3.1	He's gonna give him food. He's gonna get wet.
3.2	He will make a popsicle pop and he smack him.
3.3	Bring it to him. He's going to hold the rain in his hand.

For this child from 2.6 to 3.1, the only cases where verbs other than "go" were employed occurred with "gonna," and "go" never was repeated either with "gonna" or with "going" until 3.4. In this case "gonna" seems not to be a single morpheme for the child, since its distribution excludes "go," for ten months at least.

Surprisingly rare were instances of dual marking or redundancy of *–ing,* as in the following case:

| 2.9 | Deer'll eating the supper. |
| 2.11 | It going to eating the supper. |

and in another child, at 2.9, "He going putting" [referring to putting food out for the deer]. Although the use of V –ing was common without a modal or "going to," the finding from our texts that modals and –*ing* are in complementary distribution appears to hold up here in the tests.

What Did

By far the most common answer to *what-did* questions at first was the un-marked verb. Occasionally –*ing* responses indicated, as I have pointed out earlier, cases of genuine free variation. It was not the case that the unmarked verb revealed failure to comprehend the tense signal in the question, however. If this were the case, the content of the answers would change with time; instead, the same answers occurred before and after the past tense suffix appeared.

Did the children merely fail to use tense marking because of the difficulty of the question, but use it elsewhere in speech? Using the concorded past tense forms for each child on all the tests we have, I was able to establish when children used some appropriate tense contrast on forms, such as "went" or "eated," that were unambiguous both internally and in their phonetic context.

Nine children gave evidence of some familiarity with past tense forms prior to giving a past tense reply to these questions. However, in one to five months, and typically in two, the tense replies appeared. One suspects that sampling error is the problem, since tense forms do come in gradually, as single items at first. Indeed, some items, such as "he got wet," occurred disconcertingly early, compared to other forms.

In general, the auxiliary matching, like the category matching, appears to be chiefly dependent on the development of output patterns in the children. The order in which matching occurred — first the –*ing* forms, then intention and past tense — corresponds to the development within the productive system of the children. For five-sixths of the children, the –*ing* form was clearly prior. Ellipsis of course makes establishment of onset age for futurity awkward.

Can one predict what answers a child will give to verb questions as one can, to some extent, for category matching items? In the case of the auxiliary, it might be the case that children could interpret the semantic features of the input, as reflected in their selection of V, but still lack the formal apparatus to mark the aspect and tense of the auxiliary in the same way as in the input. The possibly analogous situation in category matching was in the *What-do* questions, in which some early answers seemed to indicate that the child could understand that the predicate was being questioned, but in which the child's predicates were structurally primitive and often lacked verbs.

Implicit here is the notion that it is possible for a child to recognize semantic implications of syntactic or other features but not yet be able to generate the appropriate formal output from his own semantic selectors. Whether this difference implies a different grammar of input and of output depends on the status of grammars in a well-developed theory of linguistic performance, which does not, as far as I know, exist.

Because of the semantic features of the test itself, it was often the case that a V appropriate for answering a question about the present might also be appropriate for the past or for intentions, though not for both. In pictures, where one talks often about events surrounding and extrapolated from the static event, this was bound to be the case, especially when the time span involved in our questions was very brief, that is, the next event preceding or following. For this reason, it is not easy to tell what has been the semantic interpretation of the input auxiliary. There were only a few cases, such as the earliest replies shown in Table 3.5, which were genuinely inappropriate, in this case for reasons beyond the auxiliary. The child used the subject of the question and added "eating . . ." in each case.

Another test is whether the V remains stable through changes in the auxiliary marking of replies, and in many cases this was true, indicating that semantic interpretation was not changed through time.

In general, then, we must be concerned in the analysis merely with the output in the child's auxiliary, and can assume that (by the stage of testing) aspect, mood, and tense in these items were correctly interpreted by most children.

At the time testing began, all but eleven children had generally mastered auxiliary features, so we have relatively limited data. Four of these children went directly from the unmarked verb to the same auxiliary features as in the question, with no evidence of generalization across categories. Four children showed a pattern like that in the category matching, such that they first developed an *–ing* reply for *what-doing,* and this was sometimes, but not always, carried over to other categories. When the *past* marker was developed, it generalized to the "will" or "going to" replies, if these were still unstable, or if they developed first, they generalized to the past tense question. In this group, there was no free variation, since once a matched response appeared, it remained stable.

The remaining three children, of which the case in Table 3.5 is an example, showed evidence of some free variation of responses. While her replies to *what-doing* were fairly constant, the marked instability of the replies to "will" and "did" makes it appear that the child gave nondistinctive replies to the two questions until 3.4.

These different styles of development with respect to a detail of discourse agreement make it difficult to determine any cross-child predictions about the

TABLE 3.5 Replies of One Child to Verb Questions

Age	Input question			
	−Ing	Going to	Will	Past
2.7	−ing[a], −s	−ing[a] −ing[a]	−ing[a]	−ing,−s
2.8	−ing, −s	b	−ing, NN	−ing[a]
2.9	−s, −ing	going putting, all finish	−ing[a]	V, V
2.10	−ing, doing N	going Adv	−ing, V	−ing
2.11	−ing, −doing −ing	−ing, gonna go Adv	−ing	pst, V
3.0	−ing, −ing	V (ellipsis)	V	−ing, V
3.1	−ing, −ing	going V, −ing	−ing	V, V
3.2	−ing, doing V	−ing	V, do N	do
3.3	−ing, −ing	−ing, going Adv	did that	V
3.4	−ing, −ing	going Adv	V, going Adv	pst
3.5	−ing, −ing	going Adv	doing N	pst
3.6	−ing, −ing	going Adv	gonna V, going Adv	Did N
3.7	−ing, −ing	−ing, going Adv	will do with NP	pst, pst

[a] In these instances the semantic content was not relevant to the question, usually being "NP eating" across all questions. Even if appropriate to the future questions, the perseveration suggests that the input was ignored.

[b] "Birdy held in hands" reply to question about boy.

In the rest of the table, all unmarked V and most other replies contain subject.

responses which occur. The reasons for the differences are not obvious from the limited evidence we have on each child.

SUMMARY

In an effort to discover both the order of development in discourse agreement in children, and the nature of the answers they made before agreement was similar to the adult form, we collected material in the form of texts from a small group of children and tests at monthly intervals from 24.

Our results suggest an order of development for features marking of Wh-words, namely *what, where, what-do, whose, who, why, where-from, how,* and *when.* The syntactic distinction between subject and object *who* was learned relatively early, but temporarily obscured by some changes taking place in the fourth year which affected performance on questions about *who-object.*

Before a child had a feature marking for a question word that provided him with a cue for categorization and the semantic search for an answer, he frequently replied as though the question were of a form he already had in his repertoire. These displacements could be characterized by a set of rules of strategy such that transitive verbs produce NP replies, intransitive verbs with animate subjects produced causal explanations for children who had those in their repertoire, and other intransitives produced locative replies. These strategies may be related to those that develop in comprehending or imitating other sentences, not just questions.

Once the verb questions were matched for category, they might receive unmarked (simple) verb replies, but very rapidly *–ing* and, later, past tense and intention (going to or will) are marked in replies in agreement with questions, shortly before or contemporaneous with their appearance in spontaneous utterances. The course of development of these responses included for some children the same kind of overgeneralization of newly developed auxiliary features that was found for categories, in the analysis of category matching.

REFERENCES

Berko, Jean. The child's learning of English morphology. *Word*, 1958, **14**, 150–177.

Braine, M.D.S. The ontogeny of English phrase structure: the first phase. *Language*, 1963, **39**, 1–13.

Brown, R. W. The development of Wh questions in child speech. *J. Verbal Learning Verbal Behavior*, 1968, 7, 279–290.

Brown, R. W. and Fraser, C. The acquisition of syntax. In *The Acquisition of Language* (Ed. by Ursula Bellugi and R. W. Brown). *Monogr. Soc. Res. in Child Developm.*, 1964, **29**, No. 1, pp. 43-79.

Charlip, Remy. *Where is Everybody?* N. Y.: Scholastic Book Services, 1957.

Chomsky, N. *Syntactic Structures.* The Hague: Mouton, 1957.

Cromer, R. The development of temporal reference during the acquisition of language. Unpublished Ph.D. dissertation, Harvard University, 1968.

Drach, K. The language of the parent: A pilot study. In *Language, Society and the Child*, Working Paper #13, Lang. Beh. Res. Lab., Univ. of Calif., Berkeley, 1968.

Kobashigawa, B. Repetitions in a mother's speech to her child. In *Language, Society and the Child*, Working Paper #13, Lang. Beh. Res. Lab., Univ. of Calif., Berkeley, 1968.

Pfuderer, Carol. Some suggestions for a syntactic characterization of baby-talk style. In *Language, Society and the Child*, Working Paper #13, Lang. Beh. Res. Lab., University of California, Berkeley, 1968.

Slobin, D. I. Questions of language development in cross-cultural perspective. Forthcoming in proceedings of the Conference on Language Learning in Cross-Cultural Perspective, Michigan State Univ., 1968.

Slobin, D. I. and Welsh, C. *Elicited imitation as a research tool in developmental psycholinguistics.* Lang. Beh. Res. Lab. Working Paper #10, Univ. of Calif., Berkeley, 1968.

CHAPTER 4

Carlota S. Smith

University of Texas

AN EXPERIMENTAL APPROACH TO CHILDREN'S
LINGUISTIC COMPETENCE*

Psycholinguistics is a field in which linguist and psychologist have collaborated in a rather unique way to study language behavior. The contribution of the linguist has been in the organization of linguistic material; the psychologist, in setting up and carrying out his studies, has sought to answer psychological questions about people's use of linguistic material. Generative grammar since the 1950s has provided much of the impetus for psycholinguistic work, partly because of its explicitness, but more significantly because of its abstract nature and its essentially psychological orientation. The important distinction between competence and performance allows both linguist and psychologist to relate the often fragmentary utterances of natural speech to the coherent and complete description provided by a grammar. The structural descriptions of generative grammar not only provide organization, such as the hierarchical structure of sentences; they also suggest specific psychological inquiries because they attempt to represent what a speaker knows about his language. What is the nature of psychological inquiry? Most psycholinguists would probably accept the statement that they are studying the mechanisms that underlie or form language behavior; specifically, they ask what processes are involved when a person understands or utters a sentence.

Language acquisition, as the study of children's language is usually called, is an area of psycholinguistics that has burgeoned with the others. In studying language acquisition, one focuses on the development of the human animal; one investigates the various stages enroute to adult speech and what is involved in the shift from one stage to the next; and one also seeks to shed light on some general questions of linguistic endowment and behavior.

In this chapter, I shall discuss some psycholinguistic work in the area of language acquisition; and in the course of the discussion, suggest a few general questions. In particular, I will be concerned, at different points, with the relation of generative (or any) grammar to psycholinguistic studies.

I would like first to mention two important problems that arise in investigating the linguistic competence of young children. It is generally agreed that

The experiments were part of a study of language acquisition, Grant #MH 07990, National Institutes of Health, administered by the Eastern Pennsylvania Psychiatric Institute.

109

performance, which is subject to nonlinguistic accidents of all kinds, does not reflect competence. The linguist or psychologist, in determining the competence of a native speaker, supplements records of spontaneous speech: he presents the speaker with systematically varied utterances and asks for direct linguistic judgments and paraphrases. One can't use these techniques with two- or three-year-olds; children are notoriously unable or unwilling to give direct linguistic judgments or paraphrases of their own speech or the speech of others. Thus the direct methods by which a linguist usually tests, extends, and limits his hypotheses, are useless. To study children's competence, we must develop indirect methods of obtaining linguistic judgments. This is a problem of methodology; the second problem is more far reaching.

There is a great difference between the utterances that a young child hears (which are presumably utterances of adult speech,[1] and the utterances that he produces. A description of children's linguistic competence should deal with this discrepancy, especially since their linguistic competence seems to greatly exceed their performance. Children appear to understand commands and simple speech before they speak at all; and children that speak telegraphically[2] appear to understand fairly complicated adult utterances. We need, then, to ask the question, how much do children attend to and comprehend of adult speech? One reason that this problem has been so little studied is the difficulty of devising indirect approaches to it; but there are other, more serious, reasons for the lack of attention.

The study of comprehension, child and adult, is just beginning. In addressing ourselves to the question of children's comprehension, we must therefore concern ourselves with the nature of the basic processes as well as the acquisition of them. In studying comprehension, we take as fundamental the notion, clearly stated in discussions of generative grammar, that to understand a sentence one must know its structure. For grammarians, the word *structure* covers several aspects of a sentence: the surface structure, the deep structure, the derivation or transformational history, or all three of these. It is easy to confuse grammatical and psychological questions here. When we say that to understand a sentence, a person must know its structure, do we refer to a full structural description, in the technical sense? It has been suggested for instance, that the process of understanding a sentence involves the production of a full structural description (with heuristic short-cuts of Halle and Stevens 1964, Matthews 1962). But perhaps it would be more accurate to say that when one understands a sentence one *could* produce a full structural description, not that one does so — just as we sometimes

---

[1] Although perhaps systematically simplified for the child's ears.

[2] This term was coined by Roger Brown to describe the early speech of children, in which function words do not occur.

say that knowing the meaning of a word involves knowing how and when to use it (but not actually using it in all possible ways). If this is a suggestive analogy, what it suggests is that the linguistic rules so powerful in generative grammar may not have the same importance for psychological studies.

There is no doubt about the psychological reality of linguistic units. This has been convincingly demonstrated in experiments by Miller (1956), Savin (1965), Fodor and Bever (1965), and others.[3]

I referred above to the role of linguistics within psycholinguistics; the organization of linguistic material into sentences, hierarchically ordered constituents, and the like, constitutes a major contribution of linguistics. When we adopt derivations as models for understanding, however, we are further extending the domain of linguistics; specifically, we are now looking for evidence of the psychological reality of linguistic rules. There may be a direct relation between a grammatical derivation of a sentence and a person's understanding or production of a sentence. If this is the case, then people behave more or less according to the rules stated in a generative grammar. But it is not clear that they do so. In fact, the more cautious grammarians have been careful to disavow the suggestion.

Consider briefly the early formulation of generative grammar as a model and a hypothesis for understanding.[4] The sentences of a language are reduced to a small number of simple sentences, and rules-transformations for combining and rearranging them. The result is a systematic statement that has great intuitive appeal because of its simplicity and elegance. Sentences have deep structure (the simple sentence(s) underlying them) and surface structure, the result of applying transformational rules. The two structures may be almost identical or quite different; what is understood is the deep structure of a sentence, perhaps with fixed emphasis and variations indicated by surface structure. A typical example of a type of sentence with different deep and surface structures is the passive.

But it is not *prima facie* evident that people do understand sentences with reference, somehow, to simple active declarative sentences. If they do so, then a passive, for instance, is understood as a variation of an active sentence, and is stored in immediate memory as a simplex sentence and an addendum of some kind. There have been some attempts to study this question by comparing the memory space taken up by passive and active sentences; the differences between the two types of structure is confounded with a difference in length. However,

[3] Perhaps the first demonstration of this kind is Sapir's (1949) famous essay, "The Psychological Reality of Phonemes."
[4] In speaking of *understanding,* I do not mean to suggest a difference between the speaker and hearer of speech, but for brevity's sake will refer only to understanding.

consider a comparison between an active sentence and a passive with deleted agent, such as:

(1) John frightened Mary.
(2) Mary was frightened.

If derivation is an important factor, we would expect the second of these sentences to take up more space in immediate memory, and perhaps to be more difficult to remember. Slobin (1967) has recently studied adults' and children's handling of these structures and found no evidence that they differ. And, as Fodor and Garrett (1966) point out, other recent experimental results do not point unequivocally to the interpretation that sentences are stored and understood as deep structures.

The passive with deleted agent is similar in derived structure to certain simplex sentences, such as:

(3) Mary was frightened.
(4) Mary was angry.

It seems unlikely that people understand these sentences in entirely different ways, one much more complicated than the other.

These comments do not apply to the type of generative grammar presented in Chomsky's *Aspects of the Theory of Syntax* (1965), (or to other, more recent proposals). The deep structures of *Aspects* are often very abstract; the deep structures in the type of grammar advocated by Lakoff (1966) and Ross (1967) for instance, are even more abstract. It is not clear what kind of grammatical rules would be involved if we attempted to work out a direct relation between these grammars and a psychological account of understanding.

Generative grammar has been oriented toward syntax, and so have most accounts of understanding. However, perhaps syntax has been overemphasized. Consider the way language is used in the ordinary way; usually, as sentences are spoken or read – in context – there is little room for misunderstanding of a syntactic nature. Perhaps in understanding an utterance, one uses mainly semantic information, calling on syntactic information only when necessary. For instance, there is only one plausible way to interpret the triplet of words *John, broke, glass:* this means that there is only one plausible structure to impose on it and syntactic information is in a sense redundant. However, in some cases a triplet admits of more than one interpretation, e.g. *John, followed, Bill;* to understand this, one must draw on syntactic markers for subject and object; that is, one needs syntactic information. If understanding is approached from this point of view, we find that the grammatical derivation of a sentence is less important and the surface structure of a sentence is more important. It is interesting to note that the primacy of syntax is now being questioned on several counts (see for instance, McCawley, 1968).

This discussion provides an introductory framework for a description of some work in the field of language acquisition. In studying language acquisition, I have argued, one must study understanding; and the processes involved in understanding are themselves little understood. It is important, I think, to be clear about these still-open questions.

II

I would like now to describe and discuss two psycholinguistic experiments with young children; the experiments were conducted by Elizabeth Shipley, Lila Gleitman and myself. We were interested primarily in three areas: the linguistic input for a child; the mechanisms that the child uses in organizing linguistic input; and the structures that the child imposes on linguistic input.

RESPONSE EXPERIMENT

Description

Our subjects in the first experiment were children who were just learning to talk. The experiment was directed toward finding out what constitutes the *primary linguistic input* for children at this stage. What do children listen to? What do they understand of the speech addressed to them? — were the questions that we asked. We wanted to know whether the children were aware of the difference between their own speech and the speech of adults; this seemed a necessary prefatory question to the more general question of their linguistic competence. We were looking for evidence as to whether the children's competence differed from what one would suppose from their natural speech.

The phrase *primary linguistic input* should not be confused with *primary linguistic data.* The latter may be used in several ways. It sometimes refers to the linguistic environment of a child, that is, the utterances made in his presence; or to the utterances in his environment that a child attends to. But the phrase has also been used to refer to the structural information that a child is endowed with; and, again, to the early structures (whether or not different from adult structures) that the child imposes on what he hears. These different uses blur the distinction between what is heard and how it is structured. In dealing with the speech of children, one often wants to aks whether children impose "their own" or "adult" structures, so that it is important to keep this distinction clear. We were interested specifically in what the children attended to in utterances addressed to them.

The children we studied all spoke telegraphically, that is, their speech consisted almost exclusively of nouns and verbs. We expected that some of them would notice the difference between telegraphic and adult speech; for these children, we wanted to know how features of adult speech affected them. For instance, if the children listened mainly to the high-stress content words that occur in their own speech, then function words might make it difficult for them to find the content words. On the other hand, because of their familiarity, function words might facilitate the search.

In the experiment we presented children with systematically varied utterances, and looked for evidence that they noticed the differences. The utterances varied in structure: some were well-formed sentences, some were telegraphic, and some were minimal or holophrastic. Nonsense syllables were substituted for function words and for verbs in some of the experimental utterances. This variable, familiarity, was introduced to test how closely the children attended to the adult parts of adult speech.

Since we could not solicit direct judgments, the problem was to devise utterances that called for behavioral responses. We could then look for patterns in the behavioral responses that indicated whether the children discriminated between the utterances. Commands were the experimental utterances, and we were thus able to ask, in scoring responses, whether the children followed the commands. The commands all pertained to toys that were familiar to the children and visible during the experimental sessions. The children were asked to *pick up the doll, wind up the music box,* and the like, in eight different ways; they were free to respond to or ignore the commands. The stimulus types are given below.

Free Response Experimental Stimulae

Familiarity	Structure		
	Child-forms		Well-formed
No nonsense syllables	*n:* Ball	*vfn:*	Throw me the ball
	vn: Throw ball		
	Lvn: Please Jim, throw ball		
Nonsense syllables	*Xn:* Gor ball	*vZn:*	Throw ronta ball
		Xfn:	Gor me the ball
		XZn:	Gor ronta ball

I will refer to particular stimulus types by the *italics* letters. Capital letters stand for nonsense syllables and lower-case letters stand for verbs, nouns, and function words. The stimulus type *Lvn* was included to test the importance of sheer length.

We faced many problems in presenting the commands to very young children. They have short attention spans, and their responses to relatively unknown adults and unfamiliar situations, are, at best, unpredictable. A fluid experimental situation was devised to allow for these difficulties. The sessions were held at the children's homes, and the mothers were enlisted to utter the experimental commands (the mothers were given practice so that all commands were uttered in a natural way). The stimulus toys were prominently displayed. Each session had the general form of an informal visit; the experimenter, an observer and the child's mother chatted with each other, and with the child, for about half an hour. Interspersed with the chat were the experimental utterances. After a stimulus was given, chat ceased (unless initiated by the child — absolute silence from the adults led, we found, to absolute silence from the child) for one and one-half minutes so that the behavioral and verbal responses of the child could be noted. The sessions were recorded on tape, and the experimenter and observer filled out standard question sheets for each stimulus.

Getting the child's attention proved to be another difficult problem; many children, especially the younger ones, were often so absorbed in their own activities as to be virtually unreachable. Yet we wanted to be sure that the child actually heard the stimuli. The mother was instructed to call a child's name, and then to give the experimental command only if she judged that she had the child's attention. There were many times, of course, when a child ignored his mother's call; she was, in theses cases, to say something else and wait for another chance to deliver the stimulus. These experimental sessions, although incredibly time-consuming, were quite effective; the fluid situation made it possible for the children to ignore the adults and the stimulus toys for a time, and then return for more chat and more experimental utterances.

The subjects were 13 children, ranging in age from 18 months to 2 1/2 years, all of middle-class professional families. We had fairly extensive samples of their spontaneous speech from preliminary play sessions and the experimental sessions (excluding replies to experimental stimuli). The children were ranked for verbal maturity on the basis of these samples. We found that median utterance-length was an effective gauge of verbal maturity; this measure correlated highly with other measures, such as frequency of pronouns and verbs, and inflection. All the children spoke telegraphically, but one group of children was distinctly less mature than the other. For simplicity, I shall refer to the less mature as *younger* and the more mature as *older;* in general, the children's verbal maturity did correlate with age. The two groups of children differed significantly in their responses to the stimuli.

The children did not always respond to the stimulus commands, but there were clear patterns indicating that the experimental variables did significantly affect their responses;[5] in other words, the children did notice the differences

---

[5] All differences mentioned have been found to be statistically significant. See the papers mentioned in footnotes 7 and 8 for details.

between the commands. I will describe briefly the scoring and patterning of the responses and then comment on the implications of the patterns.

Behavioral and verbal responses were scored separately. There were two types of behavioral response that could be clearly distinguished — touches, when child touched the toy mentioned in a given stimulus, or looks, when he looked directly at the toy. Any interaction with a toy was scored as a touch, but we did not further distinguish these responses (in some cases the child followed a specific command, such as *bang on the workbench,* by banging; in other cases he simply touched the workbench; and in others, of course, he did neither). A touch was considered to be a more affirmative response than a look. Verbal responses were categorized as question, negative, repetition, and reply. Irrelevant verbalizations were not scored.

Responses

We ask first, which type of command the children tended to follow. The touch responses was interpreted as following the commands, and the familiar adult form *vfn* most frequently elicited touch responses. Stimuli eliciting the touch responses fell into three different (statistically) groups, on the basis of frequency of the responses.

Touch Responses to Experimental Commands
(in order: stimuli that most frequently elicited touch responses are listed first)

vfn

vn n Lvn

vZn Xfn Xn XZn

A child was most likely to touch a stimulus toy if asked to do so in a familiar and adult way; notice also that he was more likely to follow telegraphic commands than to follow commands containing unfamiliar words (nonsense syllables). This pattern was significant for the group as a whole. There was, however, a very interesting correlation with verbal maturity. The older children most frequently followed well-formed and familiar commands; the youngest children most frequently followed familiar telegraphic commands (*vn* and *n*).

A similar pattern emerges in a second composite category of responses. These responses indicated attention to the stimulus; they were looks, touches, and relevant verbalizations. As a group, the children attended most frequently to familiar adult commands, and least frequently to commands containing nonsense material. There is one interesting difference, however, between the touch responses and the attention responses. One stimulus that contained nonsense -vZn- elicited attention responses as frequently as did the familiar telegraphic stimuli:

Attention Responses to Experimental Commands

vfn

vn, n, Lvn, vZn

Xfn, Xn, XZn

vZn is the only stimulus types, of those containing nonsense syllables, that does not begin with nonsense. We note then that the children were least likely to follow, or to attend to, commands beginning with unfamiliar words.

Verbal responses were analyzed separately. Repetitions (responses containing all or part of the stimulus, and nothing else) were the only type of verbal responses affected by the experimental variables; the other responses were equally likely after all stimuli. Repetitions were dramatically affected by the familiarity variable. They were most frequent after commands containing nonsense syllables; that is, commands with nonsense tended to elicit repetitions. Repetitions were frequently followed by touch responses – having repeated a command, the children were likely to follow it (recall that all stimuli had the name of a familiar toy).

It seemed clear that repetition was an affirmative response. We interpreted the repetitions as efforts to make sense out of the unfamiliar words (nonsense syllables). In effect, the children were replaying the stimulus.

The older children, who are presumably more efficient listeners, tended to repeat only the nonsense syllables of the stimuli; the other children, perhaps unable to separate the familiar from the unfamiliar, tended to repeat some sense and nonsense. These spontaneous repetitions are not unlike those studied by Ervin (1964). Her remarks about repetition do not conflict with the result reported here. Ervin concluded that children's repetitions are not grammatically progressive; the children in our experiment were repeating, not unfamiliar structures, but lexical items. Perhaps at this early stage, repetition focuses mainly on lexical novelties.

There was a strong correlation between verbal maturity and frequency of repetition after nonsense-containing stimuli; the older a child, the more often he tended to repeat these stimuli. Actually, the youngest children did not tend to repeat stimuli that contained nonsense syllables; to these utterances they tended to make no response at all. It seems likely that the youngest children were not able to "find" the words they knew in sentences with nonsense, that is, totally unfamiliar words.

Discussion

This completes the rather sketchy description of our experiment. It is reported in detail elsewhere.[6] From these results we are able to make certain hypotheses about primary linguistic input for our subjects, and about their strategy or habits of listening.

The younger children focused on minimal utterances containing familiar words. These utterances elicited responses of attention and affirmation most frequently (from the younger children only). On the basis of our experimental data, we doubt that these children attend very much to the adult parts of adult speech. More generally then, we doubt that their primary linguistic input is as rich or as confusing as has sometimes been suggested. For whatever complex of linguistic, conceptual and perceptual reasons, children at this stage (approximately 18 months to 2 years) can apparently handle only the high-stress-content words that they utter themselves. Perhaps their listening is mainly an attempt to "find" words they know; too many other words, even familiar ones, may make it difficult to do this, and unfamiliar words may make it impossible.

How, then, do we explain children's affirmative behavioral responses to complicated commands from adults? For instance, a two-year-old may be told that he should get his coat to go outside, and may respond appropriately, that is, get the coat. But such responses do not necessarily mean that the children "understand" the entire adult utterances, that is, that they decode it linguistically. Rather, the child may hear a word he knows and understand from situational cues what behavior is expected of him. In other words, he may understand holophrastically. This view of the linguistic competence of young children is hardly a startling one — Vygotsky (1962), for instance, discusses children's presentential linguistic behavior in somewhat similar terms.

The linguistic competence of these children does not differ markedly from their performance, at least in the experiment I have described. The older children, on the other hand, show linguistic competence that is more advanced than their spontaneous speech. Adult speech had "demand quality" for them; they were more likely to respond affirmatively to it than to their own telegraphic speech. They listened closely to (at least some) adult speech, and attempt to decode it fully, as their responses to commands with nonsense indicate. But it is important to note that they did not attend to all of the simple adult speech addressed to them in the experiment. The children's responses to stimuli containing nonsense indicates a systematic selectivity in their listening. Recall that one type of stimulus, *vZn*, elicited significantly more responses of attention than did other stimuli that

[6]E. Shipley, C. Smith, and L. Gleitman, "A study in the acquisition of syntax: free responses to verbal commands," *Language*, 1969.

contained nonsense; *vZn* is the only one of these stimuli that does not begin with nonsense.

Perhaps the primary linguistic input for these children consists mainly of utterances that begin with familiar words. This principle of listening would exclude from a child's attention a good many utterances, thus considerably simplifying his linguistic environment. When he hears an utterance beginning with unfamiliar words, he may ignore it as clearly impenetrable, even if it is addressed to him. Such a simplification makes slightly less improbable the amazing feat of learning to talk.

Our results do not give any information about how children organize, or structure, the material to which they attend — the linguistic input. However, the close attention that the older children paid to nonsense syllables (various responses of attention) suggests that, when an utterance is within certain limited bounds, they attempt to process all of it. In other words, we have demonstrated that the children attended to the function words of adult speech, but did not find out anything about the role of these words for the children. We do not know, for instance, whether they had any semantic value, or whether they somehow supported the high content nouns and verbs. Further research along these same lines might clear up questions of this kind. For instance, the function words might be varied with other function words, where the semantic import differed — *Throw me the ball* and *Throw him the ball;* they might be varied with familiar but inappropriate function words — *Throw to the ball, Throw of the ball:* and; they might be varied with content words — *Throw John the ball* (The stress pattern would change in this last sentence).

Actually, we do not have clear evidence that the verb played a semantic role at all. In most cases each toy had an activity appropriate to it and the verb used in the stimulus sentence asking for that activity (*Wind up the music box; Bang on the workbench*). However, since the children attended to the function words, and to the initial words of the stimuli which were either verbs or nonsense syllables, it seems probable that they did listen to the verbs. This might be tested with stimuli in which reasonable verbs were varied (*wind up* and *bring,* for instance) or by varying reasonable and unreasonable verbs (*wind up* or *step* on the music box).

An obvious limitation to this experimental technique is that the stimuli are all commands. We can be sure that children hear many commands; yet commands do not have the basic subject-verb-object order characteristic of English sentences. We would like to develop variations of the technique so that other types of utterances could be presented. We hope to work out games for young children in which statements as well as commands can be systematically varied, and in which we have clear behavioral responses to determine whether children discriminate between them.

III

REPETITION EXPERIMENT

Description

I turn now to a second experiment; this experiment involved older children and a different technique, but was directed toward essentially the same questions. We were interested in the children's linguistic competence, with emphasis on the linguistic input. Specifically, this experiment was designed to find out about structures that the children did not utter spontaneously. The technique was elicited repetition; children were presented with a variety of sentences, and simply asked to repeat them. From the children's successful and unsuccessful attempts, it was possible to infer a good deal about their ability to handle different structures.

The rationale behind this approach is this: we assume that in order to understand a sentence, one must be able to structure it. We set up a situation in which children are forced to structure sentences, and then compare their performance with sentences that they do and do not produce in spontaneous speech. Elicited repetition is such a situation if the stimuli are carefully chosen to strain the capacity of immediate memory. Repetition involves immediate memory, and it is well known that people can hold more material in immediate memory when they are able to structure it (Neisser, 1967; Savin 1968, Miller 1951). The experiment was conducted with three- and four-year-old children. The children repeated a variety of structures; some occurred in their natural speech and some did not.

We hoped to develop a profile of relative competence for the structures used; if successful, such profiles could be constructed for different developmental stages. A more general and more interesting goal was to discover what structural properties make sentences easy or difficult for three- to four-year-olds to repeat (and, presumably, to understand). Finally, we hoped to gain some insight, from the errors the children made, into the processes involved in their listening and structuring of language.

The situation in which a child repeats sentences after an experimenter is not, of course, a normal speech situation. Perhaps the most important difference is that there are no contextual cues in the experimental situation; the content of the stimulus sentences doesn't matter. (This may be one reason why the responses show as much attention to structure as they do.) However, to note that in normal situations context does matter does not invalidate experimental results. The point is that children *can* attend to particular structures, and perhaps a somewhat artificial situation is the best way to get them to do so.

Stimuli

The sentences that were presented varied in structure, and also in grammaticalness. The children heard grammatical and ungrammatical versions of each structural type. We expected the children to find it relatively difficult to repeat the ungrammatical sentences. We hoped that they would bring out some of the passive competence we were most interested in.

There were seven different structural types. They varied in transformational history, but none was maximally simple. Globally, the surface structures were the same; each had the surface form of a simplex with one complex area, that is, one in which one node or constituent had a somewhat complex internal structure.

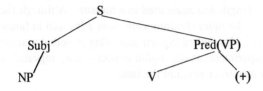

Repetition Experiment Stimuli:

Structural Types

Adjective	They played with long yellow blocks.
Conjunction	Sam and Ronny built the sandbox.
Conjunction inversion	Not George but Danny came along.
Number	Two of the marbles rolled away.
Object complement	Mary wants to play the piano.
Relative clause	The lady who sneezes is sick.
Verb auxiliary	Daddy may have missed the train.

The adjectives occurred in all stimuli containing adjectival complexity. Adjective and conjunction complexity occurred in both subject and object noun phrases.

There were ungrammatical sentences of each structural type. These sentences had a grammatical error in the area of complexity. There were three types of errors:

Constant   Harry likes ride the horses.
Auxiliary   Harry wants to riding the horse.
Inflection   Two of the marble rolled away.

Length was held constant at six to eight syllables. We found in preliminary work that shorter sentences are usually repeated accurately by three and four year olds, and that longer sentences are usually repeated inaccurately. Simple familiar words were used in each sentence. The children heard several grammatical and ungrammatical instances of each structural type, but never the same sentence twice.

The subjects were 18 children, three to four years old, all from middle-class, professional families. We collected samples of natural speech for each child and, on the basis of the samples, ranked the children according to verbal maturity. Median utterance length was again used as a measure. Although there were exceptions, generally the older children were more advanced in linguistic development. The children who ranked highest according to verbal maturity performed the best in the experiment, as one would expect — they repeated accurately most often, made few serious errors, and the like.

Results

Both of the experimental variables, structure and grammaticalness, significantly affected the children's responses. Certain structures were consistently easier for them to repeat; others were consistently more difficult. The two groups of structures are represented as A and B respectively in the table below. As expected, the children were much less accurate in repeating grammatical than ungrammatical stimulae. The main results, in summary form, are these:

Repetition Experiment: Responses[7]

	Accurate or peripheral error	Serious error	Inadequate response
A Structures			
Grammatical stimuli	92%	5.4%	2.6%
Ungrammatical stimuli	60%	32%	8%
B Structures			
Grammatical stimuli	60%	26%	14%
Ungrammatical stimuli	33%	36%	31%

[7]The experiment is reposted in detail in C. Smith (1969), "A study of the syntactic knowledge of young children," ed. T. Bever and W. Weksel, *Studies in Psycholinguistics,* in press.

The responses were scored as accurate, inaccurate, or inadequate. Responses including less than 3 words of the stimulus, in proper order, were scored as inadequate, as were the occasional cases when the child refused to respond or asked the experimenter to repeat a sentence. Inaccurate responses were subdivided into groups containing serious and peripheral errors (such as a change of number from singular to plural, or a change of tense from past to present). For overall scoring, the peripheral errors were grouped with accurate responses; this grouping did not change the general pictures of the data.

The A and B structures emerged solely on the basis of the children's responses. They also differ on other grounds for these children; A structures occurred in our records of their spontaneous speech, and B structures did not.

A Structures

Conjunction	(Sam and Harry built the house.)
Complement	(Susie likes to ride in the bus.)
Number	(Two of the marbles rolled away.)

B Structures

Adjective	(The little green frog jumped out.)
Relative	(The boy who was running fell down.)
Verbal Auxiliary	(Daddy may have missed the train.)
Conjunction Inversion	(Not Jane, but Mary, spilled the milk.)

Discussion

I will consider first the question of the children's ability to structure different types of sentences, or, in other words, which structures were within, and which beyond, their competence? The response to grammatical stimuli show that A structures were much easier for them to repeat than B structures; for an answer to the question of whether they knew more about the structures of A sentences, let us consider in some detail responses to ungrammatical stimuli.

The ungrammatical sentences were difficult for the children to repeat accurately, but they usually attempted to repeat them, and usually made mistakes in doing so. One type of mistake occurred with striking regularity — the children tended to respond to an ungrammatical sentence with a grammatical version of the same sentence. For instance:

> (5) (Stimulus) Mine old green coat has holes.
> (Response) My old green coat has holes.

I will refer to responses of this kind as *normalizations.* They were frequent, especially with A stimuli. There was an interesting correlation between normalizations and accurate repetitions of grammatical stimuli: if a child tended to accurately repeat grammatical sentences (of a given structure), he tended to normalize un-grammatical sentences.

A normalization indicates that a child has recognized the structure of the stimulus sentence – that is, that he has successfully disentangled the structure from the error. Such responses indicate, at the least, that the children were organizing the stimuli as sentences, rather than as sequences of words. And the correlation between effect of grammaticalness and normalizations shows that the A sentences were easier for the children to recognize in ungrammatical form than were the B sentences.[8]

Since it was relatively easy for the children to repeat grammatical A sentences, we must ask what the extra burden on the faculties is, in an ungrammatical A sentence. The answer is obvious – the grammatical error. Consider the repetition of a sentence in terms of a scheme of the repetition process.

Scheme for Repetition Process

$$\text{Input} \longrightarrow \text{Storage} \longrightarrow \text{Output}$$
$$\text{(Identification)} \qquad\qquad \text{(Reproduction)}$$

In terms of this familiar scheme, repetition involves three stages. At each stage, an ungrammatical sentence presents more material than does a grammatical sentence. At the stage of identification, the child must disentangle the structure and the grammatical error – we can think of the error as a kind of footnote to the structure. He must store both structure and footnote, which is more cumbersome than the storage of structure alone; he must reproduce both, which must at the least involve an extra operation. And since the children respond with normalizations to A stimuli, we infer that the difficulty comes with storage, or production, rather than with identification.

The children's responses to ungrammatical stimuli suggest strongly, then, that they do impose structure on the A sentences, and that the structure does not differ from adult structure.

The B structures are more problematic and more interesting; recall that the A structures occur in the children's spontaneous speech, but the B structures do not. Since the responses to each type differ, the B structures must be considered separately. Of the four types, sentences with verbal auxiliaries were probably most beyond the competence of the children. They were rarely repeated accurately, when presented in grammatical form; they were rarely normalized or repeated accurately when presented in ungrammatical form. Notionally, of

---

[8]The question of whether or not the children actually heard the grammatical errors may legitimately be raised – our data indicates that they did hear the errors.

course, the verbal auxiliaries are complicated and relatively adult, so that this result is not surprising. A second type of B structure was sentences with two prenominal adjectives. The children's responses suggested that the density of the adjectives caused difficulty, but not the adjective structure (they frequently left out one of the two adjectives). We might say, then, that the adjective sentences were difficult for mechanical rather than grammatical reasons; the recursion overloaded the children's capacities in some way.

The other two B structures, conjunction inversion and relative clauses, elicited uneven responses. There were accurate responses, but they did not occur with the frequency and regularity and normalizations of responses to A stimuli. Still, children certainly recognized the structures some of the time. Perhaps with these structures we have cases of sentences that the children understand but do not use — sentences that are within their competence, but not to be found in their natural speech. Relative clauses and conjunctions such as *not... but* occur rarely in the speech of three to four years old. The children's responses indicate that they have some control of these structures, although not as much as they have of the A structures.[9]

A profile of relative competence for all seven sentence types would show three different levels of competence: group 1 structures the children know best, which elicit accurate repetitions of grammatical sentences and normalizations of ungrammatical sentences; group 2 structures the children know least, which elicit accurate repetitions of grammatical sentences and few normalizations; and group 3 structures of which the children have uneven control, which sometimes elicit grammatical repetitions and sometimes elicit normalizations. Group 1 sentences occur in the children's natural speech; these are structures the children both comprehend and produce. The children neither comprehend nor produce group 2 sentences, we hypothesize, since they do not occur in natural speech and the repetition data does not indicate that the children know their structure. Group 3 sentences are within the competence of the children, according to the repetition data, even though the children do not produce them spontaneously. It is this last group, of course, that the analyst of children's speech has difficulty in discovering. With a suitable range of structural type as stimuli, one could use repetition to assemble quite complete profiles of linguistic competence for different stages of development.

I consider now the more general question of the linguistic input for our subjects. It seems likely that children have some kind of listening strategy that limits linguistic input; that they do not attempt to process or structure everything

---

[9] Slobin has pointed out that children sometimes utter sentences that they do not comprehend. The additions presumably are not understood with the familiar material, and may simply sound pleasantly adult.

that they hear. The profile of linguistic competence gives some notion of which utterances the children were able to structure, of a variety addressed to them. To discover something of the strategy they used in listening, we shall look at what happened when the children did not correctly structure what they heard — that is, did not correctly repeat or normalize the stimulus sentences.

There was a tendency to simplify the complex area of a sentence, in responses which were neither accurate repetitions nor normalizations. If the children did not successfully identify a structure — grammatical or ungrammatical — they tended to ignore the complex aspects of the structure altogether in their responses. For example, a typical pair of complex stimulus and simplified response:

(6)   (Stimulus)   The boy who was running fell down.
       (Response)   The boy fell down.

To discuss this matter further, it is necessary to explain the scoring of inaccurate responses (these contained at least three words of the stimulus sentence, in the order in which they occurred). Inaccurate responses that did not contain a peripheral error were scored as structure-preserving or structure-violating; these categories pertained only to the complex part of the sentence. In structure-preserving responses, the children usually omitted some material but retained some that was structurally important, such as:

(7)   (Stimulus)   The old gray wolf chased rabbits.
       (Response)   The old wolf chased rabbits.

(8)   (Stimulus)   The lady should have gone home.
       (Response)   The lady should gone home.

(9)   (Stimulus)   The boy who was running fell down.
       (Response)   The boy running fell down.

Structure-violating responses indicated by omission that the children did not "understand" the stimulus sentence; that is, that they were unable to impose the correct adult structure on it. If a response simply omitted the complex part of a constituent, it was scored as structure-violating. For instance:

(10)   (Stimulus)   The old gray wolf chased rabbits.
       (Response)   The old gray chased rabbits.

(11)   (Stimulus)   The boy who was running fell down.
       (Response)   The boy who was fell down.

There are several interesting aspects to this classification. The first is that we were able to make it at all, that is, that children's responses fell only into these categories. Quite a different classification, including errors in various parts of the sentence, might have been required. But the errors were almost uniformly located in the complex parts of the sentence. The children did not leave out the complex constituent altogether, nor did they repeat the complex part of a sentence but omit the rest. They might also have made disorderly errors, garbling crucial words, for instance; but in fact they did not make such errors.

Structure-violating responses occurred almost entirely after B stimuli. (This is consonant with our finding that children may have difficulty reproducing ungrammatical A stimuli, but are able to identify them easily). Of the structure-violating responses, some *reduced* the stimulus to a simplex sentence (as in 10) and some *confused* the complex constituent of the stimulus (as in 11). There were twice as many reduced responses as confused responses.

The children tended to pick out simple structures from complex structures, then, when too complex a sentence was presented to them. We might say that they imposed their own structure on the sentence, that is, a structure that they know. As a result, part of the sentence is ignored. Two other examples of reduced responses may make the phenomenon clearer:

(12) (Stimulus) Mommy could have lost her purse.
     (Response) Mommy lost her purse.

(13) (Stimulus) Not Jane, but Betty, called you.
     (Response) Betty called you.

It seems likely that such responses are due to identification or decoding failures. The children structured only the simplest part of the sentences; they omitted the complex parts, perhaps not hearing them clearly. Generalizing, we can say that children tend to omit, or even not to hear, material that they cannot handle. This may sound rather mysterious; how can children know what material they will not be able to handle? It becomes less so when we realize that adjectives, relative clauses, verbal auxiliaries, and the like receive less stress than the head noun of a noun phrase or the main verb of a verb phrase. Intonation may provide cues to the important and familiar parts of sentences. In attending to these, the children may simply ignore the unfamiliar and more difficult parts.

The responses of these three and four years old suggest that the listening of children may be selective; if children tend to notice what they do know, they may in consequence eliminate what they don't know. In the response experiment discussed earlier, we found also evidence of the selective listening of children.

The results we obtained in the repetition experiment indicate that the linguistic competence of three to four years old is greater than their spontaneous speech indicates. The A stimuli exemplified structures that the children produce and understand; some of the B stimuli exemplified structures that the children probably understand, but do not produce. We inferred that the children had only a limited ability to handle sentences with relative clauses and with conjunction inversion. They were not always successful in repeating grammatical stimuli of these types; ungrammatical versions tended to elicit reductions rather than normalizations. The children apparently tended not to recognize these structures with the additional factor of the grammatical error to cope with.

I have pointed out that children frequently responded to B stimuli with reductions. In these responses the children may be said to have imposed a structure on what they heard; as McNeill (1964) puts it, they seem to have been "looking for" simple structures (and finding them). In another vocabulary, the children decoded the stimuli according to their own ability to structure sentences.

I turn finally to the problem of characterizing the structures that were easy and difficult for the children to repeat. We seek a structural property that differentiates the two groups of structures; in other words, we would like to know whether the various easy structures were similar in some way, and the various difficult structures similar in some way. Knowledge of such a property might enable us to predict, on structural grounds, the order in which grammatical structures are acquired. Such knowledge might also help us to separate three factors in linguistic development that have so far been inextricably tangled; these factors I will call the mechanical, the grammatical, and the notional.[10] Let us consider briefly the different types of stimulus sentences.

The stimuli had similar surface structures, but they differed in deep structure and transformational history. There were two expanded simplex sentences; the other structures had two or three simplex sentences, and involved the application of different transformations. The sentences can be compared in several ways according to the number of simplex sentences involved, the number of transformations required to generate them, or the type of transformation involved. I give below a classification made according to the number of simplex sentences in each structure.

> One Expanded Simplex Sentence
> > Number
> > Verbal Auxiliary
>
> Two Simplex Sentences
> > Complement Embedding
> > Relative Clause Embedding
> > Conjunction
> > Conjunction and Inversion
>
> Three Simplex Sentences
> > Adjective Embedding

[10]It is appropriate to separate the grammatical and notional, at least tentatively, since a child may understand a notion but not understand a particular grammatical expression of that notion.

As we expected, sentences with longer transformational histories were relatively difficult for the children to repeat. But this criterion of complexity does not explain any of our results. It does not explain, for instance, why sentences with relative clauses fell into one category (B stimuli) and sentences with complements fell into another (A stimuli); both are derived from two simplex sentences, and both involve embedding transformations.[11]

It is necessary to consider the surface structures of the stimulus sentences, to explain our results rather than their deriviation. This is hardly surprising. The children's task was, in a sense, to impose a structure on the sentences they heard. In emphasizing surface structure, we suggest that sentences differ in how easy they are to hear; some sentences may be more transparent, more accessible to the imposition of structure, than others. Consider the surface structure properties of the relative clause sentences (difficult) and the object complement sentences, for instance. The relative clauses were all interposed between the subject and main verb of the sentence, whereas the object complement followed the main verb and did not disrupt the main structural elements of the sentence. Such a difference might well make the latter type of sentence easier to repeat than the former. This example suggests location of complexity as a factor in surface structure; location may be important but was not in fact, the decisive factor in separating the easy and difficult in our data.

We differentiate between A and B surface structures in terms of a property I will call *compression*. Compression refers to the way semantic information occurs in a sentence. When sentences have low compression, semantic information is distributed fairly evenly throughout the sentence; when sentences have high compression, semantic information is bunched together, or compressed, at the noun-phrase or verb-phrase level. In terms of tree structure, highly compressed sentences have NP or VP nodes dominating several information-carrying elements; in less compressed sentences, NP or VP nodes dominate relatively few information-carrying elements. For example, the sentence below has low compression. The information-carrying elements are underlined.

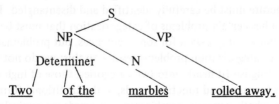

---

[11] There are differences between the embedding transformations that produce relative clauses and object complements.

This sentence has high compression.

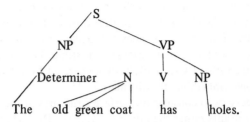

The A structures have relatively low compression, and the children found them easy to repeat. The B structures have relatively high compression, and the children found them difficult to repeat.

Latencies of the children's responses were measured (timed from the end of the stimulus to the beginning of the response). In general, responses to B stimuli took longer than responses to A stimuli. This was especially true for the younger children. Perhaps the children's faculties are overburdened if much information is compressed into a single noun phrase or verb.

The effect of compression suggests a hypothesis about children's acquisition of structure, namely, that degree of compression may be a factor in the order in which structures are acquired. Structures of relatively low compression may be learned earlier than structures of relatively high compression. In transformational terms, this would mean that transformations resulting in surface structures of high compression may be learned relatively late.

The effect of compression is confounded with other aspects of surface structure in the examples given here. Structure, location, length, and discontinuity (as in the relative clause of a subject noun phrase) undoubtedly interact with compression, and there may be additional factors as well. Compression appears to be dominant for the task of repetition but we are, after all, interest in repetition because of its relevance to understanding; perhaps under other circumstances the factor of compression would be less important. If the notion of compression is to have more than a rough usefulness, the different factors of surface structure must be carefully identified and disentangled. The notion of compression has certain problems of categorization that must be solved; it is easy to compute compression for some sentences, but problematic for others. Roughly, the categorization problems resolve to this: we do not know whether all words of English fit neatly into two categories, those of high or low information carriers (content and function words, in the traditional formulation); nor do we know whether various combinations of words are equivalent in compression (for instance, do two low-information words have the same compression as one high-information word?). These are rather clear problems that will, I hope, be investigated in the near future. With this caveat, I would like now to discuss some implications of the notion of compression.

Our subjects' ability to deal with sentences was affected by how compressed the sentences were — that is, by the amount of semantic information in the noun phrase and verb phrase constituents. *Noun phrase* and *verb phrase* are abstractions that partly explain how language is organized in memory and understanding. We may recall in this connection the "chunks" that George Miller (1956) discusses in his classic paper on memory and processing limitations in adults. Noun phrase and verb phrase constituents are analogous to Miller's chunks, and the results of our experiment show that children can handle only chunks of limited size. As children's linguistic and other faculties develop, they are able to handle larger chunks—sentences with higher degrees of compression.

Limitations on the memory and processing abilities of children account for the bound on compression, apparently; therefore, we may call it a mechanical constraint rather than a grammatical or notional one (although further investigation may show interaction between grammatical structure and compression). Extralinguistic constraints such as this are often referred to in the literature on language acquisition. But usually discussion of their specific nature is inextricably linked to a particular account of understanding, namely, a close generative model. Thus it has been suggested that children are able to perform only a limited number of transformational operations and, therefore, are unable to handle sentences that have complex derivations. Assumed is the doubtful explanation that people generate sentences much as a grammar does. Unless we accept this doubtful viewpoint, the discussion of specific constraints on numbers of transformational operations has no value.

We need not commit ourselves to a particular account of understanding before we study it. Our finding of the importance of compression shows, for instance, that certain extralinguistic constraints may be isolated more or less independently of such matters. On the other hand, we expect that the discovery of such constraints may affect the focus of studies of understanding. In the present experiment it is noteworthy that compression is a property of surface structure, not of deep structure of derivational complexity.

Mechanical constraints may limit a child's linguistic competence in more than one way. Notional, grammatical, and mechanical faculties do not necessarily develop at the same rate; although a child may understand a particular notion, and its expression, extralinguistic factors may prevent him from using it linguistically.[12] I do not mean that only extralinguistic factors, such as memory constraints, keep children from talking with full adult competence. But it does seem possible that in some circumstances mechanical constraints may keep a child from using his full linguistic capabilities. For instance, certain structures may be

[12] McNeill apparently has a similar idea in mind when he refers to children's knowledge of basic grammatical relations before they can indicate that they have this knowledge.

relatively inaccessible for mechanical reasons; a child may not understand an expression in a highly compressed sentence that he would understand if it were presented in a sentence with less compression. This suggests another reason for disentangling mechanical from other factors, insofar possible; otherwise, we may systematically mistake a child's linguistic capabilities.

Children may be able to handle grammatical expressions thought to be beyond them — if they are broken into small units that the children can process. Consider, for instance, the passive. Brown has demonstrated that young children do not "understand" passive sentences, that is, they do not correctly identify actor and acted-upon. But this is odd, for it seems likely that children understand the *notion* expressed by the passive. For instance, we would expect them to understand a passive with deleted agent such as *Mary was hurt.* It would be interesting to repeat Brown's experiment, presenting children with two sentences and then asking them to identify the actor and acted-upon. Suppose, for instance, stimuli such as this were presented: *Mary was hurt; Mary was hurt by the boy;* or *Mary was hurt and she was hurt by the boy.* Perhaps the simple structure of the first sentence, and the repeated words in the second, would allow enough mental time for a young child to process all the material. It seems likely that children fail to comprehend passive sentences because they are too compressed, and not because of notional gaps or ignorance of linguistic signals.

CONCLUSION

Surface structure was the most important factor determining whether a sentence was easy for the children to repeat accurately, and, we assume, to understand. This perhaps unexpected result suggests a general point — that surface structure deserves more attention than it has heretofore received, both in speculative and experimental approaches to the problem of understanding. It is often noticed that certain recursions (self-embedding, for instance) are difficult to understand because they make stringent demands on immediate memory. But other aspects of surface structure that are more subtle or difficult to isolate have been little studied. An important first step will be to clarify somewhat the relation between linguistic and extralinguistic factors in surface structure. This would make it possible to investigate notional and linguistic development on the one hand, and the development of the memory and computation abilities that I have called "mechanical" on the other.[13]

---

[13] It seems unlikely that these factors can be entirely separated.

There are probably two senses in which the importance of surface structure has been underestimated. First, as I have argued above, mechanical factors may make certain sentences more or less accessible to analysis and understanding. But second, surface structure, rather than derivation, may be the vehicle for understanding. In terms of generative grammar, what I am saying is that the structures that result from the applications of grammatical rules may be the proper focus of study; the question for psycholinguistics is, how do people impose an interpretation on surface structure? It is relevant here to recall an insight of Zellig Harris (1964). Harris has pointed out that most English sentences, however complex their derivation and internal structure, have the global structure of simplex sentences. Harris was not concerned with a psycholinguistic account of understanding; but I suggest, as an extrapolation, that global structure may be of primary importance for understanding.

One might speculate that, to understand a sentence, a person must know its global structure. There are other rearrangement transformations, besides the notorious passive, that do not result in the typical global structure of English. Perhaps it is necessary, for understanding, to recover a certain global structure for sentences such as these: *It surprised me that he came, It was a book that John lost,* and *Modern music he does not like.*

I do not propose that we abandon entirely the notion that, in understanding, people recover underlying sentences; but it might be fruitful to consider how much recovery is necessary, rather than how much recovery is possible.

In this presentation and discussion of two experiments I have tried to suggest an approach to some important problems in the field of language acquisition and of psycholinguistics in general. Experimental studies of linguistic behavior, in which utterances can be systematically varied, are required for serious study of linguistic competence. Also required, I think, is a conscious attempt to keep separate grammatical and psychological explanations of linguistic behavior. The structural descriptions generative grammar may represent what people know about sentences, rather than what they do in understanding and producing them.

REFERENCES

Brown, R., and Bellugi, U., "Three processes in the child's acquisition of syntax," in Lenneberg, E., ed., *New Directions in the Study of Language,* Cambridge, Mass.: M.I.T. Press, 1964.

Brown, R., and Fraser, C., "The acquisition of syntax," in Bellugi and Brown, ed., *The Acquisition of Language,* monography of the Society for Research in Child Development, 1964, 29, No. 1.

Chomsky, N., *Aspects of the Theory of Syntax,* Cambridge, Mass.: M.I.T. Press, 1965.

Ervin, S., "Imitation and structural change in children's language," in Lenneberg, E., ed., *New Directions in the Study of Language,* Cambridge, Mass.: M.I.T. Press, 1964.

Fodor, J., and Bever, T., "The Psychological reality of linguistic segments," *Journal of Verbal Learning and Verbal Behavior 4,* 1965, 5, 414-421.

Fodor, J., and Garrett, M. "Some reflections on competence and performance," *Psycholinguistics Papers,* proceedings of Edinburgh Conference 196, University of Edinburgh Press, Edinburgh, 1966.

Halle, M., and Stevens, K. N., *"Speech recognition: A model and a program for research,"* reprinted in Fodor and Katz, eds., *The Structure of Language,* Englewood Cliffs, N. J.: Prentice-Hall, 1964.

Harris, Z., "Co-occurrence and transformation in linguistic structure", reprinted in Fodor and Katz, eds., *The Structure of Language,* Englewood Cliffs, N.J.: Prentice-Hall, 1964.

Lakoff, George, "Deep and surface grammar," 1966, unpublished paper.

McCawley, J., "The annotated respective," unpublished paper, 1968.

McNeill, D., "Development psycholinguistics, 2" in F. Smith and G. Miller, eds., *The Genesis of Language,* Cambridge, Mass.: M.I.T. Press, 1966.

McNeill, D., "The creation of language," in Lenneberg, E., ed., *New Directions in the Study of Language,* Cambridge, Mass.: M.I.T. Press, 1964.

Matthews, G.H., "Analysis by synthesis of natural languages," *Proceedings of the International Congress on Machine Translation and Applied Language Analysis,* London: H.M.S.O., 1962.

Miller, G. A., "The Magical number seven, plus or minus two," *Psychological Review 1956,* 63, 81-97.

Miller, G. A., and Isard, S., "Some perceptual consequences of linguistic rules," *JVLVB,* 1963, 2, 217-228.

Miller, G. A., and Selfridge, J., "Verbal context and the recall of meaningful material," *American Journal of Psychology,* 1951, 63, 176-185.

Neisser, Ulric, *Cognitive Psychology,* New York: Appleton-Century-Crofts, 1967.

Ross, John, "Auxiliaries as main verbs", 1967, unpublished paper.

Sapir, E., "The psychological reality of phonemes," Mandelbaum, D., ed., *Selected Writings of Edward Sapir,* California: University of California Press, 1949.

Savin, H., and Perchonock, E., "Grammatical Structure and the immediate recall of English sentences," *JVLVB,* 1965, 4, 348-353.

Shipley, E., Smith, C. S., and Gleitman, L., "A study in the acquisition of language: free responses to commands," *Language,* 1969.

Slobin, D., "Recall of full and truncated passive sentences in connected discourse," 1967.

Smith, C. S., "A study of the syntactic knowledge of young children," ed. Bever, T., and Weksel, W., eds., *Studies in Psycholinguistics,* in press, 1969.

Thorne, J., "On hearing sentences," in Lyons, J., ed., *Psycholinguistics Papers,* Edinburgh: University of Edinburgh Press, 1966.

Vygotsky, L., *Thought and Language,* Cambridge, Mass.: M.I.T. Press, 1962.

CHAPTER 5   *W. C. Watt*

Carnegie-Mellon University

ON TWO HYPOTHESES CONCERNING
PSYCHOLINGUISTICS*

"...You may depend upon it that there are things
going on inside us that we understand mighty little
about."
"Jupiter! you make my flesh creep!" cried Tristram.
From a novel by Henry James

0.   INTRODUCTION

The two hypotheses which form the subject of this chapter are not, *per se*,
entirely novel; indeed, to anyone who has been following the course of psycholinguistics for the past few years they may long have been a familiar part of the
landscape. Familiar, but in such a way as to be ignored. The first hypothesis
concerns the nature of the speaker's (or "idealized" speaker's) mental grammar;
in particular, it concerns the relation between that grammar and the grammar for
English under construction by linguists. The "Correlation Hypothesis," as I will
term it,[1] has in one version been formulated explicitly in that well-known version holding essentially that the grammar of "English" is an "axiomatization"
of the (idealized) speaker's mental grammar: that is, the two grammars have an
exceedingly close relationship. However, while this version of the Correlation
Hypothesis has achieved wide currency, it seems never to have been defended in
any depth, except against completely irrational alternatives; thus, though but a
hypothesis, this version has enjoyed the status usually accorded a foundational
assumption, an axiom without which the science could not proceed. This status
alone provides us with enough reason to take a fresh look at the hypothesis.

*This work was supported by the Advanced Research Projects Agency of the Office
of the Secretary of Defense under Contract No. F 44620-67-C-0058. I acknowledge with
pleasure the helpful comments of H. H. and E. V. Clark.*

[1] The "Correlation Hypothesis" (or Hypotheses) must not be confused with the
"Correspondence Hypothesis," Hayes's term (see Introduction to this volume) for the hypothesis which holds that "...the derivational history of the sentence corresponds step by
step to the sequence of psychological processes that are executed when a person processes
the sentence" (ibid., p. 5).

The second hypothesis, the "Strong Inclusion Hypothesis," has had a much more peculiar history, since it appeared in early writings as a tacit assumption, and then yielded in later writings to the corresponding null assumption, without ever (to my knowledge) having been exposed to light, examined, and accepted or rejected. As a result, the downfall of the Strong Inclusion Hypothesis (which I do not think many, apprised of the nature of the hypothesis, would now dispute) has come about without occasioning a general awareness of the *consequences* of this downfall. And this is the reason for our here examining the hypothesis in some detail, and the corresponding null hypothesis as well; we will thus be able to determine what corollaries, if any, had the Strong Inclusion Hypothesis as their sole supporter.

It is probably superfluous, but I should like to note at the outset that, although I will try to mount as strong a case as possible for each of my arguments, on the other hand, presently available evidence on almost any psycholinguistic point is so scanty as to blunt any claim that this or that hypothesis has truly been disconfirmed. (If enough future evidence is to be concentrated on a given point, research directed at gathering that evidence must be provoked by formulating hypotheses that seem worth rejecting or upholding.)

This chapter proceeds in three sections. Sections 1 and 2 examine, independently, the two hypotheses; Section 3 concludes.

1.   THE CORRELATION HYPOTHESIS

1.0.   The "Correlation Hypothesis," as I will term it, concerns the nature of the relation between the grammar constructed for English (for example) in accordance with principles of linguistics, and the mental grammar of the ("idealized") speaker of English. As far as modern linguistics is concerned[2] the contemporary approximative notion of the nature of the linguistic grammar (hereafter, LG) was born simultaneously with the notion that speakers do have mental grammars (MG) in some sense similar to that of the LG. Indeed, LG and ("idealized") MG were tied very closely together, for the essential business of the LG was seen as accommodating in an ("idealized") MG the linguistic information available to the ("idealized") native speaker.[3] This view of the LG/MG relation has been encapsulated in a version of the Correlation Hypothesis: the LG differs from the MG

----

[2]For coverage of some notions ancestral to this idea, see Chomsky (1966)

[3]I am using the annoyingly parenthesized term "idealized" to indicate that it need not be held that the MG thus qualified is, in fact, the possession of any one speaker of English. Individual MG differ from each other in idiosyncratic ways corresponding to idiosyncratically affective facets of the individual language-acquisition process. Trivially, no two

only in that the LG represents "axiomatically" (Fodor and Garrett, 1966, p. 139) what the MG represents in some other way. LG and MG generate the same set of sentences and assign those sentences the same structural descriptions and derivational paths; the sentences transformationally related (derived from equivalent or identical deep structures) in the LG are similarly related in the MG; and in general LG and MG differ *only representationally*.[4]

speakers have exactly the same lexicon — the same words with exactly the same definitions (Harris, 1954, p. 150); less trivially, speakers differ on minor syntactic points. Unless the LG is specifically geared to capture just the MG of some particular speaker (the grammarian), then it will probably capture the MG of no speaker. Moreover, if speakers vary much in their MG, then the LG cannot represent a *composite* speaker without losing some of the very "simplicity" that contributes to its adequacy as a (putative) representation of the MG.

This point is related to, but quite different from, two other points due to Chomsky. First, it is evident that the speaker's MG and, more generally his linguistic competence, must be considerably abstracted from his actual performance, since the latter's set of "utterances" only *intersects* with the set of sentences of competence; there must be (infinitely many) sentences too complex or too stilted or just too long ever to be used — no performance will ever contain them—and then, actual discourse consists less of "sentences" as such than of ". . .interrupted fragments, false starts, lapses, slurring, and other phenomena. . ." (Chomsky, 1962, p. 531). Second, the LG is an "idealized" MG (Chomsky, 1967a, p. 398), in that the LG expresses in compact and formal notation what the MG doubtless expresses in some other (and far more abstract) way. Contrasting my point with the two just outlined, I was claiming that the performance of speakers belies, and the LG idealizes, not a set of identical MG, but rather a set of slightly differing MG. The point is obvious enough, and will not be referred to again.

[4]". . .every speaker of a language has mastered and internalized a generative grammar that expresses his knowledge of his language." (Chomsky, 1965, p. 8); ". . .a reasonable model of language use will incorporate, as a basic component, the generative grammar that expresses the speaker-hearer's knowledge of the language. . ." (ibid., p. 9); "A general linguistic theory. . .must therefore be regarded as a specific hypothesis, of an essentially rationalist cast, as to the nature of mental structures and processes" (ibid., p. 53); "The generative grammar represents the information concerning sentence structure that is available, in principle, to one who has acquired the language. It indicates how, ideally — leaving out any limitations of memory, distractions, etc. — he would understand a sentence. . ."(1963, pp. 326f.); and ". . .the technical term 'competence' refers to the ability of the idealized speaker-hearer to associate sounds and meanings strictly in accordance with the rules of his language. The grammar of a language, as a model for idealized competence, establishes a certain relation between sound and meaning — between phonetic and semantic representations. ...To discover this grammar is the primary goal of the linguistic investigation of a particular language" (1967a, p. 398).

Chomsky's conception of the nature of the speaker's MG must be sharply distinguished from two other conceptions that abut on it. First, he does assert that speakers have an MG, not just the products generated in accordance with the corresponding LG; they have a grammar, not a set of "grammatical" sentences. They have neither a mere inventory of words and phrases with their grammatical (combinatory) properties — this notion, which may be ascribed to de Saussure, Chomsky rejects (1963, p. 328) — nor do they have some

The MG in question could only be a competence grammar (CG), as contrasted with a means of making and parsing sentences (or worse yet, utterances). Further clarifying this contrast, we see that between our MG and what we say there must be interposed a performative mechanism, whose "use" illustrates one sort of performative factor, whose "misuse" betrays another sort. Having access in some way to the MG, this performance mechanism composes sentences whose analyses accord with those given them by the MG, and imposes on input sentences the analyses they would have had if generated by the MG. In so doing, the performance mechanism obeys what we might call "positive performative factors," in that knowing how to speak English involves knowing how to select and utter, from the vast synonymous paradigms generally offered by the language, a sentence that can be controlled in speaking and understood by the auditor; a sentence, moreover, that, through sequencing its main elements, focuses attention in the way desired.[5] The mechanism is also constrained to reveal what we might call "negative performative factors," in that its (mental) productions, in the course of being realized as sound, are often distorted by memory lapses and other performative difficulties.[6]

The performance mechanism must produce sentences (apart from the "negative performative factors") which will be *as if* they had been produced by invoking the rules of the MG in their prescribed order; but their composition need not have consisted of actually invoking those rules in that way.[7] To take a

inventory of sentence-blanks into which appropriate words can be put, a notion which may be ascribed to Bolinger and which Chomsky also rejects (1964, p. 54, *n*.). That is, Chomsky means just what he says when he refers to ". . .the rules of the grammar represented in the brain. . ." (1963, p. 330). But on the other hand he specifically enjoins against the interpretation that, therefore, the MG's model of generation is a model of production (or, reversed somehow, a model of reception). For further remarks on this, see below.

[5] See, for example, Chomsky (1965, pp. 11; 221, *n.* 32; 224-5, *n.* 9) for further references to these aspects of performance; cf. Firbas (1959, 1964) and Halliday (esp. 1967).

[6] See, for example, Chomsky (1965, pp. 4, 10-15).

[7] Present-day linguistic terminology has bred endless misunderstanding of this issue, in that "generate," "rewrite as," and so on, are naturally and persistently misconstrued as describing *production* rules, the result being that the generative grammar is regarded as, in fact, a set of instructions which a speaker follows in order to compose sentences. This has happened despite the fact that from the very beginning Chomsky emphasized that this was a misconstruction; for example, "A grammar does not tell us how to synthesize a specific utterance; it does not tell us how to analyze a particular given utterance. In fact, these two tasks. . . are both outside the scope of grammars. . ." (1957, p. 48). He has returned to this theme many times (e.g. 1964, p. 10; 1965, pp. 3-9; and elsewhere), restating it with increasing asperity. Most recently (1967 *a*, p. 399), he put it in these words: ". . .although we may describe the grammar *G* as a system of processes and rules that apply in a certain order to

simple example, in the LG and in the CG, pronominalization must follow passivization, in order that an abstract structure of the form "John killed John" may
be converted into the grammatical "John was killed by himself" rather than into
the ungrammatical "*Himself was killed by John." But the accepted model of
the overall linguistic capacity does not insist that speakers, in composing such
sentences, actually first ready an intermediate structure through passivization,
and only then invoke pronominalization. (This would be the fallacy *Propter hoc,
ergo post hoc.*)

In sum, taking as our text the grammatical sentence "That that that that
Byron detested Hunt distressed Shelley saddened Clare will perturb Dr. Psoriasis
would have amused Byron," we see that the CG accounts for the correct surface
analysis of this sentence and for its deep structure, transformational derivation,
and meaning; while the performative mechanism accounts for how the sentence
was actually composed, and in so doing shows which "positive performative
factors" were disobeyed and which "negative" ones were thereby run afoul of,
hence in effect accounting for the fact that a paraphrase of this sentence is
likely to be easier both to utter and to comprehend; for example, "It would
have amused Byron that Dr. Psoriasis will be perturbed at Clare's being saddened
by Shelley's distress at Byron's detestation of Hunt."

We have sketched, then, a version of the Correlation Hypothesis that we
will call CH_{CG}, a version based on the presumption that the basic human MG is
a competence grammar, served by and in service to a performance mechanism,
which grammar is the grammar that the LG is an (attempted) account of. This
version may be expressed as:

$$MG \equiv CG = LG$$

where "=" means "is isomorphic to," "is essentially equivalent to," "is no more
than representationally different from," "is idealized by," "is axiomatized by,"
or something of the sort.

relate sound and meaning, we are not entitled to take this as a description of the successive
acts of a performance model. . .in fact, it would be quite absurd to do so. . . . The grammatical rules that generate phonetic representations of signals with their semantic interpretations
do not constitute a model for the production of sentences, although any such model must
incorporate the system of grammatical rules."

Even so, the mistake has been made many times, even by Katz (1964), if I read him
correctly. Thus, the latter scholar at one time felt *at least* that in composing a sentence a
speaker necessarily *first* produces a full syntactic structure, and *then* ". . .utilizes the phonological component of his linguistic description to produce a phonetic shape for it" (p. 132;
reiterated on the following page, and see especially the footnote on that page). Vestiges of
this notion are still active.

Note, that, while the accepted notion of performance does not insist that the MG's
transformational rules be invoked one-by-one in sequence, neither does it insist that they
not be, as see below in 1.1.1.

We have explicitly acknowledged that the MG need not be identical to the performance mechanism, and we cannot demand that the composition of sentences consist of invoking the MG's rules one by one. However we have already noted, in n. 4, that a "reasonable model of language use," according to Chomsky, "will incorporate, as a basic component, the generative grammar that expresses the speaker-hearer's knowledge of the language."[8] This must mean that, in some way, the performance mechanism *refers to* the MG in the process of composing and parsing sentences. (If it did not, then the MG would have no use at all.) This in turn means that, while it is a mistake to identify the generations of the MG with the productions of the performance mechanism, it would, on the other hand, be a mistake of equal magnitude to completely dissociate the two. And, in fact, if the MG *is* actually "incorporated" into the "model of language use", then the relation must be rather close.[9] We can imagine a very abstract relation between the two components which, still, is a very close relation. For example, suppose that the set of generations of the MG were finite and that the full generation of each sentence were available on a mental 5 x 8 index card; and that the performance mechanism had "only" to find the right card to connect incoming sound to interpretation or intended meaning to outgoing sound. This notion completely divorces the MG's rules from the rules of performance, since the latter rules consist of ways of checking 5 x 8 cards, in whatever manner is most efficient, from bottom to top or top to bottom or from the middle in both directions. Even so, a sentence that the MG generates with a very complex derivation would (to continue the analogy) occupy more of the 5 x 8 card than would a simple derivation; and *ceteris paribus* should take more performative time and effort to recover. Thus, again *ceteris paribus*, "generative MG complexity" would bear a direct relation, even in this maximally abstract "index-card" notion, to "performative complexity." Then, if everything else *were* equal, we could experimentally observe performative complexity, establish whether our account of MG complexity corresponded properly, *and adjust the MG derivations accordingly.* We would have to make adjustments, if we believed our experimental results, since the alternative would be to exile the MG to an absurdly peripheral status in which its existence would be *defined* to be beyond even the most indirect proof — exactly as with the soul.

[8] A later comment (Chomsky, 1967*a*, p. 399): "...it is important to distinguish clearly between the function and properties of the perceptual model *PM* [the input aspect of the performance model] and the competence model *G* that it incorporates. ...*PM* makes use of much information *beyond* [italics supplied] the intrinsic sound-meaning association determined by the grammar *G*... ."

[9] "The psychological plausibility of a transformational model of the language user would be strengthened, of course, if it could be shown that our performance on tasks requiring an appreciation of the structure of transformed sentences is some function of the

As it happens, everything else is *not* equal (we will shortly devote a few pages to this topic), and so the proposed measure of related complexity is somewhat snarled. But, as is obvious, this does not free us from the burden of explicating that relation; we must ultimately be able to show what factors complicate the relation, and to show this in such a way that, when everything else is *made* equal (by being taken into account), then the relation will indeed hold: performatively complex sentences will be complex in the MG. If the relation still does not hold when we have taken everything into account that is at all plausible, then we must again think of changing the MG to fit the facts, if this can be done.

Our purpose in the rest of this Section on the Correlation Hypotheses can now be summarized: we will show that there are many discrepancies between reasonably hypothesized performative complexities and MG (= current LG) complexities; we will examine a variety of possible complicating and distortive factors that must be taken into account by any attempt to explain these discrepancies without changing the MG; we will conclude that these factors are not enough, or are not germane; we will consider that alterations to the MG are thus implied; and we will conclude that, apparently, these alterations cannot be made without changing the MG into something other than a CG, that is to say other than a grammar " = " to the LG; and we will then suggest that the MG is, by virtue of these alterations, an "Abstract Performative Grammar," whose nature we will try, very tentatively, to sketch.

1.1. On the CH_{CG}

1.1.1. If we compare Chomsky's comments of nn.7 and 9, above, we see that while the *general* thesis that production mirrors generation is labeled "absurd," nonetheless the issue of whether or not producing sentences involves invoking the (generative) sequence of *transformations,* is left open. There is no paradox here. The notion that in producing a sentence one converts the sentence's MG-generation directly into a production algorithm, producing the sentence by beginning with "S" and ending with a phoneme-to-sound conversion, may be naturally divided into separate notions concerning separate parts of the derivation. One notion holds that a speaker produces a sentence's deep structure by starting with "S," expanding "S" to "NP + Predicate," and expanding each node in turn until the categorial component of the base is exited from and the lexical items are added, resulting in a specification of the sentence's full deep structure. A second notion, distinct from the first, holds that one then takes that deep structure and

nature, number, and complexity of the grammatical transformations involved" (Miller and Chomsky, 1963, p. 481).

produces from it a surface structure by rewriting the deep structure through the successive application of appropriate transformations purloined from the MG. These two notions are distinct in the sense that the first can be rejected on grounds that leave the second unscathed. Within the conventional sense of generative grammar, syntax is generative and semantics only interpretive; and before lexical substitution takes place the deep structure's meaning is not fully specified, in that any lexical item, of whatever meaning, can be substituted for a given node *unless* the substitution (taking context into account) is unlawful. Thus the first notion insists, utterly contrary to sense, that a person must initially "...select sentence type, then determine subcategories, etc., finally, at the last stage, deciding what he is going to talk about..." (Chomsky, 1965, p. 197, n.8). Given the currently-accepted notion of grammar (which is not in dispute here),[10] the first notion is thus utterly ridiculous, as Chomsky makes manifest. But the second notion is not subject to the same criticism, since it only maintains that a speaker uses the rules of the MG to alter a structure whose meaning is already established into another structure with the same meaning. The second notion is not at all contrary to sense, and it was obviously worth subjecting to experimentation. Since mental activities are not accessible to direct observation, however, it was tested only in the weaker "5 x 8 index-card" version sketched above; the experiments were designed to show, not whether performance mirrored competence, but whether performative complexity mirrored competence complexity. This is the weaker version in the sense that, if it were upheld, the stronger version would remain still in doubt; but, (of more immediate importance) if it were disconfirmed then the stronger version would be seriously threatened.

[10]It is, of course, in dispute elsewhere; representative recent papers in marked opposition to major aspects of the *Aspects* model(s) are Ross (1967), Lakoff (1968), McCawley (1968), and Fillmore (1968). These works, and others by these and other like-minded authors cited in them, do not present a unified front; but they are similar in that they essentially propose that behind the deep structures of *Aspects* there lies much more abstract complex structure than could be accommodated at all convincingly in an *Aspects*-like base component. These abyssal structures clearly need transformations just to reach the level of Chomsky's deep structure. I have used one of the two *Aspects* models because it provides a firm and moderately well-known basis in linguistics for the variety of psycholinguistic comments on which this chapter is partly grounded, and because these comments are not, in general, falsified by any of the new models currently under debate. (The comments would have to be greatly altered, but not so as to be replaced by their contraries.) Lastly, it seems possible that the psycholinguistic reality of the "abyssal structures" is different from that of the "deep structures." The deep structures, to a large extent, have forms influenced by the notion of "kernel," or "elementary sentence" — the canonical and maximally simple sentential surface (Harris, 1957, pp. 334-336; 1965, pp. 364-367 *et passim;* Chomsky, 1957, pp. 45f, 61-84; 1965, pp. 17f.). But the abyssal structures scarcely betray any such influence. If there is any psycholinguistic reality to the "kernel sentence," as has sometimes been suggested (Chomsky, 1955, p. 23; 1957, p. 104, *n.* 11; Miller and Chomsky, 1963, p. 483; Chomsky, 1965, p. 18), then the "abyssal structures" might indeed have a psycholinguistic

The weaker version easily withstood early experimentation. These results were first summarized, cautiously, in Miller and Chomsky (1963, pp. 481-483); some of them, with later ones, have more recently been summarized by Fodor and Garrett (1966, pp. 143-148). The latter exposition may be consulted for details; here it must suffice to say that these experiments indeed seemed "impressive successes", as Fodor and Garrett put it (ibid., p. 143); they showed, or seemed to show, for example, that active sentences, which in the CG are more simply derived than passives, take performatively less time to produce (Miller, 1962; Miller and McKean, 1964), are performatively easier to remember (Mehler, 1963), and require less memory storage (Savin and Perchonock, 1965). Results like these were obtained for some (few) other sentence types; and, in general, results were consistently favorable to the thesis that performative complexity mirrors the generative complexity of the CG (that is, of the current version of the LG).

But, Fodor and Garrett (1966) claim, other experimental results undermine these early successes; results which show, for sentence "A" derived in a more complex fashion in the CG than sentence "B", either that "A" and "B" are performatively equally complex, or that "A" is performatively the *less* complex of the two. However, some of the results they cite are afflicted with the evanescence that seems to characterize so much work in this field.[11] In fact, only one of their cited pieces of evidence seems valid; it is that the sentence "John phoned the girl up" is more complex in the LG than the sentence "John phoned up the girl," though performatively they are of equal complexity. That is, their counterevidence consists of the one example, plus the fact that "John runs faster than Bill does" and "John runs faster than Bill" are performatively of equal complexity, which could be explained by the fact that, while the former is less complexly derived in the CG (see the discussion of "Deletion" below), the latter, on the other hand, is shorter.[12]

reality, even under the CH_{CG}, that is distinctively more abstract in some way. (A more abstract psycholinguistic reality could be attained, outside the MG proper, in the "archival linguistic competence" proposed below in 1.2.2.4.) Some of the examples cited below, as affecting the plausibility of CH_{CG}, are drawn from the literature opposed to *Aspects;* but in these cases it seems to me that the analyses proposed are incorporable into an *Aspects*-like grammar.

[11] They cite a result due to Mehler (1963) and to Miller and McKean (1964): more complex auxiliaries are no higher in performative complexity than are simple ones. But this result is now put into doubt by some work by Clark and Stafford (in press). They also cite an unpublished result from Fodor, Jenkins, and Saporta: "John runs faster than Bill runs" is harder to recognize (process) than "John runs faster than Bill" or "John runs faster than Bill does." But Fodor and Garrett (1966), p. 150) provide for this result the partial explanation that speakers of English find the first sentence strange, hence hesitate over it.

[12] They also (p. 150) cite Slobin (1963) as authority for the "fact" that truncated passives ("John was found") takes less time to process than do full Passives (no example).

However, though they had no solid data, I think Fodor and Garrett were right in concluding that the evidence favoring a close relation between generative and performative complexity was weak, and in inferring, from the threat to this relation, a threat to the stronger notion that performance mirrors generation rule-by-rule. From these conclusions they drew the further inference that the relation between the CG and the performance mechanism must henceforward be assumed to be "more abstract," a term that they leave quite vague but that seems to entail that the performative recognition routine include (or have access to) all the rules of the CG, and additionally include special performative rules for imposing surface structure on raw incoming sentences.[13]   (As many readers will recognize, this proposal is strongly reminiscent of one from Miller and Chomsky [1963, pp. 476-480].)

In a second attack on the problems of complexity relations, Fodor and Garrett (1967) report the results of an experiment and suggest two ways in which those results could be accounted for. Identifying the notion that performance complexity must mirror the transformational complexity of the CG as the "Derivational Theory of Complexity," or DTC, they return to their example of the truncated passives and point out that, according to DTC, if sentence X has a more complex transformational derivation in the CG than sentence Y, then DTC must predict X to be performatively more complex, *even though* X's extra complexity consists of the fact that X is derived from Y by *deleting* part of Y. DTC must predict "The boy was hit by someone" to be *less* complex (p. 290) than the shorter "The boy was hit," which derives (according to Fodor and Garrett) from the former sentence by transformationally deleting "by some-one."[14]   This DTC prediction is counter to sense and probably incorrect; since DTC is discredited, when it makes a correct prediction it probably does so by accident. Thus, their experimental result that (for example) "The man the dog bit died" is more complex than "The man *whom* the dog bit died" from which it derives by deleting "whom" − this result, predicted accidentally by DTC, is in want of a more satisfactory explanation.

However, I have it from Slobin (personal communication, October 2, 1968) that neither in the cited reference nor anywhere else has he demonstrated this "fact," or tried to do so. Fodor and Garrett, in a subsequent paper (1967, p. 290), cite this "fact" as an assumption, or rather, they (quite correctly) state its contrary as "counterintuitive."

[13]They specifically suggest (p. 140) that the CG/performance relation is more "abstract" than the "analysis-by-synthesis" model would imply (this is scarcely surprising). Some of their other comments are sensible enough (such as the discussion on p. 141 of the necessity for the recognition routine to recognize NP of derived phrase-structures); but (since the recognizer seems to *incorporate* or have full access to the CG) they do not seem to demonstrate a "particularly abstract relation between the grammar and the recognizer" (ibid.) such as they claim characterizes the human language faculty.

[14]These examples will be returned to below.

The first explanation to be found in their pages is a simple and persuasive
one. They conjecture (pp. 290f.) that relative pronouns ease parsing, so that
their absence increases performative complexity. (It is their absence, not the
deletion bringing about that absence, that results in the complexity increase.) As
they say, the presence of the relative pronoun ". . .is evidence of the application
of an embedding transformation, and that transformation can apply only where
certain grammatical relations hold between the noun phrases in the sentence."
That is, if I understand what they are saying (their subsequent remarks are confusing), a function of relatives is to provide a strong clue to the derived phrase
structure of an incoming sentence, enabling the auditor to impose a unique
"labeled bracketing" from which, in turn, he can retrieve (however he does this)
the correct deep structure and from that an understanding. The labeled bracketing, for instance, takes a raw incoming string (relatives italicized) like "The tiger
which the lion *that* the gorilla chased killed was ferocious" and turns it into the
derived (surface) phrase structure, with its characteristic polytomy, that is shown
simplified in Fig. 5.1. That derived structure is evidence of the action of the
transformations that derived it from the deeper structure, simplified, of Fig. 5.2;
and when the structure of Figure 5.2 has been gained the sentence has been parsed
deeply enough to receive a semantic interpretation.

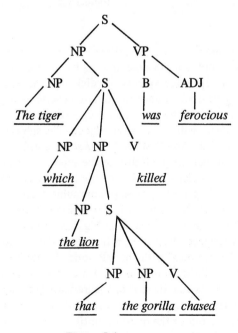

Figure 5.1

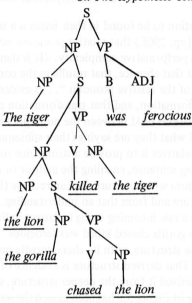

Figure 5.2

Fodor and Garrett (1967) do not go at all deeply into how the relatives actually help here, but presumably they help in this way: "The tiger *which* the lion...," as an opening sequence, predicts that the predicate for the subject "The tiger" will be postponed until the end of a clause modifying "The tiger," which clause can tentatively be assigned a deep structure, including a verb phrase, in which "the tiger" will appear as an object. The subject of that verb phrase may or may not be "the lion." When "...*that* the gorilla..." is added, there is added the prediction that the predicate for the subject "the lion" will be postponed until the end of a clause modifying "the lion," which clause will have a deep structure including a verb phrase (whose subject may or may not be "the gorilla"), in which "the lion" will appear as an object. The tentatively assigned deep structures are, simplified, as in Fig. 5.3. As we see, a fair amount of deep structure is assigned. Moreover, a further tentative assignment would make each " ? " VP identical with the VP node already known to dominate it (so that, by way of illustration, the anticipated deep structure for the second example in Figure 5.3 would be that of Figure 5.4.) We might expect probability — that is, frequency — to play a part here; indeed, without it, some unique assignments would be out of the question until virtually the whole of the sentence had been processed. Notice that "The tiger *which* the lion *that* the gorilla..." could also, very rarely, serve to open; for example, "The tiger *which* the lion *that*

(a) "The tiger *which* the lion. . ."

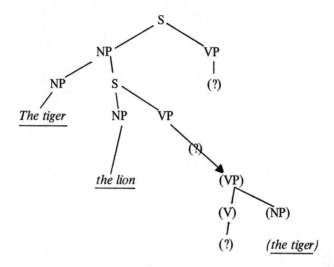

(b) "The tiger *which* the lion *that* the gorilla. . ."

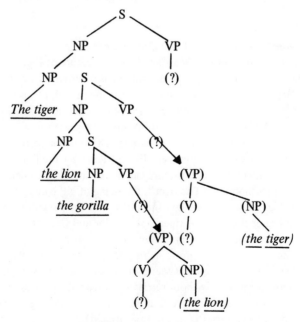

Figure 5.3

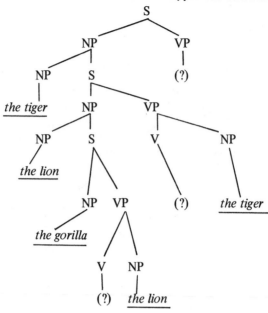

Figure 5.4

the gorilla strangled ate, I was glad to see the last of"; and this sentence has little to do with the tentatively assigned deep structure of Figure 5.3(b). That is, a very early unique tentative assignment is often unwarranted *except* psycholinguistically. We might then suppose that the rare and thus mispredicted sentence type is parsed after rescinding a prior unique tentative assignment.

In any case it is clear, I think, that the presence of the relatives greatly reduces the number of high-probability alternatives; certainly removal of the relatives increases that number. From "The tiger the lion the gorilla..." no part of the ultimate correct structure can be tentatively assigned except the (presumptive) subjecthood of "The tiger"; the string of NP could just as well open a sentence like "The tiger the lion the gorilla and the pangolin make better pets than the cobra or the Gaboon viper" (see Fodor and Garrett's sentence 11, p. 290). Thus correct deep structure cannot tentatively be assigned until later in the incoming string. Whence, presumably, the greater complexity inflicted by the absence of the relatives; for it seems quite reasonable to suppose that the longer the auditor must go without retrieving correct deep structure, the more unprocessed sentence he will have to hold in memory (having perhaps "cleared the register" after a misassignment now vitiated), and the more effort will be required of him. That is, psycholinguistic parsing complexity increases with the amount of deep structure whose correct assignment is postponed; with the length of sentence over which the postponement must be carried; and with the complexity of misassignments whose rescission returns the processor to an earlier point in the sentence.

This, at least, is (roughly sketched) a theory that has some credibility; its formulation, above, was directly inspired by remarks of Fodor and Garrett in the paper cited. I will term this theory the "Theory of Cumulative Assignments," or TCA; to summarize, it maintains that as we process a sentence (whether or not concurrently with our hearing/reading of it) we tentatively assign to it a surface structure consistent with as much initial string as it takes to *uniquely* determine such an assignment (which must, then, be fragmentary until the end of the sentence is reached, though that fragmentariness diminishes); this surface assignment tacitly implies a deep structure from which that surface is transformationally derived; and — as to "complexity" — the more quickly the correct surface (hence deep) structure can be assigned (the fewer constituents it takes to support a unique assignment), the more easily parsed a sentence is: *performatively, the less complex.* (If Fodor and Garrett should refuse to champion TCA, I would do it.)

Notice, incidentally, that TCA predicts (rightly or wrongly) that certain sentences types are performatively more complex than we might have guessed from their LG complexity alone. Suppose a sentence were such as to open with a sequence that systematically spawned roughly equiprobable assignments, so that no definite assignment could be made until later in the string. For example, the sequence "Floyd Thursby was shot by..." could open any of these four sentences: "Floyd Thursby was shot by a streetlight," "Floyd Thursby was shot by midnight," "Floyd Thursby was shot by misadventure," and "Floyd Thursby was shot by a vixen." If these four sentence endings were equally probable, then the auditor would have no (noncontextual) reason to settle on any one of the four kinds of "by..." phrase that are possible here. It would follow directly that, *though none of these sentences is linguistically ambiguous,* the "performative ambiguity" just described would increase the psycholinguistic complexity of each. Thus, to the usual explanations of the complexity of the passive, we would be forced to add that of "performative ambiguity," an aspect of TCA.

Fodor and Garrett's second explanation for their experimental results — which, however, they do not distinguish from their first — is essentially an unnecessary appendage to TCA. This explanation, their only explicit one, holds that in processing a sentence we render special homage to the sentence's verbs, making "direct inductions" of a set of "base configurations" on the basis of how each verb is classified in the lexicon "...according to the base structure configurations it may enter" (p. 295). Let us term this variant the "Theory of

Verb-Dominated Direct Inductions," or TVDDI. As we see, TVDDI differs from
TCA on two main issues: (1) TVDDI assigns special processing importance to
verbs; and (2) TVDDI insists, at every point "v" in the sentence being analyzed,
where "v" is any verb, that the processing mechanism consult its lexicon, list all
of the possible "base configurations" that that verb could fit into, and then return to the sentence under analysis, determining which of the possible "configurations" fits the already-analyzed *surface* of the sentence, and also, presumably,
matching each listed possible configuration against new pieces of sentence (as
these are analyzed), if those pieces could be commanded by the verb (as by being
in the verb's complement). Thus TVDDI, to refer to our Figure 5.4, above,
would have us get to the sentence's first verb, "chased," consult the lexicon, list
all possible "configurations" that "chase" can have, compare each of these to the
"configuration" actually assigned to that verb by the structure defined thus far,
and then choose the "configuration(s)" (and attendant predictions) that match.
(Whereas the alternative, a natural part of TCA, would have us, rather, consult
the MG's lexicon to ascertain simply whether "chase" can occur in the "configuration" already determined by the previously-analyzed structure). TCA could,
in addition, have the processing mechanism simply leave *blank* any part of the
sentence not yet analyzed, rather than, as with TVDDI, necessarily listing possibilities for such parts if those parts fall into potential complements for an
already-reached verb. Thus, under TCA, if a verb (e.g., "chase") were revealed
by the lexicon to have a "configuration" that met the requirements of the assigned structure, then the processing mechanism, once a "matching configuration"
were found, would be oblivious to all other possibilities; while under TVDDI *all*
possibilities would first be "listed," a match being attempted only afterwards.

TCA is to my mind the more plausible explanation of the processing of
"chase" as integrated into the deep structure of Figure 5.4. There, the V is determined to be one that can take NP as a (direct or indirect) object; thus the
verb "know," had it been met instead of "chase," would have been acceptable
also, since "know" has a possible "configuration" that matches the requirements
of the deep structure assigned thus far. Notice that in TCA there *is* a (partially
completed) deep structure; the processor is not constrained, as under TVDDI, to
compare possible deep structure "configurations" only with derivable *surfaces:* [15]

[15]". . . the program [that speakers] use to recover the grammatical structure of
sentences. . .must consult a lexicon which classifies the verb in the sentence according to
the base structure configurations it may enter. Second, it must run through each such deep
structure configuration, *asking whether the surface material in the sentence can be analyzed
as a transformed version of that deep structure"* [italics supplied] (Fodor and Garrett,
1967, p. 295).

But on the other hand, TVDDI is not utterly implausible as a model of the processing of extremely complex sentences; for example, of those made very confusing by loss of several relative pronouns. For in these sentences, the amount of structure assigned before the verb is reached may, owing to the complexity, be very slight, so that when a verb is reached the processor might possibly, if only in desperation, consult its lexicon, list possibilities, and then (lacking any deep-structure hypothesis) compare these possibilities against the surface to see whether that surface could be derived from one of them. That is, TVDDI may represent the strategy of the processing mechanism *faute de mieux:* failing TCA. TVDDI would thus be resorted to only when control over the sentence-processing had already been lost, and when the respondent was clutching at straws.

This much more limited role for Fodor and Garrett's TVDDI is, in fact, the most that could be supported by their own evidence. Their postulation of TVDDI was principally based (p. 295) on the fact that, where a sentence had a verb whose complement elsewhere in English could be other than the sort of complement — direct-object NP — it had in the sentence at hand, then, among the errors that respondents made occasionally, there would be an error in which the verb was, in fact, given the wrong sort of complement. (Fodor and Garrett remark [ibid.] that *only* in such cases do errors of this sort crop up, which fact, since they could crop up in other of their experimental sentences only at the cost of producing gross ungrammaticality, is not too surprising.) But this fact does not at all imply, as Fodor and Garrett think it does, that TVDDI is a basic processing maneuver used by speakers of English; it only implies that when TVDDI *is* used, it sometimes engenders mistakes. For if TVDDI were used consistently, as a basic strategy, sentences containing "versatile" verbs (capable of more than one complement- "configuration") should always be rather more complex than otherwise similar sentences containing less versatile verbs. Such sentences are predicted even by TCA to be *slightly* more complex — two or three "configurations" must be searched and compared with the sentence's accumulated deep structure — but TVDDI must predict them to be *much* more complex: the several "configurations" must be searched, then listed, and then compared with a piece of surface structure; and this, if it is a typical such piece of surface, will have undergone great distortion in the course of being transformed from the canonical — that is, deep — form in which any lexical "configuration" is given. (In Fodor and Garrett's experimental sentences the transformation-induced distortions were severe.) This complexity prediction must hold, if TVDDI is to be upheld as a basic processing strategy, even when the presence of relatives makes processing easier. But on Fodor and Garrett's evidence this is simply not so; their sentences 1 and 9, the only ones containing "versatile" verbs, are, by their own criteria, adjudged to be on the average *less* complex than sentence 2 (whose verb is not "versatile"), where all three sentences have their relatives.[16] That the "versatile" verbs have not been shown to cause greater complexity when the relatives are present means that TVDDI has not been shown to be a basic processing maneuver.

But if TVDDI did take over when TCA failed, serving as an abnormal processing maneuver for the difficult derelatived sentences, then sentences 1 and 9 should show a *dramatic* decrease in complexity when, having had their relatives restored, they are amenable to TCA methods instead of the more demanding TVDDI ones. But this seems not to be true either (p. 292).[17] Thus, while TVDDI could be *at most* an abnormal processing tactic, it does not seem, on the admittedly slender evidence we have, even to be that.

But if TVDDI is not used, even in desperation, how are we to explain the errors in which a "versatile" verb was fitted with a complement it could only have acquired from the general MG lexicon? I do not really have an alternative to TVDDI to offer, but from Fodor and Garrett's evidence I think we can glean some indication of where to look for one.

As they remark, three of their experimental sentences were such that each of the sentence's three nouns could be matched sensibly with but *one* of the sentence's three verbs, if only because prior unique matching of the other two verbs had eliminated all save one possibility for the third. Thus one could completely lose track of the surface and still recapture the only rational deep structure, using what we might call 'puzzle-solving' methods. Such methods should

---

[16]The "versatile-verb" sentences are minutely more complex than sentence 2 when all three are denuded of their relatives; this may or may not have some significance elsewhere, but in any case it cannot affect the outcome of the present argument (see the remainder of this paragraph). (Sentence 1 is, by a negligible margin, the most complex sentence of all, when without relatives; but since the only other "versatile-verb" sentence, 9, is not next-most-complex, we can scarcely attribute sentence 1's position to its containing a "versatile" verb. In fact, sentence 1's position appears to be of no independent significance at all.)

[17]It may be pertinent to recall Slobin's finding (1966) that passive sentences whose surface actor-object pair could not be mistaken for deep subject and deep object were easier to process than the "reversible" passives susceptible to this error. ("The cat is being chased by the dog" is reversible because "The cat is chasing the dog" is sensible, hence a likely error; "The flowers are being watered by the girl" is *ir*reversible because "The flowers are watering the girl" is *not* sensible, hence an unlikely error.) Possibly the irreversible passives need not be *detransformed,* in any sense, to the activelike deep structure in order to reveal their deep-subject and deep-object; the deep structure can be seized "logically," as it were.

Turner and Rommetveit found (1967*a,* 1967*b*) that "reversible" pictures (containing an actor-victim pair that would have been well-formed in another picture as victim-actor, for example two humans) did not affect performance in quite this way, so that Slobin's result seems to apply specifically to *linguistic* irreversibility.

work about as well, I should think, if the respondents were to be presented with a mere list of the sentence's chief words – preferably in order – and told to make a sensible sentence out of them. In any case these three sentences were, without their relatives, the least "complex" of the lot. (They were the least "complex" when their relatives had been restored, too – indicating that TCA may receive help from unexpected quarters.) But such a "puzzle-solving" method might have been tried also with the "versatile-verb" sentences, though (predictably?) with less success; once control over the surface were lost, respondents might well, on a partial recollection of the surface's chief words only, construct a deep structure, hence a new surface, where most of the old words turned up but where the relations among them had suffered a change.[18] Certainly a respondent would have to have recourse to his lexicon to do this – as in the three sentences containing unique assignments, for that matter – though apparently in much less exigent a way than would be predicted by TVDDI. But with this speculative remark we must close this discussion.

We entered upon this lengthy discussion of TCA, and therefore, in contrast, of TVDDI, because TCA seems to be a very serious and far-ranging hypothesis that might explain many discrepancies between the comparative sentential complexities predicted by the "Derivational Theory of Complexity," based firmly on CH_{CG}, and the performative complexities actually observed in experiment. That

---

[18]Unhappily, both of their sentences containing "versatile" verbs were such that the "versatile" verb was followed by another $verb_2$, which was such that $verb_2$ *could* occur in some other sentence as the "versatile" verb's complement, so that the sequence (versatile verb) + (other verb) bid fair to be error-producing. Thus, in "The pen which the author whom the editor liked used was new," a plausible mistake is "like to use"; while in "The man whom the girl that my friend married knew died," a possible mistake is "knew to have died." (Or, ignoring or lacking "whom," "knew had died.") The same broad method used in desperation to construct a correct deep structure for the three "unique-assignment" sentences might, if tried on these two "versatile-verb," sentences have permitted construction of a deep structure on the same rough principles; but a deep structure, in this case, that was the wrong one.

Certainly any tendency to give "like," for example, the wrong complement – because all the lexical entries for "like" were being rifled – would have been if anything encouraged by the presence to the right of "like" of the possible complement "use." *If* the claimed tendency (essential to TVDDI) were actually to exist, it might be observed even when no possible complement was present to offer encouragement. This could be tested; subjects could be given a sentence like the one in question, but in which "used" was replaced by "owned"; since "*liked to own" is impossible, any error in that direction would have to be in obedience to a (strong) tendency to give "like" the wrong complement. Unfortunately, as needs hardly be said, *failure* of the tendency to produce the named result would be of next to no significance, since the result would be ungrammatical, a consequence that speakers shy away from.

is, TCA cannot be ignored when matching complexities; it may be of help in explaining discrepancies and so in saving much of the Derivational Theory. Certainly the relation between the linguistic grammar and speakers' performances has proved, not surprisingly[19], to be other than the simple relation predicted by the Derivational Theory; and certainly TCA is a step in the right direction. However, it is the wrong step.

1.1.2. We are coming presently to the question of why TCA is the wrong step, but before doing that we must ask whether DTC itself, which still has some life in it, cannot be improved by trying to refine somewhat its gross "count of transformations" as the way of assessing transformational complexity. Certainly such a refinement is proposed unequivocally by Miller and Chomsky's reference[20] to the "number and complexity" of the transformations used to derive a sentence. Since each transformation is a sequence of (one or more) "elementary operations," an obvious way of improving the calculation of transformational complexity would be to stop counting transformations and, instead, count elementary operations. These are of four kinds: deletion, adjunction, substitution, and permutation.[21] Each of these can be counted separately, and if justified, weighted; certainly permutation is the most complex of these operations and should presumably be weighted more heavily. Indeed, as to the permutations, further refinements can easily be envisaged. Thus it is certainly reasonable to suppose that an operation that permutes a large string segment over a long distance is psycholinguistically harder to handle than one that permutes a brief string segment over a short distance. Still further possible refinements come to mind; for instance, one might suppose that DTC would be improved if its calculations of transformational complexity took into account the relative complexities of the structural descriptions mandatorily matched by the transformations in order for them to apply.

In short, DTC could probably be bettered in a number of ways, and so be better fitted to accommodate observed disparities between CG complexity and apparent psycholinguistic complexity. Certainly, at the very least, in asserting DTC to be incapable of coping with this fact or that, we must try to show that *no* DTC, including all envisaged improvements (such as those sketched just above), could cope with the facts adduced.

[19]See, again, Miller and Chomsky, 1963, pp. 476-480; cf. n. 9, above.

[20]Quoted in n. 9 above.

[21]Chomsky has proposed (1965, p. 144) that permutation be eliminated from this set, being replaced by combinations of the other elementary operations. We will continue to use the term "permutation" here, but the term can be interpreted in accordance with Chomsky's proposal, and it may well be that the best way of gauging the complexity owing to a given permutation would be to sum the complexity owing to its component operations.

1.1.3. We have been examining problems in the way of accepting CH_{CG}, that version of the Correlation Hypothesis in which the mental grammar is a competence grammar and is therefore " = " to a linguistic grammar like the one now under construction by linguists. We have observed that one can affirm belief in CH_{CG} without accepting the notion that one uses the CG to produce sentences by invoking its rules in sequence, somehow reversing this procedure to parse sentences (and somehow piecing out the CG, for parsing, with an ability to impose surface structure on raw incoming strings). But we noted that refusal to accept this version of CH_{CG} does not entirely free predictions of sentential complexity based on the LG from according with the psycholinguistic sentential complexity indicated by performance; we gave the "5 x 8 index-card" model as a version of CH_{CG} that still made the two complexities identical. Then we quoted Fodor and Garrett (1967) to the effect that there were discrepancies between the two complexities. Though we disputed the evidence on which they decided this point, we suggested that nonetheless their position was probably well-taken, in that it seemed plausible that evidence for such discrepancies would be forthcoming. Anticipating such evidence (we have presented hardly any as yet), we examined in some detail a proposal, suggested by some remarks by Fodor and Garrett, introducing into complexity calculations a principle, here called TCA, which looks as if it might explain some of the expected discrepancies. (In Fodor and Garrett, it explained phenomena that were *not* discrepant.) We also mentioned another such proposal, and we cited some of the obvious ways in which a straightforward "DTC" sort of measurement might be refined. In summary, we will have forearmed ourselves with these ways of dealing with the expected discrepancies, should we meet them: (1) refining the way in which psycholinguistic complexity is calculated as a function of linguistic complexity, by improving the Derivational Theory of Complexity; and (2) introducing, as needed, purely performative determinants of psycholinguistic complexity, such as TCA.

At this point in our exposition the CH_{CG} is still perfectly viable, in its weaker version; TCA was meant to "save" CH_{CG}, and it may appear to have done so. But it has not; and we have devoted the preceding sections to ways of mitigating discrepancies chiefly in order to prepare the way for an exhibit of discrepancies that no envisaged "refinements" appear able to account for. We have explored at some depth the means of defending CH_{CG}, but we have not explored at any depth the really telling evidence against CH_{CG}.

This now becomes our purpose. We have reserved this discussion until now, a bit out of logical order perhaps, so that the evidence against CH_{CG} can be used immediately as evidence in favor of what to my mind is the most obvious counterhypothesis. We know of course that, as has been mentioned above, all evidence on any psycholinguistic point is excessively scanty; but now we will present what evidence we can, concentrating on a single case (the truncated Passives) that has the status, in the literature on this troubled topic, of a minor classic.

1.2. On the CH$_{APG}$

In this section we consider a new version of the "Correlation Hypothesis" which states that the (idealized) "mental grammar" is not a "competence grammar" at all, but rather something of mostly-unknown properties that I will term an "abstract performative grammar," or APG. I will maintain that the APG is far, however, from exhausting the (idealized) linguistic capacity, in that the APG is as it were sustained by a competence abstract knowledge *about* the APG. The CH$_{APG}$, stated roughly, hypothesizes two components, then — the APG itself, and a necessary "archival" competence faculty.

The hypothesis will be defended on two rather different grounds: (1) the APG hypothesis appears to explain predictable performative discrepancies which any performative explanation based on a conventional CG — however strained that basis — cannot explain or cannot explain as well; and (2) the APG hypothesis appears to accord better with the learning sequence of certain syntactic devices, when we take into consideration the fact that any *CG* hypothesis must seemingly predict, as late stages in the acquisition of those devices, certain events which are wanting in plausibility.

1.2.1. We first takè up some complexity discrepancies that do not appear to be reconcilable with any account of performance that is tied, in any reasonable and consistent way, to a CG.

1.2.1.1. The first and best-known such case is touched on by Fodor and Garrett (1967). They remark (p. 290) that truncated passives like "The boy was hit" are "transformationally derived" from "The boy was hit by someone," and so are predicted by the DTC to be more complex, a judgment that Fodor and Garrett correctly label as "counterintuitive." Fodor and Garrett, however, though it at first seems that this example is introduced to illustrate the sort of problem they are attacking, do not return to it again in their paper, and indeed their suggested supplement to DTC — TVDDI (or even TCA) — does not seem to promise much in this area. Of course this fact does not of itself mean that *every* CG-based performative explanation must deliver a "counterintuitive" judgment in such cases; we cannot conclude this until possible revisions of the primitive DTC have also been taken into account. And this we will do.

First of all, however, we must clear up Fodor and Garrett's (and many others') exposition of these truncated passives, for it is seriously in error on precisely the issue at hand — the correspondence between full passives and their truncates. This becomes plain when we ask what complex symbol is associated with the word "someone," and when we ask what complex symbol is substituted for the "Δ" dominating the "agent" that is to be deleted to form the truncate. If that complex symbol is such that "someone" is the associated word, then "...by someone" could underlie a truncated passive like "John was hit"; but if that complex symbol is not one that "someone" is associated with in the lexicon, then "John was hit" must *not* be underlain by "...by someone." To consider the matter in its more basic aspect, the question is whether or not the deep subject which is to become a "...by agent" phrase and is then to be deleted can have the complex symbol of "someone." That is, can its complex symbol contain such factors as (+object), (+animate), (+animal), and (+human)?

The Passive "agent" could be "someone," and still be deleted, only if "someone" were *recoverable* after the deletion.[22] This entails, first, that from for example "The boy was hit..." we be able to recover "...by agent," that is "...by NP"; and we can, because the grammar identifies the truncation as a truncation — as having resulted, precisely, from deletion of "...by NP." But it also entails that we be able to recover, as factors in the complex symbol dominated by that "agent" NP, all of the factors of the complex symbol of "someone" — for this is the only sense in which we can say that "someone" is recoverable. In particular, we must be able to recover the fact that the "agent" NP, as the deep subject of the underlying base, headed a complex symbol containing (+human). This would be possible only if the verb "hit" *had* to have, as its deep subject, an NP whose complex symbol contained (+human), for it is from just the fact that the verb is "hit" that (+human) must be recovered.[23] If "hit" could have had a deep subject whose complex symbol did *not* include (+human) — which included (-human) — then just from the fact that the verb is "hit" we could not recover the fact that the deep subject was (+human). But of course "hit" *can* have a (-human) deep subject/surface agent, as in "The aging diva was hit by an egg."[24]

---

[22]Only "recoverable" deletions are allowed because (Chomsky, 1965, esp. pp. 144-147) otherwise deletion, a transformation, could introduce meaning-changes (in this case, meaning-losses); but since it is the deep structure and not the transformations with which the semantic component is associated, these changes would go unnoticed by that component, so that, for a sentence allowing such a deletion, the semantic component would be ascribing a meaning to the sentence which the surface, containing the lacunae introduced by deletion, could not sustain.

[23]It could not be recovered from the mere fact of truncation or from, say, the nature of the deep object (= surface subject, in the passive).

[24]This example argues, in addition, that "hit" can in its deep structure have an (-animate) subject: for example in the deep structure representable as "An egg hit the aging diva." Counterarguments to this thesis can be mounted, but in general it seems to me that

So then "The aging diva was hit" cannot derive from an underlying structure whose ". . .by agent" phrase included (+human) in the complex symbol of the source (the deep subject) of the 'agent' NP.

But the so-called "*full* passive" with ". . .by someone" — for example, "The aging diva was hit *by someone*" — demands an underlying structure whose ". . .by agent" phrase contains, precisely, a complex symbol that includes (+human). From this it follows immediately that "The diva was hit" and "The diva was hit by someone" do not have the same underlying structure. They are not paraphrastic. "The boy was hit" *cannot* derive, by "truncation," from "The boy was hit by someone"; in fact, the two sentences are not directly comparable, either linguistically or — more to the point — psycholinguistically.

In view of the psycholinguistic importance ascribed to the truncated Passives, the facts just cited impel us to undertake a brief examination of the issue of recoverable deletion; in particular, of what it is that is deleted. As Chomsky has said (1964, p. 42), each truncated passive must derive from an underlying structure containing (in the "by. . ." phrase) an "unspecified noun phrase;" and in fact our task largely resolves into that of determining the nature of this noun phrase's degree of specificity. At one time (ibid., p. 41), Chomsky asserted that such an unspecified noun phrase was to be realized by its appropriate "designated element," either by some maximally unspecific word like "it," "someone," or "something" — realizable on the surface — or else, in the absence of any appropriate surface word in the language, by a mere "abstract 'dummy element'." We have already observed that for "hit" (and many other verbs) "someone" (and therefore "something") is overly specific; and "it" is too specific for the same reason that "something" is: it is not recoverable. So the only choice open to the "by agent" - phrase for "hit," there being no candidate for an "appropriate" unspecific word, is the "abstract dummy," "Δ." Any such "Δ," since it has no way of being realized on the surface by a word, must be *obligatorily deleted* (Chomsky, 1965, p. 222, n. 1).

In one of the two models of grammar that Chomsky alternately entertains in *Aspects* (see esp. pp. 120-123), we find that every lexical category is rewritten, as the last act of the base component's categorical subcomponent, as "Δ"; but that most of these "Δ" elements will be rewritten by the lexical subcomponent as a "lexical entry" of the form (D, C), where ". . .D is a phonological matrix and C a complex symbol" (p. 122). The observations of (1964) and (1965) can now be fitted together: if the "Δ" of the passive's "...by Δ" phrase has *not* been rewritten as a lexical entry — roughly, as a word — then "Δ" is the only terminal

they fail. English appears to invest with a special character any (-animate) object that is, or appears to be, moving under its own power; and the most fundamental aspect of this character is the ability of such objects to occur as real underlying subjects of certain verbs. This might be stated in the grammar by inclusion of a factor (animated), having the positive value (+animated), when an (-animate) noun is to serve as deep subject.

and it automatically triggers deletion of the "...by Δ" phrase. Of course failure
to rewrite "Δ" has to have happened while the passive was still a deep structure,
as yet unpassivized, with "Δ" occupying its deep structure position of subject.
In sum, then, if a "passivizable" sentence in its deep structure has a vacuous unrewritten "Δ" Subject, and is passivized, then the resulting "...by Δ" phrase is
obligatorily deleted.[25] (This synoptic view can be seen explicitly in 1965, pp.
128f., 137.)

Now, one could impose either of two conditions on the connection between deletion and recoverability. The one would hold that nothing can be deleted that cannot be recovered; the other would hold that everything that
can be recovered must have been deleted. We might call these the "weak" and
"strong"conditions, respectively. Clearly the use of "Δ" just cited meets the
"weak" condition: we can always recover "Δ." But it utterly fails to meet the
"strong" condition, since *from the typical truncated passive we can recover
linguistic information much more specific than is conveyed by mere "Δ."* Even
from "John was hit" we can recover "...by (-abstract) (+object)." From "John
was divorced" we can recover "...by (-abstract) (+object) (+animate) (+animal)
(+human)" and, presumably, (-male). Even singularity and plurality are sometimes recoverable. In English there are verbs that, by lexical definition,
describe transitive actions that can be performed upon one only once and by
only one person, and these verbs therefore, when with singular deep objects,
take only singular deep subjects. Five of them are: "sire," "father," "beget,"
"bear" (= *give birth to*), and "deflower." Thus from "Gladys was deflowered"
we can recover nearly everything about the missing agent but his name. Similarly, there are verbs that, by lexical definition, require plural subjects (and do
not accept mass subjects, apparently); two of these are "bracket" and (when
synonymous with that verb) "flank." From "Make sure each adverse comment
is bracketed [by Δ]" we can recover the fact that the missing "Δ" is (+plural).
Even more specific recoveries may be possible; thus, from "George was gored"
we might plausibly claim to be able to recover, among other factors, (+animal),
(+large), and (+horned) (I am indebted for this example to H. H. Clark), and
also of course, barring cuckolds, (-human). In short, so much specific linguistic
information is recoverable from truncated passives that "Δ" will fail the strong
condition of recoverability *much of the time.*

---

[25]It would seem a natural next step to specify that if a "passivizable" sentence has an
unrewritten "Δ" deep subject, then passivization is obligatory and subsequent "...by Δ"
deletion is also obligatory. The alternative, letting passivization be optional and then having
any *un*passivized "Δ"-subject sentences be aborted, seems awkward. However, Chomsky
does not take this further step.

I submit that only the "strong" condition pertaining to recoverability is intuitively satisfying, and that only the "strong" condition is consistent with the many other ways in which the LG reflects the competence of the idealized speaker; for if we can recover this linguistic information we must be recovering it in the deep structure (where else could it reside?), and so it must be *in* the deep structure to be recovered.

As we see, neither "someone" nor "Δ" can (abstractly) be the "agent" that is generally deleted to form truncated passives, since "someone" is too specific (not all of its factors are actually recoverable, as from "hit"), while "Δ" is not specific enough (as for "deflower," "flank," "divorce," etc.). "Someone" fails the weak recoverability condition; "Δ," the strong. The needed corrective, quite clearly, is to incorporate the "strong" condition in the grammar, but without violating the "weak" condition. It now remains to ascertain how this may be done.

We continue, as above, with the *Aspects* model, in which the lexical subcomponent is called upon to substitute, for each of the "Δ" symbols that the categorial subcomponent generates as its terminal string, a (D, C) "lexical entry" consisting of a word in abstract phonological specification (D), together with (C), the word's meaning (and fine syntactic function), in the form of a complex symbol of factors (such as [human]) headed by values (let us assume + or -). In this scheme the only source of semantic factors of present interest to us is this substitution maneuver, which automatically carries with it the abstract phonological specification of a word; yet, as we have seen, we will sometimes want to associate some factors (C) with some "Δ" symbols *without* at the same time substituting a word (D); there *is* no D.

We want to substitute for "Δ" exactly the factors that can be recovered after "Δ" has obligatorily been deleted — no fewer factors, and no more. Thus for the ". . .by Δ" phrase of "hit" we will want (+object), but not (+animate) or (-animate). For the phrase of "divorce," we will want (+human), but not (+plural) or (-plural), and in addition we will want (+male) if the superficial subject (deep object) is (-male), but (-male) if the subject is (+male); generally, (∝male) for "agent" "Δ" when the surface subject is (-∝male), with ∝ ranging over + and - . For the phrase of "deflower," which demands a (+human) deep object, we will want (+human) and (+male); and furthermore, if the deep object (surface subject) is singular, then we will want (-plural). For "flank" we will want, whatever the surface subject, (+plural). For "gore" we will want, among other factors, (+animal) and (+horned).[26]

[26] It might seem that to use "gore" correctly we would now require that the grammar include an encyclopedic knowledge of which animals are and are not horned. But this is false. We insist only that the grammar tell us, if someone says "I was gored by a canary," that that person thinks canaries weigh a ton and have horns.

Now, most of these recoverable factors will be recovered, quite obviously, just on the strength of the verb; the restrictions on the verb's deep subject are known, and this is the way we (or the grammar) will recover the missing factors. Moreover, even when the nature of the deep object (surface subject) contributes to determining what can be recovered, as when the "agent" of the passive of "deflower" must be (-plural) if the surface subject is (-plural) — this restriction can be incorporated into a restriction on the verb. In fact, it *must* be so incorprated, since it is a restriction on "deflower" that the deep subject be (-plural) if the deep object is.

The fact that recoverable "agents" are recovered from restrictions on the verb directs us toward an efficient way of providing in the grammar for preservation of the "strong" recoverability condition. Since we are attempting to have the grammar generate deep subjects whose complex symbols are totally anticipated by the lexical restrictions on what can occur as deep subject of the verb, and since therefore the complex symbol of such a deep subject is effectively provided by the lexicon's contextual statement of the verb, it is entirely natural to *derive* such a subject's complex symbol *from* the contextual statement of the verb.

The verb remains selectionally restricted according to what deep subjects and deep objects it can take (Chomsky, 1965, esp. pp. 95-99, 165), and so the usual procedure will be for the NP to gain their complex symbols before the verbs do. Optionally, however, the "Δ" dominated by NP need *not* gain a complex symbol from the lexicon; it will remain devoid of factors after the generation has passed through the NP-substitution rules. (So far, there is nothing novel.) But, when the verb gains its complex symbol in conformity with the contextual constraints specified in the lexicon, I propose that, if the deep subject is "blank" (has no complex symbol), then all of the factors specified in the verb's contextual restriction for deep subject be copied out under [NP, S] to form a complex symbol dominated by the verb's deep subject. (We ignore for the remainder of this paper the possibility of similarly treating the deep *object.)* That is, if the deep subject is "blank," it automatically acquires all and only the factors specified for deep subject in the lexicon's selectional restriction on the verb. Thus any verb being introduced into a sentence with a "blank" deep subject (1) must have a contextual statement that accords with the non-blank categories — such as, here, the deep object — and (2) must impose its own requirements on any "blank" categories.

As we noted, only the deep subjects that the process of lexical substitution left "blank" can derive a (thin) complex symbol from "copying" in this way. The usual deep subject (e.g., "the professor," "the wart-hog," "the King of Zembla") is far more specified (has many more factors) than is required by the verb, hence is far more specified than could be determined by (or recovered from) the verb. For all such "Δ" the more orthodox method of substituting a complex symbol will prevail; for our present purpose that method can consist entirely of substituting, for the "Δ" of [NP, S], any (D, C) that the lexicon makes available for such a substitution.[27]

After introduction of the verb's complex symbol, with copying into the deep subject if called for, the sentence will have for its deep subject either a complex symbol drawn conventionally from the lexicon, or else a complex symbol copied from the lexical entry for the verb. If a verb makes a dual requirement of its deep subject and deep object ("divorce" insists that they have different values for [male]; "deflower" insists that the deep subject have [-plural] if the deep-object does), then this requirement is reflected exactly in the factors that are drawn from the verb's contextual statement for insertion into the deep subject's complex symbol. Suppose that the deep object has a complex symbol that includes (-plural) and (-male); then "deflower" can be introduced as the verb, but only, according to its lexical context-statement, if also the deep *subject* is (-plural) and (+male). If the deep subject already has a complex symbol, it must not include (+plural) or (-male). If the deep subject is "blank," then (-plural) and (+male) are copied from the verb's contextual statement *into* the deep subject's complex symbol. Thus, when all of these operations are over, "divorce" will have either a conventional deep subject – e.g. "Agatha" or "the heartless scoundrel" – or else it will have just a "thin" complex symbol containing, among a few other factors, (-male) and (-plural), for example.

Now, we could insist on treating these "thin" C's just as, before, we treated the "Δ" that had no C at all; that is, we could insist that all such C's be deleted, after passivization. But some of the deep subjects resulting from "copying" will have complex symbols C very similar to some C in the lexicon to which a lexical item D is joined. The "copied" deep subject of "deflower," if the deep object is singular, will have very nearly the complex symbol C of the D "someone" provided by the lexicon. The two C's will differ only in that the "copied" C of the singular deep subject of "deflower" will be specified (+male), while the C given in the lexicon for "someone" will (obviously) not have this specification. Let us see how these two C's might be matched. "Someone" is no more specific than (+human) (-plural), being indiscriminate respecting (male)ness; it should

---

[27]Among these lexical substitutions will be the (D, C) for "someone." Since, for example, "hit" does not specify that its deep subject be (+human), no (+human) deep subject (such as "someone") can be conferred on "hit" through "copying;" thus unless for "hit" the deep subject can acquire "someone" from the lexicon, it can never acquire "someone" at all. We will shortly return to this point from another angle.

consequently appear in the lexicon with a *nonvalued* factor: (male) rather than either (+male) or (-male). Since the (+male)ness of the copied deep subject of "deflower" is, by definition, recoverable, obviously it does not matter what D we adjoin to the "copied" C, so long as that D does not carry with it new, hence irrecoverable, factors, or new *values* on factors. That is, to any "copied" C we can adjoin any lexical D whose lexical C (1) contains no factor not included in the copied C; (2) contains every factor included in the copied C; and (3) contains no value on any factor — if it designates a value for that factor at all — that is different from the value on that factor in the "copied" C. Returning to the D "someone," it can now be substituted for the singular C copied into the deep subject from the verb "deflower."

Some such operation must be possible, for if it were not, the grammar would claim that in the sentence "Moll has been deflowered by someone" we could not absolutely recover the fact that her deflowerer was (+male), and this would be, in fact, manifestly false. So there is strong motivation for the modification of the accepted version of the grammar (for example, Chomsky, 1965, p.165, Rule 21-ii) needed to accomplish such a solution.

Three final points.

(a) "Someone" can be withdrawn from the lexicon to fit a copied C; but also of course it can be withdrawn as a (D, C) pair, in a conventional lexical substitution, to instantiate a deep-Subject "Δ." The severe selectional constraints on the verb that permit copying of "someone" must be imposed on the deep subject *in any case;* if the deep subject has a C gained in the lexicalization pass, then the verb's contextual restrictions must countenance that C (or else that verb cannot be introduced); if the deep subject is "blank" after the lexicalization pass, then the verb's contextual restrictions "copy" a C into the deep subject. The contextual restrictions in question are really a dual constraint on the deep subject and its verb, imposed by the deep subject if that is first to be introduced, imposed by the verb if it is first. This means that whenever "someone" can be gained from "copying," it could also have been gained from direct lexical substitution (a verb that forbade its deep subject to be "someone" could scarcely have specified such a deep subject through "copying"). Thus, in permitting the D "someone" to be adjoined to a *copied* C, we have introduced an undoubted redundancy into grammar.

The redundancy is not difficult to remove, and the manner of its removal has ancillary advantages; but to go deeper into this topic would require more space than we have here and so, for the present, having pointed the redundancy out, we will ignore it.[28]

---

[28] The redundancy in question cannot be removed, as we have noted before, just by eliminating "someone" from the lexicon, since there are many cases in which "someone"

(b) To provide in the most natural way for the generation of both "Gladys was deflowered by someone" and its paraphrase "Gladys was deflowered," we have allowed the deep subject's finding a D in the lexicon to be an option; if, for example, "someone" *is* substituted, then the full passive will result; but if no D is substituted, then the unlexicalized "Δ" and the thin complex symbol it heads will, most simply, be deleted, and the paraphrastic truncate will result. Notice then that it is not quite right to say, even for a truncate like this, that the word "someone" can be recovered. More accurately, a C can be recovered with which some C in the lexicon does not "disagree," and to the latter the D "someone" or the D "somebody" is joined.

(c) For any C drawn conventionally from the lexicon, a D is provided by the lexicon; indeed, conventionally, the pair (D, C) is withdrawn together. But for some of the C's that result from "copying", no D exists; in fact, the copied C to which a D can be joined is the exception rather than the rule. Any C containing (+human) but omitting (-plural) cannot acquire the D "someone," which requires (-plural); any such C will not find a D at all. (It is just such a C that "divorce" has for its "copied" deep subject.) For such cases, where the C has no way of breaking surface, we have two choices. The first and simplest one is to insist, as in (b) just above, that such a D-less C be obligatorily deleted (with the result, for example, "Gladys was divorced"). The second choice is to introduce a way of deriving from such a C, where possible, a phrase like ". . . by *one or more persons*" or the like. The C would have to undergo one or more segmentalization transformations (Postal, 1966*a*); but this would be possible, and might well be desirable. We cannot take this subject further here. But we will assume that "one or more persons," if not actually *derived* from the C of an appropriate "copied" deep subject, would be identified in the grammar as synonymous with it.

We have taken this discussion far enough now, skipping only minor details, to return to our main point. But first let us summarize the series of steps involved in the generation of sentences exhibiting recoverable deletion: (1) the categorial subcomponent terminates, leaving each lexical category (noun, verb, and

---

occurs in a sentence where it cannot have been generated through "copying" – for example, in "The actor Farine d'Avoine was divorced by someone last year." Nor can the redundancy be removed just by eliminating "copying" as a source for "someone," since to do so would make deletion of a "copied" C obligatory even when that C matched the lexicon's C for "someone," where this obligatory rule would, altogether artificially, be introduced just to remove the redundancy (and where the relation between the paraphrases "Moll was deflowered" and "Moll was deflowered by someone" would be made unnaturally remote).

This and other questions are taken up, with a consideration of some residual problems, in Watt, forthcoming.

so on) represented by a "Δ" symbol; (2) for every "Δ" *noun* symbol, the lexicon substitutes, optionally in the case of deep subjects, a (D,C) pair of complex symbol *cum* phonological matrix; (3) for every "Δ" *verb* symbol, the lexicon substitutes a (D,C) pair conformable to the verb context and also (4) copies, if the deep subject has no C, into the vacant C of the deep subject all the factors that the lexicon stipulates for the verb's deep subject in that sentence; (5) for such a "copied" C, there may now, optionally, be substituted any D whose C in the lexicon "agrees" with that C; (6) any D thus substituted will be realized on the surface; and (7) if no D is substituted, then — unless segmentalization is introduced as another option — deletion is obligatory (and this is the only source of the truncates' recoverable deletions).

We now return to the main issue of determining what full passives are directly related to what truncates. We see that, formally, a full passive corresponds to a truncate if the agent of the full passive contains, in its complex symbol, all — and only — the factors, with no discordant values, specified in the lexicon for inclusion in the deep subject of the agent's verb. Informally, the Agent is "someone" only for the rare "singular deep subject of singular deep object" verbs, like the five cited above. If there were similar verbs for (-human) or (-animate) subject-object pairs, then the truncate's corresponding full passive would have a ". . .by something" agent phrase. For any verb whose deep Subject must be (+human), but which is indeterminate as to plurality,[29] the surface overt agent is, minimally, "person or persons" or the like. For many verbs (such as "hit"), the minimal surface agent is, alas, "one or more persons or things" or the like. There are, of course, the sentences like "Dwayne was hit (struck, kicked, flunked, exonerated, ...) by someone," but such sentences are *not* directly related to any truncate, since from "Dwayne was hit (struck, kicked, flunked, exonerated, ...)," one cannot recover (+human), because, for "hit" and "strike" a (-human) rock could have served; for "kick" a (-human) ostrich could have served; and for "flunk" and "exonerate" either a (+plural) group ("the professors"/"jurymen") or a (-count) group ("the Department"/"Army") could have served. For a common verb picked at random, the chance that that verb occurs in a directly related truncate/full-passive pair of sentences is rather remote.

However, such verbs are not that difficult to find, by any means (see n. 29), and certainly there are quite enough for meaningful psycholinguistic testing. But that testing has been somewhat complicated by the findings summarized just above. Heretofore, the problem of testing the comparative psycholinguistic complexity of full passives and truncates has been construed as that of comparing

---

[29]For example, "divorce," "marry," "assassinate," "dub," "knight," "plagiarize," "traduce," "manumit," "catechize," "shrive," "harangue," "indite," "abdicate," and countless other equally common verbs.

each truncate with a full passive consisting of the truncate augmented by ". . .by someone." In this way the great imponderable of all psycholinguistic investigation — the comparative influence on sentential complexity of meaning-differences — has been entirely avoided, since the assumption was that the truncates and their ". . .by someone" counterparts were paraphrastic. But now, as we see, there are very few verbs (such as "deflower") for which this assumption was warranted. On the other hand, many verbs (like those in n. 29) take only (+human) agents, and for these the truncate, at least, has the counterpart in ". . .by one or more persons," or the like. One difficulty is that, while it is not hard to stretch out a truncate so that it occupies the same amount of recording tape as that truncate plus ". . .by someone," on the other hand ". . .by one or more persons" is more difficult to compensate for, if the stretched truncate is not to sound peculiar. (Of course the *proportion* by which the latter agent is outsized could be reduced by using much longer truncates than has been customary.) In addition the slight unnaturalness of the phrase, for many, might slow responses and so skew results. But it is clear how the revised experiments might proceed.[30]

[30]That is, it is clear how the experiments might proceed rigorously in the context of present knowledge. However it is quite possible, I think, that the complexity experiments could be considerably simplified, without being vitiated by the factors sketched above in this subsection, if one or two experiments were first conducted on aspects of language use related to truncation.

We have shown that, for example, "John was divorced" is directly related, not to (1) "John was divorced by someone," nor to (2) "John was divorced by some people," but only to (3) "John was divorced by one or more persons" or the equivalent. Does this mean that "John was divorced" is *ambiguous* with respect to plurality of the agent? If it were, and were a paraphrase of (3), then (3) would have to be ambiguous too (Hiż, 1964). But this would be ridiculous; we say a sentence is ambiguous when it could have more than one meaning, not when (a) it overtly specifies a choice of meanings and specifies that no choice between those meanings can be made, as in "...by one or more persons", nor when (b), as in the truncate, it tacitly *(contextually)* specifies the choice of meanings and remains silent on which choice is correct. It is clearly preferable to describe both (a) and (b) as "indeterminate" rather than as "ambiguous."

About "ambiguity" we have a little psycholinguistic data; about "indeterminateness" we have none. The "prior experiment" mentioned above, then, involves testing whether or not indeterminateness affects linguistic performance in the same way that ambiguity does. Ambiguity apparently slows processing when two (or more) interpretations are about equally likely (MacKay, 1966), but does not do so when only one is likely (Foss, Bever, and Silver, 1968). If indeterminateness proved to be like ambiguity in this respect, then the testing of truncates whose indeterminateness is narrow and known could be greatly simplified. At the very least, many truncates could be limited to but one "likely" interpretation by being read in a prejudicial context; for example, "John was divorced" could be given in a context in which the auditor would be heavily disposed to think that only one agent did the divorcing. Since "John was divorced" is indeterminate *only* with respect to plurality of the (necessarily [+human]) agent, this truncate could then be tested for complexity against

Having come back to our main topic, we now ask if it seems likely that the truncates will be found through experiment to be in fact, as predicted by DTC, more complex than the full passives from which in essence they derive. This does not seem likely. What does seem likely, on the contrary, is that experiment will at last confirm what has so often been declared, namely, that truncates are more complex in the LG, but simpler in the MG, even when the length difference has been compensated for[31] — unless, of course, mitigations for these predicted data can be found, such as TCA (or even TVDDI). Since we must consider·some other cases much like the truncated passives — cases which should also be mitigated if the truncated passives are — we defer for the moment a consideration of whether the anticipated discrepancy between LG and MG can still be attributed to some 'mitigation' or other.

1.2.1.2. There are other apparent discrepancies between LG and MG complexities; the number of cases is easy to multiply, and none is very surprising.

(a) One observed discrepancy is from Fodor and Garrett. They found (1967, pp. 293f.) essentially that the comparative complexity predicted by DTC, on the LG, for sentences like "The tired soldier fired the shot," was not confirmed by an experiment they ran; that is, sentences containing prenominal

---

the simpler ". . .by someone" full passive, the latter having been made the truncate's local paraphrase (in essentially the sense of Harris, 1965, p. 388, n. 35; and see p. 390, n. 41). Furthermore it is probable that, psycholinguistically, sentences containing verbs like "divorce" could be made still easier to experiment with. For example it seems likely that the sentence "John *has just been* divorced" would invariably be interpreted as having a singular agent, even though it is (remotely) possible that John was just divorced by three women simultaneously. Such a sentence, if "performatively univocal" as we might term it, could then be tested without bothering to prejudice its prospective auditors.

However, it should be kept in mind that such simplifications of the psycholinguist's task have no *linguistic* warrant whatever.

[31] This essentially assumes that prior experiment will establish what contribution length alone makes to performance time, testing numbers of different string lengths of similar or identical immediate constituent structure; for example, "William Henry Harrison" vs. "John Tyler"; "My adversaries are very persistent" vs. "My adversaries are very, very persistent" (Watt, 1968); and so on.

We also assume that care will have been taken to guard against complications due to the constraint imposed by context, or by general expectancy, jointly on the deep structure and the surface, which makes for example the truncate "John has just been divorced" derivable from a deep structure additionally specified so as to coincide with the deep structure that, in the grammar, underlies "John has just been divorced by someone." I foresee no real difficulty here — the effect is that of narrowing the versatility of "divorce" by insisting that its deep subject be (-plural) — but then unforeseen difficulties have been the bane of psycholinguistic experimentation in this area.

adjectives (e.g., "tired") did *not* exhibit the comparative complexity they should have to be derived, as in the LG from a structure representable as "The soldier, which soldier was tired, fired the shot."[32]

(b) "John hammered the nail" and "Charlotte Corday knifed Marat" derive from sources representable as "John used a hammer to act upon the nail" and "Charlotte Corday used a knife to act upon Marat" (for essentially this view, see Lakoff, 1968); but it is implausible that the first pair of sentences should be psycholinguistically more complex than the second pair.

(c) "Mary grows flowers" and "The heroes cracked the glass" derive from sources on the order of "Mary causes flowers to grow" and "The heroes caused the glass to crack" (Chomsky, 1965, p. 189), but the first pair of sentences is certainly, counter to prediction, simpler.

(d) "Dee is hard to please" derives from a source on the order of "For anyone to please Dee is hard," with the first sentence, counter to sense, predicted to be the more complex.

(e) "Dee is eager to please" derives from a source very like "Dee is eager to please," and should therefore be demonstrably less complex than the more distantly-derived "Dee is hard to please"; again, a prediction counter to expectation.

(f) "There's a dragon in the street" derives from an ultimate source on the order of "A dragon is in the street" via an intermediate string of the form "In the street there is a dragon" (Watt, 1967); the first sentence is further from the ultimate source than is the third sentence, and so it is predicted, again counter to sense, to be more complex.

(g) "I read the book while in England" probably derives from a source something like "I read the book while I was in England" (Chomsky, 1965, p. 219), with the shorter sentence therefore predicted to be the more complex.

(h) "Brutus killed Caesar" has a source that we can represent as "Brutus caused Caesar to be (become) dead" (Lakoff, 1965, IX, pp. 9-12), but if we realize that source on the surface, in the "representative" form just given, sense tells us that "Brutus killed Caesar" is simpler.

---

[32]The experiment compared the complexity introduced by inserting two adjectives (three transformations @) with that due, as before, to two deletions (with Fodor and Garrett, one transformation @). Contrary to DTC, the "adjectived" sentences proved less complex than the deleted ones, according to Fodor and Garrett. One must own, however, that their evidence does not justify great confidence in their claim. If their Table 5, p. 293, pertains just to the "adjectived" sentences, as it seems to on internal evidence (Fodor and Garrett say otherwise, ibid.), then the "adjectived" sentences were proven less complex than the deleted-relatives sentences of their Table 1 (p. 292), but *not* less complex than the same sentences of Table 2 (ibid.). The latter sentences were identical to the former ones except that they were read "expressively," whatever that may have come to.

(i) "Guy Grand ate the pickled eel with revulsion" perhaps has an intermediate source on the order of "Guy Grand had revulsion while he ate the pickled eel" (Chomsky, ibid.), and in any case it has a deeper source like "Guy Grand was revolted $\begin{Bmatrix} \text{while eating the pickled eel"} \\ \text{by eating the pickled eel"} \end{Bmatrix}$; this form, since it is clearly a passive, must derive in turn from something on the order of $\begin{Bmatrix} \text{"The pickled eel} \\ \text{"Eating the pickled eel} \end{Bmatrix}$ revolted Guy Grand $\begin{Bmatrix} \text{while he ate it"} \\ \underline{\hspace{2cm}}\text{"} \end{Bmatrix}$ and the second (more likely) of these structures has a still deeper source on the order of "Guy Grand's eating the pickled eel revolted him" or, more deeply, "(Guy Grand ate the pickled eel) [and it] revolted him."[33] This means that, under DTC, we must expect these sentences to *decrease* in complexity roughly in the order of their citation here; whereas sense suggests that experiment will show exactly the opposite to be true.

And so on.[34]

In short, there are probably many sentences that are more complex in the LG but (discrepantly) of less performative difficulty, even when the unequal sentence lengths have been taken into account (see n. 31, above). (Here, the shorter sentences are generally the more distantly derived ones.[35])

1.2.1.3. We now ask whether this apparent set of exceptions can be explained in such a way as to leave CH_{CG} unjeopardized.

(a) We first take up the case of the full passives and the truncates, according to the account of these forms sketched above in 1.2.1.1. We assume that the truncates will be shown empirically to be psycholinguistically less complex, as a

---

[33] As always, these illustrative sentences are used only to *suggest* their respective structures; the deeper the structure, the more strained is the attempt to provide an illustrative (surface) sentence. In the last illustration, I have inserted "[and it]" to make a viable surface.

[34] There is also the result, reported by Fodor and Garrett (1966, p. 150), that "John phoned the girl up," while "derived from" "John phoned up the girl," is no more complex. This result is impossible to evaluate, however, since "phone" is (at least in my speech) much more common than "phone up," so that the "up" at the end might have come as a surprise, after the sentence had seemed to be finished, or else just struck auditors as strange. It would be crucial to the demonstration of this discrepancy to test some verbs that occur *more naturally* with, for example, "up," and verbs that occur *only* with "up"(or "down", "out", and so on) – for example, "single *out*," "eke *out*," "jot *down*," and "divvy *up*." Lacking such evidence, we must decline to accept the discrepancy as a proven generalization, though it is certainly plausible enough.

[35] Of course case (f) and part of (i) differ from the others in this regard.

rule, than the corresponding full passives, even when the differences in string length have been taken into account. That is, we assume that the truncates will, as a rule, take less time to parse or compose. Now we ask if this discrepancy appears to be explainable by the contemplated revisions in the DTC. The answer is in the negative. If the truncate derives by deleting a "copied" deep subject, which the full passive does not delete, then no revised DTC can account for the discrepancy. If the full Passives in question derive their overt agents via segmentalization, as with "by one or more persons" or the like, then for these passives (but only these), DTC offers a possible explanation, since segmentalization might be more complex an operation than deletion. Thus DTC might explain some discrepantly complex full Passives, but it cannot explain all. Moreover, no other plausible revision of the treatment of the truncates looks to be more amenable to explanation in terms of a revised DTC; for example, we might propose to derive truncates more distinctively than is done in the account given above, having them result, not from "copying" plus deletion, but from a failure to "copy." But this would afford little improvement in any DTC measurements. The truncate represents a deletion, not just of the deep subject's "copied" C, but also of the deep subject's NP node (formally, the head of the C); and it was never proposed to derive the NP by "copying," so that a mere "failure to copy" would not deprive the deep subject of its NP. But suppose that the deep subject *were* so deprived — that is to say, suppose there were no deep subject at all, in deep structures destined for truncation. Such an omission would require introduction of a special passive rule (one requiring no deep subject) to generate the truncations; this is not a desirable move. Furthermore, even if it were proposed that truncates be derived by just failing to "copy" a C into the deep subject, the DTC measurements would still not be much improved; though it is a moderately complex operation considered in isolation, "copying" does not *add* much complexity, since it is only part of the already complex operation (a transformation) of introducing the verb (see above). In short, no way comes to mind of revising DTC so as to force DTC to predict with general accuracy the comparative performative complexities of full passives and truncates.

TCA will not help either, since every full passive that fully corresponds to a truncate (of *n* words), *includes* that truncate as its first *n* words; any TCA-predicted delays in assigning surface and deep structure must affect such sentences equally. Passing to questions of relative probability, we see that it is certainly true that truncates are more common than full passives by a factor of four to one (Svartvik, 1966, p. 141); but this factor is, beyond question, less than that by which, for example, "The tiger. . .was ferocious" is more probable than "The tiger. . .I was glad to see the last of" (see 1.1.1, above). Thus, though the full passives are clearly the less probable, with completion "surprising" to that mild extent, the margin of likelihood is scarcely so great as to promise much in mitigation of an overturned DTC prediction.

In sum, none of the mitigations we have looked at promise to palliate the predicted discrepancy between the truncates' greater LG complexity and lesser performative complexity.[36]

(b) We continue with a brief inspection of the other discrepancies mentioned above. The "Mary grows flowers/ $\begin{Bmatrix} \text{causes} \\ \text{makes} \end{Bmatrix}$ flowers $\begin{Bmatrix} \text{to} \\ \ \end{Bmatrix}$ grow" case (1.2.1.2.[c]) is another discrepancy not easily explained. No revision of DTC promises much, because the longer sentence is very close to the deep structure, while the shorter sentence is rather clearly a distorted (hence more distant) version of that structure. TCA does not offer much either; for example, from the first two words ("Mary causes. . ." or "Mary grows. . ."), more correct deep structure is obtained for the "causes" sentence than for the "grows" sentence, because the "grows" sentence could, up to "Mary grows," be an intransitive sentence like "Mary grows an inch with every doughnut." Neither "shorter" nor "longer" sentence appears to continue, at any point, in so improbable a way as to cause rescission of a prior deep structure assignment made on a "probabilistic" basis. In sum, the discrepancy stands.

The "Dee is hard to please" case appears equally unyielding. Taking all the sentences of 1.2.1.2.(d), together with the more complex paraphrase "It is hard [for anyone] to please Dee," it is obvious that TCA essentially predicts the sentences to be about equal by its standards. DTC, however modified, must gauge "Dee is hard to please" and "It is hard to please Dee" as of highest derivational complexity (yet we anticipate these to be performatively no more complex than the others). The transitional probabilities are unpredictable in this case, but it does not seem at all likely that the factor that complicates the performance of "To please Dee is hard [for anyone] " is the unlikelihood of "Dee," "hard," "anyone," or any other element in this sentence. This case, too, cannot be dismissed.

[36]It is almost certainly true that, while the truncates are only four times more common than full passives in general, their likelihood is greater still when they are compared with just their *paraphrastic* full passives (such as "Moll Flanders was deflowered *by someone* last year"). But it is hard to believe this to be relevant. The unlikelihood of the paraphrastic full passives is surely not so extreme as to cause them to be resisted because of being bizarre; and it cannot be maintained very plausibly that, while completing a truncate with a lexical NP is not very "surprising," nonetheless completion with, for example, ". . .by someone" is so "surprising" as to mitigate DTC.

Verbs seem to vary in the extent to which their naturalness in a passive is increased if an overt "by agent" phrase is given. ("There has never been a time when France *was* not *governed*" sounds more awkward than "Nixon *was elected* to the Presidency in 1968"). If it is more "surprising" for a verb that needs no overt "by agent" to have one than for a verb that does need such a phrase, it should not be hard to lend empirical verification to this fact.

The "Dee is eager to please" sentences of 1.2.1.2.(e) were predicted by the simple DTC to be *less* complex than the "Dee is hard to please" sentences just examined. TCA finds no distinctions here; DTC cannot be revised in any obvious way to remove the discrepancy; again the probabilities seem irrelevant; and so again the case stands.

The "There's a dragon in the street" sentences of 1.2.1.2.(f) seem just as impervious. TCA appears irrelevant; DTC appears beyond the needed modification; and probability seems to be as irrelevant as TCA. Again, the discrepancy stands.

The several other discrepancies noted in 1.2.1.2 — just over half of the total — are subject to more uncertainty of judgment than those just considered, and the few statements that one can now make about their mitigation might better be postponed. Case 1.2.1.2.(a) is hard to evaluate because it seems that "The tired soldier fired the shot" might be derivable from a structure like "The (soldier was tired) soldier fired the shot" rather than from a structure like "The soldier who was tired fired the shot"; this change would alter the DTC prediction rather violently, since the permutation that (presumably) contributed most heavily to the predicted complexity would now have been removed. The cases of 1.2.1.2.(b), "John hammered the nail/used a hammer to act upon the nail," seem particularly hard to compare because of their inequality as to string length; for the time being we pass these by, then. Case 1.2.1.2.(g) involves a simple deletion ("I read the book while [I was] in England", but deletions of this sort seem so minor that the undoubted DTC prediction seems subcritical. The cases of 1.2.1.2.(h) are more interesting. Certainly DTC cannot be revised in any obvious way so as to predict "Brutus caused Caesar to be(come) dead" to be performatively *more* complex than "Brutus killed Caesar"; but TCA appears to predict the shorter sentence to be simpler, a possible mitigation. As to probability, it does seem completely unlikely that any sentence fragment "Brutus caused Caesar to. . ." should actually be completed with ". . .be dead," or that "Brutus made Caesar. . ." should be completed with ". . .dead." So reception of these sentences might be slowed because of this "surprise" element. But before pronouncing this a case of mitigation on "surprise" grounds, we ought to test the comparative complexity of other sentence pairs that are like "kill"/"dead" except that their "surprisingness" is reversed: for example, "Brutus angered Caeser"/ "Brutus made Caesar angry." Lastly, the complex case 1.2.1.2.(i) seems to me to require further linguistic analysis before we can base any DTC prediction on a firm LG account of these sentences. But for the time being it does not at all seem likely that "Guy Grand's eating the pickled eel revolted him" or "To eat the pickled eel revolted Guy Grand" will be predicted by DTC, on *any* LG account, to be more complex than "Guy Grand ate the pickled eel with revulsion"; and if not, the predicted discrepancy will stand.

(c) Considering just the *processing* aspect of performance, we have several fairly clear cases where LG complexity and performative complexity seem unalterably at odds. If we now turn briefly to the *compositional* aspect of performance, the number of discrepancies if anything increases. TCA can no longer mitigate the discrepancies, since the composer of a sentence can hardly run into the problem of assigning deep structure to his output; the output has its *origin* in that deep structure. Nor should "probabilistic" factors play a role, since the speaker of a sentence is unlikely to run into performative difficulties caused by his surprise at how the sentence turns out. Yet the same DTC-predicted discrepancies, with the same difficulties of sufficiently altering the DTC, obtain for the composition of sentences as obtain for their reception. Thus, for example, DTC (revised or unrevised) predicts that truncates should take more time to compose than full passives, stringwise length aside. If, as anticipated, this prediction fails, then the receptive discrepancy will be matched by a compositional or productive discrepancy. In like manner, each performative discrepancy considered above from its receptive aspect has a compositional aspect; and, as we see, it is even harder to propose mitigations for compositional discrepancies than it is for receptive ones.

(d) In sum, the discrepancies we noted earlier (now expanded to have both receptive and compositional facets) do not all have explanations such as to leave CH_{CG} unthreatened; indeed, roughly half of these discrepancies remain, after a number of proposed "mitigations" have been tried, as discrepant as ever. Certainly it would be exceedingly unwise to claim that no other mitigations can plausibly be put forward;[37] but our attempt, and failure, to find such mitigations effectively shifts the *onus probandi* to the opposing position, that of the defenders of CH_{CG}. And this comment, by reminding us that the CH_{CG} has now a rival hypothesis, returns us to our main theme.

---

[37]For example it might quite plausibly be contended that purely semantic complexity in the deep (or abyssal) structure might affect performative complexity. (But we have sidestepped this possibility, in all cases save 1.2.1.2.[a] and [e], by comparing *paraphrases* only.) Or again, it might be suggested that performative complexity might be partly a function of Miller and Chomsky's "N(Q)" measurement (1963, p. 480) of sentential simplicity. (But this measurement gauges only constituent structure, whether deep or derived; in gauging the complexity of a derived constituent structure, it ignores completely the manner — simple or complex — in which that structure was derived, except insofar as that derivation conforms to the rough over-all judgment that transformation decreases the number of branches per node and so increases N(Q).) Or yet again, there is the proposal due to Harris (1968, pp. 186f.) that sentences increase in performative difficulty upon their greatly diverging from the simple high-frequency formats (such as SAAD); ". . .in *He went home, I think* one is less sure what is the subject." (Most of the discrepancies noted here are not subject to this mitigation, it seems; and note that while "There's a dragon in the street" is quite divergent from the SAAD, it is itself of a high-frequency format, and so is not predicted to be

1.2.2. If there are discrepancies between the complexity predictions of the MG and those observable in the behavior of the users of that MG, and if no mitigating explanations can be found for those discrepancies, then we must change our model of the MG. We must design a new MG in which the performatively simpler truncates are more simply derived than the performatively complex full passives; in which performatively simpler sentences like "Mary grows flowers," "Dee is hard to please," "There's a dragon in the street," and all the other cases we may expect future experimentation to disclose, have the simpler derivation. In general: it does not appear that the MG actually derives these sentences (even in the "5 x 8 index-card" sense) in the way we have thought, and so we must consider changing the MG so that these sentences receive new and simpler derivations. Afterward, if the result of our changes could also be an LG, as customarily constrained by metatheoretic considerations, then we can change the LG too and thus restore the equation MG = LG (with the usual freedom of interpretation of "=").

(Incidentally, the demand just made does not quite correspond to the demand that all "brief" paraphrases, being the performatively simple ones, be entered as simple in our new MG, the more complex sentences either being derived from them or, perhaps, having independent derivations. For it is not always the case that the briefer paraphrase promises to be the performatively simpler one, as we have seen in 1.2.1.2, just above. There is nothing particularly distinctive, linguistically speaking, about the set of sentences [taken in its entirety] that are to be given simpler derivations in the MG.)

Pursuing this idea, we see that in the new MG the truncated passive must, rather than being derived from deletion of a "copied" "by agent" phrase, be related to the full passive in quite another way. If the truncate were to be derived by a passivelike transformation from a deep structure like the active, then that transformation could not convert the deep subject into a "by agent" phrase, since that phrase would only have to undergo deletion, exactly the discrepancy-producing operation we want to avoid. In short, to introduce into the new MG a truncate whose derivation is of the simplicity apparently required, we must essentially introduce the truncate *as a new variety of deep structure.* But we have no mandate to make the full passive a new variety of deep structure. Then we are speaking of two deep structures for transitive-verb sentences — one like the active, and one like the truncate; and we are speaking of three derived surface structures for transitive-verb sentences — one the active (from the first-named

more complex by this criterion.) Certainly Harris's proposal seems more than reasonable; and it does not (cf. the "There's a dragon" case) reduce to yet another statement about divergences from deep structure or about transitional probabilities.

deep structure), one the truncate (from the second-named), and one the full passive (derived in the usual way from the first-named).[38]

1.2.2.1. Setting aside for the moment any reservations we might have about this step, let us determine what is to be done to accommodate the other discrepancies in the revised MG. Clearly, in general, the performatively simpler sentences ("Mary grows flowers," "Dee is hard to please," perhaps "It is hard to please Dee," and "There's a dragon in the street") are to be entered as new deep structures, or very close to deep structures, with their performatively complex counterparts ("Mary makes flowers grow," "[For anyone] to please Dee is hard," and "In the street there's a dragon" or "*A dragon is in the street") either removed from the set of deep structures or, possibly, left there in the expectation that, thus reduced, the discrepancy between the MG prediction and actual performance might be explained on other grounds.

Assuredly, the resulting MG looks rather little like the LG we are accustomed to. It seems natural enough, in fact, to ask at this point whether we should not debate jettisoning the notion of the MG altogether, substituting for it some much looser abstract linguistic faculty: a set of sentences (with recursive rules to extend that set indefinitely), or some way of generating (determining) sentences that is so disorganized as not to constitute a "grammar" at all, in the usual sense of that partially defined term. That is, why not take to their logical extreme the alterations proposed here, moving all sentences' derived constituent structures into the deep structure, and so having no explicit way at

---

[38] Postulating that, in the MG, the deep structure for the truncate is quite dissociated from that for the full Passive implies that while the passive tends to be detransformed in memory to the underlying activelike deep structure, the truncate should not exhibit the same tendency, inasmuch as it is not, in the MG, underlain by an activelike deep structure at all. And, in fact, Slobin has reported experimental results (1968) that lend strong empirical support to just this conclusion.

Note that, by strict DTC, a truncate is now predicted to have (*ceteris paribus*) the same performative complexity as its paraphrastic active, if any (for example, "Moll was deflowered" and "Somebody deflowered Moll"). This prediction, while not implausible, deserves careful checking, especially in view of Gough's finding (1966, pp. 494-496) that truncates and *non*paraphrastic actives are *not* equal in performative complexity. In Gough's experiment the actives paraphrased the truncates except for having full-fledged subjects (for example, "the girl"); this fact, of course, makes the complexities incomparable, and, as Gough himself points out (p. 495), the experiment was biased in favor of the active in any case: his subjects were asked to verify whether presented sentences described subsequently presented pictures, and the pictures were ones to describe which ". . .a speaker of English normally uses the active voice. . . ." That is, the pictures displayed overt actor and overt acted-on; so perforce did the actives; but of course the truncates did not.

all of coupling sentences together as having the same subcategorial and cooccurrence constraints? The full passive, for example, would (just like the truncate) be added directly to the set of deep structures. However, this extreme move has no psycholinguistic justification at all; quite the contrary. The set of anticipated discrepancies is far from encouraging it and the performative complexity of the full passive militates against it; while on the other hand there is at least enough tendency for people to remember complexly derived transforms as simpler ones (Mehler, 1963; Clark and Clark, 1968; but cf. Turner and Rommetveit, 1968) that a *general* detransformation toward the deep structure is well attested. Moreover, there are other facts about the linguistic behavior of individuals that lead one to believe that people do have an MG, a complex grammar in which such unobvious facts as the constituency of the verb phrase in the deep structure are "psychologically real" beyond the possibility of doubt. Lakoff and Ross (1966) have made some observations about the benefactive object in English that illustrate this point. As they say, the benefactive object ("Baron Geauxbois bought a new Cord *for Tom*") must not be inside the Verb Phrase (VP) in English, since if it were, by a reasoning they defend, it would behave like the direct object ("Baron Geauxbois bought *the jury*") or the indirect object ("Baron Geauxbois gave a new Cord *to Tom*"), which *are* inside the VP. For instance, it would resemble them in becoming the surface subject of a passive ("*The jury* was bought by Baron Geauxbois" and "*Tom* was given the new Cord by Baron Geauxbois"). But it does not resemble them, since "**Tom* was bought a new Cord by Baron Geauxbois," the equivalent passive on the benefactive object, is ungrammatical. And, since the benefactive object is *not* therefore in the VP, it *can* (like other elements not in the VP) be referred to in a "do so" construction; hence, "Baron Geauxbois bought a new Cord for Tom, and will *do so* for Barbara next Tuesday" is grammatical, while the same construction using a direct or indirect object — these *are* inside the VP — would not be grammatical: "**Baron Geauxbois gave a new Cord to Tom, and will do so to Barbara next Tuesday," and "**Baron Geauxbois bought the jury, and will do so [? to] the judge next Tuesday." The two facts — no passive, yes "do so"; yes passive, no "do so" — are coupled, in Lakoff and Ross's treatment, and are explicitly predicted by whether or not the object — benefactive or direct/indirect — is inside the VP. It might still, I suppose, be argued that these facts would make as much sense in some other and much looser account — one in which the formation of passives and "do so" sentences was oblivious to the constituency of the VP — but any such notion is completely overthrown, to my mind, by the following facts. In my own speech the passive on the benefactive object which Lakoff and Ross condemned — for example, "Tom was bought a new Cord by Baron Geauxbois" — is *perfectly grammatical.* There can be no doubt on this score, since I find completely grammatical the benefactive-object passives of a number of verbs: "obtain," "procure," "steal," and others. Thus, according to Lakoff and Ross's criterion, in my MG the benefactive object *is* inside the VP. Then following Lakoff and Ross, I should find ungrammatical the (to them, grammatical) "do so" sentences like "Baron Geauxbois bought a new Cord for Tom, and will *do so* for Barbara next Tuesday." Now, if I should find this sentence ungrammatical this would be a striking fact, since usually if many other American speakers find a sentence type grammatical, then I do too — mine is generally an "inclusive" idiolect. I do not find the benefactive object "do so" sentence grammatical. (In fact, I even have trouble understanding it and am slightly incredulous that everyone else is not similarly puzzled.) Thus the claim that, for my MG, the benefactive object is in the deep VP, turns out to have a rather immediate verification, one which strengthens in turn the claim that the MG of the speakers with whom Lakoff and Ross were concerned is such that the benefactive object is *outside* the VP. Then, if so unobvious a fact as the constituency of the deep verb phrase can be demonstrated to have psychological reality in the MG, one is not at all disposed to assume that transformations lack this reality, in some sense. Notice that, on the basis of VP constituency in the deep structure, one can predict facts about surface-structure elements which are not in the surface VP at all — for example, the surface subject of the benefactive-object passive — *though they are elements withdrawn from the deep VP by, precisely, transformation.* Thus, in conclusion, there is good evidence that the MG is in form very like the LG, with its complex interplay of rules and elements, and there is no evidence to the contrary. There is only the evidence, developed above in this paper, that the contents of the MG seem not to be exactly those of the LG to which we are accustomed.

1.2.2.2. It is clear that the kind of MG we are moving toward must be judged by criteria of economy different from those by which the LG is now judged. This kind of MG — let us now begin to call it the "abstract performative grammar," or APG — is quite uneconomical on the points where it differs from the LG (or CG " = " to the LG). In developing the truncates, for example, without regard to their extremely close linguistic relation to the full passives, the APG will fail to exploit that close relation in the obvious and natural manner — by giving the two types of sentence a common derivation up to the point (deletion) where they must part ways. It is a commonplace of linguistic discussion that an irrefragable argument for inclusion of transformations in the grammar is that only transformations permit capture of this basic economy, for only transformations can operate upon essentially one underlying structure (like the active), properly alter it into two other structures (the abstract surface active and the abstract common passive/truncate), and then alter the common passive/truncate into passive and truncate. Thus the severe restrictions that determine actives containing (roughly speaking) transitive verbs and their objects, and that determine passives containing surface subjects and, sometimes, a surface-by+Agent — these restrictions can be made into one set of restrictions essentially on one underlying structure, the one underlying Active, Passive, and truncate. (Thus, to say that a verb is transitive in an active sentence with an object is tantamount to saying that the same verb can occur passivized in a normal passive sentence; information about the active and the passive is reduced to information about the set [active, passive]). This has been the view since the outset of transformational work (for example, Chomsky, 1957, p. 43) and it has been maintained up to the present day. That is, despite the uncertainties about the precise nature of evaluative measures and about the precise form of the grammars to which these measures are to be applied, there has been the persistent notion that a grammar that made correct generalizations (that collapsed duplicative rules into fewer and nonduplicative rules) should turn out to be more highly valued than a grammar that failed to make such generalizations.[39]

An APG does not include all of the generalizations that the LG includes, and so it is definitely less highly valued by the criterion referred to in n.39 just above. In particular, the APG is not economical in its treatment of the set of sentences (passive/truncate), and in general we can see that there are sets of sentences (x, y) such that there are possible "generalizations" about them that are realized in the LG but not in the APG. Thus we may say that the LG and APG differ most basically in that insofar as the sentences *x* and the sentences *y* are taken as a single set, and insofar as the *set* (x, y) is that to which the evaluation measure is applied, to that extent the LG will *consistently* be more highly valued than the APG.

However, the APG was clearly introduced to effect another and quite different sort of economy. For we have concluded that if truncates are performatively less complexly derived than the LG "predicts," then there is warrant, provided no mitigations for this discrepancy can be found, for changing the MG so

---

[39]"We have a generalization when a set of rules about distinct items can be replaced by a single rule (or, more generally, partially identical rules) *about the whole set* [italics supplied], or when it can be shown that a 'natural class' of items undergoes a certain process or set of similar processes. ... The problem is to devise a procedure that will assign a numerical measure of valuation to a grammar in terms of the degree of linguistically significant generalization that this grammar achieves. The obvious numerical measure to be applied to a grammar is length, in terms of number of symbols [that is, symbol-tokens]." (Chomsky, 1965, p. 42.) Chomsky then proceeds to remark that if length is to be the criterion, consistent notations and rule formats must be adopted so that the criterion can be correctly applied.

as to simplify the derivation of the truncates; and thus, tacitly, we have taken the position that the MG must realize certain economies of derivation not realized in the LG (CG). Taking the Passives and truncates as our (x, y) example, the LG minimizes the number of rules by which the set (x, y) is derived; but the APG minimizes the number of rules by which the set (x) is derived and, separately, the number of rules by which the set (y) is derived. Implicitly so far, but now explicitly, we have been saying that the APG is at least sometimes to be measured by an "abstract performative" evaluation measure in which a set of rules is more highly valued if it individually derives each paradigm of sentences with the fewest number of rules. Thus in the APG the truncates receive a generative treatment that is essentially the treatment they would receive in the LG *if there were no full passives in English* (and if the residual generalizable similarities between truncate and transitive Active – such as identity of their verb sets – were ignored). To take another example, "Mary grows flowers" receives a treatment in the APG equivalent to the treatment that that sentence would receive in the LG if none of the sentences like "Flowers grow" or "Mary makes (something happen)" were included in English.

How far the APG is to be evaluated by the proposed "abstract performative" evaluation measure is still an open question, since there is no *a priori* way of prescribing the extent to which the APG should obey "abstract performative" rather than "competence" or "linguistic" simplicity criteria. Certainly at this point there seems to be no reason to insist that the APG derive the full passive by the minimum number of steps, since the full passive (taken as a monolithic set) seems to be performatively complex. However, conversion to an APG highly valued *only* on the "abstract performative" criterion is a (remote) possibility.

By the same token, the actual form of the rules specific to the APG will not be stated here beyond the kind of more-or-less obvious descriptions exemplified in discussions above. Presumably the truncate will have a direct APG derivation much like N – is – adjective sentences; and "Mary grows flowers" will, with a complex underlying lexical entry for "grows," have an APG derivation like "He buys cars." "There's a dragon in the street" might in the APG have a directly derived pleonastic "there-is" (there + be + Tense) adjunct. These investigations are scarcely begun, and attempting to state such rules with any finality would be entirely premature.

1.2.2.3. Two of the fundamental facts to be learned about a language in the course of its acquisition are (1) which sentences of superficial similarity must in fact be distinguished as different, and (2) which sentences of superficial difference must be generalized as being basically similar. Thus the learner of English must realize that "Dee is hard to please" and "Dee is eager to please," despite their superficial similarity, must be viewed as being quite different at a more basic level (the level we call deep structure); see 1.2.1.2.(d) and 1.2.1.2.(e), above. Thus also, the learner of English must realize that "The King of Zembla rewarded the winning athletes" and "The winning athletes were rewarded by the King of Zembla" are, despite their dissimilarity on the surface, basically the same at some deeper level (again, that of deep structure). To quote Chomsky (1967a, p. 433) on differentiation, ". . .the grammar of English, as a characterization of competence, must, for descriptive adequacy, assign different deep structures [to sentences superficially similar but fundamentally different]. The grammar that each speaker has internalized does distinguish these deep structures. . ." And on generalization (1965, p. 45), ". . .a certain empirical claim is made, implicitly, concerning natural language. It is implied that a person learning a language will attempt to formulate generalizations [for sentences superficially different but fundamentally similar or identical] that can easily be expressed. . . . in terms of the notations available in [the theory of grammar], and that he will select grammars containing these generalizations over other grammars. . ."

Evidence that speakers differentiate and generalize is not hard to find. That the speaker "knows" there to be a profound difference between the superficially similar sentences "I *persuaded* the doctor to examine John" and "I *expected* the doctor to examine John" is shown by the fact that all speakers find the difference manifest when the embedded sentence (The-doctor-examine-John) is passivized, since the resultant Passives have distinctively different relations to their active counterparts just cited. "I *persuaded* John to be examined by the doctor" does not have the same truth value as the corresponding active (one of the two sentences can be false, the other true). But "I *expected* John to be examined by the doctor" does have the same truth value as the corresponding active (if one is true the other is; if not, not) (Chomsky, 1967a, pp. 432f.). The latter fact about paraphrasticity is, in turn, one kind of evidence favoring generalization. Other evidence in favor of generalization is that speakers also commonly "know" that for every sentence of type *a* (e.g., active) there can be constructed a sentence of type *b* (e.g., passive) with the same meaning or (as with affirmative/ negative) a constant difference or increment of meaning. (Informants do not have trouble turning actives into passives.)

As to the above-noted differentiations, no psycholinguistic evidence that I know of encourages us to think that they are not incorporated directly into the MG (now identified as an APG), in some way. On the other hand, we have evidence that seems to indicate that some *generalizations* (for example, that truncates correspond to full passives) are *not* incorporated in this way. Yet surely the manifest nature of the generalization must be (unconsciously) realized by everyone who learns English. How then can we possibly explain the seeming failure to form the appropriate rule in the MG?

The sentences of performative simplicitly that we propose to enter in the APG as derived (like the active) "directly" from deep structures have in common another attribute in addition to their comparative simplicitly: they are learned early. For most of the cases considered here, this must remain for now just a plausible assumption; we assume, then, that a child acquiring English will acquire "Mary grows flowers" before "Mary makes flowers grow"; "There's a dragon in the street" before "In the street there's a dragon"; "John hammered the nail" before "John used the hammer to act upon (or hit) the nail"; and so on.[40] But one of these assumptions has some support, since it is known (Harwood, 1959, pp. 248f.; Brown and Hanlon, this volume, pp. 14-17) that children at least *use* truncated passives before full ones. This fact alone does not entail that children use truncated passives before they are *able* to use full ones, since it is a well-known result (Fraser, Bellugi, and Brown, 1963) that comprehension precedes production and therefore that the abilities of the MG can outstrip those of the compositional performative mechanism (McNeill, 1966, pp. 76-82). Indeed, one of Fraser *et al.*'s results is specifically that children comprehend full passives before they produce them; but these comprehensions, it seems, might have been achieved just by comprehending the truncate portion of the full passives concerned. Pending further evidence we find, as stated, "some support" for our conjecture that MG's command truncates before full passives.

[40]There may well be exceptions to this pattern, however (the assumption may be risky in any case). For example, children are often observed making sentences like (an actual example) "He made her dead," meaning "He killed her"; but this does not at all entail that the child cannot make sentences with "causative" verbs ("kill" = "make [be] dead"; "grow" = "make grow"). This would have to be determined empirically, of course, but it might be only that the child initially has trouble with "causative" verbs which have a form different ("dead"/"kill") from that of the "caused" predicate ("be dead"; "grow"). This at least seems to be an avenue of investigation worth pursuing. (It is perhaps worth remarking that the children of Harwood's study [ibid.], whose age ranged from 4.11 to 5.8, had both kinds of construction. "Make" plus a verb or adjective ["You make me sick", cited on p. 239] was common, and so was, for example, "break" in the "causative" sense of "make. . .break." The "causative" verbs [*incorporating* "make"] seem to have been more common than the construction "make + verb" [ibid., pp. 246f.]; but this of course does not demonstrate anteriority of the former construction.)

It is also worth remarking that empirical failure of this generalization would not jeopardize the APG hypothesis itself, but only the hypothesis, here being proposed, concerning the explanation for the apparent failure of the MG to embody all possible generalizations. If it should turn out that some of the performatively simple sentences here in question are learned late rather than early, a more complex explanation for the failure to generalize would have to be put forward. That step may perhaps await the empirical disconfirmation.

What shall we suppose the child's truncate-formation rule to be at this early pre-passive stage? Shall we assume that he has what we might call a "pre-passive passivization" rule which acts like the true passivization rule except that it attacks only actives that are to be turned into truncates? This is a possible assumption, perhaps. But in formulating such a transformation within his MG a child must (unconsciously, of course) be formalizing (and maximally exploiting) the generalization that for every active of a certain form there is a paraphrastic truncate.[41] But such actives scarcely exist — only those, in fact, with a verb like "deflower" or "beget" and a very indefinite Subject (like "someone"). That is, truncates do not correspond to active sentences in anything like a simple way, except in cases which the child can hardly have come into contact with. Then, since truncates have neither surface forms like the active nor an obvious relation to the active's deep structure, there is no good reason to suppose that a child who makes truncates (and actives, of course), but no full passives, has made the generalization needed to permit him to construct those truncates by recourse to a "pre-passive passivization" rule.[42]

[41] He might, just conceivably, be formulating the sort of "meaning-change" generalization such as may underlie the awareness of the similarity between, for example, affirmative and negative, which sort of similarity is realized in the LG as a systematic similarity of deep structure. That is, he might be forming the generalization that the truncates, while not synonymous with the actives, can be viewed as preserving all of the active except what is irrecoverable from the active's deep-subject, so that each truncate would be seen as incorporating a diminution of the semantic content of any one of a set of actives. (For example, the truncate "The *Hindenburg* was sabotaged" corresponds "by diminution" to the infinite set of actives including, for example, "A maniac sabotaged the *Hindenburg,*" "(*n*) maniacs sabotaged the Hindenburg" (where *n* is any positive integer), and so on; but it does not correspond to, for example, "*The Julian calendar sabotaged the *Hindenburg.*") The relationship does not seem to be a simple one, though for a possible further simplifying factor see n.42, just below.

[42] The paucity of actives corresponding paraphrastically to truncates is exactly matched, of course, by a paucity of matching full passives in the speech of the older child who uses full passives. The older child's generalization "truncate = (full passive minus by-Δ)" — a necessary step to achieving the LG account — could not be one formed on the basis of overwhelming *linguistic* evidence as such. But notice that a generalization to the truncate from the corresponding full passive is aided — as the generalization from the corresponding active is not — by the very close correspondence of surface-form. And note further that in language *use* ("*parole*"), the missing agent is often recoverable from deictic context or from preceding linguistic material; and this, in a way that is not at all obvious at present, must play a role in promoting the correct LG generalization. However, as we have noted, it seems likely that the generalization is never made at all in the APG.

It seems more than reasonable, in fact, to think that the child is constructing truncates ("Those cookies were baked") by the same rules he uses to construct simple predicate-adjective sentences ("Those cookies were good"). The
surfaces are very similar, and participles like "baked" are quasi-adjectival[43]. But
if this is in fact the way the child makes truncates, his truncate-information rule
is as simple and direct as is his rule for forming the predicate-adjective sentences;
that is, both come directly from a deep structure on the order of "subject-NP +
(Be-verb + tense) + predicator," where a predicator is either a participle
("baked") or an adjective ("good").[44] That is, the child has a much simpler
way of making truncates than the adult would *if the adult's MG were " = " to
the LG.*

We see then that to demand that the child later acquire the LG's way of
making truncates is to insist that he abandon a simple way of making truncates
in favor of a more complex way. It is to insist that he forego the simplicity of
his (putative) original derivation of the truncates in order to achieve a simplifying generalization holding for truncates and full passives together; it is to insist
that he give up a simple way of deriving the set of sentences *x* because, when he
acquires the set *y*, the set (x,y) can be more simply derived if he uses the necessarily more complex derivation of *y* to derive *x* also, amplified (as by providing
for recoverable deletion) where needed. It is to insist, in short, that CG or LG
or "competence" simplicity is superordinate to APG or "abstract performative"
simplicity, and to insist that the efficiency with which individual sentences are
composed and parsed is subordinate to the efficiency with which *sets* of sentences are *stored.* In sum, the presumptive abandonment of the early derivation of

---

[43]Some past participles are more adjectival than others; for example, some ("interested," "tired," "annoyed") can be modified by "very," while others ("baked") cannot. But
generally they can all be compared ("more interested"; "more tired" or even "tireder";
"more baked"); modified by "quite"; and so on. The subject has been studied elsewhere,
and need not be dwelt on here.

[44]This comment on the APG is manifestly derived from the LG analysis of Postal
and Lakoff (Lakoff, 1965, Appendix, A, *passim*) in which verbs and adjectives (and not
just past participles and adjectives) are essentially the same "VERB" grammatical category,
differing (ibid., 0, p. 15) only by one syntactic feature: conventional verbs are (+V) and
(-adjectival), whereas conventional adjectives are (+V) and (+adjectival). Notice that if the
ruling grammatical category were "predicator" rather than "verb," so that (+V) would not
automatically head this category's complex symbol, then verbs could be (+predicator)
(+verb) (-adjective); adjectives could be (+predicator) (-verb) (+adjective); and past participles could be (+predicator) (+verb) (+adjective). That is – without necessarily advocating
this description for the LG – the close relation between LG and derivative APG descriptions
is easily demonstrated.

the truncates in favor of the LG derivation is not an event of linguistic ontogenesis that inevitably accords with intuition; in fact, especially in view of the probable performative simplicity of the truncates in the adult MG, the event is somewhat lacking in plausibility. And, as we see, defenders of the CG hypothesis are not spared the burden of proof, for the CG hypothesis must include an explanation of why (x,y) generalization is paramount, just as the APG hypothesis must include an explanation, presumably along the lines sketched here, of why (x,y) generalization is sometimes subordinated.[45]

CG and APG criteria of economy are competitive by nature, no matter how we refine their definition. They need not always come into conflict; the set (x, y) is often such that a single derivation is possible (obeying CG simplicity) that is still very simple by the APG criterion; for example, when x is the set of transitive-verb actives and y the set of intransitive-verb actives, or perhaps when x is the set of simple affirmative sentences and y the set of corresponding negatives.[46] But sometimes, we have supposed, the two criteria do conflict, as in the cases considered above. In the case of the truncates, it appears that the APG criterion is the stronger. But we are not obliged to assume that the APG criterion is always the stronger; it would be rather more reasonable to anticipate that determination of which is stronger is at least partly contingent on the degree of

[45] For a persuasive account of some CG generalizations see n. 46, just below.

[46] McNeill, in his penetrating study of linguistic development in the child (1966, pp. 61f.), proposed a specific reason for the child's development of a negative transformation (that is, one that forms negative surfaces from negative deep structures). "The pressure. . . to devise transformation rules may come from the cognitive clutter that results from not having them" he remarks. "In Period 1 [a stage of acquisition] the child had to remember only two rules for the placement of the negative ['no' or 'not']. In Period 2, he had to remember five. By Period 3, if it were not for the transformations, he would have had to remember six or seven. It is possible, then, that the load on the child's memory by Period 2 was so great that the. . .transformational rules we observe in Period 3 were precipitated." And he continues, "The child needs to process sentences in short intervals of time; presumably it takes less time and a child tends to forget less when the placement of the negative is done by transformational rules rather than by independent. . .[deep structure] rules."

Essentially the transformation that McNeill proposes replaces a burgeoning number of special phrase-structure rules for positioning of the negative. The new rule consists of a single instruction which takes the negative particle from the beginning of the sentence and adjoins it to the auxiliary ("does", and the like). Thus the different ways of making different negative sentences are collapsed into one, so that the child's need "to process sentences in short intervals of time" is plausibly served by this simplifications.

But if we grant that the child already knows how to make correct truncates, modeled on "noun – is – adjective" sentences, then no analogous economy can be achieved by substituting a new transformational account of the truncates for the old "direct" account. He has no burgeoning set of special-purpose rules to be gotten rid of; he has only the freedom expressed by the node "predicator" in the rule – needed for predicate-adjective sentences

complexity that an (x,y) generalization would introduce into the derivation of *x* alone. Investigating this possibility must assuredly be an early task in any exploration of the APG hypothesis.[47]

In conclusion, we see that the chief difference between CG and APG boils down to this: the CG puts a premium on overall economy and so makes all significant generalizations; and the APG puts a premium on economy of derivation of individual sentential paradigms, and so balks at incorporating some of these generalizations.

1.2.2.4. Having determined what must apparently be altered in the MG — having determined that the MG is apparently an APG — we now ask whether or not the LG could be revised in turn so that, once again, the formula MG " = " LG could be restored (as see 1.0., above). To continue with the example of the truncates, could the APG "direct" analysis of that set of sentences replace their conventional treatment in the current LG? We see at once that if the APG analysis of the truncates were to replace the present LG derivation (from the full passives via by-Δ deletion) then the LG would fail to make the obviously correct (x,y) generalization (necessary to preserve high-valuedness by a "competence" criterion of simplicity) about the truncates and full passives, unless the LG also gave up its present account of the full passives and adopted an (x,y) account in which both truncates and full passives derived directly from a passivelike deep structure. But then the LG would only have to abandon the obviously correct (x,y) generalization about the full passives and the actives.[48] In short, there is no escaping

in any case — "S $\rightarrow$ NP + be + predicator," plus other rules (question; negation...) also needed anyway. Thus the child, by McNeill's criterion, has nothing to gain from a new (and more complex) derivation of the truncate. McNeill's explanation for the addition of transformations to the MG, which to me is quite persuasive for the negatives, seems to have no bearing on the truncates, and so this best explanation of CG generalization seems to have a systematic set of exceptions, those we have been claiming to be *un*generalized in the APG. The two explanations — McNeill's of cases favoring generalization and hence "competence" economy, and mine of cases opposing generalization because favoring "abstract performative" economy — are far from mutually exclusive and evidence that supports one criterion does not necessarily refute the other.

[47]It is also possible that other factors play a role in determining, for a given case, whether CG or APG criterion shall prevail: for example, length of time between acquisition of *x* and acquisition of *y* (= length of time for the derivation of *x* to harden); relative frequency of *x* and of *y*; nearness of *x* and/or *y* to some *z*; and so on.

[48]This is a simplification, since some truncate*like* sentences do have a derivation like the one the APG seems to provide for the true truncates: NP — be+tense — predicator. Thus "The glass is broken" or "The glass has been broken for some time" seem to contain, not a participle derived from a verb via passivization (with absence of the deep subject arranged by deletion), but rather just an adjective, "broken." The meaning of such sentences

seems to be on the order of "The glass (has a crack) (is not whole)" and "The glass has (had a crack) (not been whole) for some time," respectively. Thus, when the LG analyzes a "*pseudo*truncate" in this fashion, since no passives are involved, the LG's (truncates, full-passives) generalization is unaffected. (But, it seems, in the APG both pseudotruncates and true truncates have the "adjective" ["predicator"] analysis, with the consequence that the LG, though able to adopt some of the APG's analyses, cannot adopt all.)

Obviously the sentence "The glass broke" might now be resolved into "The glass became broken", thus appearing as an inchoative sentence subject to the analysis of Lakoff (1965, IV, pp. 4-14). The deceptively simple active "John broke the glass" would now be seen to have a deeper source like "John made the glass (be, become) broken", revealing itself to be a causative sentence in Lakoff's sense (ibid., pp. 14-18). Thus, introduction of the adjective "broken" suggests an LG analysis for the true truncate along these lines: "The glass was broken" ← "The glass was broken by Δ" ← " Δ broke the glass" ← "Δ made the glass (be, become) broken." But this analysis is perfectly captured by the (x, y) generalization just indicated, and so the LG easily changes over to this analysis of these truncates without losing any part of its "Competence" status.

Of course if the LG should adopt this analysis, then such a sentence as "The glass was broken" would be ambiguous, meaning either "The glass wasn't whole" or else "The glass was broken by Δ." But this seems perfectly in order. Notice, however, that many superficially similar sentences are *not* ambiguous in this way: "The house was broken into" absolutely requires an agent, a deleted "Δ." With some verb/adjective pairs (such as "divorce"/ "divorced"), there will be both ambiguous sentences ("John was divorced") and unambiguous sentences ("John was being divorced at this time last Monday"). The latter, again, can *only* be a truncated passive; "divorced," when a pure adjective, is a "stative" (no activity) adjective like "tall" rather than a "nonstative" adjective like "noisy" or "foolish" (Lakoff, ibid., Appendix, A, pp. 9f.); and a "stative" adjective cannot occur in such a "nonstative" (*activity*) environment.

We have gone into this matter at this length (while at the same time oversimplifying and omitting many details) because it directly affects our psycholinguistic measurements of the performative difficulty of the putative truncates. For now we see that it would be possible to conclude that true truncates were performatively simple when in fact it was only *pseudo*truncates like "The glass is broken" that were being tested. Or the sentences being tested might be ambiguous (might be sets of nonparaphrastic homonymous strings), as "The glass was broken" seems to be, in which case (a) the "prejudiced" reading would, quite covertly, be the "adjectival" one, thus again yielding a misleadingly "simple" performance; or (b) the sentence would be (tacitly) recognized as ambiguous, in which case either "truncate" or "*pseudo*truncate" reading would be complicated by this covert ambiguity (see n. 30, above). In testing speakers' performances on the truncates, then, these factors must be carefully excluded. Once the risks are identified, however, this is easy to do. Most sentences can quickly be typed as "truncate," "pseudo-truncate," or "both" (ambiguous): such as, respectively, "That window was broken deliberately"; "That window has been broken for weeks"; and "That window was broken on Friday."

There appears to be no way, with regard to these sentence types, to reconcile APG and LG; if the LG incorporates the APG's analysis of the truncates, it does so only for the superficially similar *pseudo*truncates. As I hope is obvious, there is no way of merging truncate and pseudotruncate by claiming that, for example, "The glass was broken" is both purely adjectival and *also* has, as a complement to the adjective "broken," a deleted passive "by Δ" phrase. (For a different proof that the related "The glass broke" could not have such a source, see Lakoff, ibid., IV, p. 17.) This claim would entail — pretending illustratively the conclusion — manifest in the preceding discussions, in fact — that if the MG is to become an APG, then the MG can no longer be "=" to the LG, because the LG could not, itself, become an APG (without changing a fundamental characteristic — high-valuedness by a "competence" simplicity criterion — that it has been assumed, from the beginning of generative transformational studies, to possess).

That is,

$$MG \equiv APG \neq LG.$$

But then the LG must embody many generalizations that the MG does not; yet the LG is supposed to be a representation of the human linguistic faculty. We are therefore constrained either to renounce this representative function of the LG, or else to identify where in the human linguistic faculty the LG's now-distinctive generalizations, absent from the APG, are after all represented. There can be no question of renouncing the representative function of the LG, since there is no reason whatsoever to claim that speakers have not, tacitly, made the generalizations at issue; it is impossible to believe that tacit realization of the full-passive/truncate relationship can fail utterly to be made. Then we are obliged to infer that the LG is perfectly correct in making its non-APG generalizations; and so we must seek to identify how these generalizations are represented in the linguistic faculty if they are exiled from the MG where they were formerly lodged.

It would clearly be premature to attempt any definitive answer to this question; but it is at least obvious, under CH_{APG}, that the linguistic faculty must contain, besides the MG (APG), knowledge *about* the MG. The linguistic faculty must include the *knowledge* that actives and truncated passives, though they are independently derived in the MG, are closely related under the paraphrase bond. This, then, is the archival competence faculty anticipated in 1.2, above.[49] Thus

but counterfactually that "Δ" can in this instance be realized as "someone" — that "The glass was broken" would derive from "The glass was broken by someone," which, like any passive, would have an activelike source like "Someone broke the glass," (which, we have said, in turn has the source "Someone made the glass be broken"). But if "broken" always has a deleted "by Δ" phrase, then the last sentence must, in its turn, come from "Someone made the glass be broken by someone," which comes from "Someone made someone make the glass be broken," which comes from "Someone made someone make the glass be broken by someone," and so on in an infinite regress.

[49]Many readers will at this juncture be reminded of Zellig Harris' model of transformational grammar and of his way of commenting on that model (1957, 1965, 1968). The reminder is apt. It is very probable, to my mind, that the archival competence faculty just postulated will in many respects have the "equilibrium" character (Harris, in lecture, about 1962) of this model, in which sentences are not derived from abstract (nonsentential)

the linguistic content of the CG is now redistributed over two components —
the MG, now an APG; and the archival faculty just mentioned. And the content
of these two components taken together is, quite properly, represented "axiomatically" in the LG.

This should not really be a surprising result. That the generalizations of
the LG should be uniformly represented in the linguistic faculty could not be
an *a priori* assumption. The facts that the LG is a grammar, and that the linguistic faculty appears to include a grammar, never strictly entailed that the two
grammars were essentially identical; this might have turned out to be the case,
but it seems that it cannot. The MG seems not to bear the direct relationship
to the LG that it has generally been thought to; but neither the existence of the
MG nor the form and content of the LG has been in any way jeopardized. This
point is perhaps worth emphasizing. It means that the fundamental notions of
linguistics, concerning the LG, have been in no way threatened by the APG hypothesis. It also means, of course, that the nature of the MG can no longer be
inferred directly from the nature of the LG; in many cases (in *all* cases, at first)
it must be discovered independently, but this in turn means that one can try to
find out what is actually *in* the MG without being hampered by the assumption
that everything in the LG is (in some isomorphic way) also in the MG.

I have referred to the new sort of MG as an "abstract performative grammar" and have used the term "abstract performative" criterion of simplicity.
The term was adopted for the obvious reason that an important concern of the
MG seems to be to conserve on the derivations of individual sentence-paradigms,
an issue which does seem to be basically performative. But the APG has been
clearly distinguished from the mechanism actually used to parse sentences; that
is, it is not to be confused with the mechanism that *makes use of* or *refers to* the
rules of the MG in the course of acts of linguistic behavior as such. (We opened
this discussion by specifying that the MG we were going to concern ourselves
with would be, in the most abstract sense possible, the MG *whose analyses* were
imposed on outgoing and incoming sentences, by whatever mechanism and in
whatever way; we emphasized that this was the MG that must be " = " to the

underlying structures but are rather related (psycholinguistically, "tacitly *known* to be related") to other sentences. I would insist that the sentences thus archivally related be assigned their ("derived") constituent structures, and that these structures be related; and I cannot agree with Harris that two sentences bound by this relationship must, for any n-tuple of
words occurring in both together, be identically ordered (identically sequenced with all
other like sentences) on a scale of grammaticality (Harris, 1957, pp. 288f.; 1965, p. 368, and
n.) Some actives improve with passivization, but most do not. But in general it seems to me
that an "Harrisian" or "equilibrium" archival competence faculty may well be what is indicated.

For readers unacquainted with Harris' concept of transformational grammar, insofar
as it contrasts with Chomsky's, Grunig's account (1965-1966) may serve as a useful introductory comparison.

LG if any MG is; and it is *this* MG that we have now hypothesized not to be
" = " to the LG.) The APG is no less "abstract" in this sense than the CG was:
it too is a passive faculty, it too could just as well be assumed (but for the non-
finiteness of its output) to exist in the maximally abstract "5 x 8 index-card"
version cited facetiously above. Hence the "abstract performative grammar" is
both "performative" and "abstract." It is also envisaged to be, in every respect
but that of obeying a "competence" or LG simplicity criterion for sentential
generalizations, a "grammar." Thus, I submit, the APG is fitly so named.

If the APG hypothesis were to be definitively upheld, it might be natural
to distinguish two kinds of "competence": "abstract performative" competence
(not an oxymoron), and "archival" competence; but this thorny issue were better
postponed.

1.3. We began by specifying, as the object of our interest, the abstract MG
whose analyses (derivations) were the ones that the performance mechanism,
in whatever way, imposed on sentences being composed and on sentences being
parsed. We readily accepted the notion that the rules of this MG are probably
not used one after the other to compose or in reverse order to parse; indeed, we
postulated a somewhat facetious model in which sentential derivations were
printed out on 5 x 8 cards and in which parsing and composing consisted of
finding the right card. We concluded that even this model strongly supported
the notion that MG complexity would be reflected in performance (behavior)
complexity — unless distortions intervened — because the more complex sentences would occupy more of the 5 x 8 card and thus take longer to access. These
preliminaries defined the nature of our problem — to ascertain whether or not
available and reasonably predicted evidence supported the hypothesis (CH_{CG})
that this abstract MG was in fact the LG. The problem first resolved into that
of seeing what performative factors (for example, TCA) might intervene between
MG and performance in such a way as to distort the correlation, as by making
sentences that were relatively simple in the MG, relatively complex to parse or
compose. Having discussed what seemed to be the most plausible of the possible
significant distorting factors, we then listed a number of (predicted) discrepancies between MG and performative complexities. And then we asked whether
these discrepancies seemed all to be "mitigated" by the distorting factors already
discussed. We concluded that they were not all mitigated. This led to our conclusion that therefore CH_{CG} was wrong, that the MG was not a CG " = " to
the LG, and that an alternative hypothesis should be advanced, conformable to
evidence of performance and evidence of children's learning sequences, about the
nature of the MG. We stated a new hypothesis, that the MG was in fact an abstract performative grammar. This version of the Correlation Hypothesis,
CH_{APG}, was then further discussed, a very tentative sketch of the APG was
given, and it was suggested that the linguistic faculty consisted of (at least) two

components, the APG and an archival competence faculty. The latter was briefly outlined.

I have agreed with Fodor and Garrett (1966, 1967) that there is little
promise in the notion that the complexity of the sentential analyses of the LG
will be directly reflected in the complexity of the human performance of those
sentential analyses. From this point on, however, our opinions radically diverge.
Where they persist in the assumption that the MG is a CG is an LG, and further
assume that the performance discrepancies are to be accounted for by an "abstract" relationship (1967, p. 296) between the CG and performance, I on the
other hand have rejected this assumption, because no plausible performance
factor actually seemed capable of accounting for all discrepancies and because,
in any case, the assumption has no *a priori* warrant; and I have proposed the new
hypothesis just summarized. Thus the predicted discrepancies between LG and
performance are explained in completely different ways: in Fodor and Garrett's
account the discrepancies occur between MG (=LG) and performance, whereas
in my account, CH_{APG}, the basic source of these discrepancies occurs between
LG and MG (= APG). As I made clear, however, none of the possible performance distortions of comparative complexities – such as TCA or even, conceivably, TVDDI – can be ignored; indeed, some discrepancies will be wholly or
partially mitigated by taking such distortions into account.

Since the LG/performance discrepancies are, by CH_{APG}, asserted to occur
chiefly between LG and MG, the new hypothesis must, to be complete, include
an account of how the APG can be one thing and the LG something else, where
both are correct. The main outlines of that account have already been indicated:
the LG must include the linguistic content (such as the [x, y] generalizations) of
both MG (= APG) *and* the archival competence faculty. But the details of this
proposal – hence its confirmation – very much remain to be worked out.

The contention between CH_{CG} and CH_{APG}, as I hope is clear, is no mere
terminological issue. The two hypotheses propound quite different notions
about the nature of the MG, about the nature of the relation between MG and
LG, and about an important aspect of the ontogeny of the rules being integrated
into the MG. These, surely, are the most serious issues confronting present-day
psycholinguistics.

2.   THE STRONG INCLUSION HYPOTHESIS

2.0. The question to be raised below is, briefly, this: To what degree is the observer entitled to assume, of a "well-formed English sentence" emitted by a
child, that that sentence is assigned by the child's mental grammar the structure

(the derivation) assigned the same sentence by the adult mental grammar? I resume use of the term "mental grammar" (MG) to avoid argument over whether this device is a CG or an APG; but I note in passing that, under the CG hypothesis, the question at hand has the following form: to what degree is the observer entitled to assume that a child's "well-formed English sentence" is assigned by the child's CG the structure (derivation) assigned the same sentence by the LG, the grammar of English constructed by linguists? Because our question is quite divorced from both CG or APG hypotheses (or so I will maintain here), I will generally develop this section as if the CG were the MG at issue, chiefly because this tactic permits appeal to familiar examples from the linguistic literature. Where it seems advisable, I will insert tentative comments on the possible effect of a substitution of APG for CG.

Ignoring the APG for the moment, then, and thus feigning belief in the proposition that the (idealized) adult MG is in some sense (perhaps the "axiomatic" sense) the linguistic grammar, we broaden our basic question and restate it in this way: is the child's (idealized) MG "strongly included" in the adult's (idealized) MG?

To many, the meaning of "strong inclusion" will be plain from the term and the context; but an informal definition will render that meaning more explicit. We first quote, for a similar set of properties, an informal definition from Chomsky and Miller (1963, p. 197): "Two grammars will be called *weakly equivalent* if they generate the same language [set of strings]; they will be called *strongly equivalent* if they generate the same set of structural descriptions." Each such structural description is of a string; thus, "strong equivalence" is also expressible as holding for two grammars if they generate the same set of strings-with-structural-description. Let us, following Katz and Postal (1964, pp. 24-26), single out the notion "string with one structural description" — that is, "unambiguously derived string" — and let us term anything answering that description "a sentence." (Thus our "sentence" is identical to Katz and Postal's "sentoid" [ibid.].) So every "sentence" is unambiguous. (And what is called an "ambiguous sentence" in conventional terminology would for us be a "set of homonymous sentences.") So, finally, two grammars may (at first) be called *weakly equivalent* if they generate the same set of strings, and *strongly equivalent* if they generate the same set of sentences. A language such as English, or such as the English subsets controlled by children, can be regarded as a set of strings (sentential surfaces) or as a set of sentences (strings with structural derivations). Since it is natural to apply Chomsky and Miller's terms to languages as well as to their grammars, we derive the following statement: two languages will be termed *weakly equivalent* if they contain the same strings (are *stringwise* identical), and *strongly equivalent* if they contain the same sentences.

We adopt the abbreviation "p-inclusion" for "proper inclusion." We now state the meaning of the term "strong inclusion": One language will be said to be *weakly p-included* in another language if all its strings are p-included, and *strongly p-included* if all its *sentences* are p-included. The strong and weak p-inclusion of grammars, as distinct from languages, is defined analogously.

The "Strong Inclusion Hypothesis" (hereafter, SIH) can be simply described as holding that, if a language is weakly p-included in another language, then it is also *strongly* p-included. Thus, according to the SIH, the set of well-formed strings generated by a child (whether or not the child's MG also generates some ill-formed strings) is strongly p-included in the language generated by an adult's MG, hence (unless the APG hypothesis is adopted) is strongly p-included in the set of sentences constituting the English language. Or, in particular, since any one string constitutes a (one-member) set of the kind in question, every well-formed string produced by a child must be assumed to be assigned, by that child's MG, the structural description, or derivation, assigned that string by the adult's MG, hence by the CG hypothesis by the grammar of English.

2.1. As we see immediately, these notions of "strong" and "weak" p-inclusion are overly simplified, for there are several ways in which a set of sentences can be p-included in English in one way but not p-included in another. A sentence may exhibit:

(i)   *Stringwise well-formedness.* The sentence is weakly p-included in English.
(ii) *Surface-structural well-formedness.* A sentence that is weakly p-included in English may be:
    (a)   A parroting;
    (b)   A quasi-holophrase;[50] or
    (c)   A sentence with an orthodox constituent structure, which may be:
        (c')   an incorrect surface structure, or
        (c")   the correct surface structure, in which case the sentence is *strongly,* as well as weakly, p-included.
(iii) *Deep-structural well-formedness.* A sentence may have:
    (d)   No deep structure — for example, a parroting; or
    (e)   A deep structure, which may be:
        (e')   incorrect or
        (e")   correct (the sentence is *"deeply* p-included").
(iv) *Derivational well-formedness.* If the sentence is of both surface-structural and deep-structural well-formedness — if it is both "strongly" and "deeply"

[50]We define and discuss these terms in n.52, below.

p-included — then it will have transformationally derived its correct surface from its correct base through a transformational path which is:

(f')   an aberrant path, or

(f")   the correct one; in which case we will say that the sentence is *maximally* p-included. (NB that *maximal* p-inclusion entails *strong* and *deep* p-inclusion.)

The Strong Inclusion Hypothesis, stated too simply above, now breaks down into these hypotheses:

SIH_1: If a language (set of sentences) L_1 is *stringwise* (weakly) p-included in another language L_2, then L_1 is *surface-structurally* p-included in L_2 (L_1 is *strongly p-included*).

SIH_2: If a language L_1 is *surface-structurally* p-included in L_2, then L_1 is deep-structurally (*"deeply"*) p-included in L_2.

SIH_3: If a language L_1 is *surface-structurally* and *deeply* p-included in L_2, then L_1 is *maximally* p-included.

SIH_4: If a language L_1 is *weakly* (stringwise) p-included in L_2, then L_1 is *maximally* (surface and deep-structurally and derivationally) p-included.[51]

Clearly the SIH version of greatest utility, were it only valid, is SIH_4, since SIH_4 hypothesizes that any sentence that has the *appearance* of being in every sense a correct English sentence, *is* one in every sense. IF SIH_4 were upheld, then whenever a child emitted a stringwise-well-formed sentence he would necessarily have emitted a completely well-formed English sentence; whereas if SIH_4 fell, but, say, the weaker SIH_1 were upheld, then all that could be decided, of a stringwise-well-formed utterance, would be that that utterance had the correct surface structure.

2.2.   The four Inclusion Hypotheses need only be stated to be put into doubt, as it seems to me, for it is perfectly clear that all of them can be disconfirmed by counterexamples.

2.2.1. On formal grounds:

(i) SIH_1 is disconfirmed because there are sentences stringwise-identical but surface-structurally dissimilar, so a sentence may be stringwise identical with some English string (hence weakly p-included in English), but not strongly identical (hence not strongly p-included). A "parroting" or a quasi-holophrase is

---

[51] For completeness, we ought to list such further inclusion hypotheses as:

SIH_5. If a language L_1 is *stringwise* (weakly) p-included in another L_2, then L_1 is *deeply* p-included; and so on. But the range of plausible inclusion hypotheses seems to be covered by $SIH_1 - SIH_4$, and so the others, though formally on a par with those, will be ignored here.

such a string;[52] elsewhere, weak identity without strong identity produces one kind of ambiguity; such as "They are flying planes," whose surface structure is either something like "NP − are+flying − planes," or else something like "NP − are − flying + planes."

[52] A "parroting" is a sentence emitted by a child in direct imitation of a sentence just heard; such an emission, which need signify nothing whatever about the child's MG (compare the adult's imitation or burlesque of a phrase in an unknown foreign language, as in, for example, "Have you seen Slava Domnulu's new opera *Acest om nu ştie nimica*?") has long been recognized by students of developmental psycholinguistics as an obvious counterexample to any hypothesis like the one under view. (However, McNeill asserts [1966, pp. 68f.], on the basis of a finding of Ervin-Tripp [Ervin, 1964], that children may not imitate forms their MG's do not already generate, in which case, of course, "parrotings" would *not* fail of strong p-inclusion. For a contrary view, cf. Turner and Rommetveit, 1967*b*, pp. 654ff.)

A "quasi-holophrase" is a sentence or sentence part that contains, as an unanalyzed lump, a string that in the English LG is broken up into a sequence of distinguished segments (Hiž, 1961, pp. 44f.) − essentially, of morphemes. A quasi-holophrase contains at least one distinguished segment, however, and so fails to be a complete holophrase; this seems to be true in the case cited by Brown and Hanlon (this volume, p. 000): the "you" segment of "D'you. . .," as Brown and Hanlon point out, is certainly a distinguished segment.

For another instance, the subject I call Language Acquisition Device #6 made extensive use at the age of 3.1 of the form "Would you mind. . ." (doing, getting, putting on, and the like). All of his sentences containing "would you mind. . ." were, stringwise, quite grammatical, and they were used under, and only under, the right circumstances. But his understanding of this phrase was incomplete. If, in signifying compliance with his request, one said "No," meaning "No, I wouldn't mind. . .," then he showed disappointment, for his grammar demanded "Yes" as the affirmative reply. Superficially, his MG could have contained either of two mistaken notions: (1) the word "mind" was misunderstood as its antonym, thus replacing an antonymous V able to occur, with the intended meaning, in the phrase "would you____doing. . ."; or (2) the entire phrase "would you mind" was underparsed, with "mind," in all probability, going completely unanalyzed. Now, (1) insists that LAD #6 substitute "mind" for one of these verbs: "favor," "sanction," "indorse," "countenance," or the like; none of these V are in common use in LAD #6's household, and I think the likelihood of his having the antonym of "mind" as an inferred (or universal/innate) semantic concept, is remote. Then (2) is the more reasonable explanation, and "would you mind. . ." was a quasi-holophrase.

(The upshot of numerous disappointing responses to his use of the locution was that LAD #6 despaired of his respondents' obduracy, and at 3.3 relinquished the expression.)

To avoid possible confusion it should be pointed out that the term "holophrase" has been used in two completely different (but related) senses. Commonly (for example, here, and in Lenneberg, 1953) the term is applied to cases where a string that could be analyzed (*is* analyzed in the LG) is apparently used as if a single morpheme; examples are "all right," "everybody," "scarecrow." The second use appears in McNeill (1966), who applies the term (pp. 63f.) to cases where a single word is used to stand for an entire phrase or sentence, as where the utterance "Milk" can mean, for a one-year-old, " 'I want some milk,' 'The milk is on the floor,' 'Don't give me any more milk; I want Pablum,' etc."

(ii)   SIH$_2$ is disconfirmed because there are sentences surface-structurally identical but basally (deep-structurally) dissimilar; for example, the two sentences of the form "The cops must stop drinking by midnight," which have surface structures something like "NP − must − stop − drinking − adverb" but which have one of these two deep structures, approximately: "NP − must − stop − themselves − from − drinking − adverb" or "NP − must − stop − (unspecified human-NP) [for example, "everybody"] − from − drinking − adverb."

(iii)   SIH$_3$ is disconfirmed because it is certainly possible for a sentence to be *structurally* and *deeply* p-included in English, but yet not *derivationally* p-included; it would have the right surface and the right deep structure, but would have derived the latter from the former in the wrong way. Suppose that both in the LG of English and in some aberrant, weakly p-included APG, the deep structure of the truncated passive were something like:

$$[_S \; [_{NP} \; {}^\Delta]_{NP} \; [_{VP} V \; {}^{NP}]_{VP} \;]_S$$

And suppose that the surface in both LG and weakly p-included APG is NP − be+tense − participle. Deep and surface structures are identical, but LG and APG can still differ by having different transformational paths. For example, in *this* APG, deletion + special-passivization: a vacuous-deep-subject-deletion transformation, which transforms the above deep structure to:

$$[_S \; [_{VP} \; V \; {}^{NP}]_{VP} \;]_S$$

− plus an obligatory passivization transformation that would attack any structure of this form. As against, in the LG, passivization + deletion: a transformation that passivizes normally (yielding a conventional "Gladys was deflowered by Δ" sort of structure) and a transformation that then deletes the "by+Δ" phrase.

In sum, on the basis considered, there is no warrant for *any* of the Strong Inclusion Hypotheses.

2.2.2.   However, it might still be maintained that there is a specifically *natural-language* basis for one or more of the SIH; it might be maintained that one or another SIH applies whenever both including and included sentence sets are "languages" in the same sense. Of course the defender of any such thesis would be obliged to admit immediately that the notion "natural language" is utterly ill-defined, necessarily so for the present; perhaps he could provide a rough idea of what he meant by stipulating that a "natural language" L must have a grammar G that is obviously "economical" in the "competence" or LG sense; but even so, this would be a necessary but not sufficient condition, since many sentence sets, while "economically" describable, are too small to be a natural language; or they might lack attributes of which we are entirely ignorant. The only way of being sure that it is a "natural language" that is at issue is to provide the notion with a sort of *ostensive* definition (Kotarbinska, 1960; Grice, 1968, p. 240) and then to restrict oneself to the appropriate ostensions (examples). So let us take, as our including L_2, that ill-defined sentence set "English";[53] and as our weakly p-included L_1, let us take what appears to be a dialect of English — that dialect in which transitive-verb sentences can be passivized ("That '37 Hudson Terraplane *was bought by* a born sucker") but in which passivizations of locative verbs ("That chair *was sat in by* Dr. Psoriasis as he chuckled over the misdeeds of the locative verbs") are either disallowed completely or else, no less exigently, consistently labeled as much less natural. English, we will assume, is the broader dialect in which both passivizations are altogether grammatical.

We assume that the grammar G of L_1 and the grammar G of L_2 are both highly valued by (intuitively understood) LG criteria of simplicity; this means no more, in actuality, than that neither $G(L_1)$ nor $G(L_2)$ will fail to realize obvious generalizations or to achieve obvious reductions in the number and/or complexity of rules.

Rather than trying to disconfirm, one by one, a "natural-language" defense of each of the SIH, let us see whether we cannot show, on "natural-language" grounds, that *at least one* of the SIH must be false.

We assume, in the absence of any discernible reason to the contrary, that L_1 is weakly and structurally p-included in L_2, so that the passivized transitives and the *un*passivized locatives ("Dr. Psoriasis sat in that chair. . .") have the same respective surface structures in L_1 and L_2. Now we ask if, from that fact and the fact of the status of L_1 and L_2 as "natural languages," we can infer (a) that they have the same deep structure, and (b) that their surfaces are derived via the same transformations. We make the elementary observation that an optimal $G(L_2)$ will derive passivized transitives and passivized locatives via the same passivizing transformation; that transformation, in $G(L_2)$, will be general enough to attack either sort of verb. But in $G(L_1)$, which cannot passivize locatives, the

[53]That English is a language is not so self-explanatory an assumption as it might seem. It is easy to find statements to the effect that a natural language can include phenomena not amenable to the sort of generalization found generally in the grammar of that language (Harris, 1951, pp. 346f.; Chomsky, 1962, p. 543, n. 28; Valdman, 1968, p. 125). Even such large paradigms as the benefactive-object passive might fall under this heading. Nevertheless, the existence of these exceptional phenomena does not affect our definition of the notion "natural language," since that definition is ostensive. (It must be noted, incidentally, that this ostensive definition is not a conventional one, in that, though we can point to many *parts* of the illustrative object — that is, English sentences — we cannot ever actually point to the object itself, the English language, except in the peculiar sense of pointing to a device [an MG, ideally] capable of enumerating all the parts of the object. But this appeal to the notion of ostensive definition seems strained to so slight an extent that, in view of its possible clarificatory function, I have let it stand.)

application of the passivizing transformation must be more restricted. Either in $G(L_1)$, the transitives and locatives have the same deep structures as they do in $G(L_2)$, but the passivizing transformation in $G(L_1)$ refers specifically to the verb's transitiveness [a reference absent from $G(L_2)$] ; or else in $G(L_1)$ the passivizing transformation has the same form as it does in $G(L_2)$, but is prevented from attacking the locatives because, in $G(L_1)$, the locatives have a non-passivizable deep structure [hence a Deep Structure different from the one they have in $G(L_2)$]. Then $G(L_1)$ either has a passivizing transformation different from that of $G(L_2)$, or has a locative deep structure different from that of $G(L_2)$; and so either SIH_3 or SIH_2 has been disconfirmed (on "natural-language" grounds), and, in any case, SIH_4 has been disconfirmed.[54]

[54] A further word on the locative verbs. It was maintained by Chomsky (1965, pp. 104-106, partly revising an earlier treatment) that verbs like these, though "intransitive," when co-occurring with a V-complement (but not with a VP-complement), may be passivized by the ordinary passive transformation, because in Chomsky's 1965 formulation the passivization transformation specifies, not that the verb be transitive with a direct object in its complement, but only that the verb be followed, in its complement, by both an NP and a manner adverbial instantiated as "by+*passive*." This rule, which has V-Locative passivization as a desirable by-product, was created to account "...automatically," in Chomsky's words, "for the restriction of passivization to verbs that take manner adverbials freely." The underlying assumption was, apparently, that the "by NP" phrase of the passive is a manner adverbial, so that if a V could take such an adverbial in the passive, it ought to be able to take other such adverbials in the active.

Lakoff, however, has shown (1965, Appendix, F, pp. 1-3) that there is a class of verbs – the "Stative" verbs like "know," "believe," "see," and "hear" – that do not occur "freely" with ordinary manner adverbials but that, nevertheless, freely passivize, as in "That Vieuvathit is Luxembourg's greatest composer *is believed by* all Andorrans." We note that the "Locative" verbs also do not occur freely with manner adverbials. In fact, "sleep in" seems to me to occur no more freely with such adverbials than does "sleep" itself, which was for a long time used by Chomsky, in the familiar "Colorless green ideas sleep furiously," to *illustrate* (among other like facts) that such verbs do not co-occur with such adverbials. Nor can either Lakoff's observation on the "statives" nor mine on the 'locatives' be palliated by Chomsky's statement (1965, p. 218, n. 28) that "...the generalization that relates manner adverbials to passivization...[is not] invalidated by the fact that certain items must be listed, in the lexicon, as conflicting with this generalization...." For in both cases it appears that the verbs in question are, *as a class,* unable to occur "freely" with manner adverbials. Thus to list in the lexicon, individually, each such verb as being "deficient" in this regard, would be (exactly in the sense endorsed by Chomsky) to miss a generalization.

In addition, Lakoff has also shown (ibid., *passim*) that adverbs do not occur as such in the deep structure at all, typically, hence cannot be available in the deep structure in the way Chomsky described them (though they might still be correctly sited *through prior transformation* to cue passivization). However, this fact is almost irrelevant in view of the facts presented above and their inescapable consequence; if the passive's "by NP" phrase is indeed a manner adverbial, it is of an entirely different type from the ordinary adverbs like "furiously," "mechanically," "briskly," or the like. So cueing passivization by the presence

Since both SIH_4 and either SIH_2 or SIH_3 are shown to have no "natural-language" basis, clearly there is *in general* no natural-language basis for the set of SIH, and one is not encouraged to expect that a natural-language basis for one of the other SIH (say, SIH_1) will be forthcoming.

2.3. We have disconfirmed all of the SIH on general counterexamples, and have disconfirmed some (and by extrapolation, all) of the SIH on specifically "natural-language" counterexamples. We now briefly take up the appropriate *contrary* hypotheses, discounting just the strongest of these — "If a natural language L_1 is weakly p-included in a natural language L_2, then L_1 is NOT *maximally* p-included in L_2" — and letting the rest fall by inference. We will do this by showing that an L_1 can be a natural language (someone's dialect) and yet be maximally p-included in an L_2 (another dialect). This in fact can be granted immediately on trivial examples; for instance, English less one word ("inconcinnous") or some one aphorism ("The more the merrier") is, clearly, a natural language that could be the L_1 of some speaker; and clearly this L_1 could be maximally p-included in English. But English itself, standardly speaking, can be maximally p-included in a dialect that includes all of English *plus* some peculiar outgrowth of its own. General American English has sentences like (1) "Your transmission needs fixing" and (2) "Your transmission needs to be fixed," but none like (3) "Your transmission needs fixed." But (3) is common in the Pittsburgh and general Western Pennsylvania dialect, and some Pittsburgh speakers (of an "inclusive" dialect) have all three sentence types, seemingly with equal grammaticality. Their G differs from English, presumably, not in surrogating any English rule or structure with another rule or structure, but only in *supplementing* the English G with an optional rule for deleting "to be" from (2); hence the L_1 English is maximally p-included in the L_2 "inclusive" Pittsburgh dialect, and the contrary hypotheses are overturned.

2.4. As we have seen with the quasi-holophrases and, perhaps, the "parrotings," it has always been clear that in at least these few aberrant cases a child's superficially well-formed sentence might, covertly, be not well-formed at all; that a sentence might be weakly p-included in English but not p-included in any deeper way. (This limited observation holds equally, of course, for LG and APG alike.) But, as we have also seen, the *general* case for the deeper p-inclusions has no *a priori* warrant whatever. This fact seems only twice to have been brought out into the open, but, even so, there is manifest in the psycholinguistic literature a growing (if tacit) awareness of the dubiety of the deeper inclusion hypotheses as

of a manner adverbial is not a good idea in any case.

     This leaves the account of V-locative passivization still open. Lakoff and Ross (1966, p. 7) have suggested that perhaps "remain in" (for example) is a transitive verb, taking NP as its object. However, a passive sentence with "remain in" had earlier been labeled by Lakoff (1965, Appendix, F, p. 13) as ungrammatical, so that it is not clear that this Lakoff-Ross suggestion is meant to provide a means of V-locative passivization.

they apply to children's language. Thus, for example, Brown and Fraser (1964, p. 71) specifically defend a Strong Inclusion Hypothesis; but Brown and Hanlon (this volume, pp. 14-17) take pains to show that the (LG) analyses that they assign children's stringwise well-formed sentences are defensible on the basis of a demonstrated consistency with the rest of the children's language. Thus the present discussion does not appear in a climate of wholesale (but tacit) acceptance of the inclusion hypotheses (and, as we mentioned at the outset, it is not our main purpose to overturn them, though clarifying the degree to which they are in doubt is a necessary step toward our goal of exhibiting the consequences of the hypotheses' downfall).

As was said just above, the inclusion hypotheses (to generalize them, vaguely, as a set) have been specifically discounted twice in the literature, though without being specifically formulated; I refer to the rejections of Chomsky and McNeill. Chomsky, for his part, has made comments (1965, p. 202, n. 19; 1967*b*, pp. 86f.) to the effect that a child's superficially well-formed sentences, in the early stages of acquisition, need not be underlain by the same deep structures as underlie them in the speech of an adult; that is, to particularize, Chomsky has in effect denied SIH_2, hence SIH_4 as well. McNeill (1966, pp. 55f.) reaffirms the rejection of Hypotheses 2 and 4, pointing out that such a child-sentence as "I don't see you", for example, probably does not have the transformational or deep structure history that it has in the LG (or in the adult MG). (For future ease of reference, let us tag this the "Chomsky-McNeill Null Hypothesis.") McNeill also (in effect) states another null hypothesis which counters the SIH from another (and, on the surface, contradictory) direction; he holds that at the earlier stages a child's sentence (whether or not superficially well-formed) is generally *a pronunciation of the deep structure* — the result of applying the phonological rules directly to the sentence's deep structure with no intervention of transformations and so no (distinct) surface structure at all (McNeill, pp. 54-65). If McNeill's Null Hypothesis should prove valid, then at this early stage, when such a deep-structure pronunciation resulted in a stringwise well-formed sentence, SIH_2 alone would be upheld, though vacuously, accompanied by the fall of SIH_3, SIH_4, and (presumably) even SIH_1. Since in fact McNeill's Null Hypothesis seems quite plausible, having been ably defended by its author, and since by allowing deep structures an ontogenetic development we can make the two null hypotheses mutually compatible, it seems that the literature already contains statements interpretable as holding that at one stage or another a child's speech disconfirms every one of the inclusion hypotheses, without exception.

2.5. If, however, the Strong Inclusion Hypotheses fail in the case in which all of a child's utterances (when normalized, of course, to MG sentences) are stringwise well-formed, how much greater and more certain must be their failure when only *some* of a child's utterances have well-formed surfaces. For in such a case the whole of the child's "language" cannot possibly be p-included (even weakly) in English; all "natural-language" basis for an individual sentence's deeper inclusion is therefore forfeit, and the formal bases of the inclusion hypotheses can now be dismissed out of hand.[55]

2.6. Above, we have seen that the set of stronger inclusion hypotheses fails on both general (2.2.1.) and natural-language (2.2.2.) grounds, so that in a young child's speech a superficially well-formed sentence may be assigned by the child's MG, covertly, a deeper analysis completely at variance with that assigned it by the English LG and/or the adult MG. But we have also seen that, even in the speech of a child who controls rather little of English, it cannot be assumed that every sentence *will* be covertly misanalyzed, since, though the stronger inclusion hypotheses fail, so also (2.3.) do the corresponding contrary hypotheses. We have noted (2.4.) that failure of stronger p-inclusion has long been acknowledged in the case of the distinctively childish quasi-holophrases and, though now doubtfully, in the case of "parroting"; and we have noted that, perhaps partly due to what I have termed the Chomsky-McNeill and McNeill Null Hypotheses, faith in the stronger p-inclusion hypotheses is now on the wane. Finally, we noted (2.5.) that if some covert misanalyses could be expected even when all of a child's sentences were superficially well-formed (weakly p-included), this could be expected all the more, of a superficially well-formed sentence, when the child's set of generated weakly p-included sentences comprised only a subset of the set of his generated sentences.

We have thus covered one way in which a child's generations may be misleading; but there is, of course, another side of the coin; certainly the young child generates sentences which are not even weakly p-included in English but

----

[55]I assume that no one could adhere to the notion that a child's partial set of stringwise well-formed sentences forms a language in its own right, hence a set of sentences subject to whatever tenuous support the "natural-language" basis can lend to the inclusion hypotheses. To assume this, one would have to assume that the child's language L_1 in fact consists of two sublanguages, $+L_1$ and $*L_1$, containing the well-formed and ill-formed sentences respectively, and that the child's MG in fact consists of two subgrammars, $G(+L_1)$ and $G(*L_1)$ respectively. But this notion is, clearly, preposterous. If a child says "I fixed up it," it is not because he has a special grammar, $G(*L_1)$, devoted to generations of this sort, but because he has a defective $G(L_1)$, one which incorrectly fails to distinguish those NP that can follow Verb+remora (e.g. "fixed+up") from those — e.g. "it" — that cannot. (If it should be maintained that a child in his very earliest stages generates each sentence by a rule idiosyncratic to that one sentence, thus in a way having as many [one-rule] "grammars" as he can generate sentences, we could still avoid the quibble over whether such devices are indeed "grammars" by pointing out that we are not concerned with such cases in the the present instance, since at so early a stage the child will scarcely emit any stringwise well-formed sentences at all.)

which are nonetheless *maximally* p-included in the child's own MG. (And, to generalize and "idealize," in the MG of the English-speaking child at the stage in question.) We have already noted one such case; for when the child generates "I fixed up it" he generates a sentence which is not weakly p-included in English but which is, by definition, maximally p-included in the child's MG; and any sentence generated by the child's MG yet not (at some level) identically generated by the English LG, falls into a similar class. In fact, the case in which a child's generation *is* weakly p-included in English but not p-included in English at some deeper level (thus violating one or another of the stronger inclusion hypotheses) is only a special case, as we see, of a more general phenomenon found in the speech of the younger child: generations that are maximally p-included in the child's MG but not maximally p-included in the English LG.[56] Thus, while generations from the child's MG that are stringwise well-formed may be misleading in one way (inducing the unwary to assume them well-formed on *all* levels), on the other hand the child's generations that are *not* stringwise well-formed are misleading in a quite different way, since their utter lack of superficial well-formedness with respect to English disguises a *total* well-formedness with respect to the child's own MG.

Naturally this sort of deceptiveness is (in the context of the discussion thus far) quite without importance, since "well-formedness with respect to the child's own MG" can simply be assumed, just because the sentence was in fact generated by the child; that is, it is maximally p-included in the child's MG by definition. A veneer of LG stringwise-well-formedness may be a trifle misleading because from it one might infer LG *maximal* well-formedness; but if a sentence is stringwise *ill*-formed, then it is also surface-structurally and transformationally ill-formed and it is probably also deep-structurally ill-formed: its overt ill-formedness cannot hide a thoroughgoing covert well-formedness, and since its maximal p-inclusion in the child's MG is "guaranteed" anyway (as see just above), its LG-ill-formedness cannot deceive us on this score either. Nothing about a sentence can lead us to falsely infer that it was generated by the child's MG, in the present context, since it either was or wasn't; superficial ill-formedness is always underlain by at least partial deeper ill-formedness; and so the most deceptive cases are still those we considered first, those where superficial LG-*well*-formedness in child productions covers their deeper LG-*ill*-formedness.

[56]Our use of the phrase "maximally p-included in the child's MG" must, of course, include the vacuous cases when a "maximally p-included" sentence has no deep structure (as distinct from surface structure) at all.

We want now to change our angle of attack slightly, and to do this with greater clarity we want to condense to its rudiments that part of the preceding discussion that concerns p-inclusion in LG and in the child's MG. We see that a given string, surface structure, deep structure, or transformational path can be well-formed in the English LG or the child's MG — let us tag these conditions "E" and "C" respectively — or ill-formed in one or the other: "*E" or "*C," let us say. Joining these conditions, we say that a string (or surface structure, and so on) may be well-formed in both LG and child's MG, in one or the other, or in neither; that is, may have the set of properties (E, C); (E, *C) or (*E, C); or (*E, *C). The sentence sets thus defined are represented diagrammatically in Figure 5.5. One's reading of the diagram is much simplified, of course, if one considers string, surface- and deep-surface, and transformational path all together, ignoring the fact that a given sentence may be, say, (*E, C) as a string but (E, C) as a deep structure. That is, we can concentrate on maximal p-inclusion alone, and then "a sentence" — at every level — would be uniquely assigned to one of the four sentence sets of Figure 5.5. In this case, where we assume that covert ill-formedness is detected and tagged as *E and where emission by a child assures the tag C, assignment of "a sentence" to one of the four sets is quite mechanical.

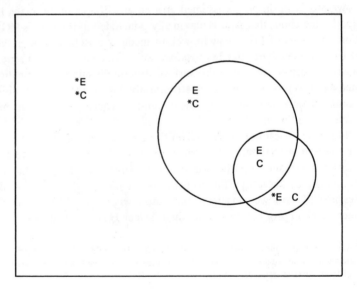

Figure 5.5.

2.7. It is hardly necessary to add, however, that in actual practice the assignment of a child's sentence to either (E, C) or (*E, C) is not mechanical at all; any such assignment, as we have noted, presupposes that the sentence has been generated by (and so is maximally p-included in) his MG, and of course this presupposition has no *a priori* warrant whatsoever. A child's having produced a sentence is no assurance that his MG generates it, since between what his MG generates and what he produced the child's performative mechanism may have intervened in such a way as to distort the generation, producing an utterance not identical with the underlying MG-generation and so misrepresentative of it. In fact, that such distortions are common occurrences is widely acknowledged by developmental psycholinguists. It is well known that the young child's ability to comprehend surpasses his ability to produce (his grasp exceeds his reach), and the most natural way of explaining this fact is to assume that his MG generates all that he can comprehend, but that in trying to gain access to that MG for composition his performative limitations intervene and limit his output (Fraser, Bellugi, and Brown, 1963; McNeill, 1966, pp. 76-82; and see section 1.2.2.3, above). One example of the consequence of such limitations is, possibly, the so-called "telegraphic speech" to be observed in the speech of young children: as Chomsky has conjectured (1967*b*, p. 88), it may be that "telegraphic" sentences (they omit material somewhat in the manner of a telegram) owe their deviant surface forms partly to the intervention of a defective performative mechanism which (chiefly because of specific memory limitations) is unable to pass through to the surface the full complexity of what the mechanism can compose by gaining access to the MG, with the result that the performative mechanism acts as a "filtering device" that "operates on deep structures in some non-normal fashion" so as to produce the "telegraphic" result.[57]

Even if there were no plausibility to this argument at all, however, one would manifestly have no reason to assume that the speech-productions of young children are completely undistorted replicas of compositions based on the child's MG. Such, certainly, is not the case with adults, whose speech is full of errors and distortions of all kinds (see n. 3, above); there is scarcely a sentence in an adult's casual speech that is not refracted by performative factors, down to and including cases where, plainly, the speaker has completely lost track of where in the sentence he is, and either trails off or veers in the wrong direction.[58] It is

[57]McNeill (1966, pp. 18f.), however, argues at one point, though a bit ambiguously, that "telegraphic speech" results, not from the interposition of a defective performative mechanism, but entirely from defects in the accessed MG. It would, of course, be quite possible for a defective MG and a defective performance mechanism to work in consort, yielding jointly deformities which neither would yield alone.

[58]The very common "whom...is" ("whom" as subject) sentences are of this sort; for example [italics supplied], "Can a 40-year-old double divorcee find love and happiness married

entirely reasonable to expect that children also have MG whose generations, when accessed by the compositional performative device and then performed as speech, become garbled; and probably in the earlier stages, as plausibly in the case of "telegraphic speech," garbled in ways peculiar to the speech of children. What this means is that some of the sentences that a child produces are not generated by his MG at all — they are only refractions of such generations, and only the (recovered) generations themselves are properly labeled C; the refractions are properly left outside the (C, *C) set of categories altogether.

Thus, where in preceding sections we observed that a child-produced sentence might have covert irregularities, being therefore covertly (*E) rather than (E), now we see that a child-produced sentence may covertly be (*C) rather than (C).

Moreover, this potential of a covert *C status obtains both for *E and for E items; and both for outputs that are not English and for outputs that are. For we have no real reason to suppose that the interposition of performative error results inevitably in the production of non-English — of *E sentences — since it is in theory perfectly possible for performative error to produce the appearance of a full-fledged English sentence. And this is possible, moreover, whether the MG's generation was (E, C) or (*E, C), since performative error could in theory either distort one well-formed English sentence into the outward form of another — as in the first case — or, as in the second case, distort an ill-formed (*E, C) sentence into the outward form of some *well*-formed sentence — whether (E, C) or, quite deceptively, (E, *C). *Neither possibility is in the least far-fetched.* Certainly cases of the performative distortion of one sentence into another sentence (from the MG-generated sentence into a sentence other than the one intended) can actually be observed in the productions of adults. Thus we find this sentence addressed to "Dear Abby": "I would like your opinion, which I respect highly."[59] It is of course clear that the opinion the writer would like, and the opinion the writer already respects highly, cannot be the same opinion; the writer has constructed what we may call a "portmanteau sentence" by mistakenly merging two different (and differently-indexed) occurrences of the word "opinion."[60] But the result of the confusion is a sentence, nonetheless; or at least the appearance of one. (What the deep structure of this

to a 22-year-old boy *whom* everyone thinks *is* interested in her daughter?" — from an inquiry in *Playboy*, April 1969, 16, No. 4, p. 56.

[59]*The Pittsburgh Press*, October 10, 1968, p. 40. The comma is mine.

[60]Note also that, to be correct, the first "opinion" should be a count noun, the second a mass noun.

product might be is an open question.)[61] But then, if adults can hit upon the the semblance of a sentence through error, so can children. And, as to the second case, in which an ill-formed deep structure can be distorted into a well-formed sentence — this surely can happen also.[62] Thus on both counts it is to be expected that children, even more than adults, produce a set of sentences having in part only the most deceptive kind of relationship to the generations of the MG. And since these problems can arise unpredictably with any child-emitted sentence, they must be assumed possible with *every* such sentence; and so every sentence, if one is to be sure of its analysis and assignment, must be scrutinized rather closely.

We will take a brief look at such scrutiny in a moment; but first we should summarize all of the foregoing discussion as succinctly as possible. Pretending (for clarity's sake only) that the primary problem in treating a child's sentence is its proper categorization, we present such a summary in the decision-diagram of Figure 5.6.

It is, I think, obvious that the diagram of Figure 5.6 has two main divisions: that below the conclusion "C AT ALL LEVELS," in which all of the decisions about E and *E at all levels are perfectly straightforward; and that above the cited conclusion, where the decision as to C, *C, or "no assignment" is made. The latter division rather clearly constitutes a Gordian knot which can either be cut — by making the simplifying assumption that *of course* what a child says is generated by his MG — or else unraveled, through testing the sentence under examination to ascertain, as best one can, whether a judgment as to MG generation can be made. As we see, the most difficult and delicate decisions, almost undoubtedly, are those made at the outset of the diagram in answering the question "Generated by the child's MG?." Though this statement does not blunt the manifest difficulty of deciding (for example) whether the sentence, if stringwise and surface-structurally well-formed, is also deep-structurally and transformationally well-formed, hence maximally p-included — a question, again, better settled non-arbitrarily.

2.8. We have gotten far enough to have outlined some of the main problems involved in analyzing and categorizing child-uttered sentences and to have seen,

---

[61]We might suppose, however, that the deep structure is quite orthodox, bearing the correct complex symbols for both nouns associated with the D "opinion," and distinctively indexing them. But the rest of this distorted composition — the nature of its transformations and of its surface structure — is completely opaque.

[62]For example, a mistake near the surface might correct a deeper error of the sort that gives a plural verb to a singular noun; this kind of "corrective" error would seem reasonable to expect on the basis of the similar errors in the other direction, such as the error that, from a correct deeper structure, derives the incorrect "They think having a million dollars *make* them qualified for public office."

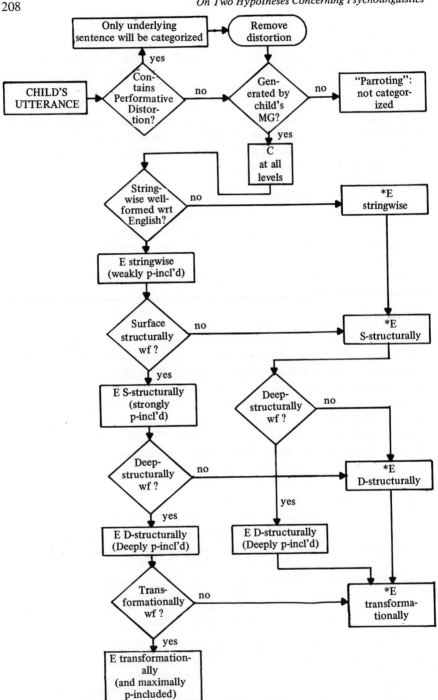

Figure 5.61. Decision-Diagram for Categorizing Child-Produced Sentences.

in brief, that there is great need for *methods* here: heuristics for aiding the determination of C or *C and of the well-formedness of sentential levels hidden from the ear. The developmental psycholinguist is willy-nilly a "field worker" in the old-fashioned sense of working systematically through a body of data and returning to his subjects to elicit further data. The introspection that is helpful or even essential (Postal, 1966*b*, pp. 92f.) for much of modern generative work is almost totally lacking when an adult analyzes the language of the child, since the adult no longer commands the language that the child commands and his knowledge of sentencehood and of meaning and connection of meaning – generally, his intuitions – are not serviceable to him; he is not a fluent speaker of the language under analysis.[63] And so the greatest single present need in this field is for a *Methods in Psycholinguistics.* The need for such a manual is all the greater in view of the fact that young children (whose language is most distant from our intuitions) are unusally recalcitrant interviewees. At the risk of repeating it once too often, we may cite here the engaging dialog reported by Brown and Bellugi (1964, p. 135):

Interviewer: Adam, which is right, "two shoes" or "two shoe"?

Adam: Pop goes the weasel!

It will not, however, surprise the reader to find that while we have come far enough to delineate this problem, we have no panaceas at hand. There is no manual and we cannot compile one now. Still, there are a few useful heuristics available, and I should like, in drawing toward a close, to invite attention to one or two of these in particular. They are to be found in Brown and Hanlon (this volume, pp. 14-17); these scholars have been unusually punctilious in giving their reasons for settling on specific analyses of child-produced sentences. (1) One Brown-Hanlon heuristic was used to determine whether a child who said "Me and Diandros are working" had an MG in which "me and Diandros" was (a) the superficial Subject and (b) plural in number. As they note, both (a) and (b) are supported by the "we" of the related produced sentence, "Me and Diandros are working, aren't we?". The use of "we" seems to refer to "me and Diandros" as one NP; the NP of the tag "...aren't *we*," for example, commonly refers directly to the superficial subject of the antecedant declarative ("*Me and Diandros* are working...") to which the tag is attached; and "we" is of course plural and inclusive of the speaker. (2) A similar heuristic was used to determine what the

---

[63]There are, perhaps, limited exceptions to this generalization. For example, McNeill (1966, pp. 37f.) reports that adults presented with two (paraphrastic) ill-formed childish sentences can judge which is further from English (hence, by implication, earlier-learned) in about four out of five cases.

MG under study had to say about the verb phrase and auxiliary. Since ". . .are working . . . " was tagged with "aren't . . . ", and " . . . made . . . " was tagged with "didn't. . .," Brown and Hanlon rightly infer that the MG that generates these correct tags probably embodies knowledge approximately to the effect that "n't" is attached to the first segment of the auxiliary, which is "are" in the first example and "did" in the second; and they further infer that the MG must know that the "do + tense" auxiliary corresponds to a "0" auxiliary accompanying "make + tense" in the sentence "I made a mistake, didn't I?"

These are, to reiterate, heuristics and not what Chomsky has called "discovery procedures" (1957, pp. 50-56); they are not litmus-paper tests to be applied mechanically. Thus, for example, the first heuristic will not always work because the "we" of an "aren't we?" tag need not refer to the superficial subject of the antecedent declarative or, indeed, to a single NP in the underlying deep structure; cf. "I'm working and Diandros is working, aren't we?" And the second heuristic involves appeal to a simplified notion of how tags relate to their antecedents — a notion which may be correct for fledgling MG's but which has not yet been shown to be so — for it is not the case that the form of the tag need have any simple relationship to the surface-form of the antecedent; witness, for example, "Let's go to the movies, shall we?" But I think Brown and Hanlon could well contend that these exceptions do not invalidate their heuristics; they only show areas of weakness that bear closer attention. It is in the nature of heuristics to fail once in a while, and it is no criticism of Brown and Hanlon's suggested heuristics to observe that they are obviously meant to permit only rough analyses.[64]

Thus, while the thoroughgoing uncertainties of dealing with the linguistic productions of children urge the development and formalization of as much method as possible, on the other hand what we could list at present would be only a small set of rather thin heuristics,[65] and it follows that, pending availability of deeper theoretical understanding and, equally, completion of the

[64]Brown and Hanlon's own description of their set of heuristics shows, I think, the proper mixture of confidence and caution: "We propose to treat the child's production of a construction, in quantity and over a good part of its proper range, together with evidence that he understands the construction when others use it, as *signs* [italics theirs] that he has the grammatical knowledge represented formally by the derivation of that construction in the adult grammar [the adult MG]."

[65]It must be noted that the heuristics in question are "thin" in a respect other than that discussed above — their not being foolproof — for their already-imperfect reliability declines steadily in proportion as contact with a sentence's surface is less informative about underlying structures. Thus, compositional command over a sentence and its related sentences, together with details observable on the surface, suffice to reassure the analyst that the sentence is stringwise and surface-structurally well-formed (or ill-formed); but

suggested *Methods* text, the uncertainties discussed above will continue in full force.

2.9. In conclusion, we have in this section on the stronger inclusion hypotheses established that none of these hypotheses has either formal or natural-language warrant, and we have observed (2.6) that, in addition, a child's sentence can be ill-formed with respect to the English LG at any level but still be, at the same level, well-formed with respect to the child's own MG. The dissociations between E and C, and *E and *C, we exhibited graphically in Figure 5.5. We have made special note (2.7) of the distinctive ways in which children's performances can disguise the true nature of their MG's generative capacity, to such an extent that, predictively, it is as great a problem to determine whether a given production betokens MG-generation of the string in question as it is (*given* that the sentence is at least stringwise well-formed with respect to the child's MG) to determine what structure the MG assigns that sentence at the levels beneath the surface. This discussion was summed up in the "decision diagram" of Figure 5.6. Having seen the logical consequences of the fall of the inclusion hypotheses, together with the nature of human linguistic performance (that of children in particular), we passed (2.8) to the *practical* consequences – namely, the need for more and better discovery heuristics to aid in analyzing these refractory data.

This brings us to the end of our two tasks of elucidating the unspoken assumptions that, so I have argued, underlie contemporary developmental psycholinguistics to a greater or lesser degree, and of setting forth the most essential details of what follows when those assumptions, revealed as groundless, are withdrawn. It remains to say that our treatment of these problems has not been exhaustive, and certainly there are other problems in this area that we have not

---

"understanding" is impossible to gauge with much accuracy when one cannot, as one can with adults, elicit paraphrase sets. Behavior is but an uncertain indication of understanding, as may be seen in the fact that two utterly dissimilar sentences can effect the same action: for example, "Please pass the ketchup" and "If you don't pass the ketchup I'll poison your coffee." (For comments on this problem in an experimental situation where it is much reduced, see Shipley, Smith, and Gleitman, 1967.) So a child's deep structures are more inaccessible than his surface structures; and his transformations (which, as we have seen, can be LG-ill-formed independently of both deep and surface structures) are still less accessible. With all of this I am sure Brown and Hanlon would agree, and my aim in mentioning these points has, again, only been to elucidate further the uncertainty they voice.

[*Postscript.* Since completing this paper I have learned of the availability of what seems to be the "Methods" text called for above: Slobin, D.I. (Ed.), *A Field Manual for Cross-Cultural Study of the Acquisition of Communicative Competence,* obtainable from the ASUC Store, University of California, Berkeley.]

even touched on;[66] here, as in linguistics as a whole, no one study much reduces the amount of work yet to be done.

3.   GENERAL CONCLUSION

In the two preceding chapters we have treated as separate problems the relationship between the adult MG and the LG of English (1), and the relationship between both LG and adult MG on the one hand and the child's MG on the other (2). Now, in conclusion, we pause very briefly to knit these two strands together. We see that we have been studying but two aspects of a single problem: the nature (broadly considered) of the human linguistic capacity — both MG and archival linguistic faculty — as this relates to the LG of English. In the first section we treated mainly of adult competence and performance, and in the second mainly of those of the child; but of course the MG that the child forms is the MG that he will have as an adult, and the two competences and performances are concomitantly close. If performative criteria of economy play a role in shaping the adult APG, as we have hypothesized, then they play that role by shaping the way in which the child's developing APG takes form. Indeed, there is no other way in which such criteria could have any influence.

This said, it seems proper to examine one sort of doubt concerning the most basic characteristic assumed of the adult MG: its status as a grammar. We know that the English LG must include some marginal peculiarities (see n. 53, above); but some MG's clearly betray peculiarities that are more central. This fact alone is not astonishing; there is no reason to assume that the gradual process of improving one's grammar, observable in the child, terminates in a grammar amenable to no further improvement. (No one has ever claimed that it does; in fact, I know of no one who has addressed himself to this question, with the partial exception of Halle, as seen just below). But, while suboptimalities do not

---

[66] As examples of questions that must eventually be taken up but which we have not touched on here, we might cite these three: (1) To what extent can a child's speech (MG) be influenced by an idiosyncratic family or parental dialect (if there is one), if such a dialect reduces the generality of the rules of English (by introducing special exceptions) and so impedes generalization? (2) To what extent can childish language-play like that reported by Weir (1962) become conscious with the child, producing, if not poetry, at least conscious linguistic play like that reported by Stene (1934) for adults? (I have never been able to find out whether the happy coinage "porculant" — said of the author by Language Acquisition Device #5 at 5.2 — was the product of accident or design.) And (3) to what extent is it accurate to think of a child's linguistic development as passing from one MG to another (larger and better) MG, thence to another, rather than as passing from one MG to a quasi-grammatical (hence unstable?) state, *thence* to a new MG?

run counter to what we "know" about acquisition, they might seem to run counter to what we "know" about *grammars* as such, depending on how extensively we expect grammars to obey competence criteria of economy. Let us, then, inspect a particular MG suboptimality and try to estimate its adverse effect on the MG's status as a grammar.

In fact, examples of general adult suboptimality are exceedingly easy to find, and we have one ready to hand. In 1.2.2.1, above, we considered the case of the benefactive objects of English, after Lakoff and Ross (1966); we observed that, while in the dialect they analyzed the benefactive object must not be within the verb phrase, in my own MG the benefactive object, just as clearly, *is* within the verb phrase. The criteria for establishing the structural locus of the benefactive object were two: the object is in the verb phrase if it can become the superficial subject after passivization and cannot be referred to in a "do so" construction; it is *outside* the verb phrase if it cannot become the passive's subject and can be referred to in a "do so" construction. As I made clear in the initial presentation, the facts in the matter seem quite unequivocal; in my own speech I can freely form benefactive-object passives with any number of different verbs ("buy," "obtain," "procure," "steal," "find," and many others); and on the other hand, the "do so" construction with the benefactive object is, to me, utterly ungrammatical. (To me, it has roughly the befuddling quality of Ross's [1966, p. 1] well-known "Relativization in extraposed clauses [is] a problem which evidence is presented that help is needed to solve.")[67] Presumably, the speakers on whom Lakoff and Ross based their contrary analysis were just as fixed in *their* MG. In short, given the facts, two rather different MG's must be postulated. Of course each can be considered to be, for its language, of optimum simplicity or economy.

But there are speakers who readily accept "John was bought a new Cord by his doting father," yet cannot accept such a passive with many other verbs: not with "obtain," not with "procure," and not with "steal" or "find." Such speakers, it is my experience, *do* find acceptable the, to me, forbidden "John's

[67]Naturally this is not the whole story. While it seems that any transitive V with benefactive object can, in my dialect, spawn a benefactive-object passive, nonetheless I would certainly avoid such a generation for any V that could take both a "to" indirect object and a "for" benefactive object, since in the case of the resultant ambiguity, my interpretation would so favor IO as to eclipse BO, unless something else in the sentence were disambiguating. Thus, "John peddled an old Chevy for me last week" and "John peddled an old Chevy to me last week" can both, according to my MG, be passivized to "I was peddled an old Chevy by John last week," but my interpretation of this passive would heavily favor an IO reading (the second given). It is, I suppose, possible that I would disambiguate in favor of BO rather than of IO if the remainder of the sentence leaned that way, as in, for example, "I was written a fine letter by my amanuensis last week." As is plain, the matter is far from exhausted.

father bought a new Cord for John in 1938 and will do so for Gertrude next Saturday." That is, they can passivize on the benefactive object with the common verb "buy" (and "make" and perhaps a few other verbs not cited here), but this ability has not affected their inability to form other passives on that sort of object or their ability to "do so" with such objects. Then clearly their MG's are inconsistent; they have a special rule for the (otherwise undistinguished) set ("make," "buy," . . .). This being so, it seems entirely appropriate to say that, by any likely criteria of economy, these MG's will be suboptimal, and this in a rather nonmarginal case: formation of the passive.

How does this happen? Quite speculatively, we might conjecture that while there is indeed a general tendency, as one acquires a language, to optimize the MG one is building,[68] on the other hand the acquisition process does not go

[68] It might seem that we have maintained a systematic ambiguity in these pages by speaking of the process of optimizing one's MG with regard both to coming up with the optimally economical account of the language (English) one is acquiring, and to optimizing one's MG *beyond* that point, instituting changes in English to conform with the more highly-valued MG thus formulated. But the ambiguity is only apparent, in my view: only at the very earliest stages (in fact, when there are no recursive rules in the MG) can it be said that an MG is being formulated so as to generate, with maximum simplicity, a language actually observed; the "ambiguity" disappears when we realize that the child's MG, at a relatively early stage, generates a set of sentences that ranges far beyond anything the child has actually heard. Thus, it seems quite reasonable to say that the child does indeed attempt to optimize his MG *and* have that MG generate what he "knows" to be in English. When these two goals conflict, as when English is suboptimal, then one of two things happens: (1) the fact that English is suboptimal is manifest, and the over-optimized grammar is adulterated to fit the facts; or (2) the fact that English is suboptimal is not manifest, and the over-optimized grammar is allowed to stand, with − if all speakers over-optimize − a consequent increase in the economy of the LG itself. As an example of (1), we may take the fact that children invariably overgeneralize (overoptimize) their rule for forming the past and past participles of English "strong" verbs (e.g. "break/breaked/breaked" instead of "break/broke/broken") and then, at least in the usual environment, adulterate their verb-formation rules to allow for the English irregularities (Ervin, 1964, pp. 177-179; McNeill, 1966, pp. 70-72). As an example of (2), we may suppose that a failure of English (that is, the speech of familiar speakers) to optimize might tend to go unnoticed if its effect were either very rare ("do so" with benefactive objects) or else purely negative (nonoccurrence of passives on benefactive objects with verbs other than "buy"); thus, for instance, an adult speaking the "inconsistent" dialect noted earlier might still have a child who, purely through contact with the parent's speech, could, with optimization, derive the more powerful MG.

That children are strongly impelled to achieve a maximally economical MG has been stated forthrightly in various places, most succinctly perhaps in Halle (1964, p. 344, after Chomsky): ". . .language acquisition by a child may best be pictured as a process of constructing the simplest (optimal) grammar capable of generating the set of utterances [sentences] , of which the utterances heard by the child are a representative sample." (The rest of Halle's discussion on this and the following page is well worth rereading.) This comment does not directly suggest that languages change in the direction of permitting simpler grammars, but the inference is a natural one and it fits neatly with our general apprehension of

on indefinitely, and it need not stop at just that point when every aspect of the grammar is maximally economical. We have no particular reason to suppose that every rule, however late, is absorbed all at once for all possible cases, and so it is quite conceivable that some late rules are left, when the grammar has stabilized, in an arrested state of development. Such, if accession of the benefactive-object rules is late, might be the case with the "inconsistent" MG's just mentioned: once started with "buy," they should have moved all the way to my dialect or else dropped "buy"-passives for benefactive objects and receded to the dialect analyzed by Lakoff and Ross. But, it may be hypothesized, they did neither, and so were left with an inconsistent and suboptimal grammar.

Whether or not the Benefactive Object rules are indeed late — and what "late" means[69] — must remain subjects for further inquiry. At least the fact of suboptimality of many adult MG's seems irrefragable; and the explanation proposed above is consistent with that fact and is not inconsistent with what little has been hypothesized about the acquisition of language.

many changes — with, for example, our apprehension that the uniquely-inflected verb "dive" ("dive/dove/dived" in the United States) may well change, receding to "dive/dived/dived" or else advancing to "dive/dove/diven."

It is perhaps worth remarking in this connection that, conceivably, some well-known diachronic phenomena may illustrate a language's changing to optimize performative economy rather than, as in these examples, to optimize competence economy. Epenthesis and hypercharacterization (Malkiel, 1957-1958) may be steps toward optimizing production and reception, respectively, rather than steps toward optimizing competence economy of rule statement; and it might be that some of these changes are better explained under the APG hypothesis than under the conventional hypothesis supporting the CG. But further speculation along these lines would be otiose at this time.

For a comment on the inconsistency of children's MG's, and on the fact that this inconsistency gradually diminishes with increasing age, see Turner and Rommetviet, 1967*b*, pp. 656f.

[69]Rather little effort has been directed at determining the age at which people stop making significant additions to their MG's. (Of course, *non*significant additions, like new lexical items or idioms, may continue to be acquired up to senility, at whatever age that commences.) That is, when is what we may call one's "linguistic majority" reached? The standard answer appears to be "12" (see Lenneberg, 1967, pp. 164-181), but clearly, for some speakers, the figure is as late as 14. Or this at least is a reasonable guess based on the fact that at 12 and 13 these speakers appear to lack little of the full English apparatus and to be acquiring at a slow rate. (But they *are* still acquiring.)

One might suppose that these last two (or more) years of acquisition are optional, and that they are at least partly responsible for the greater grammatical richness observable in some people's capacity.

But we must be perfectly clear about what this finding means. It does *not* mean that what speakers have in the way of a linguistic faculty is a disorderly congeries of rules; what it means, from all we know, is that speakers do have MG's that are basically "grammars" in the full sense in which the English LG is a "grammar" — see again all of the discussion of this point in 1, above — but that these MG's can be, at various places, suboptimal by either CG or APG criteria of simplicity. But note well that these restricted effects are conspicuous precisely because they are exceptions to the overwhelmingly general case — the coherence and (given its scope) the simplicity of the grammar.

Thus, even the view that insists on allowing for every plausible way in which the MG can depart from the LG — first by being an APG, then by being a suboptimal APG — ends by postulating a grammar much like the familiar one (but one optimized, at least in part, in accordance with criteria of performative simplicity). In the end, though now from a new angle, we return to an overall view more like the orthodox one than might at first have seemed likely. Whether the new angle is a more correct one, of course, is a judgment that we cannot make with any finality until we can avail ourselves of the results of further experiments — including the several outlined in these pages — and of further insights into the domain of grammar.

REFERENCES

Brown, R., and Bellugi, U. Three processes in the child's acquisition of syntax. *Harvard Educational Review,* 1964, **34,** 133-151.

Brown, R., and Fraser, C. The acquisition of syntax. In Bellugi, U., and Brown, R. (Eds.), *The Acquisition of Language.* (Monographs of the Society for Research in Child Development, 92). Lafayette, Ind.: Purdue University, 1964.

Chomsky, N. Transformational analysis. Unpublished doctoral dissertation, University of Pennsylvania, Philadelphia, 1955.

Chomsky, N. *Syntactic Structures. (Janua Linguarum* 4). The Hague: Mouton and Co., 1957.

Chomsky, N. Explanatory models in linguistics. In Nagel, E., Suppes, P., and Tarski, A. (Eds.), *Logic, Methodology, and Philosophy of Science.* Stanford: Stanford University, 1962.

Chomsky, N. Formal properties of grammars. In Luce, R. D., Bush, R. R., and Galanter, E. (Eds.), *Handbook of Mathematical Psychology,* Vol. II. New York: John Wiley and Sons, 1963.

Chomsky, N. *Current Issues in Linguistic Theory. (Janua Linguarum* 38). The Hague: Mouton and Co., 1964.

Chomsky, N. *Aspects of the Theory of Syntax.* Cambridge: M.I.T., 1965.

Chomsky, N., *Cartesian Linguistics.* New York: Harper and Row, 1966.

Chomsky, N. The formal nature of language. In Lenneberg, E. H., *Biological Foundations of Language.* New York: John Wiley and Sons, 1967*a.*

Chomsky, N. The general properties of language. In Darley, F. L. (Ed.), *Brain Mechanisms Underlying Speech and Language.* (Proceedings of the Princeton Conference on Brain Mechanisms Underlying Speech and Language, 1965.) New York: Grune and Stratton, 1967*b.*

Chomsky, N., and Miller, G. A. Introduction to the formal analysis of natural languages. In Luce, R. D., Bush, R. R., and Galanter, E. (Eds.), *Handbook of Mathematical Psychology,* Vol. II. New York: John Wiley and Sons, 1963.

Clark, H. H., and Clark, E. V. Semantic distinctions and memory for complex sentences. *Quarterly Journal of Experimental Psychology,* 1968, **20,** 129-138.

Clark, H. H., and Stafford, R. A. Memory for semantic features in the verb. *Journal of Experimental Psychology* (in press).

Ervin, S. M. Imitation and structural change in children's language. In Lenneberg, E. H. (Ed.), *New Directions in the Study of Language.* Cambridge: M.I.T., 1964.

Fillmore, C. J. The case for case. In Bach, E., and Harms, R. T. (Eds.), *Universals in Linguistic Theory.* New York: Holt, Rinehart and Winston, 1968.

Firbas, J. Thoughts on the communicative function of the verb in English, German, and Czech. *Brno Studies in English,* 1959, **1,** 39-68.

Firbas, J. From comparative word-order studies. *Brno Studies in English,* 1964, **4,** 11-126.

Fodor, J. A., and Garrett, M. Some reflections on competence and performance. In Lyons, J., and Wales, R. J. (Eds.), *Psycholinguistics Papers.* Edinburgh: University of Edinburgh, 1966.

Fodor, J. A., and Garrett, M. Some syntactic determinants of sentential complexity. *Perception and Psychophysics,* 1967, 2, 289-296.

Foss, D. J., Bever, T. G., and Silver, M. The comprehension and verification of ambiguous sentences. *Perception and Psychophysics,* 1968, 4, 304-306.

Fraser, C., Bellugi, U., and Brown, R. Control of grammar in imitation, comprehension, and production. *Journal of Verbal Learning and Verbal Behavior,* 1963, 2, 121-135.

Gough, P. B. The verification of sentences: the effects of delay of evidence and sentence length. *Journal of Verbal Learning and Verbal Behavior,* 1966, 5, 492-496.

Grice, H. P. Utterer's meaning, sentence-meaning, and word-meaning. *Foundations of Language,* 1968, 4, 225-242.

Grunig, B. Les theories transformationnelles. *La Linguistique,* 1965, #2, 1-24; 1966, #1, 31-101.

Halle, M. Phonology in generative grammar. *Word,* 1962, 18, 54-72; reprinted in Fodor, J. A., and Katz, J. J. (Eds.), *The Structure of Language: Readings in the Philosophy of Language.* Englewood Cliffs, New Jersey: Prentice-Hall, 1964.

Halliday, M. A. K. Notes on transitivity and theme in English, part 2. *Journal of Linguistics,* 1967, 3, 199-244.

Harris, Z. S. *Methods in Structural Linguistics.* Chicago: University of Chicago, 1951.

Harris, Z. Distributional structure. *Word,* 1954, 10, 146-162.

Harris, Z. S. Co-occurrence and transformation in linguistic structure. *Language,* 1957, 33, 283-340.

Harris, Z. S. Transformational theory. *Language,* 1965, 41, 363-401.

Harris, Z. S. *Mathematical Structures of Language.* (Interscience Tracts in Pure and Applied Mathematics, 21). New York: John Wiley and Sons, 1968.

Harwood, F. W. Quantitative study of the speech of Australian children. *Language and Speech,* 1959, 2, 236-271.

Hiż, H. Congrammaticality, batteries of transformations, and grammatical categories. In Jakobson, R. (Ed.), *Proceedings of Symposia in Applied Mathematics,* XII. Providence: American Mathematical Society, 1961.

Hiż, H. The role of paraphrase in grammar. In C.I.J.M. Stuart (Ed.), *Monograph Series on Languages and Linguistics,* 17. Washington: Georgetown University, 1964.

Katz, J. J., Mentalism in linguistics. *Language,* 1964, 40, 124-137.

Katz, J. J., and Postal, P. M. *An Integrated Theory of Linguistic Descriptions.* (Research Monograph 26). Cambridge: M.I.T., 1964.

Kotarbinska, J. On ostensive definitions. *Philosophy of Science,* 1960, 27, 1-22.

Lakoff, G. *On the Nature of Syntactic Irregularity* (doctoral dissertation, Indiana University). *Mathematical Linguistics and Automatic Translation Report* NSF-16. Cambridge: The Computation Laboratory of Harvard University, 1965.

Lakoff, G. Instrumental adverbs and the concept of deep structure. *Foundations of Language,* 1968, 4, 4-29.

Lakoff, G., and Ross, J. R. A criterion for verb phrase constituency. In Kuno, S. (Ed.), *Mathematical Linguistics and Automatic Translation Report* NSF-17. Cambridge: The Computation Laboratory of Harvard University, 1966.

Lenneberg, E. H. Cognition in ethnolinguistics. *Language,* 1953, **29,** 463-471.

Lenneberg, E. H. *Biological Foundations of Language.* New York: John Wiley and Sons, 1967.

MacKay, D. G. To end ambiguous sentences. *Perception and Psychophysics,* 1966, **1,** 426-436.

Malkiel, Y. Diachronic hypercharacterization in Romance. *Archivum Linguisticum,* 1957, **9,** 79-113; and 1958, **10,** 1-30.

McCawley, J. D. Concerning the base component of a transformational grammar. *Foundations of Language,* 1968, **4,** 243-269.

McNeill, D. Developmental psycholinguistics. In Smith, F., and Miller, G. A. (Eds.), *The Genesis of Language.* Cambridge: M.I.T., 1966.

Mehler, J. Some effects of grammatical transformations on the recall of English sentences. *Journal of Verbal Learning and Verbal Behavior,* 1963, **2,** 346-351.

Miller, G. A. Some psychological studies of grammar. *American Psychologist,* 1962, **17,** 748-762.

Miller, G. A., and Chomsky, N. Finitary models of language users. In Luce, R. D., Bush, R. R., and Galanter, E. (Eds.), *Handbook of Mathematical Psychology,* Vol. II. New York: John Wiley and Sons, 1963.

Miller, G. A., and McKean, K. A chronometric study of some relations between sentences. *Quarterly Journal of Experimental Psychology,* 1964, **16,** 297-308.

Postal, P. M. On so-called "pronouns" in English. In Dinneen, F. P. (Ed.), *Monograph Series on Languages and Linguistics,* 19. Washington: Georgetown University, 1966*a.*

Postal, P. M. A Note on "Understood Transitively." *International Journal of American Linguistics,* 1966*b,* **32,** 90-93.

Ross, J. R. Relativization in extraposed clauses. In Kuno, S. (Ed.), *Mathematical Linguistics and Automatic Translation Report* NSF-17. Cambridge: The Computation Laboratory of Harvard University, 1966.

Ross, J. R. *Constraints on Variables in Syntax,* doctoral dissertation (dittoed). Cambridge: M.I.T., 1967.

Savin, H., and Perchonock, E. Grammatical structure and the immediate recall of English sentences. *Journal of Verbal Learning and Verbal Behavior,* 1965, **4,** 348-353.

Shipley, E. F., Smith, C. S., and Gleitman, L. R. *A Study in the Acquisition of Language: Free Responses to Commands.* (Technical Report VIII). Philadelphia: Eastern Pennsylvania Psychiatric Institute, n.d. [1967].

Slobin, D. I. Grammatical transformations in childhood and adulthood. Unpublished doctoral dissertation. Cambridge, Harvard University: 1963.

Slobin, D. I. Grammatical transformations and sentence comprehension in childhood and adulthood. *Journal of Verbal Learning and Verbal Behavior,* 1966, **5,** 219-227.

Slobin, D. I. Recall of full and truncated passive sentences in connected discourse. *Journal of Verbal Learning and Verbal Behavior,* 1968, 7, 876-881.

Stene, A. The animate gender in modern colloquial English. *Norsk Tidsskrift for Sprogvidenskap,* 1934, 7, 350-355.

Svartvik, J. *On Voice in the English Verb.* The Hague: Mouton and Co., 1966.

Turner, E. A., and Rommetveit, R. Experimental manipulation of the production of active and passive voice in children. *Language and Speech,* 1967a, 10, 169-180.

Turner, E. A., and Rommetveit, R. The acquisition of sentence voice and reversibility. *Child Development,* 1967b, 38, 649-660.

Turner, E. A., and Rommetveit, R. Focus of attention in recall of active and passive sentences. *Journal of Verbal Learning and Verbal Behavior,* 1968, 7, 543-548.

Valdman, A. Review of Guiraud, P., *Le français populaire. Language,* 1968, 44, 123-127.

Watt, W. C. English locative sentences. Paper given at the Forty-Second Annual Meeting, Linguistic Society of America, 1967. Abstract in *Handbook* of the Meeting, p. 62.

Watt, W. C. English reduplication. *Journal of English Linguistics,* 1968, 2, 96-129.

Watt, W. C. Lexicalization and recoverability. Forthcoming.

Weir, R. H. *Language in the Crib.* The Hague: Mouton and Co., 1962.

CHAPTER 6

John R. Hayes

Carnegie-Mellon University

Herbert H. Clark

Stanford Univeristy

EXPERIMENTS ON THE SEGMENTATION OF AN ARTIFICIAL SPEECH ANALOGUE

The word, as an "object" of language, seems almost as real to our auditory experience as a ball does to our visual experience. Yet, on close examination, words appear to be only segments of the continuous flow of speech we hear around us. The word is, nevertheless, real. To quote Sapir (1921):

> Linguistic experience, both as expressed in standardized, written form and as tested in daily usage, indicates overwhelmingly that there is not, as a rule, the slightest difficulty in bringing the word to consciousness as a psychological reality. No more convincing test could be desired than this, that the naive Indian, quite unaccustomed to the concept of the written word, has nevertheless no serious difficulty in dictating a text to a linguistic student word by word; he tends, of course, to run his words together as in actual speech, but if he is called to a halt and is made to understand what is desired, he can readily isolate the words as such, repeating them as units. He regularly refuses, on the other hand, to isolate the radical or grammatical element, on the ground that it "makes no sense."

The experiments we are reporting here are concerned with the ontogeny of the word as a psychological unit; how do we come to perceive that the utterances of our language are segmented into words?

The segmentation problem might first appear to be no problem at all; language can be segmented because it is already segmented — either by pauses or by other well defined markers which identify the beginnings and endings of the words. While this suggestion is an obvious one, it has received surprisingly little empirical support. Consider the case for pauses, for example. Phenomenologically, we usually think of the words in speech as being separated by very short pauses, just as the words in print are separated by spaces. Examinations of sound spectrographs (for example, Lieberman, 1967), however, show that words in sentences most often flow into one another without any intervening pauses. We might say, however, that we perceive the segmentation because we know that it is possible to pause between the words. But this brings us back to the beginning problem: we have to know the segmentation before we can know where it is possible to pause.

221

A second candidate for segmentation is stress. As Jakobson, Fant, and Halle (1963) note, "in languages where the stress is bound to the initial. . . syllable. . .it functions as a boarder mark which denotes the beginning (or end) of the word." English, of course, is not such a language. In English, the rules for stress within a word depend in a very complex way on the abstract function of that word within the sentence as a whole (see Chomsky and Halle, 1968). In this sense, stress is a very imperfect indicator of word boundaries in English; one must know the syntactic rules themselves before one can use the stress rules in order to segment a sentence correctly. Lieberman (1965), indeed, has shown that linguists can judge the stress values of the words within sentences with very high consistency; however, these stress values are apparently not present in the acoustic signal itself, but are inferred by the linguists from their grammatical knowledge of English. Stress is therefore not in the spoken sentence itself, but in the mind of the listener; as such, it is of little help for the initial segmentation of speech.

Another possible segmentation device depends on the differences in the distribution of phonemes at the beginnings and endings of words. These differences could be used as cues for segmentation. For example, the "ng" sound is common at the end of English words but never occurs at the beginning. This kind of cue, however, does not seem very promising, since the overlap in the distributions is more striking than the differences.

As yet, none of the proposed segmentation markers, either separately or in combination, has been shown to be adequate to account for the phenomena of segmentation. Since the search for segmentation markers has been rather discouraging, we have turned in this paper to the examination of an alternative class of theories which do not require that a marker be present whenever a segment is perceived. We will call these the "recognition" theories. Recognition theories hold that a word is perceived as a segment not because markers currently delimit its beginning and end, but rather because the listener has recognized a pattern of phonemes (in the speech stream) that constitutes a word.

The speaker of any language must *learn* the phoneme patterns that constitute words. If segmentation is accomplished by a recognition mechanism, then he must necessarily learn the patterns from his experience with the language. It is widely recognized, in fact, that segmentation does depend on familiarity with the language that is being segmented (Neisser, 1967).

There are many possible mechanisms that would depend on linguistic experience in identifying words. We will define three types and distinguish them according to the kind of linguistic experience they employ.

1. Any *bracketing mechanism* identifies as words those phoneme sequences which have frequently been "bracketed" by segmentation markers. It should be noted, however, that this mechanism does not require that the markers be

present in the utterance currently being segmented, but only that they have been present in the listener's previous linguistic experience.

2. The *reference mechanisms* are those that identify as words the patterns of phonemes that have been strongly correlated with an external event or reference. Osgood and Sebeok (1965) have proposed such a mechanism, for in accounting for the unity of words, they say, "The word *apple* is heard. . .in a variety of constructions. . .but it is associated with a common perceptual sign and/or proximal experience (e.g., is accompanied by seeing and/or manipulating the same object apple)."

3. *Clustering mechanisms* are able to detect the recurrent patterns that constitute words, even without the aid of pauses or of meanings. These abstract mechanisms are able to measure crude correlations and to differentiate between the strong interphoneme correlations found within words and the weaker correlations across word boundaries. They identify as words the strongly correlated clusters of adjacent phonemes in the speech stream.

Harris (1955) has proposed just such a procedure for use by linguists in discovering the words of an unfamiliar language. His procedure is best described by working through one of his examples. He considered the utterance "He's clever," and its phonemic representation /hiysklever/. He then turned to informants in the language (as the source of his correlational information) to determine how many different phonemes can follow /h/. He found that there were 9 different phonemes that could act as successors to /h/. In the same way, Harris found that 14 phonemes could follow /hi/, 29 could follow /hiy/, 29 could follow /hiyz/, 11 could follow /hiyzk/, 7 could follow /hiyzkl/, and so on. High successor counts correspond to little constraint from the context and hence to low correlations among phonemes. Harris interpreted high successor counts as indicating that a segment boundary had been crossed. Hence, he located these boundaries just before the peaks in the successor count, as in the sample utterance /hiy.z.klever/, where the periods indicate boundaries.

We are especially interested in the clustering mechanism for three reasons. First, both the clustering mechanism and the bracketing mechanism have a property not shared by the reference mechanism. Since they operate solely on the auditory input, these two mechanisms have a capability of segmenting words before the words have been associated with a referent or have acquired a meaning, and therefore may play a role in the acquisition of reference and meaning. Suppose, for example, that a child is to learn the meaning of the word *milk* by understanding sentences such as "Drink your milk," "Here's our milk," and "Want some cold milk?" in the presence of milk. The child's task will be very much easier if the sentences are segmented into words before he starts correlating, since he would be able to eliminate such potential correlates as "rmilk" and "ilk" without testing them. Presumably, the task of acquiring grammatical information would also be simplified if sentences were segmented beforehand.

One could also argue from music that a reference mechanism, if such a mechanism exists at all, could not exist prior to a more abstract clustering or bracketing mechanism. Music has much the same superficial structure as does language in that it consists of notes, figures, leitmotivs, phrases, melodies, themes, and the like. For almost all kinds of music, there is nothing we could call the "referent" of a musical phrase, yet we can distinctly recognize the various hierarchical musical units — the recurrent themes of a fugue, the repeated occurrences of rhythmical patterns, and so on. This argues that there must be a nonreferential mechanism for the segmentation and recognition of at least some sound sequences.

The second reason for interest in the clustering mechanisms is an esthetic one. We originally became interested in this mechanism through analogy with a visual phenomenon. Even to a careful observer, an animal who remains motionless may merge perfectly into its background, but it will be quite visible as soon as it moves. When it moves, the correlations among the elements within its visual boundaries are much stronger than correlations between it and its surroundings. Given a clustering mechanism, the same difference in correlation would establish the boundaries of auditory objects, that is, words. We very much prefer to appeal to such general cognitive processes in explaining linguistic phenomena than to more special processes which apply uniquely to language.

Finally, we feel that it is scientifically more useful to try to demonstrate the existence of the clustering mechanism than of the bracketing mechanism. If patterns can be detected without segmentation markers, then we would assume that they can certainly be detected with segmentation markers. Thus, if we can demonstrate a clustering mechanism, we can very likely also demonstrate a bracketing mechanism.

THE EXPERIMENTS

We have set our goals in the following experiments at a very modest level. Our aim is merely to demonstrate the existence of a clustering mechanism in humans and to uncover some of its properties. We want to show that humans, given experience, can in fact identify recurrent patterns in a previously unfamiliar language and that they can do so simply by listening to the language without the aid of segmentation markers, reinforcements, referents, or teachers.

To demonstrate these points clearly, we had to meet the stringent requirement of (1) finding a language in which we could be sure that there were no segmentation markers of any kind, and (2) insuring that the speaker of the language would insert no extraneous markers, as he might do, for example, by unintentionally modifying the stress pattern at word boundaries. To satisfy these requirements, we constructed an artificial language entirely without segmentation markers and hired a computer to speak it to the subjects.

The Speaking Program

All of the sounds used in our experiments were combinations of square waves generated by a DDP-116 computer. To produce an audible square wave, the computer cycled repeatedly through a counting loop, alternately turning a voltage on or off. The modulated voltage was then amplified and fed either to a tape recorder or to a loudspeaker that transformed it into audible sound. The resulting sound resembled a rather poor quality organ or oboe. Changing the setting of the counting loop enabled the pitch of the tone to be changed in steps or to be made to vary slowly or rapidly to produce glides, warbles and trills. The available frequencies ranged from 250 to 2000 c.p.s. The computer could operate four such variable counting loops simultaneously. Thus, it was capable of accompanying itself in a quartet, a task which our artificial languages in fact required it to perform.

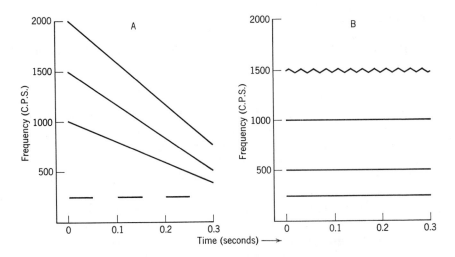

Figure 6.1. Frequency-time patterns for two phonemes.

The stimulus materials which we presented were organized at three levels. By analogy with natural language, we will call these the level of the "phoneme," the level of the "word," and the level of the "language." The artificial phonemes were complex sounds in three or four voices which lasted between 0.2 and 0.3 second. Typical phonemes are shown in Fig. 6.1. We divided the phonemes into two classes in rough analogy to the vowels and consonants of human speech. Our artificial consonants were phonemes that changed markedly from beginning to end, such as the phoneme in Fig. 6.1A. The artificial vowels were the ones which, like that shown in Fig. 6.1B, changed little from beginning to end, that is, maintained approximately the same quality of sound throughout its duration.

The "words" were fixed sequences of 6 to 8 phonemes. All of the words were constructed by starting with a consonant and alternating consonants and vowels in the phoneme string. A word, then, might consist of consonant #3, vowel #5, consonant #2, vowel #1, and so on.

A language can be defined as a fixed set of words and their rules of combination. In the experiments described here, the languages were simply finite-state grammars with equal transitions between each word and another word and between each word and itself; in other words, the probability of any one of the four words occurring after any given word, including itself — that is, sampling with replacement — in this sequence was equal. What the subject (S) actually heard was a continuous stream of words, one right after the other without pause in between words, for a duration of about 45 minutes.

Experiment 1

The purpose of the first experiment was simply to attempt to demonstrate that humans can segment our artificial language into its component words by listening to it.

Procedure. The language used in Experiment 1 consisted of four words. Three of them were 8 phonemes long and one was 6 phonemes long. The phonemes used in constructing the words were 12 consonants and 7 vowels. Thus, many phonemes were used in more than one word.

The experiment involved two phases, a listening phase and a testing phase. In the listening phase, the S listened for about 45 minutes to the artificial language. The Ss were told that they were to be tested after the listening phase to determine if they could recognize what they had been listening to. They were also told that they would win a prize of $5.00 if they got a perfect score on the test. The Ss were not told that the language consisted of four words nor were they told that the language consisted of units three to four seconds in length.

At no time during either the learning or the testing phase did the experimenter (*E*) give the *S*s any information concerning the correct segmentation of the language.

The premise of our testing procedure was that *S*s who had segmented the language appropriately would know where pauses ought to be placed, even though they had never heard pauses in the language before. In particular, they should be able to recognize that a string of phonemes with pauses placed at the word boundaries was more "familiar" than a string with pauses placed in other locations, that is, in the middle of words.

The test consisted of 40 items. Each test item consisted of two sets of four words, an "A" set and a "B" set. One of the sets consisted of the four words of the language in random order separated by pauses at the word boundaries. The other set consisted of four new words constructed from exactly the same string of 30 phonemes as the first set. There were just two changes: (a) each pause was shifted two phonemes to the left, and (b) the last two phonemes (29 and 30) were placed first. All of the words generated by this procedure consisted of sequences of phonemes that could occur in the original language and that had in fact been presented many times during the listening period. Furthermore, any combination of these words would yield a sequence of phonemes which was legal in the original language. The new set of words, then, contained no unusual transitions from one phoneme to another that might have served as a cue for discrimination.

The *S*'s task in the test was to indicate for each test item which set of words sounded most similar to the language he had heard in the listening phase. The positions of the two sets were counterbalanced over the 40 test items.

Results. The results provide clear evidence of segmentation. The distribution of test scores (shown in Fig. 6.2) was biased strongly in the "correct" direction. A sign test (Siegel, 1956) on the number of *S*s achieving better (or worse) than the chance score of 20 revealed a bias in the expected direction at the 0.02 level of confidence.

Fig. 6.2 also shows that none of the *S*s come even close to achieving a perfect score on the test. The effect obtained with 45 minutes of listening was a small but measurable *tendency* to recognize the appropriate segmentation.

Our initial hope that the 40 test items would provide independent measures of *S*s' discrimination proved to be quite unfounded. A control *S*, given the test without the listening period, achieved a score (of 10) which would have been significantly poorer than chance if the successive judgments were independent. *S*s who had not been exposed to the materials in the listening phase could still adopt a consistent response strategy and score either well above or well below chance. They could not, of course, determine the *direction* in which their scores differed from chance. Therefore, we treated the scores on the 40-item test simply as indicating the direction in which each S differed from chance.

Discussion

By serving as pilot subjects, the experimenters were able to obtain a subject's-eye-view of the segmentation process. In the experimenters' subjective view, the process seems to proceed roughly as follows. At first, the sound stream seems quite amorphous and featureless. After perhaps a minute of listening, an event — perhaps a phoneme or part of a phoneme — stands out from the stream. When

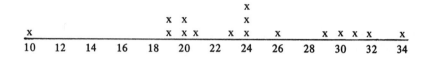

Fig. 6.2. Distribution of scores in Experiment 1.

the event has recurred several times, the listener may notice that it is typically preceded or followed by another event. The combination of events can in turn be related to events that happen in its neighborhood. Recognition of a word, then, seems to proceed from perceptually distincitive foci outwards in both directions toward the word boundaries. Presumably, the process would tend to stop at the word boundaries because the correlations across the boundaries are weak.

If segmentation does proceed by relating a growing focus to neighboring event, then we would expect that any operation which reduces the uniqueness of the relation between the focus and its neighbors would impede segmentation. One way to reduce the uniqueness of this relation is to reduce the number of phonemes. If there are few phonemes, each must occur in several different combinations. We must expect, then, that a language constructed from many phonemes will be easier to segment than a language that is constructed from few phonemes. The second experiment was conducted to test this hypothesis.

Experiment 2

Procedure. In the second experiment, we employed three languages — a 16-phoneme language, and two four-phoneme languages. Each language consisted of four words. In the 16-phoneme language, the consonants were selected from a list of 12 alternatives, and the vowels from a list of four alternatives. In the four-phoneme languages, consonants and vowels were each chosen from lists of two alternatives. These lists were sublists of those used for the 16-phoneme language, and they were chosen so that the phonemes in each language would be as distinct as possible.

The words of the 16-phoneme language and of one of the four-phoneme languages (to be called 4-short) were six phonemes in length. The words of the other four-phoneme language (to be called 4-long) were 12 phonemes in length. We included the language 4-long in the experiment as a test of the hypothesis that the critical factor in segmentation is the information content of the words rather than the number of phonemes in the language. Notice that 4-short has six bits of information per word, 4-long has 12 bits per word, and the 16-phoneme language has between 16 and 17 bits per word. If the number of phonemes is the critical factor, then we would expect 4-short and 4-long to be equally difficult to segment and the 16-phoneme language to be less difficult. If it is the information content of the words that is critical, then we would expect that 4-short would be most difficult to segment, 4-long next most difficult and the 16-phoneme language least difficult.

The three languages were each constructed as in Experiment 1, that is, as finite-state languages with all transition probabilities equal. Each language was presented to a different group of Ss in the same manner as in Experiment 1, but in this case the tests were shortened from 40 items to 24.

Results. The results are shown in Fig. 6.3. Sign tests on the numbers of Ss who achieved scores above (or below) the chance score of 12 revealed significant segmentation at the 0.05 level of confidence for the 16-phoneme language, but not for either of the four-phoneme languages. Mann-Whitney tests revealed significant differences in segmentation scores between the 16-phoneme language and each of the four-phoneme languages at the 0.05 level of confidence, and no significant difference between the two four-phoneme languages.

Discussion

The results are consonant with the hypothesis that difficulty of segmentation depends on the number of phonemes in the language, and they are not consonant with the hypothesis that difficulty depends on the information content of the words. The results, therefore, provide support for our position that segmentation is a process which proceeds by relating a growing focus to neighboring events.

We hope to test this position further in future work by attempting to identify and to control the occurrence of the highly distinctive events with which the focus starts. If our position is correct, it should be possible to control the order in which the words of a language are segmented by controlling the occurrence of these events in the words.

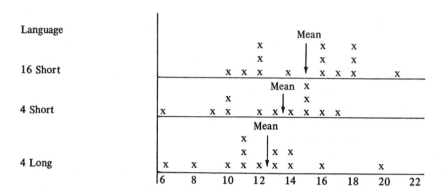

Fig. 6.3 Distribution of scores by language in Experiment 1.

DISCUSSION

These two experiments demonstrate that humans do, in fact, have a clustering mechanism able to segment artificial speech. It is a mechanism which (a) can segment completely unutterable sounds, (b) works on "speech" that has no semantic and no significant syntactic structure, and (c) requires relatively little time — about three-quarters of an hour in our experiments — to come to at least some parsing of the speech. It seems to us that these are important properties of a mechanism that would be useful to a child first trying to sort out the sounds he hears around him. That is, if we could assume that very young children relied on such a mechanism — at least in part — we could make substantial progress toward understanding the very first stages in the child's acquisition of language.

It is important, first, that the sounds that our subjects parsed into words were speechlike, although unutterable. This situation is analogous to the one the child faces in his first encounters with language. It is very unlikely that he has the repertoire of sounds necessary to produce the first words he is able to understand. To segment his parent's speech successfully, he need only be able to *hear* the various distinctions that are being made in the phonological structure. Then, by listening for the correlations, which is what the clustering mechanism does, he is able to decide just where the word boundaries are in the adult speech.

It is just as important, however, that this mechanism is able to operate completely independently of semantic and syntactic considerations — except for the simple syntactic constraint that speech *is* made up of words. This frees the initial segmentation mechanism in the child from necessarily being a complicated device which, say, "associates" what is said with what is seen, as Osgood's reference mechanism would have it do, or which makes and tests hypotheses about the syntactic structure of speech.

Finally, it is significant that our *S*s were able to segment speech in a relatively short period of time. Granted, the languages they were able to segment had a very small vocabulary, but they also contained no additional cues, like pauses between sentences or phrases as in natural speech, to help the segmentation along. This adds to the plausibility that the clustering mechanism might be a basic part of the young child's mental apparatus.

The clustering mechanism is almost certainly not the only device used by children. Another device the child could use, for example, is one which notes the possibility of pauses within sentences. It is well known that when a speaker breathes he will do so between words, not within them. Even hesitations — the interruptions in speech typical of someone trying to think of the next word — will almost always occur at word boundaries (Maclay and Osgood, 1959). A mechanism that is able to note these pauses and hesitations, then has additional information for the segmentation of speech into words. It could be argued, however, that this device is really only a specialized clustering mechanism. In noting speech interruptions, it is still only attending to the high intercorrelations of the sounds within words, that is, to the integrity of the word as a unit, just as a clustering mechanism would do. In similar mechanisms, however, the child could make use of other kinds of information about words, such as, phonological and syntactic properties, in conjunction with the simple clustering mechanism.

This conception of how the child first comes to segment speech leads to several suggestions for future work in segmentation of artificial speech. Most of the following suggestions are aimed at a clustering mechanism used in conjunction with other phonological and syntactic features of speech.

1. Very little is known about what makes a phoneme "distinctive" in our artificial speech, but it is certain that we hear particular sounds that stand out over the background of the other sounds. In several preliminary studies, we have attempted to identify the more distinctive sounds in our language and have done so with some success. Further experiments are needed, however, to show whether the distinctiveness of these phonemes can be helpful to the segmentation process. Our conception of the ongoing process of word perception is that the listener starts with a distinctive sound and then begins to notice its correla-

tions with the sounds around it. Now, if each word of a language began with a distinctive phoneme, the listener would have the greatest opportunity to notice (a) that the sounds before that phoneme were not correlated with it and (b) that those after it were. This would immediately give him the word boundaries. But if the phoneme came in the middle of the word, he would not perceive the boundaries so quickly, for they would emerge only after he had built up all the correlated sounds around the distinctive phoneme. Thus, we would expect distinctive sounds to be most advantageous at the beginning or ending of words, not in the middle of words.

2. Pauses of various kinds should make segmentation much easier, for if the pause is treated as a marker — and a very distinctive one at that — it should be a great help to the clustering mechanism. The first question to be answered is whether pauses help at all. This could be tested by comparing a language without pauses between words, such as the one in Experiment 1, with the identical language but with pauses between each word. If markers do help segmentation, the second language should be segmented with greater ease than the first. We could also follow the suggestion made previously about the value of pauses and hesitations in natural language. One could compare one language with no pauses with another in which pauses occurred between words some part of the time. Our prediction would be that the second language should be more easily parsed than the first.

3. Adult speech abounds with prefixes, suffixes, and inflections, but children in their first attempts to speak ignore them completely. The tendency to ignore them could occur because children really do not perceive affixes and inflections as an integral part of the words they are attached to; instead, children hear them first as segmentation markers.

This conception of the function of affixes and inflections for the child can be tested in an artificial speech analogue. Two languages could be constructed so that the first has no inflection whatsoever, like the language in Experiment 1, and the second has one or more affixes that are tacked onto each of the words in the language interchangeably. The affixes in the second language would serve almost the same function as pauses in that both affixes and pauses occur very frequently in the language, always at word boundaries, and uncorrelated with any particular word in the language. The single test for both languages would be one that does not include affixes, but which is otherwise analogous to the text in Experiments 1 and 2. Even though the test for the second language would not include the affixes, the second language should show better segmentation than the first, for the affixes, acting as highly redundant markers, allow the segmentation to take place more quickly.

4. Other grammatical properties should presumably help in the segmentation process too. One hypothesis, for example, is that languages with phrase-

structure grammars should be easier to parse than those with finite-state grammars. Furthermore, in languages with phrase-structure grammars, the word boundaries which coincide with the greatest number of constituent boundaries should be the most quickly perceived, for it is at these boundaries that there is the greatest possibility of noticing the lack of correlation between the sounds on either side of the boundaries. Intonation is another natural language property which undoubtedly aids segmentation. Although intonation contours are a problem for our artificial speech synthesizer as it now exists, the presence of such contours — or their analogues — should also help in the perception of the surface structure constituent boundaries, and hence in the segmentation of words within these constituents. It should be noted that these grammatical considerations can be tested independently of, or in conjunction with, the previous considerations of affixes, pauses, or distinctive sounds.

Finally, we sound one note of warning: the conclusions from these experiments on adults may possibly not be applicable to children at all. The present experiments, and their accompanying discussion, argue only for the *plausibility* of the mechanism in children's acquisition of language, not for its precise existence. To complete the case, experiments like the present ones must be repeated, under the appropriate conditions, on children of about a year old. The technicalities of these experiments, of course, would be very difficult, yet there are available methods that make such experiments feasible. This, too, we leave to the future.

In conclusion, the present experiments have demonstrated the existence of a very primitive clustering mechanism for the segmentation of artificial speech into words. This mechanism appears to operate only on the information available in the intercorrelations between the successive sounds in the speech stream; it identifies as words the clusters of sounds that consistently recur in an unbroken sequence. We have suggested some of the implications of this kind of mechanism for the ontogeny of segmentation in the child and some of the directions research on this problem might take in the future. In a word, however, it is clear, that, in our quest for the child's quest of his first word, we have barely uttered the first word.

REFERENCES

Chomsky, N., and Halle, M. *The Sound Pattern of English.* New York: Harper & Row, 1968.

Harris, Z. S. From phoneme to morpheme. *Language,* 1955, 31, 190-222.

Jakobson, R., Fant, G., and Halle, M. *Preliminaries to Speech Analysis.* Cambridge, Mass: M.I.T. Press, 1963.

Lieberman, P. *Intonation, Perception, and Language.* Cambridge, Mass.: M.I.T. Press, 1967.

Lieberman, P. On the acoustic basis of the perception of intonation by linguists. *Word,* 1965, 21, 40-55.

Maclay, H., and Osgood, C.E. Hesitation phenomena in spontaneous English speech. *Word,* 1959, 1, 19-44.

Neisser, J. *Cognitive Psychology.* New York: Appleton-Century-Crofts, 1967.

Osgood, C. E., and Sebeok, T.A. *Psycholinguistics: A Survey of Theory and Research Problems.* Bloomington, Ind.: Indiana University Press, 1965, pp. 55-56.

Sapir, E. *Language.* New York: Harcourt, Brace & World, 1921.

Siegel, S. *Nonparametric Statistics for the Behavioral Sciences.* New York: McGraw-Hill, 1956.

CHAPTER 7   *Margaret Donaldson and Roger Wales*

University of Edinburgh

ON THE ACQUISITION OF SOME
RELATIONAL TERMS*

McNeill, in a recent review of work on the development of language (in press), remarks that, while much attention has been given to the question of how language influences thought (the problem of "language and cognition"), little or nothing has been done so far about the converse problem of "cognition and language." That is, there has been little attempt to account for the fundamental features of language acquisition in terms of a general theory of cognitive development. McNeill doubts whether at the moment we are in a position to carry this enterprise far; and his doubt seems well-founded. Donaldson (1966) has, however, already argued that, even in the present state of knowledge, we ought always to try to relate what is said about language acquisition to other aspects of cognitive development instead of considering it in isolation. This chapter has been prepared with this in mind.

The chapter, as the title indicates, is concerned primarily (and exclusively in so far as it contributes empirical findings) with the acquisition of *some* relational terms — indeed, with a limited, though possibly a very important, set. But given the objective just stated, it is obviously advisable to undertake some preliminary consideration of relational terms in general and of what may be involved in the acquisition of the ability to make relational judgements and statements.

It can reasonably be maintained that most of language is composed of relational terms. This was the position reached by C. S. Peirce, for instance, as he developed his relational logic. Peirce (1933) appears to allow that "indexical words" such as proper nouns or demonstratives are strictly nonrelational, and he seems to be prepared to admit this of words referring to certain attributes which

We here report part of a study supported by a grant from the British Social Science Research Council. George Balfour, Robin Campbell, John Taylor and Brian Young have been our colleagues since the project started in 1966. Eve Clark was responsible for the collection of much of the spontaneous speech recorded in the first year. Julian Dakin helped with some analysis of the speech data. We are indebted to all of these, and to David McNeill, Bernard Meltzer, John Marshall, and James Peter Thorne, who read and commented on an earlier draft of the manuscript.

235

can be described as one-place predicates. But otherwise, for him words are, in essence, relational. This claim is more obviously incontrovertible in the case of some words than of others — more evidently true of "lover," for instance, than of "tree." All common nouns might be held to be relational in that they are class names, though some of them, like "lover," have a further relational property which others, like "tree," do not possess.

This raises a question central to the present discussion. Within the class of relational terms, many different subdivisions have been proposed — and used for various purposes. For instance, distinctions can be drawn in terms of number of predicate places. Then the relation may be classified as reflexive or irreflexive, symmetrical or asymmetrical, transitive or intransitive, and so on. Peirce himself indulges on occasion in much more complicated and obscure classificatory exercises, but at present there is no need to be concerned with these. The question that has to be asked is: what distinctions are significant for questions of development? Are there some relational terms that are acquired very early? If so, what are their general features? How do they differ from those acquired later? And how can we relate these features to what we know — or may be led by available evidence to postulate — about the general nature of developing cognitive processes?

It is widely accepted that the earliest one-word utterances of children are holophrastic, which is, of course, to say that the single word somehow functions as a whole statement — although the word "statement" suggests a degree of conceptual articulation that is presumably quite lacking. McNeill (op.cit.) remarks of this earliest period: "Except for those occasions when children's speech is purely expressive, it is invariably predicative. Children cry, or comment, and sometimes both. But they never utter mere labels." It may be hard to prove this last claim.. But the predicative nature of two-word utterances, when these begin to appear, is, on the other hand, very clear. What is quite commonly lacking, indeed, is explicit statement of the subject. The following samples of the speech of a child of 27 months, quoted by McNeill from data collected by Brown and Bellugi, illustrate this:

> *up dere; in ere; read dat; hit hammer; hurt ...;*
> *no down there; get broom; put suitcase.*

In each of these utterances a preposition or a transitive verb occurs. The child seems to be expressing relations in space (and usually in proximate space: *up dere, in ere, down there*); or else to be describing actions directly concerning physical objects. Now it is known that by this age the child has a considerable ability to manage spatial relations on the level of action — to make detours, to look for objects behind or under other objects, and so on. He also, and by the same token, has a rich repertoire of types of action available for the manipulation of physical objects ("schemas of actions," as Piaget would call them). And he appears to have developed some conception of a world of enduring objects. We have only to suppose him (1) capable of relating action to object perceived (which involves, of course, differentiating the two) and (2) capable of relating one perceived spatial position to another, in order to provide him with cognitive capacities that are at least consistent with the production of utterances of the above kind. That is to say, no major discrepancy seems to be revealed here between his known nonlinguistic cognitive skills and his linguistic utterances. One relational term included in the above list is, perhaps, not quite covered in this way, however – and that is the negative in *no down there*. There is also another utterance, not so far quoted but drawn from the same source, that seems to contain in it the germ of a relational cognition of a new kind: the phrase *Yep, it fit*. The context in which this was uttered is not made clear (except that the statement was an answer to the question *Does that one fit?*), and it is obviously important to know what the context was. But if the child is really engaged in a consideration of whether "x fits y," then he is involved in a kind of relational activity that goes beyond the linking of action schemas and physical objects.

It should also be observed that, although in the beginning physical actions and physical objects dominate the linguistic scene, nevertheless, at an early age, words which refer to attributes of objects rather than to objects themselves (or which would certainly do so in the adult language) begin to appear. Thus, phrases like *green coat* and *wet sock* are reported. These, if they are to be regarded as predicative, can be classed as one-place predicates. A more complicated – and particularly interesting – situation arises because of the early occurrence of phrases like *big boat* and *more milk*. Both *big* and *more*, as they occur in the adult language, could logically be considered as two-place predicates, though they may not take this overt form. Whether the reference is made explicit or not, X "has more" or "is big" by reference to some standard of comparison.

The making of comparative judgements seems to be pervasive in thinking, yet the acquisition of the ability to comprehend and produce terms that are relational in this last sense – namely, in that they imply comparison across space or across time – has, until now, been the object of very little direct inquiry, in spite of the fact that they have figured in crucial ways in much cognitive research. However, the explicit study of such terms has been a focal topic in the research project that has yielded the data to be reviewed and discussed later in this chapter.

In the context of such a study, it would help greatly if a full formal linguistic analysis of comparative constructions were available. It would help if we had such an analysis even for English alone, and would help still more if an analysis of wider application had been proposed. However, given the great diversity of the linguistic constructions through which comparative judgements may be expressed, it seems hardly surprising that attempts to encompass them within the scope of a (possibly universalizable) set of syntactic rules have not yet met with universal success! At present, there is not even any reasonable consensus about what such an analysis would require to account for (see Jespersen, 1924; Smith, 1961; Lees, 1961; and Chomsky, 1965). It has usually been considered that an attempt should be made to include such forms as *more* and *less* (both as separate comparatives and as one way of forming a comparative in English by conjunction with other adjectives); comparatives of the *X-er* variety; the relation of comparatives with superlatives; the forms *too-X* and *X-enough;* the equative construction *as. . .as*; and possibly such sentences as *John is tall*, on the argument that, in their deep structure, these are implicitly comparative and so should be assigned an analysis which reads (roughly!) *John is taller than average.* Arguably, however, certain verbs (such as *exceed*), and expressions like *to the right of*, might also need to be included; and the words *same* and *different* can hardly be ignored.

In reporting our findings, we shall be concerned with this last pair of terms, and with *more* and *less* in their use as separate comparative forms. We shall also be considering a number of spatial comparative adjectives such as *tall* and *short*, and *high* and *low*; and in connection with this last group, we shall be concerned not only with the *X-er* comparative forms but also with superlatives, with *too-X* and *X-enough* and with the equative construction. Linking all of these studies is a common theme to which it will be necessary to return frequently — the fundamental importance of the distinction between the different (positive and negative) poles of the contrasted terms.

In the case of the spatial adjectives, we shall be in a position to report the children's performance on a number of different tasks. It will become clear that we have been led by our research to regard this as a matter of considerable methodological importance in a study of this kind.

Logically dominating the use of relational terms that involve comparison is a question that seems to have a good claim to a position of central importance in the operation of cognitive processes: "Is X the same as Y in some specified respect or respects — or is it not?" The way in which this question is answered opens or closes certain further possible paths of inquiry. Clearly, if X is asserted to be the same as Y with respect, say, to quantity (X and Y supposedly being sets of discrete entities), then it is possible to seek further specification by asking some such question as "What is the number that each set contains?" However, it is when X is asserted to be not the same as Y that the search for more precise specification makes it appropriate to go on to questions involving further comparative terms. For instance, in the present example, the question "Does X contain more elements than Y or less elements than Y?" may then be asked. It is perhaps advisable to remark at this point that the question of the relations between *same* and *different* will be treated more fully at later points in this chapter; and that this will involve consideration of the possibility that *sameness* may be derivable from complex conjunctions of difference. Furthermore, it should be noted that nothing which has been said is meant to imply that the terms *not the same* and *different* function in strictly equivalent ways within the language.

The question of sameness may or may not be limited to the consideration of certain specified attributes, depending on one's purpose; and accordingly, the word *same* is used in a variety of different ways. An attempt will now be made to indicate the complexity of the situation.

First, there is the sense of *same* in which the reference is to full identity — the identity of one enduring object. This notion has traditionally perplexed philosophers, and it is easy enough to get into considerable entanglements of thought over it, as both Locke and Hume, for instance, discovered. The problem, of course, is that in the case of one entity, when we are led to ask if it is the same (one), we are normally making a temporal comparison — and across time objects change. So how can they change and still remain the same? This, as Vlastos (1965) suggests, is one of the reasons why Plato considered the Forms to be more real — or "cognitively reliable" — than their sensible instances, since the latter, by being F at one time and not-F at another, are "logical monstrosities, systematically violating the principle of noncontradiction." Vlastos (op. cit. p.15). However, if we were to allow this kind of consideration to lead us to deny enduring identity, we would be brought to what Penelhum (1967) calls "the extreme language-destroying consequence that no predicates which cannot be simultaneously ascribed to one subject can be ascribed to a subject at two different times." So it seems best to simply adopt the opinion, apparently reached by most children of 18 months, that we live in a universe in which objects do endure, though they may change, and consider that it makes sense to ask "Is this the same pen that I had here yesterday — or is it a different one?" Notice that we are in much greater difficulty if we want an answer to a question such as "Is this the same idea that I had here yesterday — or is it a different one?" Problems of the latter kind have, of course, also received a great deal of attention from philosophers, and various attempts have been made to define identity in a way that extends beyond consideration of the primitive identity of concrete objects. (See, for instance, the discussion in Reichenbach [1947] of Russell's proposed definition.) For present purposes, however, these arguments are not of great relevance. What is important is to consider the further complexities that attend the word *same*, even when only concrete objects and their physical properties are in question.

1. We commonly speak of two (or more) objects as being *the same* when they are alike with respect to all observable attributes. (By virtue of the very fact that at least two objects are specified, this statement may be held to exclude from "observable attributes" likeness in respect of locus in space-time).

2. We use the word *same* with reference to two (or more) objects when they are alike with respect to at least one observable attribute, but different with respect to at least one other.

3. We say that two concrete entities are *the same* in some respect that is not directly observable.

Under this third heading many possibilities of subdivision arise. Recognition of the respect of sameness may involve the combined consideration of attributes, each of which, taken separately, is observably different — as seems to occur in Piaget's conservation tasks, for instance. Or the judgement of sameness may depend on previous perception of an attribute which is not actually observable at the time the judgement is made. This can be illustrated by reference to a test devised for use in the Edinburgh Cognition Project. The material is six cards, three of which are blank on both sides, while three are blank on one side and have pictures of aeroplanes on the other. If the cards are first inspected on both sides and then arrayed with six blank sides showing, it is appropriate to judge that the cards are still *the same* with respect to the number of aeroplanes on them. So the test, though not devised primarily for this purpose, allows number conservation — or "maintained sameness of number" — to be assessed in a situation in which the critical change is perceptual disappearance rather than shift in configuration. In all cases of this last kind, of course, the sameness, not being directly perceptible, must be inferred.

It is perhaps reasonable now to conclude (even without pushing on to a consideration of, say, analogies, where the same relation holds between the terms of two different pairs) that the achieving of mastery of the relational terms *same* and *different* looks like a task of very considerable complexity. "Sameness" and "difference" must always be judged with respect to certain criteria, and the criteria shift — both with our purposes and (in a different way) across time in a changing universe.

The Edinburgh Cognition Project is a study (currently in progress) of the development of cognitive and linguistic skills in children between the ages of three-and-a-half and five. The experimental group consists of fifteen subjects who come daily for two-and-a-half hours to a nursery school specially set up for the purposes of the research. In social background, the children represent the middle range of the population. They come neither from culturally deprived homes nor from homes that are especially intellectually stimulating. Examples of parental occupations are plasterer, miner, and laboratory technician. When the work began about a year ago (at which time the children were around three-and-a-half years old) the children were given a set of 15 pretests that had previously been prepared and pilot-tested. Some of the tests were inspired by tasks used by Piaget to assess the change from preoperational to concrete operational thinking; others were specifically devised for use in the project. The objective was to sample a wide range of skills that there was reason to think were likely to be of fundamental importance for later cognitive development. Also, the aim was to construct the tests in such a way that children of three-and-a-half would be able to make some attempt at tackling them, while most children, as they attained the age of five, would still have some difficulty with them. Analysis of these tests, after they had been constructed on the above general principles, showed that all (except perhaps one which was a test of imagery) involved, as an important feature, some judgement of sameness or difference. Findings from six of these tests will be reported here. First, however, it may be well to mention that, after a period of approximately six months of systematic training (which is just ending), the same tests will be administered again. The general aim of the research, as will by now be plain, is to assess the effects of this experimental intervention (which has been much more prolonged than that in most "training studies" of a controlled kind) on the capacity to perform these tasks. For present purposes, however, it will be possible to refer only to a very limited part of the data from the pretests and to some evidence obtained from the spontaneous speech of these children, samples of which are recorded daily in the nursery.

One of the tasks was a test of classification. Four sets of material were used, sets I and II being composed of common objects (toothbrushes, eggcups, and the like), and sets III and IV being composed of formal geometrical shapes. In sets I and III, there were four kinds of objects (with three exemplars of each) and four colors; and there was no overlap between groupings by form and groupings by color — that is, all the toothbrushes were blue, all the egg-cups red, and so on. In sets II and IV, the same categories of objects were used as for I and III, but this time the color attribute assumed only three values instead of four; and each of these values was represented by one exemplar of each type of object — that is, there were three toothbrushes, one red, one white, and one yellow, and so on. This arrangement is shown in Fig. 7.1.

	Form and color coincident	Form and color not coincident
Common objects	Set I	Set II
Formal shapes	Set III	Set IV

Fig. 7.1 *Materials used in classification task.*

The test included a free sorting task, but the results of this will not concern us here. The first part of the procedure, however, which does concern us, required the child to pick, from a given set, an object that was related in a specified way to a standard selected from the set by the experimenter.

A formal analysis of the task is first presented. The notation follows that of the lower predicate calculus. For our purposes, however, we adopt Quine's (1953, p. 108) approach to the interpretation of predicates or general terms, namely: "We can look upon . . . (the) forms simply as schemata or diagrams embodying the form of each of various true statements." No claims concerning the usefulness of the calculus for other than present descriptive convenience are intended.

1. The four sets of material already described constitute four domains of discourse, to be referred to as I, II, III and IV.

2. The symbols x, y . . . . stand for variables within a domain, and the symbols a, b . . . . stand for constants, or specific individuals, within a domain.

3. The following predicate letters are used and are to be interpreted as indicated:

S^u = "same in some way," that is, alike with respect to at least one, and possibly all, observable attributes.

D^u = "different in some way," that is, different with respect to at least one, and possibly all, observable attributes.

S = same with respect to all observable attributes.

D = different with respect to all observable attributes.

P = same with respect to at least one observable attribute and different with respect to at least one.

All of these are two-place predicates. S (a,b), I, for instance, will be interpreted to mean that two individuals *a* and *b* from domain I are the same in all observable attributes.[1]

On this analysis: (i) S^ueq. (PvS)
                     (ii) D^ueq. (PvD)

The expressions S^u(a,–) and D^u(a,–) will be used to code the instructions given to the children, which is to say that the task is to fill the blank place.

---

[1] It should be noted at this point that form and color were meant to be the only attributes involved, but some children observed and commented on other properties of the material – for instance, very slight differences between shades of red. In such a case, red may be regarded as an attribute that is assuming different values (cf. Reitman, 1965). Another kind of case arose when a child, asked why he had chosen a yellow and a white pencil as being different, answered that one was sharp and one was blunt! It is further worthy of note, though details cannot be given here, that two children who produced idiosyncratic responses in a perceptual discrimination task produced similarly idiosyncratic responses in the classification task. We are grateful to John Taylor (who worked on the discrimination task) and to Robin Campbell (who worked on classification) for calling our attention to this as an illustration of the importance, in interpreting these results, of looking at the separate tasks, not in isolation, but for the evidence they may yield concerning the development of cognition as a system.

Observe that the relations between elements in domains I and III are necessarily either S or D (taking into account only the intentionally varied attributes of form and color); those between elements in II and IV are either P or D. So there is a certain asymmetry in the situation which should be noted. $S^u(a,-)$, I or III, can yield as correct response only a choice of x such that S(a, x); $S^u(a,-)$, II or IV, can yield as correct response only x such that P(a,x); and $D^u(a,-)$, I or III, can correctly yield only x such that D(a,x). However, $D^u(a,-)$, II or IV, can correctly yield either x such that D(a, x) or x such that P(a, x). This amounts to saying that the child cannot make a wrong choice in response to $D^u(a,-)$, II or IV, though he can, of course, offer faulty — or no — justification.[2] Also, it carries the implication that it is possible for an element *b* to be correct both in response to $S^u(a,-)$, II or IV, and in response to $D^u(a,-)$, II or IV, which is merely to point out again that two objects may be alike in one respect and different in another.

A final point of some importance is that in all cases a subject may respond by denying that there exists in the domain an object that stands in the required relation to the standard. That is, he may respond with an assertion to the effect that:

$$\overline{(Ex) \; [D^u(a, x)]} \quad \text{or} \quad \overline{(Ex) \; [S^u(a, x)]}$$

In the discussion of results that follows, the occurrence of responses of this kind will be reported in the abbreviated form $\overline{(Ex)}$.

There are features of the procedure, in addition to those specified by the above analysis, which should be briefly indicated.

1. The child was initially given an opportunity to talk freely about the objects in each set and was encouraged to name them. Irrespective of what the child was able to say, the experimenter (E.) then pointed to each object in erratic order, naming the object as he did so — for instance: *That's a blue toothbrush.*

2. A correct choice was rewarded with: *Good, that's right.* Whenever the subject (S.) made a wrong choice, he was told that it was wrong and a correct choice was demonstrated by E., with accompanying verbal explanation.

3. Where P-relations between elements obtained, attempts were made to discover which attribute was determining the choice and whether the other attribute would also be judged acceptable as a criterion. This was done by asking the child why he had made a given choice; by inviting him to make further choices after the element he had originally picked had been removed from the set (in cases in which his original choice was correct and he had been told so); and by

[2] Arguably, he cannot make a wrong choice in response to $D^u(a,-)$, I or III, either, since any two objects whatever are "different in *some* way." This is relevant to the interpretation of the responses actually obtained (cf. Table 7.1 and p. 248).

asking him whether certain choices made by E. were acceptable. The results of this part of the inquiry are complex and will not be presented here.

Finally, it should be noted that the instructions "same in some way" and "different in some way" were chosen, after much preliminary consideration and pilot-testing, as the clearest form of wording that could be maintained throughout the test.

Since there were 15 subjects, 30 initial choices were obtained for "same in some way" and 30 for "different in some way" for tasks I and III considered together; and the same number for tasks II and IV combined. Table 7.1 summarizes the choices.

TABLE 7.1

Instruction	Domains I and III				Domains II and IV			
	S(a,b)	D(a,b)	$(\overline{\text{Ex}})$	No Response	P(a,b)	D(a,b)	$(\overline{\text{Ex}})$	No Response
S^u	28	0	2	0	28	0	2	0
D^u	25	5	0	0	24	2	3	1

It should be noted that the two cases of denial of the existence of an object "the same in some way" in domains I and III came from the same child, and she changed to S(a,b) responses after explanation. A second child gave the two $(\overline{\text{Ex}})$ responses to S^u instruction in II and IV, but his response on both these occasions resisted explanation. Two children were involved in the $(\overline{\text{Ex}})$ responses to D^u instruction in II and IV. One of these changed to P after explanation and subsequently gave a D(a,b) response in IV. The other child again resisted explanation on both occasions. There were five cases (involving four children) of changes from S(a,b) to D(a,b) responses to D^u instruction in I and III; but only one of these cases occurred in I and also had the effect of making further explanation in task III unnecessary.

The tendency to avoid a D(a,b) choice for all sets of material and both instructions is clearly pronounced. Most of the children appear to make no distinction between the instructions *Give me one that is the same in some way* and *Give me one that is different in some way*. Comment on this finding will be delayed until results for the second test have been reported.

The next task to be considered was specifically devised to assess the children's comprehension of the terms "more" and "less." The results obtained when this was administered as a pretest are reported in full in Donaldson and Balfour (1968). Here, a considerably abbreviated account will be given.

The first study had the following characteristics.

1. Discrete units were used. There was no investigation of continuous quantities.

2. There were always two sets involved in the comparison.

3. Both static and changing situations were used.

4. The sets were sometimes initially equal to one another and sometimes unequal.

5. The subject was sometimes asked to effect a change himself and sometimes merely to observe and judge it. Sometimes he observed the change as it actually took place, and sometimes only the outcome of the change.

6. When change was effected by the experimenter, only one set was altered.

7. The direction of change sometimes accorded with the final state of the sets relative to one another and sometimes did not.

In a second supplementary study, carried out approximately six months later, subjects were asked to deal with only one set and to effect a change (in this case, a decrease) in its quantity.

In the main study, eight different stimulus situations, involving the variables described above, were used. On the first occasion, the children were asked questions about each of these situations, all of the questions involving the term *more.* On the second occasion a day or two later, questions of the same form, but now using *less,* were put to them.

The material used consisted of two cardboard apple trees, with six hooks in corresponding positions on each; and twelve red apples which could be hung on the trees. The trees could swivel, when this was desired, so that the child could not see the apples being hung on them. When the sets of apples were made equal by E., the spatial distributions always corresponded. For each stimulus situation there were a number of trials involving different numbers of apples. The numbers used to make up a set on a given tree ranged from one to five and the differences between sets ranged from one to four.

The following descriptions illustrate the kinds of procedure used.

1. S. was asked to judge a situation of static equality presented by E. S. did not see the apples being put on the trees. When they were swivelled round for him to observe, he was asked: *Does one tree have more (less) apples on it than the other?* If he answered *Yes* he was asked *Which tree has more (less) apples?* If he answered *No* he was asked *Is there the same number of apples on each tree?*

2. S. was shown a situation of initial inequality, prepared, as before, out of his sight. He was told: *Now make it so that there are more apples on*

this tree (lesser number) *than on this tree* – or else . . . *so that there are less apples on this tree* (greater number). . . . When S. had finished he was asked: *Does one tree have more (less) apples than the other?* If he said *Yes* he was then asked: *Which tree has more (less) apples?*

Other tasks involved, for example, the presentation of situations of static inequality with a simple request for comparative judgement; the presentation of initial equality with a request to the child to *make it so that there are more (less) apples on this tree than on this one;* the presentation of initial inequality with subsequent addition by E., while S. watched, of one or more apples to the lesser set (or, alternatively, subtraction by E. of one or more apples from the greater set) followed by the usual request for comparative judgement. In this last case, the direction of change did not accord with the final state of the sets; that is, the tree to which more apples had been added still always had less apples than the other tree after the addition had been made – and similarly for the operation of subtraction.

The supplementary study was simpler in conception and design. Only one tree was used and there were only two stimulus situations: (a) four apples on the tree, two on the table; and (b) three apples on the tree, three on the table.

Each of these was presented twice, the order of presentation being (a), (b), (a), (b). The child was asked in each case: *Make it so that there are less apples on the tree.*

This additional test was given for two main reasons.

1. To see if there had been change in the typical response patterns over the interval of six months.

2. To check on the possibility that the responses to *less* questions on the first occasion had been influenced by the fact that they had been preceded (though, it will be recalled, not on the same day) by questions involving *more*.

The complex data obtained from these two studies cannot readily be presented in summary form. However, there are two main findings that are relevant to the present discussion. In all the differing situations that were used on the first test, the great majority of the responses gave no indication that the children were making any distinction between *less* and *more*. Only one child answered *less* questions with a high degree of success throughout. The remainder of the children (that is, thirteen, since one child gave so few responses that he cannot be included) responded to these questions just as they did to the corresponding questions containing *more*; and their responses were typically of kinds that constituted correct response to *more* and, consequently, incorrect response to *less*.

The position may be illustrated by giving a detailed analysis of responses to the stimulus situation in which S. had to pass judgement on a situation of static inequality presented to him by E. In this situation, a few children completed as many as seven trials with *more* and six trials with *less*. But other children would not continue for so long. The total number of responses available is 69 for *more* and 55 for *less*. The results are presented in Table 7.2.

TABLE 7.2

	Yes	No (subsequently changed to Yes)	Same	Total
Does one have more?	65	3	1	69
Does one have less?	55	0	0	55

	Correct Choice	Incorrect Choice	No Choice	Total
Which one has more?	63	5	1	69
Which one has less?	15	40	0	55

On 40 trials, then, the child, having judged that one set contained less apples than the other, proceeded to choose, as the one that had less, the one that in fact had more. The 15 correct choices of the tree with *less* were contributed by five children, of whom only one was correct on all presentations attempted. Two additional children were correct in more than half the responses they made.

It was a marked feature of the results that in the "active" tasks (that is, those in which the children themselves were asked to effect a change), children very rarely removed apples from the trees, but almost always added, whether the request was to *make it more* or to *make it less*. But in the stimulus situation described above, in which the child was asked to *make it so that there are more apples* on the tree that initially had less (and vice versa), even the instruction containing *more* proved very difficult, and only three children carried it out without error. If there is a tendency for the children to take *more* as meaning "larger present quantity," then the phrase *make it so that there are more. . .* may well be expected to prove difficult for them to interpret. Many children made alterations which differed in type from one trial to the next (they might add to one tree, or to both, and end up with equal or unequal sets) and there was, in general, much inconsistency. However, the task gave further confirmation to the view that *less* was generally regarded as equivalent to *more*. One child made this explicit. Asked to make three less than two, he said: *But it is less on that tree.*

The results of the supplementary study indicated that, for many of the children, the interpretation of *less* as meaning *more* still persisted. Fourteen subjects were tested, one of the group being at this time in hospital. One of the 14 responded to the initial instruction by saying: *How can I?*, and then made no further response to urgings by E. that he should try. At one point he said *Take them off, you mean?* but then made no move to do so. However, he readily added apples when E. finally tried replacing *less* in the instruction by *more*. Clearly, for this child *less* and *more* were no longer synonymous, but the opposition of the two did not seem to be effectively established as a relation between language and action.

From the 13 remaining children, 52 responses were obtained. The distribution of these is shown in Table 7.3. The third column reports the frequency with which the response of removing apples and then putting some back on again occurred.

TABLE 7.3

Instruction	Response by			
	Addition	Subtraction	Addition followed by subtraction	Subtraction followed by addition
Make it less	41	6	1	4

The one child who had consistently differentiated *less* and *more* on the original pretest accounts for three of the six subtraction responses. Three children contributed the four cases of "subtraction plus addition." It may be worth observing that two of these made remarks which referred explicitly to *trying to make it less,* while indicating that they thought they had failed.

There is, then, in this second test, slightly more evidence of perplexity over *less* than was provided by the first test (where signs of perplexity were almost wholly lacking). But the general pattern with respect to that feature of the results that we are at present considering remains substantially unchanged.

The second finding to be considered here concerns the responses to the situation in which the two sets are initially equal and the child is asked: *Does one tree have more (less) apples on it than the other?* In this case, three subjects denied on every trial that one had more and likewise denied on every trial that one had less, responding, as might have been anticipated, by a simple *no* or shake of the head or by some such assertion as *They're the same.* However, a further six children gave evidence of denial of inequality, if responses such as *both of them, both the trees, that one does an' that one, they two ones, each tree,* and *these two have* are accepted as a form of denial. Of the six children who made assertions of the above kind, two, at one point or another, spontaneously asserted that the sets of apples were *both the same* or *both the same number,* and all answered *Yes* to the question *Is there the same number of apples on each tree?* However, it should be noted that three of these children gave answers of this kind only in response to the question *Does one tree have more . . .?*, whereas in answer to *less . . . ?* they simply chose one of the trees. The other three responded to *less . . .?* in the same way as they did to *more . . .?* using, once again, such expressions as *on each tree* and *both the trees.*

The evidence that has been presented so far indicates that, in the case of two pairs of antonyms, the children studied manifested in their responses a failure to differentiate between the two opposing members of the pair, showing in each case, a strong tendency to interpret both members in a way that would be correct for one of them in the adult language. In other words, the expected oppositions did not seem to be established.

The two pairs of antonyms may logically be related to one another in a way that has already been briefly indicated. Judgements of "more" and "less" already imply a judgement of difference. To use the terminology of the calculus of relations (Tarski, 1965), the relation "more than" and the relation "less than" are both included in the relation of diversity.

Further observations may be made about the logical properties of the relations. To take the most obvious, "same" is symmetrical, reflexive and transitive. "Different" is also symmetrical, but it is irreflexive and intransitive.

"More" and "less," on the other hand, are each symmetrical, irreflexive and transitive. That is, considered logically as relations, they resemble one another more closely than do "same" and "different."

Yet indifferentiation of the antonyms occurs in both cases. It is probably necessary, then, to turn, in the search for an interpretation of the findings, to a consideration of the highly complex functioning of relational terms in the language. Although *same/different* and *more/less* are certainly antonyms, they are by no means straightforwardly opposite to one another, even for adults. If we took only the above formal properties into account, then it would seem that, at least for *more* and *less* where these properties coincide, this ought to be the case. But it is sufficient to reflect that you can *put more in* to a glass, whereas you cannot (in the same sense) *take less out* for it to become evident that this is not so. In effect, *more* is ambiguous. It may be used in a simply additive sense as well as in a strictly comparative sense. It should be noted that ambiguity of this kind is not confined to *more.* This will be further discussed later (see p. 253).

In the attempt to interpret the findings, it may be best to begin by discussing what seem likely to be, ontogenetically, the most primitive contexts of the words we are considering.

More seems to be that one of the four that is normally produced soonest. Brown and Bellugi (1964) report, among the earliest noun phrases noted in the speech of their subjects, *more coffee* and *more nut*. It seems very probable that *more* is first comprehended — and produced — by children with reference to a context where one entity is changing — say, when the child wants food in addition to what he has already been given — and that judgement of one entity or set as having *more than* another is an appreciably later event. Notice that the word *less*, if heard by the child in the context that is here being postulated as the earliest for *more*, might well carry some such meaning as *more, but not so much more*. One adult might say to another, *That's too much. Give him less*. But there is no way of determining, on available evidence, whether this might have any connection with the findings reported here. However, a point that is in some ways similar may be made with respect to *different* and *same*. In everyday speech, sentences such as *Give me a different one* can — and commonly do — mean *Give me another one that is of the same kind*. In other words, the emphasis here is on difference in identity combined with some sort of similarity — and in this case, the phrase *a different one* is very close in meaning to the phrase *another one*. Now, while the word *different* does not seem to occur commonly in the early utterances of children, *other* is perhaps less rare. A child of 17 months, fetching the second of a pair of slippers, was observed to remark *other one* as she did so; and she then proceeded to fetch a pair of shoes, place them beside the slippers and again say *other one*.

It is possible, then, that *different* is first comprehended as implying a denial of object identity along with the presence of some sort of similarity; and that when the children in our group respond to the instruction *different in some way* in sets II and IV by preferring P(a,b) to D(a,b), they are in fact interpreting the instruction in this way. It is worth noting that the set of eleven objects from which they have to choose (the standard constituting, of course, the twelfth of the 4 by 3 matrix) contains six objects that satisfy the relation D(a,b) against five that satisfy the relation P(a,b). The preference for P(a,b) reported in Table 7.1 is therefore very marked.

It may, on the other hand, be that *different* and *same* are being treated as synonyms — which is what seems to happen in the case of *more* and *less*, as will shortly be discussed.

Before going on to this, however, it seems appropriate to make some reference to evidence concerning *same* and *different* as they occurred in the spontaneous speech of our subjects in the nursery over a period of eleven months from February to December 1967 — that is, from roughly three-and-a-half to four-and-a-half years of age.

In the first place, utterances containing the word *same* are appreciably more frequent than those containing *different*. *Different* is recorded only five times.

1. *I've been to a different one, not the same as that.* Here the child is denying that a picture represents a beach he has visited. The two beaches are not identical (not "one and the same") though obviously similar in many respects.

A second child uses *different* in the same sense and context three days later:

2. *A different seaside.*

3. *They're all the same, but they're different.* Here the child is speaking of books, and it again seems possible that *different* carries the meaning "not identican" or "different individuals." But this is less likely. Neil might be saying that though they are all alike in belonging to the class of books, they are different with respect to observable attributes such as size.

4. **Neil:** *What color, Maureen?*

   Maureen: *Yellow. There's different colors on mine.*

Here, beads are under discussion and, plainly, comparison of attributes is involved.

5. *I'm going to mend the car, because it's a different car.* The function of *because* here is obscure, but "different individual" is once more clearly implied. So this seems to be the sense carried by *different* in three out of the five recorded instances.

The word *same* occurs in sixteen utterances (excluding (1) and (3) above, where it occurs along with *different*). These may involve comparisons of objects or of actions, though the former are more common. In general, two objects are compared with respect to some attribute; that is, *same* is not used to mean "same individual." Examples are given below.

1. *I've got the same color,* referring to beads which two of the children are playing with.

2. *You've got the same as Alan.*

3. *We've all got the same* (with reference to color of straws).

4. *I want one the same* (with reference to a toy car).

5. *His looks the same size.*

6. *And if you turn the pages, you'll get the same thing again.*

7. *The airplanes are going the same way.*

8. *I can do the same as you.*

Most of the utterances are well-formed, but two are not;

9. *Got whiskers, a rabbit, same's mine.*

10. *This slide's the same like the slide when I go to Grannie's.*

The general conclusion is that the children show a greater tendency to use *same* than to use *different* where comparison of the properties of objects or actions is at issue. However, at this point a further consideration seems relevant.

It has already been remarked that relations expressing a precise kind and direction of difference are included logically within the general relation of diversity. So then it may be that when the children recognize — and want to speak about — differences in attributes, there is a tendency for them to move directly to the greater degree of specificity — to say, for instance, *mine's bigger than yours* (a very common type of statement in their spontaneous conversations) rather than to make the more general statement, *mine's different from yours.*

This, in turn, suggests some further reflections. It seems reasonable — and in accordance with available data — to suppose that it is easier to predicate one attribute of one object than to predicate one attribute of two (or more) objects at once. Children typically make utterances like *that's a blue flower* (Brown and Bellugi, 1964) before offering plural versions of the same kind of construction. And often, at a somewhat later stage, they will say *that one's green and that one's green* instead of *they are green,* or *both are green.* Now, it is known that children dealing with the Stanford-Binet (Form L-M) question on pictorial similarities and differences at year V will sometimes make statements like *that one is the same and that one is the same* — presumably by analogy with *that one's green and that one's green.* Statements like *that one is the same and that one is the same* are, of course, not well-formed, and suggest a failure to comprehend the relational nature of *same.* Yet they might possibly be an important step in the direction of the correct utterance *they are the same* — and the ultimate correct comprehension of what this implies. (This is obviously suggestive when seen in the light of the arguments of Lyons [1963] about locatives).

Consider, however, the case of observed difference in attributes. *That one's green and that one's blue* cannot yield, by quite the same direct analogy, *that one's different and that one's different* — and hence the ultimate assertion *they are different* may have to be arrived at by an alternative route.

Another way to express a similar notion is to remark that when two things are "the same," there is, after all, at least some one attribute which they share and which may facilitate the plural form that unites them in one predicate. But when "they are different" — what is "this thing" that they are......?

The evidence concerning *less* and *more* must now be further considered. A first obvious suggestion is that children rarely hear the word *less* in ordinary conversation. (Both *less* and *more* are among the first 500 words in the Thorndike and Lorge [1944] frequency counts, but this does not dispose of the question of whether, in everyday interchange between children and adults, the frequency differs significantly.)

However, if the explanation of the responses to *less* was merely that the children had rarely heard the term, they might reasonably be expected to show perplexity when given instructions containing it — or, at any rate, to interpret it in a diversity of ways. What we have to account for is that they so regularly, and

with so little sign of hesitation, interpret it as a synonym for *more*, sometimes
making this interpretation very explicit, as in the case of the child who, asked to
make a set of three less than one of two, replied: *But it is less.* What happened
was that the children responded as if they knew the word *less* and knew that it
referred to quantity, but as if it remained for them undifferentiated from *more,*
with *more* as the consistently dominant interpretation for the undifferentiated
pair. When perplexity did appear (though even then it was rare), it was in the
supplementary test, given six months after the original one — and so it presumably represents developmental advance by comparison with the earlier untroubled
state.

An attempt to handle these issues more precisely is made in Donaldson and
Balfour (op. cit.).

In the records of the children's spontaneous speech during the first eleven
months, there were only six utterances in which *more* occurred. No use of *less*
was recorded. Only two of the uses of *more* were unambiguously comparative
in the full sense. Both were produced by the same child (the child, incidentally,
who successfully differentiated *less* from *more* in the formal task) and both
referred to number of beads:

> *I've got more on than the other boy.*
> *We've got more beads than you have.*

The other utterances involved requests for *more bricks,* and references to *getting
some more tea* or to adding *some more* pieces to a figure that was being constructed.

There was one isolated use of *most: I've got the most* (wooden shapes).
I've got most of them. You can have some.

We now go on to a discussion of the studies of the spatial comparative
adjectives.

Reference has been made at an earlier point in this paper to the current
lack of any formal linguistic analysis of comparative constructions, to the
extreme diversity of these and to the problem of giving an account of them that
will reveal the nature of their underlying relatedness. Study of the data that we
are about to report has brought us increasingly to a belief in the value of a
semantically based approach to this problem. The nature of this approach can
only be sketched here, but it has as an essential feature an emphasis on recognition of the importance of contextual reference. This is meant to imply that
comparative constructions can only be interpreted with reference to some
attribute of a given context. Thus, even *John is tall,* if interpreted as *John is
taller than average,* is likely to make different sense to different people if the
context of "taller than average" is *not* supplied; for example it will probably be
interpreted differently by Gulliver, a Lilliputian, an adult pygmy, and a four-
year-old child. If this point is accepted as even arguable, then this implies that

at least this set of constructions can only be analyzed correctly by taking into account aspects of the possible referential contexts. This is not, of course, to say that it is necessary to commit the analysis to some limited theory of reference, but rather that an analysis, in dealing, for instance, with *John is taller than average,* would have to take into account the possibility of handling *tall* semantically (for instance, as Bierwisch [1967] does); of handling a semantic (or pragmatic) specification of *than average* in this context; and also of handling the implication, carried linguistically, of the nature of the normative comparison being expressed. The point of the phrase "nature of the comparison" is that there is a distinction to be drawn between two different kinds of comparison — and the distinction is one that may prove to be of considerable significance for the study of ontogenesis. Expressions like *taller* are what we might call *descriptively comparative;* but there are other comparative constructions, notably *too-X* and *X-enough,* that may more appropriately be called *functionally comparative.* The following sets of sentences illustrate this distinction and some of its implications for the admissibility of utterances. (Asterisks mark inadmissible sentences).

1. John is taller than the wall.
2. John is not taller than the wall.
3. John is shorter than the wall.
4. John is not shorter than the wall.
5. John is tall enough to see over the wall.
6. John is not tall enough to see over the wall.
*7. John is short enough to see over the wall.
*8. John is not short enough to see over the wall.
*9. John is too tall to see over the wall.
*10. John is not too tall to see over the wall.
11. John is too short to see over the wall.
12. John is not too short to see over the wall.

If John's problem were not seeing over the wall but walking under a bar (a certain distance above the ground), then the permissible set would be:

13. John is taller than the bar.
14. John is not taller than the bar.
15. John is shorter than the bar.
16. John is not shorter than the bar.
*17. John is tall enough to walk under the bar.
*18. John is not tall enough to walk under the bar.
19. John is short enough to walk under the bar.
20. John is not short enough to walk under the bar.
21. John is too tall to walk under the bar.
22. John is not too tall to walk under the bar.

*23. John is too short to walk under the bar.
*24. John is not too short to walk under the bar.

The appropriateness of the comparatives here is closely linked to the prepositions. Notice the further interesting point that the inadmissible cases above, namely 7 and 8, 9 and 10, 17 and 18, and 23 and 24 are all inadmissible in the negative when inadmissible in the affirmative. On the other hand, if the verb rather than the comparative adjective is negated, the admissibility changes (cf. *John is short enough not to see over the wall*). These facts suggest that there are interesting semantic interconnections between comparison and negation.

It is important to observe at this point that *too-X* and *X-enough* are not always so clearly or completely asymmetric in admissibility as they are here. It depends on the functional properties of the situation. In the above illustrations, the functional comparatives are a way of marking in sentences the satisfaction (or otherwise) of some criterion of adequacy, where adequacy is bounded on one side only. But in certain circumstances — notably where "exact fit" is in question — adequacy is bounded on both sides (cf. the hierarchy of n-state comparisons suggested on p. 255), and the relations between functional comparatives are thereby altered. This illustrates what has already been said about the importance of referential context.

The complexity of the situation we are considering may be illustrated in a number of additional ways. First, while polar antonyms are in general implicitly comparative, the positive (but not the negative) pole may be ambiguous in much the same way as *more* is ambiguous (see p. 247). Certainly all the unidimensional adjectives are thus ambiguous in English, and also a few multidimensional ones such as *great* and — similarly in Latin — *maximus*. This can be seen through their occurrence in measure phrases. *Policemen are six feet tall* merely means *are tall* as determined by the arbitrary constant of being six feet or more in height. They cannot be six feet short. Thus in this example the negative pole is strictly inadmissible. However, even in cases in which the use of the negative pole is not impossible — for example, *How shallow is the lake?* — it seems intuitively obvious that a speaker would normally tend to ask *How deep is the lake?* unless there were some contextual constraint. That is, the positive pole is the preferred term in most circumstances.

A further illustration of the complexity of interconnections that has to be recognized is provided by consideration of the equative form *as. . .as*. If we say that (a) *X is not as big as Y*, we would generally take (a) to mean (b) *X is smaller than Y;* and not take it as an ambiguous utterance with (c) *X is bigger than Y* as an alternative reading. This asymmetry can be shown to be general with reference to functional contexts. If we are talking about something of size X with respect to the possibility of its fitting (exactly) into a given hole of size Y, we might say *X is as big as Y*. This would mean that *X is not too big to fit Y; X is*

not too small to fit Y; X is big enough to fit Y; and *X is small enough to fit Y.*
If, however, *X is not as big as Y* (with reference to the same functional context),
this would mean *X is too small to fit Y,* and *X is not big enough to fit Y.* (It
would *not* mean *X is too big to fit Y* or *X is not small enough to fit Y).* If we now
pursue these alternatives, together with the negation of such related expressions
as *X is big, X is bigger than Y,* and the like, it soon becomes clear that the comparatives and equatives are essentially asymmetric in their interaction with negative forms.

Note now that the equative *X is as . . . as Y* can be logically defined (cf.
Quine [1953]) as the conjunction of the negation of the contradictory comparatives. To use Quine's example: "Consider a theory of bodies compared in point
of length. The values of the bound variables are physical objects, and the only
predicate is *L* where *Lxy* means *x is longer than y.* Now where $\sim Lxy.$ $\sim Lyx,$
anything that can be truly said of *x* within this theory holds equally for *y* and
vice-versa. Hence it is convenient to treat $\sim Lxy. \sim Lyx$ as *x = y.* Such identification amounts to reconstruing the values of our variables as universals, namely,
lengths, instead of physical objects" (p. 117). Such universals "may be regarded
as entering here merely as a manner of speaking — through the metaphorical use
of the identity sign for what is really not identity but sameness *of length*"(p. 118)
[italics supplied]. This particular illustration might point to the source of some
of the difficulty, indicated earlier, that arises over *same/different.* Later we shall
also indicate that the strong and necessary use of a sameness relation is a logical
consequence of the conjoining of the negation of contradictory comparatives
only when there is reference to a given physical system. That the use of *same*
does not always hold as a strong *same* relation in the language is pointed out by
the fact that we have expressions like *exactly the same, just as . . . as,* and the
like.

The need to take account of the interrelations of comparison, negation and
particular referential contexts, and to look at the use of comparatives in terms
of the semantic function involved, should now be clear. We think it important to
stress that our awareness of these issues developed as a direct outcome of our
attempts to make sense of the child's acquisition and use of comparatives of this
complex sort. [3]

---

[3] A related issue is the role of *and* and *but* in conjoining comparative statements. Take
for illustration a situation (used in the Edinburgh Cognition Project) in which a subject has
to press a key when he sees a card that is related to the standard, X, in a way described by
such a conjoining. Consider the following:

25. as tall as X and as wide as X
26. as tall as X and wider than X
27. as tall as X and not as wide as X
*28. as tall as X but as wide as X
(Continued on next page).

A detailed discussion of relevant syntactic and semantic issues will be found in Campbell and Wales (1969); and these and other related problems will be considered with special reference to ontogenesis in Wales and Campbell (forthcoming). Meanwhile, on the basis of this preliminary survey of the issues and of what needs to be incorporated in any analysis that will be interesting from a performance point of view, we would suggest the following hierarchy of complexity of comparisons that may be expressed in the language:

1. *One-state comparison.* This is exemplified by the use of "more" in its additive sense (cf. p. 247). While this is perhaps not strictly comparative, it might be claimed that it would be unintelligible without a prior general context of comparative judgements.

2. *Two-state comparison.* The defining feature here is that there is comparison between an object and a standard (implicit or explicit), but the comparative judgement requires only a yes/no decision and the standard is not definite. Superlatives (in which the comparison is between a member and the rest of the class) and all adjectives that are implicitly comparative are included here. So also are the functional comparatives *too-X* and *X-enough,* given a context in which exactness of fit is not at issue.

3. *Three-state comparison.* Here the standard is definite and the comparative judgement involves explicit reference to one of two possible directions of departure from it, the directions being those marked by the polarities of the antonymous stems. All explicit descriptive comparatives, such as *more . . . than* and *X-er than,* fall into this category.

4. *Four-state comparison.* In this case there are functional contexts requiring not only a yes/no comparison, but also comparison of exactness of fit (or lack of it) with respect to a given standard, such as *just . . . enough* (and the like), and also *just the same as.*

Notice in the last three the issue of definiteness, and notice also, in general terms, that *enough* marks an inequality towards a norm, whereas the others mark inequalities away from a norm. Definiteness is seen to be important by consideration of the ambiguity of reference of *a bigger one,* whereas *the bigger one* is unambiguous.

(Continued from p. 254).
29. as tall as X but as wide as Y
30. as tall as X but not as wide as X
31. as tall as X but wider than X

These clearly provide still further evidence of the interconnection between comparison, negation, and reference. (They also indicate the value of the traditional notion that *but* serves not only for conjoining statements but also for denying that statements are in certain respects consistent with each other.)

Four interrelated studies of comparatives other than *more/less* and *same/ different* have been conducted, involving one direct comprehension test, one production test, and two tests that start with an attempt at elicitation and, if this procedure fails, move into testing for comprehension. The essential aspects of the procedures, and summaries of some of the results of the first two tests, will be reported. Notes on the last two will also be included. Full accounts and analyses will be found in Wales and Campbell (op. cit).

I THE COMPREHENSION TEST

There were eight items in all. In each, four objects were shown to S. and a standard procedure was used. One set of material and the form of the procedure are illustrated in Fig. 7.2.

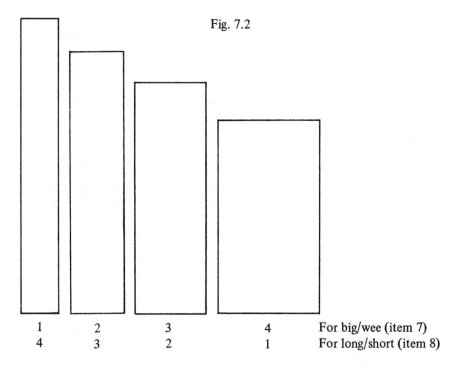

Fig. 7.2

1	2	3	4	For big/wee (item 7)
4	3	2	1	For long/short (item 8)

E.: *Point to the biggest one.*
E.: *Now point to the wee-est one.*
E.: *Now give me one that's bigger than this one* (No. 2).
E.: *Is there another one that's bigger than this one?* (No. 2).
If *No.*   E.: *Are you sure?*, and so on.
If *Yes.*   E.: *Give me it, then.*
E.: *Now give me one that's wee-er than this one* (No. 3).
E.: *Is there another one that's wee-er than this one?* (No. 3).
If *No.*   E.: *Are you sure?*, and so on.
If *Yes.*   E.: *Give me it, then.*

In the different items, various different sets of objects and different adjective pairs were used. In what follows, as implied earlier, we take *big, long, tall, high,* and the like as the positive poles of the adjective pairs.

Responses to Superlatives

There are scored 1 for correct response, 0 for incorrect. The breakdown of scores across items is:

(1)		(2)		(3)		(4)	
biggest:	wee-est	longest:	shortest	thickest:	thinnest	highest:	lowest
15	15	14	9	10	8	13	6

(5)		(6)		(7)		(8)	
tallest:	shortest	fattest:	thinnest	biggest:	wee-est	longest:	shortest
9	6	12	3	8	3	10	8

(The difference between items [1] and [7] was that [1] used three-dimensional objects [cubes]; [7] used two-dimensional ones as illustrated above, which dimensions might be said to be in "conflict." The same holds for items [2] and [8].) Notice the consistent and obviously statistically significant finding that responses to the positive pole are superior to responses to the negative pole.

We would expect the chosen object to be one of the referential extremes if the superlative *-est* was being understood correctly. The breakdown of responses looked at in these terms is:

	Nonextremes	*Extremes*
Positive pole + *est*	5	115
Negative pole + *est*	47	73

The significant entry in this table is 47. This breaks down in an interesting way: of the 47 nonextreme choices, 34 were of the object immediately adjacent in size to the chosen positive pole object. That is, having chosen object 1 from the size series 1, 2, 3, 4, as being the +ve +est one, Ss were most likely to choose object 4 as being the—ve +est one, but in the event of their not choosing object 4, they were most likely to choose object 2 ($X^2 = 9.3$, p $<.01$).

Responses to Comparatives

With the same initial simple scores, results are:

(1)		(2)		(3)		(4)	
bigger:	wee-er	longer:	shorter	thicker:	thinner	higher:	lower
14	13	12	14	11	10	13	10

(5)		(6)		(7)		(8)	
taller:	shorter	fatter: thinner		bigger:	wee-er	longer:	shorter
10	7	10	7	7	5	10	9

Again there is the superiority of performance on the positive poles, but it is not so marked as with the superlatives.

One interesting result was the failure of most subjects on most occasions to choose a second object, after having chosen a first one correctly. This was requested and always possible. Out of 162 correct initial choices, in only 38 cases did a correct second choice follow — and 3 subjects accounted for 21 of these. This raises the possibility that the S's handling of the comparative morpheme was semantically analogous to his handling of the superlative morpheme. However, this does not seem to be the case. Analysis of the number of cases in which only one correct choice was given shows that, out of a total of 124 such choices, 54 were choices of the extreme item (that is, the item that was both -er than the standard and -est of the set of four), and the remaining 70 choices were of the intermediate item.

II THE PRODUCTION TEST

This test was couched in the form of a story of some men looking for a dog and encountering various situations. At fairly regular intervals, E. would produce a picture and ask questions about it, with the aim of eliciting a choice that was appropriate — for example, when looking for the dog, *Which tree* (of the three pictured) *would be best to climb up?* – and would then attempt to elicit from the child a linguistic justification of his choice. Four of the situations are illustrated in Fig. 7.3. The figure under each drawing indicates the number of times it was chosen in response to the accompanying question. Choices that were judged appropriate are underlined. Note the discrepancy between items (2) and (3) above. In both cases it was possible to match the modal choice with the desired end: the man to reach the highest tree, and the plank to span the wider river.

Justifications

A rough classification has been made for present purposes as follows:

Type 1. The presumably most advanced type is one that is, first, *objective* (that is, refers to some characteristic of the pictured object [s]) and second, *relevant* to the end for which the object was selected (that is, refers to some aspect of the object's size). Four subjects consistently offered justifications of this type.

Type 2. Responses of this type were, in the main, *subjective* (that is, referred to some state of the subject; *'cause I just know, I like him the most* and the like) or *objective but irrelevant.* That is, they either were tautological – for example, *'cause it is* – or mentioned some strictly irrelevant circumstance – for example, *to get the dog.* Sometimes they were failures to offer any justification (such as *don't know* and no response). Seven subjects responded consistently in one or other of these ways. Subcategorization along the lines suggested does not lead to a consistent breakdown of these subjects.

Type 3. The remaining four subjects gave some responses of type 1 and some of type 2. Occasional responses here of a type 1 variety were *eliminative.* That is, the child would justify the choice by elimination of the other possibilities, for instance by saying (in item 4 above) *that one* (thick log) *would not be the easiest one.*

The breakdown of 120 justifications is as follows: no response, 10; don't know, 8; tautological, 18; subjective, 11; objective, 71; inscrutable, 2. The breakdown of the "objective" responses in relation to the immediate concern of this paper is given in Table 7.4.

TABLE 7.4

Adjectival Predicates					Other
Positive Adj. x	Comparative x-er	Superlative x-est	Too-x	X-enough	
13	2	16	6	1	27

(1) *Which man do you think eats the most?*

(2) *Which man do you think picked bananas off that tree?* (tree no. 1)

(3) *Which plank would be the best one to make a bridge?*

(4) *Which log would be the easiest one to cut through?*

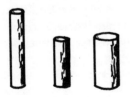

Fig. 7.3

This does not include the six eliminative responses. The *x-enough* case and two of the *too-x* cases occurred in contexts that suggested that a descrptive comparison was intended, for instance in item 4 (p. 257) *'Cos that's big enough, they're wee enough,* and *that's too big and they're too wee.* The other two tests were as follows:

III. A tape recorder was used as the material for the task itself. Ss were encouraged to describe the tape recorder to itself (that is, as it was recording). After some time had been spent establishing the procedure on details such as the operating switches, color, and the like, attention was focused on the relative size of the tape reels. A pilot study on six children of five to six years of age, who were not conservers (of amount), had established that such children tended to describe the tapes in terms of *that side* (x) *is bigger; that side* (y) *is smaller; that side* (x) *is getting smaller; that side* (y) *is getting bigger,* and the like, but would still refuse to accept that the tapes would eventually come to a point of equality *(Will they ever be the same size? – No.)* The three- to four-year-old children used in this study, however, found great difficulty in describing the tape recorder reels and in the majority of cases used descriptions like *that side is big.* The interesting thing is the relative lack of variety and structure in the productions in this situation as compared with those elicited in the story. What is clear about this situation is that the necessity for the tapes to be "the same" at some point cannot be inferred merely on the basis of conservation of length of tape (that is, by the negation of the conjuction of the contradictory comparatives). It is also necessary to have knowledge about the tape speed. That is, the conjoined use of these comparative statements does not justify, except by reference to properties of this particular physical system, the conclusion that a point of equality of size will ever be reached.

IV. The fourth test was inspired by the work of Sinclair-de-Zwart (1967), and was used to throw further light on the adjectives used by these children to talk about the relative sizes of objects in a seriation task. Sinclair-de-Zwart, starting with a complete series, found that children who were not concrete-operational subjects would correctly describe each object in an ascending series from left to right as bigger than the one on its left. If they then described a descending series, there was a crucial difference in performance according to whether the series was now descending from right to left (the inverse of the previous one) or continuing from left to right. In the former case, the Ss erroneously continued to refer to the (now smaller) objects as *bigger.* In the left to right descending series, they would shift to *smaller,* which Sinclair suggests occurs because this shift does not require a reversal of the logical operations underlying the description of the series. Instead of presenting the S. with a complete series from the outset, we added objects one at a time, and used an open-ended procedure, starting always from the request *Tell me about these two men.* While the responses are very varied, even within a series, it is perhaps possible to make two generalizations: first, a few Ss appear to have the same problem of linguistic shift as was noted by Sinclair; but in the situation that we used, the failure to shift was accompanied by an appropriate change in the pointing operation. (This also occurred in the case of the many within-series shifts.) That is, the use of *bigger* (which dominated throughout) was maintained as a correct usage. Second, the Ss in general seemed to switch less frequently from *bigger* to *wee-er* in the "continuing" series than in the "reversal" series.

There are a number of conclusions that may already be clear from the above results on the comparatives: first, the children do operate in terms of the polarities assumed in most theoretical discussions; second, even before they are used in a well-formed fashion, comparatives are differentiated from superlatives, though they are sometimes used as equivalent expressions; and third, the use and appropriateness of the comparative expressions can only be fully understood in terms of the referential contexts of their use. This latter point is very clear from the "spontaneous" use of comparatives recorded in the nursery — of which, in the first eleven months, there were 160 utterances (therefore they cannot be analyzed here!). It is very striking, however, that it is relatively easy to classify the uses in terms of the situations in which they occurred, for instance asking for things, modeling, and talking about things the children can see. Perhaps the most interesting point here is that the uses of "true" comparatives are often in (roughly) "competitive discourse" situations, such as the following (Neil is playing with a car):

Neil:	*I've got a little black one.*
Maureen:	*I've got a little black one in my house.*
Neil:	*I've got a bigger one than you . . . up to my ceiling.*
Maureen:	*So've I.*

If comparatives are used typically to *justify* certain comparative judgements, then this is precisely the kind of discourse situation in which they could be expected to occur in an appropriate form.

Finally, it seems as though the stem polar adjectives (such as *big, more,* and *tall*) are ontogenetically prior to any other comparative constructions. Perhaps the order of acquisition subsequently proceeds: superlatives, *too-x* (used descriptively), and "true" comparatives (*more than, x-er* etc.), followed by *too-x* and *x-enough* used as functional comparatives. Of course, inferences and claims about the order of acquisition of structures can only be safely made from longitudinal data. This we hope to analyze in due course.

CONCLUDING COMMENTS

It must be obvious by now that the studies summarized here are better understood as posing than as resolving problems. As a matter of fact, given the present state of developmental psycholinguistics, we would be uneasy if this were other than the case.

An immediate conclusion that may be drawn is that children's failure to respond appropriately in tasks in which they are instructed to perform in accord with such talk as *same as, different from, more than, Is there more here or more here?* and the like, may be as attributable to the structure of the child's language as to other aspects of his cognitive apparatus. Much more work needs to be done before results from such studies become, in any systematic fashion, fully interpretable. To show that similar results may be found when the "same" tasks are presented "non-verbally" merely begs the question unless it can be clearly demonstrated that the apparent convergence of the language performance and other cognitive performance misleadingly reflects two quite unrelated systems of competence. We hold that the simplest interpretation is that the apparent convergence reflects an interaction of the two systems of competence – in a noncircular fashion – because of the apparent need in considering both systems independently, to take account of referential aspects of the situation the child is immediately confronted with, together with what look like the same formal relations some of the time. Having said that is not to have said very much, except, however, that in this instance, data instead of pure conjecture have helped us to say it. What is now needed is an attempt to develop alternative formalizations that might be appropriate and also to show, through further observation and experiment, what usefulness there may be in trying to map certain cognitive relations in ways that are consistent with linguistic relations or vice-versa. On the cognitive side some valuable suggestions already exist through the work of Piaget (as in Beth and Piaget, 1966), though alternative formalizations may be required, and, anyway, evaluative criteria need to be developed to assess their appropriateness. On the language side we are strongly hinting that what psycho-linguistics needs are criteria of *context appropriateness* for *utterances* constrained by the linguistic criteria for *grammaticality/acceptability* of *sentences.* That we are not being too unrealistic in expressing these desires is shown, on the one hand, by the increased interest in the possibility that deep structure categories are semantically derived (for example, Lyons, 1968; Fillmore, 1968); and on the other, by the current interest in the possibility that *speech acts,* in Austin's sense, must be expressed in the deep structure analyses of sentences (for example, Boyd and Thorne, 1969). It is presumably quite possible that these two approaches will converge. They certainly both seem to be motivated by some of the same problems that have concerned us in this chapter when we have talked of the need to consider the referential-semantic aspects of the comparative constructions, and the need to consider the functional appropriateness of the utterances. Both approaches also seem to be involved in a shift to the hazy borderline between linguistic competence and performance. One of the reasons for our use of a fully overt performance approach is the belief that only through the study of the same kind of linguistic relation in different performance settings will a sufficiently reliable consensus of data enable us to formulate a theoretically interesting description of competence. Presumably, in fact, linguists have to start from performance in the first place in the description of competence; for example, in the partitioning of some acceptable utterances from others that are not acceptable, and the like. If this is so, then it might be a misleading methodological move to attempt to discuss what is the appropriate grammatical description of the child's language before at least a reasonably coherent rule-of-thumb interpretation of the child's performance is available. Traditional and contemporary linguistic, philosophical, or psychological theories, or our own intuitions, may serve as sources of hypotheses as to what to look for in such an interpretation. The need for a variety of ways of looking at the child's language is well illustrated by our own study in which, if we had attempted to view the child's *competence* solely on the ground of any one of our tests, or solely on the "spontaneous" utterances in the nursery, we would almost certainly have been led to serious distortions in our understanding of what sorts of structure were involved. As it is, a fairly coherent picture is starting to emerge. We will not rehash findings and conclusions already formulated in the body of the chapter since, among other things, this is merely the summary of a continuing study. It would be foolhardy to try to draw the conclusion that we have shown necessary relatedness between the linguistic and cognitive structures of the child, but our results suggest that it would be equally foolhardy to reject the possibility without much more careful study and much richer theories.

REFERENCES

Beth, E. W., and Piaget, J. *Mathematical Epistemology and Psychology.* Dordrecht, Holland: Reidel, 1966.

Bierwisch, M. Some semantic universals of German adjectivals. *Foundations of Language,* 1967, **3**, 1-36.

Boyd, J. and Thorne, J.P. The semantics of modal verbs. *Journal of Linguistics* 1969, **5**, 57-74.

Brown, R. and Bellugi, U. Three processes in the child's acquisition of syntax. *Harvard Educational Review,* 1964, **34**, 151.

Campbell, R. N. and Wales, R.J. Comparative structures in English *Journal of Linguistics,* 1969, **5**, 215-251.

Chomsky, N. *Aspects of the Theory of Syntax.* Cambridge, Mass.: M.I.T. Press, 1965.

Donaldson, M. Prepared comment on paper by D. McNeill. In *Psycholinguistics Papers:* J. Lyons and R. J. Wales (Eds.), Edinburgh: Edinburgh University Press, 1966.

Donaldson, M. and Balfour, G. Less is more: a study of language comprehension in children. *British Journal of Psychology* 1968, **59**, 461-471.

Fillmore, C. The case for case. In *Universale in Linguistic Theory.* New York: Holt, Rinehart and Winston, E. Bach and R. Harms (Eds.) 1968.

Jespersen, O. *The Philosophy of Grammar.* London: Allen & Unwin, 1924.

Lees, R. B. Grammatical analysis of the English comparative construction. *Word,* 1961, **17**, 171-185.

Lyons, J. *Structural Semantics.* Oxford: Blackwell, 1963 (Publications of the Philological Society, XX).

Lyons, J. *Introduction to Theoretical Linguistics.* Cambridge: Cambridge University Press, 1968.

McNeill, D. The development of language. In *Carmichael's Manual of Child Psychology.* P. A. Mussen (Ed.) (in press).

Peirce, C. S. *Collected Papers, Vol. III.* C. Hartshorne and P. Weiss (Eds.), Cambridge, Mass.: Harvard University Press, 1933.

Penelhum, T. Personal identity. In *Encyclopedia of Philosophy, Vol. 6.* Paul Edwards (Ed.), New York: MacMillan and Free Press, 1967.

Quine, W. van O. *From a Logical Point of View.* Cambridge, Mass.: Harvard University Press, 1953.

Reichenbach, H. *Elements of Symbolic Logic.* New York: Free Press, 1947.

Reitman, W. R. *Cognition and Thought: An Information Processing Approach.* New York: Wiley, 1965.

Sinclair-de-Zwart, H. *Acquisition du langage et développement de la pensée.* Paris: Dunod, 1967.

Smith, C. S. A class of complex modifiers in English. *Language,* 1961, **41**, 37-58.

Tarski, A. *Introduction to Logic and to the Methodology of the Deductive Sciences.* New York: Oxford University Press, 1965.

Thorndike, E. L. and Lorge, I. The Teacher's Word Book of 30,000 Words. New York: Bureau of Publications, Teachers' College, Columbia University, 1944.

Vlastos, G. Degrees of reality in Plato. In *New Essays on Plato and Aristotle.* Reinford Bambrough (Ed.), London: Routledge and Kegan Paul, 1965.

Wales, R. J. and Campbell, R. N. The ontogenesis of comparison (forthcoming).

CHAPTER 8

Herbert H. Clark

Stanford University

THE PRIMITIVE NATURE OF
CHILDREN'S RELATIONAL CONCEPTS

The previous chapter by Donaldson and Wales (henceforth called D and W), "On the Acquisition of Some Relational Terms," is a valuable contribution to our knowledge of cognition in general and to our understanding of early language development in particular. I think it is particularly important for two reasons: it presents an extensive theoretical discussion of relational terms in English and their importance; and it presents significant, new, and interesting data on the use of relational terms by children. Unfortunately, the paper does not then proceed to relate the two points—the theory and the data—to the extent that it could. It doesn't appreciate fully how the theory is to explain the data, or how the data are to test the theory. In the following discussion, I would therefore like to fill in this gap as best I can, exploring the basis for the primitive nature of children's relational concepts. In doing so, I will present other linguistic facts—and some psychological data—that can profitably be brought to bear on the children's data. In the end, I will make a few comments on methodology—essentially cautions to future experimenters in this area.

There are two main findings in D and W's research. First, in very young children, *more* and *less* are used synonymously, and they both appear to mean "more." The analogous result holds for other comparatives and superlatives; the positive end of the scale is used correctly more often than the negative end. Second, *same* and *different* are also not often used correctly. *Different* is usually taken to mean "different item with the same attributes." Both findings are well supported, since they are based on a variety of ingenious experiments, all directed at how children use and understand language, not just at what they produce.

The children's use of *more* or *less* is of particular interest to me, since I have also been working on comparatives. Although all my subjects have been adults, I have found that they have some of the same problems with comparatives—albeit not such obvious problems—as D and W's children do. Experiments with adults have also convinced me that there is much to be gained from a linguistic analysis of the comparative and of the underlying adjectives.

Such an analysis is necessary, I have found, to explain how people understand and use comparative statements in deductive reasoning and how they remember comparative sentences (Clark, 1969, in press; Clark and Card, in press). I must therefore disagree with D and W, who express the opinion that linguistics has nothing firm to say about comparative constructions. True, the analysis of comparatives is incomplete at present, but the analysis as it stands so far appears quite firm on several points. But before discussing the linguistic analysis of comparatives, I would like to look at the nature of the adjectives that enter into comparatives, words like *long* and *short*.

Long and *short* are polar opposites, with *long* positive and *short* negative. Why is *long* called the positive term? A common sense answer is that *long* indicates the presence of an attribute and *short* its absence. This answer, I think, is essentially correct, but its importance for language development comes from other linguistic properties of positive and negative adjectives. As D and W point out—and as others (Sapir, 1944; Lyons, 1963, 1968; Greenberg, 1966; Bierwisch, 1967; Vendler, 1968) have before them—*long* is also the term used in such sentences as *The board is ten feet long*. It is obviously ungrammatical to say, *The board is ten feet short*. A second point D and W bring out is that *long* is implicitly comparative, for if we say *The board is long* we mean that we have some implicit standard and that the board is longer than it.

But let us consider the sentence *The board is ten feet long* more closely. It can be paraphrased by the sentence *The board is ten feet in length* or *The length of the board is ten feet* or some other such sentence. Clearly, the term *long* in the paraphrased sentence means only that we should be measuring the length rather than the *width, thickness, distance,* or *height* of the board. This use of *long*, then, contains no implicit comparison against a standard, as the other use of *long* does. Notice that we can say, *The short elf is one foot tall*, but not *The short elf is tall*. The second sentence is incongruous just because *tall* without a quantifier can only be interpreted contrastively.

What conclusions can we draw from these facts about English adjectives? It appears that there are two meanings for *long*, but only one for *short*. First, *long* has what will be termed a *nominal* use; it means "of the dimension length." Second, *long* also has a *contrastive* use and means "longer than average." *Short* has only a contrastive use and never means merely "length."

The distinction between the nominal and contrastive uses of *long* becomes more convincing when we consider other facts about English. The name of the length dimension is, of course, *length,* not *shortness,* and *length* is morphologically derived from *long. Shortness* contrasts with *longness* (if we can use that term), whereas *length* contrasts with *width, depth, height,* and other dimensional names. Another important point is that the question, *How long is that board?*, is usually neutral; the questioner is implying that he would not be surprised if he heard that the board was either quite long or quite short. But the question, *How short is that board?*, is not neutral. Here the questioner implies that he expects the board to be short, so he is asking how short.

The nominal *long* is semantically prior to both the contrastive *long* and the contrastive *short*. We must posit the dimension *length* before we can speak of measurement on the dimension—*long* (= "much length") and *short* (= "little length"). We might characterize the nominal *long* as superordinate to the contrastive *long* and the contrastive *short*. I have argued elsewhere (Clark, 1969) that nominal *long* can also be described with one fewer semantic feature than either contrastive *long* or contrastive *short*. This agrees with traditional linguistic terminology. *Long* is called *unmarked*, since it can be used in a neutralized sense, and *short* is called *marked*, since it cannot.

Conceptually, there is one remarkable coincidence among the spatial adjectives of English: it is always the unmarked term that designates physical extension along a dimension. Notice that spatial adjectives usually come in unmarked-marked pairs, for example, *deep-shallow* for *depth, high-low* for *height, distant-close* or *far-near* for *distance, wide-narrow* for *width*, and the like. *Long* refers to extension of *length*, not lack of it. A line that has no length is not just a short line—it is nothing, it is a point. But a line without shortness is even difficult to speak of. Apparently, it would be longer than average, but would still have length. The same sort of reasoning applies equally well to *deep, high, tall, distant, far, wide,* and the other unmarked spatial adjectives. This illustration points out that extension is a physical phenomenon, not a product of the semantics of English. And most important, there is no *a priori* reason for the unmarked adjective to refer to the extended rather than the unextended end of the scale. There is also no reason why the extended end of the scale should be related consistently to the marked or unmarked adjective at all. Dimension names could denote extension on one dimension, but lack of extension on another. The consistencies here, although there *appear* to be no *a priori* reasons for them, are obviously not adventitious. There must be an explanation for them.

With this conceptualization of antonyms in mind, now consider the English comparative construction, for example, *John has more apples than Dick.* There is one point that all the linguists who have studied comparatives (Lees, 1961; Smith, 1961; Chomsky, 1965; Huddleston, 1967; Doherty and Schwartz, 1967) agree on, and that is that such a sentence is derived from two underlying "base strings." *John has more apples than Dick* is derived ultimately from *John has many apples* and *Dick has many apples.* The two primitive base strings are combined to form *John has more apples than Dick has many apples*; with obligatory changes and deletions it becomes *John has more apples than Dick has* or *John has more apples than Dick.* Notice that we can say *The desk is longer than the door is wide,* retaining the adjectives from both base strings, since *long* and *wide* are not identical.

Furthermore, the unmarked adjective can take on neutral meaning in comparative sentences, just as it can in questions (Clark, in press, *a*). Thus *The board is longer than the desk* can imply that the board and desk are long, but it can also mean merely that the board has a length that is more than the length of the desk, without implying that either is long. This ambiguity, however, cannot occur when the adjective is *short,* since *short* cannot be used nominally. *The board is shorter than the desk* implies that the board and desk are short. These generalizations, of course, hold for each pair of unmarked-marked adjectives; for example, *John has more apples than Dick* is ambiguous in this respect, whereas *John has less apples than Dick* implies that John and Dick have a paucity of apples.

These linguistic facts will now be used as a basis for an explanation of D and W's most interesting result—that *more* and *less* are synonymous for young Scottish children. *More* and *less* are the comparative forms of *much* and *little,* and apparently of *many* and *few* as well in Scottish English. (In my own American English, *fewer,* not *less,* is the comparative of *few.*) Of *much* and *little, much* is unmarked, and of *many* and *few, many* is unmarked. That is to say, *much* and *many* can be used in both a nominal and contrastive sense. *How much money do you have*? is a neutral question, meaning "What is the amount of money you have?" But *How little money do you have*? is clearly contrastive, implying the questioner expects you to have little money.

We can now posit the following developmental sequence. First, the child uses *more* and *less* in the nominal noncomparative sense only. Second, since the nominal term refers to extension rather than to lack of extension, he uses both *more* and *less* to refer to the extended end of the scale. Finally, he learns to distinguish *less* from *more* and apply it to the less extended end of the scale comparatively. Let us go into these stages in detail.

In the first stage, *more* and *less* both mean "a quantity of" or "some." A question people might commonly ask a child is "Do you want more food?" Notice that the comparison is not complete. It should continue, "than you have been given so far." Of the two underlying base strings, one is explicit—*you want much (or some) food*—and the other completely implicit—*you have been given much (or some) food so far.* To the child who cannot know the existence of the second base string, the question can only mean "Do you want *some* food?" The child probably encounters *less,* too, in elliptical utterances; for example, "I have more food, and you have less." He would interpret *less* also as "some," since it occurs as a single "adjective" modifying *food.* The senses of "a quantity of" and "some," of course, are equivalent to the nominal use of *much.* This would explain why *more* and *less* are treated synonymously, although it would not explain why both mean "more" at this stage.

Thus, to predict how children will choose among two sizes of objects, we must assume that the notion of "having extent" is best exemplified by the object having the most extent. As a consequence, when asked to choose the tree with *more,* or *less,* apples on it, the child will point to the tree with more, because it best exemplifies to him "a tree with some apples on it." This is just what D and W found in most of their subjects. There was one particular child who balked when requested to make it so that there are less apples on a tree with more on it than the other. His reply was, "But it *is* less on that tree," which could well be paraphrased, "But there *are* some on that tree."

In the final stage, *more* and *less* are at last used in their true comparative meaning. The child must attend to both objects at the same time; he must bring both base strings correctly into the same relational sentence. He understands that he must compare two things to decide which has the higher or lower measurement of extent. Only a few of D and W's children were at this stage; presumably, they will all use *more* and *less* correctly at some time later, just as all adults do.

The developmental sequence just described also explains the children's difficulties with *taller-shorter, thicker-thinner, higher-lower, bigger-wee-er,* and so on. If a child first understands both *taller* and *shorter* as meaning "having tallness," he should err more often on *shorter* than on *taller.* He should have the same trouble with the other negative polar adjectives as well. This is, of course, what D and W found, and I have observed much the same thing in adults. In my experiments, subjects comprehended positive adjectives in comparative sentences more quickly than negative adjectives (Clark, 1969). If D and W had tested children earlier, they might possibly have found as much confusion about *taller* and *shorter* as about *more* and *less.*

The three-stage development of comparatives is given independent support in other observations on children. Evidence for the purely nominal use of adjectives as the first stage of development comes from Donaldson's own book, *A Study of Children's Thinking* (1963) and from Duthie's appendix to it. Both Donaldson and Duthie observed children working through problems that required that they understand sentences such as *Dick is taller than John* and *Betty is five years younger than May.* Some children could only treat the quantified comparatives in a nominal sense. When one of Duthie's children was asked at one point how he knew that Tom was four, he replied, "Because it says that Tom is four years younger than Dick (p. 237)." His conclusion sounds baffling, but for him both *four years younger* and *four years older* could mean "four years old (or of age)"—*old* used, of course, in the nominal sense. Notice, too, that the above child appears to take account of only the first underlying

base string of the sentence—*Tom is four years young.* In other unquantified
problems, both Donaldson and Duthie noted that children would sometimes take
Betty is older than May to mean the same as *May is older than Betty* and sometimes the same as *Betty is younger than May.* The children were interpreting
these sentences to mean "Betty is different in age from May "; consequently,
all these sentences were equivalent in meaning. The senses of *old* and *young* in
these sentences are again nominal; the sentences mean simply "Betty has an age
and Mary has an age"—the two underlying sentences—and "the ages are not
necessarily the same."

There is other evidence that at the first stage in development children
understand only the nominal sense of comparatives. In one of the experiments
that D and W reported, children were shown two trees with equal numbers of
apples on them and were asked, "Does one tree have more (or less) apples on it
than the other?" Some children replied "both of them," "that one does an'
that one," "they two ones," and so forth. These answers must be elliptical
forms of *that one has more and that one has more,* or in the same sentences
with *less.* For the answers to make sense, the *more,* and *less,* in these coordinate
sentences would have to mean "some." These sentences are identical in form to
That one has many (or some) and that one has many (or some), the underlying
base strings for adults of *That one has more than that one.* These examples are
similar in structure to another of D and W's observations, that children sometimes say, "That one is the same and that one is the same." This sentence is,
of course, an explicit statement of the underlying structure of *That one is the
same as that one.* It is possible that the coordinate sentences here serve as a
primitive stage in the development of the full comparative, since the two coordinate sentences are later needed as constituents of the comparative construction.

At the second stage, we need to add the crucial assumption that the best
exemplar of a dimension is an object with the most extent. It seems quite possible that this could be a perceptually motivated fact; the best example of
something with length is something with much length, because that is the example which best distinguishes length as a dimension to be attended to from other
dimensions. Besides, there is evidence that children attend to extension first.
Farnham-Diggory and Bermon (1968), for example, found that five-year-olds,
when asked to talk about the comparative sizes of objects, almost always directed their attention toward the larger, more extended object first.

By the beginning of the third stage, it is quite likely that children fully
appreciate the two underlying sentences of the comparative, but still interpret
them separately. Evidence for this comes from some other observations found
in Donaldson's book on thinking (as well as in Burt, 1919, and Piaget, 1921,
1928). She quotes one child as saying, "It says that Dick is shorter than Tom,
so Dick is short and Tom is short too." Thus the child is making the underlying

base strings the basis for her interpretation. Presumably this child would correctly answer the question, "Which tree has less apples on it?" because she could answer the question "Which tree has few apples on it?" This, however, is still far from understanding comparatives in full, as Piaget (1928), for one, was careful to notice. He gave nine- and ten-year-olds the following problem: "Edith is fairer than Suzanne; Edith is darker than Lili. Which of the three has the darkest hair?" Piaget (p. 87) explained why children were unable to solve this problem: "It is as though the children reasoned as follows: Edith is fairer than Suzanne so they are both fair, and Edith is darker than Lili so they are both dark. Therefore Lili is dark, Suzanne is fair, and Edith is between the two. In other words, owing to the interplay of the relations included in the test, the child, by substituting the judgment of membership (Edith and Suzanne are "fair," etc) for the judgment of relation (Edith is "fairer than " Suzanne), comes to a conclusion which is exactly opposite of ours." At a later age, however, children do interpret more than the base strings—Piaget's "judgment of membership"—and come to a full understanding of the comparative construction. It is interesting to me that even in adults the comprehension of comparatives is affected by the underlying base strings of the comparative construction (and by the marked-unmarked distinction in adjectives) (Clark, 1969, in press). The ontogeny of comparative constructions has a permanent imprint on how they are comprehended.

I have argued that the child first learns the nominal use of polar adjectives, so that both members of a pair mean "having extent." Then he acquires the subordinate property of antonyms—their contrastive use. This analysis has other psychological appeal in that the most general use of the adjectives is learned first and the more specific second. The later learned contrastive uses of *long* and *short*, for example, also require a more complex syntactic structure. It takes only one proposition to assert that a board has length, but two to assert that one board has a length that is greater than the average. Furthermore, it takes three propositions to form a comparative, like *This board is longer than that one:* this board has length, that board has length, and the first length is more than the second. The comparative with the marked adjective *shorter* is even more complicated, perhaps: this board has length, that board has length, the lengths are less than average, and the second length is more than the first. The simple contrastive uses of *long* and *short* require, to use Donaldson and Wale's term, a two-place predicate; the nominal use requires only a one-place predicate.

The developmental scheme for comparatives that I have suggested obviously needs more support. As of now, it is still a hypothesis, although there are both empirical and linguistic reasons to think that such a scheme is approximately correct. One gap in its empirical verification is the lack of data on younger children. But another serious one is the lack of data on noncomparative adjectives. Since D and W point out that *long* and *short* themselves are implicitly relational, and since D and W are interested in relational terms, it is curious that they did not test children for the comprehension of these words. It is possible that children of three-and-a-half already use noncomparative forms correctly, so one would want to observe even younger children. But if the present analysis of the comparative is correct, there should be subtle but observable deficits in the use of noncomparative adjectives in children of this age as well, since the development of comparative and noncomparative adjectives is inherently intertwined.

To complete my discussion of D and W's paper, I want to comment on some methodological problems. First, it was unfortunate that the *more* and *less* questions were not alternated for different children. In D and W's major experiment, the *more* questions were always put to the children before the *less* ones. It is conceivable that if the *less* questions had been asked first, the children would have correctly used *less* in the relational sense, but perseverated on that answer to make their responses to *more* wrong. The same unbalanced procedure was also followed in questioning the children about *taller* and *shorter, thicker* and *thinner*, and so forth. The niceties of counterbalancing the questions probably did not make any difference, but we would like to be assured that it did not.

There was one place, however, that failure to alternate questions might have caused a major bias in the data. In the experiment on superlatives, D and W showed children four objects graded in size and then asked children to point to the biggest and wee-est one. The children were always asked the questions in this order—biggest then wee-est. D and W found that when choosing the biggest object children almost always picked an object at the extremes. But when choosing the wee-est object, they often pointed at the object immediately adjacent to the biggest extreme. Did they choose this object because they wanted to pick the biggest object but were hesitant to point to the same object for both questions? If this did happen, there is little significance in this result. Children might have chosen the biggest object for both *biggest* and *wee-est* except for the experimental context. This would have been clear if the questions had been asked in both orders.

D and W's discussion of what *same* and *different* must mean to the child is, unfortunately, only suggested by their data. *Same*, they say, means "the identical object" or "the same token," where *different* means "an object of the identical type, but not the same token." This could have been tested very simply. In D and W's experiment, a child had an array of objects before him, and the experimenter picked out one object and asked for an object that is the same. To the child, however, "the same object" presumably referred to the one the experimenter was holding in his hand, so the child could not give the correct answer. If the object had been replaced after the question, the child could have then picked out the *same object*—that is, the one which the experimenter had just put back. When asked for a *different object*, the child should pick up an object similar to the one the experimenter replaced, but not that object itself. This simple operation would have helped to confirm D and W's conclusions.

In sum, the point of my remarks is that a strong theory can often indicate the proper kind of experiments to run or data to collect. I think that D and W are on to a very exciting phenomenon—the primitive nature of children's concepts—something that has been studied only informally before. But I hope that future work in this area can take better advantage of the strong empirical evidence that linguists have already discovered. Linguistic theory, in a very real sense, has already mapped out the landmarks to look for in children's thinking. It remains to the psychologists to fill in the map with roads and terrain, sometimes even correcting for the main landmarks that the linguists thought they had seen.

REFERENCES

Bierwisch, M. Some semantic universals of German adjectivals. *Foundations of Language,* 1967, **3**, 1-36.

Burt, C. The development of reasoning in school children. *Journal of Experimental Pedagogy*, 1919, **5**, 68-77, 121-127.

Chomsky, N. *Aspects of the Theory of Syntax*. Cambridge, Mass.: M.I.T. Press, 1965.

Clark, H.H. Linguistic processes in deductive reasoning. *Psychological Review,* 1969, **76**, 387-404.

Clark, H.H. The influence of language in solving three-term series problems. *Journal of Experimental Psychology*, in press.

Clark, H.H., and Card, S.K. The role of semantics in remembering comparative sentences. *Journal of Experimental Psychology*, in press.

Doherty, P., and Schwartz, A. The syntax of the compared adjective in English. *Language*, 1967, **43**, 903-936.

Donaldson, M. *A Study of Children's Thinking*. London: Tavistock, 1963.

Duthie, J. A further study of overlap error in three-term series problems. In Donaldson, M., *A Study of Children's Thinking*. London: Tavistock, 1963.

Farnham-Diggory, S. & Bermon, M. Verbal compensation, cognitive synthesis, and conservation. *Merrill-Palmer Quarterly of Behavior and Development*, 1968, **14**, 215-227.

Greenberg, J.H. *Language Universals*. The Hague: Mouton, 1966.

Huddleston, R.D. More on the English comparative. *Journal of Linguistics,* 1967, **3**, 91-102.

Lees, R.B. Grammatical analysis of the English comparative construction. *Word*, 1961, **17**, 171-185.

Lyons, J. *Structural Semantics*. Oxford: Blackwell, 1963.

Lyons, J. *Introduction to Theoretical Linguistics*. Cambridge: University Press, 1968.

Piaget, J. Une forme verbale de la comparaison chez l'enfant. *Archives de Psychologie*, 1921, **18**, 141-172.

Piaget, J. *Judgment and Reasoning in the Child*. London: Kegan Paul, 1928.

Sapir, E. Grading: a study in semantics. *Philosophy of Science,* 1944, **11**, 93-116.

Smith, C.S. A class of complex modifiers. *Language*, 1961, **37**, 342-365.

Vendler, Z. *Adjectives and Nominalizations*. The Hague: Mouton, 1968.

CHAPTER 9

Thomas G. Bever
The Rockefeller University

THE COGNITIVE BASIS FOR LINGUISTIC STRUCTURES*

INTRODUCTION

We can all agree that the capacity to symbolize and communicate in language has powerful effects on how we think and behave, but how does the way we think affect the structure of our language? This article explores the ways in which specific properties of language structure and speech behavior reflect certain general cognitive laws.

Recent investigations of language have made an important simplifying assumption: the primary subject for linguistic description is linguistic *knowledge,* as opposed to linguistic *behavior.* This heuristic strategy has facilitated progress in the formal description of the "abstract" structures of language, but has left open the question of how such structures are learned by children and utilized by adults. Previous attempts to integrate linguistic structure and speech behavior have been efforts to find direct mappings of abstract linguistic structures onto language learning, speech perception, and speech production. Although the details of these mappings differ, the basic postulate is the same: actual speech behavior is some regular function of the abstract linguistic structure originally isolated in linguistic investigations. That is, grammar rests at the epicenter of all language behavior, with different functions of grammatical structure accounting for different kinds of behaviors (for example, talking, listening, memorizing, and the like).

This paper begins an exploration of an alternative approach to the study of language: as a conceptual and communicative system which recruits various kinds of human behavior, but which is not exhaustively manifested in any particular form of language behavior. That is, the concept of "language" is like those of "species" or "organ" as they are used in biological science. Consider, for example, the problem of accounting for the concept "cow" by an exhaustive description of its physiological and behavioral structures (including genetic material).

This research was supported by A. F. 19(628)-5705 and ARPA SD-187. I am particularly indebted to G. A. Miller and H. L. Teuber for their logistic and intellectual support during much of the research reported in this paper.

Such an inventory would leave untouched the species concept itself; it would merely specify the interaction among the descriptively isolable components of the organism. The fact that there is a distinct and distinguishable bovine species that organizes these components is taken as a given before the descriptive science begins. No aspect of the cow's physiology could be pinpointed as *the* "physical bovine essence." This is true even for the genetic material, which at first might be taken as *the essential physical manifestation of every species.* However, the genetic material in a fertilized cow egg "is" a cow only *given* the bovine processes of uterine nourishment, embryological maturation, postnatal behavioral development, and so on; these all *assume* various interactions which the genetic material itself would be called upon to explain without a prior concept of the species.

Analogously, in the study of language, we cannot aspire to "explain" the presence and structure of language as a composite function of various descriptively isolable language behaviors, nor is there any aspect of language which can be specified as *the* uniquely central aspect. This is true even of linguistic grammars, which at first have been taken as *the essential structure inherent in language behavior.* Yet grammatical structure "is" the language only given the child's intellectual environment provided by a society and the processes of physiological and cognitive development, which are the basis for language behavior.

Language has various manifestations, each of which draws on and contributes to structural constraints on the language created by every other subsystem. During the first decade of his life a child simultaneously learns all these systems — primarily how to talk in sentences, how to understand sentences, and how to predict new sentences in his language. These and other cognitive skills can mutually influence each other as the child acquires them and as they are integrated in adult language behavior. Consequently our first task in the study of a particular structure implicit to adult language behavior is to ascertain its source rather than immediately assuming that it is *grammatically* relevant.

Recent linguistic "grammars" are intended to describe our knowledge of a language (as revealed by our intuitions about potential sentences) rather than how we ordinarily use that knowledge. Accordingly, in recent considerations of language learning, attention has been focused on the acquisition of linguistic competence as isolated in linguistic investigations of grammar. This view of language "structure" and its development in children, isolated from the rest of cognitive development, has been too narrow. Many aspects of adult language derive from the interaction of grammar with the child's processes of learning and using language. Certain ostensibly grammatical structures may develop out of other behavioral systems rather than being inherent in grammar. That is, linguistic structure is itself partially determined by the learning and behavioral processes that are involved in acquiring and implementing that structure.

The example of such an interaction discussed in this paper is the effect of perceptual strategies in the child and adult on linguistic structure and the relative acceptability of certain kinds of sentences. Since adult linguistic ability includes the ability to talk in sentences, to listen to sentences, and to produce intuitions about sentences, the child must simultaneously acquire "concrete" *behavioral* systems for actually talking and listening as well as an "abstract" appreciation of linguistic structure itself. It is clear that the child tends not to learn sentence constructions that are hard to understand or say. Thus, some formally possible linguistic structures will never appear in any language because no child can use them. In this way the child's systems for talking and listening partially determine the form of linguistic structure even as the structure is being learned and used by the child. Thus, the way we use language as we learn it can determine the manifest structure of language once we know it.

The demonstration of this thesis proceeds in several steps. First, I outline the relationship between perceptual mechanisms and conceptual structure in the child and adult exemplified in the capacity to judge relative numerosity of visual arrays. Adults can make such judgments using three different kinds of mechanisms, basic perceptual mechanisms (for example, numerosity detectors), superficial perceptual strategies, or an internalization of the structure of integers. In acquiring these capacities, children pass through three stages, each of which is successively dominated by one of the modes of adult functioning (in the order given above).

Second, I show that language is processed by adults in the same three modes, and that in acquiring language, children are dependent on each of the three modes successively. In particular, speech comprehension in the child from two to four is relatively dependent on behavioral strategies rather than on a primitive mechanism or sophisticated structural knowledge.

Third, I suggest that the properties of the system of speech perception affect adult linguistic structure, since the young child may learn linguistic structures only after he acquires many perceptual mechanisms. Finally, I show that, in fact, many linguistic structures in adult language are clearly determined by behavioral systems like those which characterize speech perception in the young child and adult.

It would be tempting to argue that these investigations reduce the extent to which language can be viewed as peculiarly innate, since they show that certain aspects of linguistic structure are direct reflections in language of our general cognitive structure and its development. However, this would be like arguing that the physiological structure of joints and of reciprocal muscular inhibition *explains* the fact that we can walk upright. While it is true that our walking capacity depends on certain anatomical structures, it is also true that the presence of the structures themselves does not explain why we walk, nor does it explain how the anatomical structures are recruited by walking behavior. In each case in which we discover neurophysiological substrata involved in specific behavior systems, the problem is merely made more precise: how do the behavioral systems recruit and organize such neurophysiological capacities? The argument in this chapter, that language structure and behavior are the joint product of both linguistic and psychological structures, leaves us with the analogous question: how does the instinct to communicate integrate the distinct components of perception, cognition and motor behavior into human language?

I. JUDGMENTS OF RELATIVE NUMEROSITY

In our research we have distinguished three aspects of cognition for separate study: basic capacities, behavioral strategies, and epistemological structures (see Mehler and Bever, 1968b; Bever, 1969). First we investigate the *basic capacities* that appear in young children without obvious specific environmental training. Consider, for example, the two-year-old's capacity to judge numerical inequalities (Mehler and Bever, 1968a; Bever, Mehler, and Epstein, 1968), or his ability to predicate actions with verbs in speech (Bever, Mehler, Valian, Epstein and Morissey. Second, in both perceptual and productive behavior, children and adults utilize many systems of *behavioral strategies* to short-cut the internal structure implied by the regularities in their behavior. For example, to make relative judgments of large numbers, we may suspend our knowledge of integers and counting, and simply use the perceptual rule that an array that "looks" larger has more components; or if we hear a series of words with only one reasonable semantic connection (for example, "dog bite cracker") then we suspend any further perceptual analysis of the speech signal and assume that the sentence follows the usual semantic constraints on "dog," "bite," and "cracker." Finally, as adults, we have a set of *epistemological structures* — systematic generalizations of our intuitions about the regularities in our own behavior. Consider, for example, the theoretical concept of an integer and counting which we can use in justifying our judgments of quantities; or the intuition of relative "grammaticality" that a parent uses to guide a child's speech and a linguist depends on for the isolation of linguistically relevant data.

All three aspects of cognitive behavior are simultaneously present in adults. Consider first the case of number: when presented with an array such as that in (a) and asked to judge which row has more circles in it, we can either count the circles in each row and see which number is larger; use the generalization that a row that looks larger has more components in it; or depend on elementary "subitizing" strategies to come to an immediate decision (in those cases in which the absolute size of the stimuli is less than seven). Which of these strategies we deploy will depend on the clarity and duration of the stimuli, the penalty for an incorrect answer, and so on. (c.f. Volkman,)

(1)   o o o o o o

                   oooo

Children do not appear to have the choice among these three strategies that adults have. Our research into the acquisition of the ability to judge numerical inequalities in arrays like (1) shows that at different periods the child's behavior appears to be dependent on one or another of the strategies. For example, children of 2.0 to 3.0 make correct judgements as to which row has more circles in (2), although they do not count the number in each row. It does not appear that they are choosing on the basis of density in (2) *a* and (2) *b* since at the same age they have no tendency to pick the denser row in a situation like (3) as having "more."

(2)   o o o o   o o o o   o o o o

                 oooooo   o o oo o o   o o o o o o

                   (a)   (b)   (c)

(3)   o o o o

                   oooo

The children are not merely choosing the longer row as having "more," since they choose correctly in (2) *a* as well as (2) *c*. Thus we must conclude that young children have a primitive capacity to appreciate the relative numerosity of small arrays even though they cannot count and do not have an (explicit) notion of integers. Six-year-olds, on the other hand, also perform correctly on judging the more numerous row in the arrays in (2), but they generally count the two rows in each case, or they perform a 1-1 matching operation to see which row has some circles left over after the matching. Both of these operations depend on a psychological notion of integers and their relation to external objects. (Note that it is not necessary to claim that these children understand the concept of integer in any deep mathematical sense.)

Between the ages of three and five the child appears to depend on the generalization that larger arrays have "more" components. For example, their performance is worse on (2) *a* than that of younger and older children (Fig. 1), while their tendency to choose the longer row as having more in (3) goes up from 60 percent at age two to 100 percent at age three.

It is an open question at the moment as to whether such perceptual strategies are learned as inductions across experience (since it is probably true that most things that "look" larger do have more parts) or whether the strategies appear as a result of maturation. On either interpretation the child successively displays

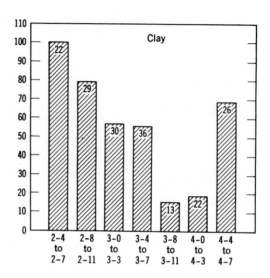

Figure 1. The proportion by age of responses choosing the row with more members in (2a) (numbers inside bar indicate the number of children interviewed at that age) (see text; taken from Fig. 2 in Mehler and Bever, 1967).

dependence on the three types of thinking: use of basic mechanisms, behavioral generalizations, and epistomological systems. Thus the study of the child at different ages can isolate and lay bare the operation of the different types of thought processes that are often integrated inextricably in adult thought.

II. THREE ASPECTS OF LANGUAGE BEHAVIOR

We have been able to pursue the same sort of combined study of adult behavior and its development in children with respect to language. In this section I first explore the interaction of three linguistic systems analogous to those for the adult's perception of numerosity, and then demonstrate that the child's behavior depends primarily on each of three systems at different points in his development.

Basic Linguistic Capacities and Epistomological Structures

In this discussion I shall largely take for granted the fact that *basic linguistic capacities* and *linguistic intuitions* are relatively clear concepts, while *perceptual strategies* of speech require more careful exposition. In the first place, it is clear that adults have the *basic capacity* to understand that words refer to objects and actions, and to understand the basic relational concepts of "actor, action, object." It is (almost as) clear that adults can make sophisticated phenomeno-logical judgements about the sentences in their languages. Thus adults can recognize that 4(*a*) is a sentence and 4(*b*) is not; that (4) *c-e* are ambiguous but in characteristically different ways; that, while (4)*f* and (4)*g* mean the same, they are not related in the way that (4)*g* and (4)*h-j* are; that the unacceptability of (4)*k* is caused by what it says, but the unacceptability of (4)*l* is caused by how it says it; and so on. All of these judgments require that the adult have the concept of the languages as a system independent of any actual use, that he

(4)   *a* He kicked the can.
         *b Can the kicked he.
         c The file is on the floor.
         d He read carefully prepared papers.
         e The missionary is ready to eat.
         f The cockroach died from the poison.
         g The poison killed the cockroach.
         h The cockroach was killed by the poison.
         i It's the poison that killed the cockroach.
         j Did the poison kill the cockroach?
    ? k The cockroach then wrote me an unwritten letter
            complaining about the poison.
       *l I be replying politely please for not to bug me.

be able to consider the potential usability of a sentence, and the relations among potential sentences. It is in this sense that the capacity to have linguistically relevant intuitions is an example of the kinds of epistomological systems we can construct to capture and extrapolate on the regularities implied by our own actual behavior.

A generative grammar attempts to provide a description of the structural basis for intuitions about sentences like the above. The basic intuition of *sentencehood* (e.g. that [4] *a* is part of the language and [4] *b* is not) is accounted for if the grammar provides a description only for those sequences that are accepted as sentences. The structural descriptions are correct insofar as they provide the basis for intuitions about the relations among sentences, such as the different types of ambiguity in (4)*c-e* or relations between specific classes of sentences, such as those represented by (4)*g* ("active"), (4)*h* ("passive"), (4)*i* ("cleft sentence"), or (4)*j* ("question").

Current transformational grammars represent the traditional notion that sentences have two structural levels of description, the basic internal relations among phrases, "actor, action, object, modifier" and the explicit relations among adjacent phrases in the actual appearance of the sentence. For example, sentences (4)*g-j* all have the basic relations outlined in (5), while the superficial relations are obviously different. A transformational grammar represents the relations between the internal and external form of a sentence with a set of rules ("trans-

(5)   actor   = the poison
                                   action = kill
                                   object = the cockroach

formations") that map abstract internal structures such as that represented in (5) onto actual sequences.

(6) | Internal | ⎰ actual sequences
        | structure | ——— transformations ——→ ⎱

For example, a passive transformation applies to (5) to place the internal object at the front of the actual sentence and the actor at the end of the actual sentence; a question transformation inserts a form of the auxiliary verb "do" at the beginning of the sentence. (See Brown and Hanlon, Chapter 1 in this volume, for a detailed exemplification of the formal operation of transformations). Thus the variety of transformations can account for the fact that a variety of actual sequences (for example, (4)*g-j* can share the same internal structure (for example, [5])).

The fact that every sentence has an internal and external structure is maintained by all linguistic theories — although the theories may differ as to the role the internal structure plays within the linguistic description. Thus talking involves actively mapping internal structures onto external sequences, and understanding others involves mapping external sequences onto internal structures.

Strategies of Speech Perception

In addition to basic linguistic capacities and systematic sets of structural intuitions, adult language behavior also appears to depend on behavioral inductions involved in these mapping operations. Our most intensive research has been devoted to exploring the role of these inductions in speech perception. In a recent paper Fodor and Garrett (1966) reviewed the experimental evidence in favor of the working hypothesis that the perceptual operations that map external sequences onto internal structures are themselves directly related to the grammatical transformations specified within a grammar; that is, the view that for every linguistic transformation involved in the linguistic analysis of the relation between the internal and external structure there corresponds one perceptual "decoding" operation. Fodor and Garrett argue that this view leads to an empirical prediction that the perceptual complexity of a sentence is proportional (or at least monotonically related) to the number of transformations involved in the grammatical description of that sentence. According to this view, the passive construction is harder to understand than the active because one more rule is used in the grammatical derivation of the passive sequence than the active sequence. Fodor and Garrett review the evidence for the general claim that the relative number of rules predicts perceptual complexity and conclude that the evidence is unconvincing. The cases in which added transformations do not involve added behavioral complexity are of two types. First, transformational rules that delete internal structures do not necessarily involve added complexity; for example (7)*a* is not more complex than (7)*b*; in fact, (7)*a* is *less* complex psychologically, although more complex grammatically.

(7)   a   The dog was called.
          b   The dog was called by someone.

The second type of failure of added grammatical transformations to predict added psychological complexity is in certain reordering transformations. Thus (8)*a* is obviously not more complex to understand than (8)*b*, (8)*c* is not more complex to understand than (8)*d* and (8)*e* is not more complex than (8)*f*.

(8)   *a*   The small cat is on the grass mat.
          b   The cat that is small is on the mat that is made of grass.
          c   The operator looked the address up.
          d   The operator looked up the address.
          e   It amazed Bill that John left the party angrily.
          f   That John left the party angrily amazed Bill.

Fodor and Garrett conclude from such examples and their review of the experimental literature that the relation between grammatical rules and perceptual operations is "abstract" rather than direct. This negative point has clarified many issues for us but has left open what the actual nature of the operations of speech perception is. In the following section I outline the positive evidence that bears on the processes of speech perception and the role of perceptual strategies in mapping external sequences onto internal structures.

Segmentation Strategies. Recently, a great deal of attention has been given to the "psychological reality" of the structures and rules postulated in transformational grammars. The most notable success has been to show both by experiment and appeal to intuition that the form in which sentences are understood and memorized corresponds closely to the internal syntactic structure internal to them (See Miller, 1963; Mehler, 1963; Mehler and Bever, 1968). Thus, any model for speech perception proposed in this tradition includes a device that isolates the internal structure corresponding to each lexical sequence.

(9)

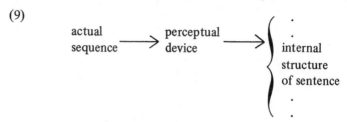

For such a perceptual device to operate efficiently, the actual sequence of words in a speech utterance must be segmented into those subsequences that correspond to a full sentence at the internal structure level. For example, if one hears the sequence represented phonetically in (10), one must decide that it has two distinct sentences corresponding to it at the underlying structure level, and not more or less.

(10)   ðəboyləyksgəlzgəlzləyboyz   (that is, *the boy likes girls girls love boys*)

Failure to separate the correct basic segmentation into sequences that do correspond to underlying structure sentences could seriously degrade comprehension. For example, suppose that a listener assumed that the second instance of "girls" above was actually a spurious repetition; then he would be faced with finding an underlying structure for the following: *The boy likes girls love boys.* The problem is that this sequence has no single underlying syntactic structure.

There is no known automatic procedure that insures the proper segmentation of actual sequences. In cases like the above, however, pronunciation often provides many cues that indicate where the segmentation into basic sentences should occur. The operation of this segmentation strategy to separate sentences in a discourse like (10) can utilize many situational, semantic, and pronunciation cues. The segmentation problem is much more complex, however, for sentences embedded within other sentences. Consider (11)*a* for example:

(11)   *a*   when he left, everybody grew sad

This has two deep structure sentences, each one corresponding to one of the "clauses" in the apparent sequence: ("When he left, everybody grew sad").
I shall represent this structure division as clauses at the surface structure level with parentheses, ( ), and the corresponding internal structure segmentation with brackets, [ ]; for example, (11)*b*.

(11)   *b*   ([when he left])   ([everybody grew sad])

If the wrong perceptual segmentation were attempted, then further perceptual analysis of the sentence would be impossible. For example, the listener might initially segment the first four words into a sequence bound together by an internal structure (that is, "When he left everybody. . ."), but would then have two words left over ("grew sad") with no possible segmentation deriving from another internal structure sentence.

A recent series of experiments have given initial support to the existence of a perceptual strategy of isolating lexical sequences that correspond directly to underlying structure sentences (Fodor and Bever, 1965; Garrett, Bever and Fodor, 1966; Bever, Fodor, and Garrett, 1966). These investigations have studied the perception of nonspeech interruptions in sentences with two clauses. The basic finding is that subjects report the location of a single click in a sentence as having occured toward the point between the clauses from its objective location. For example, Fodor and Bever found that in sentence (12), a click objectively located in "yesterday" or in "the" was most often reported as having occurred between those two words. Fodor and Bever argued that the systematic displacement of the click towards the point between clauses showed that the clause has relatively high psychological coherence, since it "resists" interruption by the click.

(12)   because it rained yesterday the picnic will be cancelled

Several experiments have shown that this systematic effect of the syntactic segmentation is not due to any actual pauses or cues in the pronunciation of the sentence. First, Garrett, Bever, and Fodor used materials in which the exactly identical acoustic sequence was assigned different clause structures depending on what preceded. Consider the sequence ". . .eagerness to win the horse is quite immature." If it is preceded by "your. . .," then the clause break immediately follows "horse." But if that sequence is preceded by "In its. . .," then the clause break immediately follows "win." The authors cross-recorded one initial sequence or the other and tested subjects on their ability to locate clicks in the different sentences. The results showed that the clause structure assigned each sequence "attracted" the subjective location of the clicks. Abrams and Bever (1969) found similar results with sentences constructed by splicing words from a random list.

Scattered through the materials in these experiments were sentences that did not consist of two entirely separate clauses in the external structure, but which had one clause embedded within another. For example, in the sentences (13) *a* and *b*, there are two sentences at the level of internal structure, but they

(13)   *a*   ([the man ([who nobody likes]) is leaving soon])
         b   ([nobody likes the man ([who is leaving soon])])

are not literally reflected in an organization into distinct uninterrupted sequences in the actual sentence. Nevertheless, Fodor and Bever found that the points at the extremes of the embedded clauses are as effective in attracting the subjective location of clicks as they are in sentences with two entirely separate clauses.

In certain cases in the previous experiments, two internal structure sentences corresponded to a sequence in which the division into two clauses was even less obvious in the actual structure. Consider (14) *a*:

(14)   *a* ([[the reporters assigned to George] drove to the airport])

         b ([the reporters ([who were assigned to George]) drove to the airport])

The sequence "... assigned to George..." does not have the same distinctiveness as a clause in the surface structure of (14) *a* as in (14) *b*. Nevertheless, sentences in which the surface structure does not obviously reflect the underlying structure, like (14) *a*, were found to affect the subjective location of clicks (for example, clicks were displaced perceptually to the point following "George").

These data suggest that an early step in the perceptual organization of a string of words is the isolation of those adjacent phrases in the surface order which together could correspond to sentences at the level of internal structure (Strategy A). This perceptual strategy would generate the experimental prediction (15) for the location of clicks.

Strategy A: Segment together any sequence X...Y, in which the members could be related by primary internal structural relations, "actor action object....modifier."

(15)   Errors in location of clicks presented during sentences are towards those points which are external reflections of (potential) divisions between internal structure sentences.

Various further experiments indicate that (15) is correct. First, some negative experiments indicate that within-clause minor phrase structure divisions do not affect perceived click-location. Bever, Kirk, and Lackner (1969) used the same technique of click location in which they systematically varied the within-clause surface phrase structure of 25 sentences. They found *no* tendency for the number of errors into a break to be correlated with the relative depth of that break in the surface phrase structure. Bever, Lackner, and Stolz (1969) found no difference in the effect on click location of three kinds of within-clause structures; adjective-noun ("red ball"), verb-object ("hit ball"), and subject-verb ("ball hit"). Finally Bever, Fodor and Garrett (1966) investigated the relative effectiveness of pairs of surface structure transitions which were superficially quite similar, but which differed by having or not having an "S" node in the surface phrase structure tree. Consider the two sentences in (16):

(16)   *a* ([they watched [the light turn green]])

         b ([they watched [the light green car]])

The relevant difference between the two structures just after the verb is the presence of an S-node in the surface structure of the first sentence. Bever *et al.* found that this difference of a single node had a profound effect on the pattern of errors in click placement. Together with the negative results from the other experiments, this finding supports the following initial conclusion: a relative increase in the number of surface structure nodes defines a perceptual unit only if the increase is due to an explicitly marked sentence-node in the surface structure.

Although negative experimental findings are always inconclusive, these experiments do indicate at least that within-clause surface structure has far less effect on click location than breaks between clauses. Several other experiments indicate that points in the surface which correspond to underlying structure divisions do attract clicks, even in the absence of major division between apparent clauses. Bever, Kirk, and Lackner found several instances among their 25 sentences in which a within-clause phrase structure break corresponded to a division between sentences in the internal structure. These breaks did attract the subjective location of clicks. In a second experiment they found that subjects locate clicks subjectively between a verb and its complement object significantly more for "noun-phrase" verbs ([17] *a*) than for "verb-phrase" verbs ([17] *b*). This corresponds to the fact that in "noun-phrase complements" the break following the verb corresponds uniquely to the beginning of a new internal sentence.

(17)　　*a*　　[they desired [the general to fight]]
　　　　　　　1　　　　　　2　　　　　　　　2 1

　　　b　　[they defied [the general] to fight]
　　　　　　　1　　　　2　　　　　1　　　2

These results demonstrate that Strategy A is correct, that perceptual segmentation proceeds primarily in terms of internal structure organization into sentences. However, there are various difficulties with each of the experiments we have reviewed and further work is necessary. Furthermore, it is not clear whether every internal structure division has an effect on perceptual segmentation, or whether this effect is limited to those internal structure sentences whose order is literally reflected in the surface structure (or which are marked by a sentence node in the surface structure); for example, it is not clear that both the first and second underlined sequences below will be treated as a perceptual unit — they both derive from the same internal sentences (*my steak is rare, my steak is tender*), but only the first preserves this order in the surface structure.

(18)　　*a*　　I like *my steak rare and tender.*
　　　b　　I like *my rare and tender steak.*

Whatever the outcome of further experimentation, it is clear that the internal logical relations are a major determiner of perceptual segmentation in speech processing. As we hear a sentence we organize it perceptually in terms of internal structure sentence units with subjects, verbs, objects, and modifiers.

Consider now the relation between Strategy A and a transformational grammar. Clearly Strategy A presupposes the distinction between internal and external structural relations. But there is no obvious way in which the grammatical transformations may themselves be transmuted into subcomponents of Strategy A. Rather, Strategy A is implemented on the basis of knowledge of the possibility that a particular external form class sequence could correspond to an internal structure; the possible external sequences are, of course, enumerated by the transformations, but not necessarily in a way that can be directly utilized in the process of perception. In fact, several experiments demonstrate that the application of the segmentation Strategy A is directly sensitive to knowledge of the potential internal/external relations that individual lexical items *can* have, as opposed to their actual deployment in a particular structure.

First, Kaplan and Kaplan showed recently (personal communication of pilot work) that subjects respond to the interruption of a sentence following an adjective like "hard" ([19] *a*) faster than they responded to the interruption of a sentence ending with an adjective like "eager" ([19] *b*).

(19)   *a*   The old general was hard . . .
        b   The old general was eager . . .

I suggest that this is because immediately following "eager" the listener is processing an internal structure unit, while following "hard" he is not. This is presumptively due to the fact that the listener makes immediate use of his knowledge that "eager" *must* terminate an internal structure sentence, while "hard" may or may not terminate such a unit. Consider the examples of the possible continuations of the sentence fragments in (19).[1] (Internal structural sentence boundaries are marked with brackets.)

(20)   *a*   The old general was [*hard to please*].
        b   [The old general was hard] and [wouldn't give up].
        c   [[The old general was eager] to please]].
        d   [The old general was eager], and [wouldn't give up].

A second example of the use of knowledge of internal/external potentialities in applying Strategy A appears in Bever, Lackner and Kirk's experiment on click location (see above). Clicks were also placed in the noun phrase following the verbs (for other groups of subjects). (The numbers in sentences

[1]There are many facts that motivate the distinction between the internal analyses of (20)*a* and (20)*c*. For example, consider the fact that (20)*a* is related to "it was hard to please the old general" while (20)*b* is not related to *"It was eager to please the general." That is, the abstract sentences internal to (20)*a* can be reflected in the actual sentences "It was hard" and "Somebody pleased the general," while the sentences internal to (20)*c* are reflected in "The general was eager" and "The general pleased someone."

[21] *a* and *b* below indicate the different objective click positions that were
used.)

(21) *a* that general desired soldiers to fight

       b that general defied soldiers to fight

Bever *et al.* found that the difference in subjective click location for the constructions in (21)*a* and *b* was primarily due to responses to clicks objectively in the
verb (position 1). The previous studies of click location had shown that clicks
following and preceding a clause break are reported as occurring in the clause
break equally often — that is, it is not the case that pre-clause break clicks are
more sensitive to structural effects. Bever *et al.* suggest that their results show
that the listener segments the sequences by using information inherent to the
potential internal structure/external structure pairs which each complement verb
can have. Verb-phrase complement verbs characteristically must have a direct
object (for example, "soldiers") that is simultaneously the subject of a complement sentence. In contrast to this, noun-phrase complement verbs can have at
least the following kinds of objects:

(22) *a* direct object which is also the subject of a complement
      sentence (....desired soldiers to fight)

    b a complement sentence as direct object (....desired that they
      fight)

    c direct object which is also the direct object of a complement
      sentence (if the complement sentence is in the passive)
      (....desired them to be fought)

    d direct object without any complement sentence(....desired them)

    e direct object which is a nominalized complement (....desired
      them fighting)

    f complement sentence which has the same subject as the main
      verb (....desired to fight)

Thus many of the possible constructions following a noun-phrase complement
verb begin a new sentence at the level of internal structure, while this is *never*
the case with a verb-phrase complement verb. The fact that in structurally homonymous sentences clicks located in the verbs are located differently shows that
listeners use the information contained in the verb to predict the internal structure segmentation. When a listener hears "defy" he *knows* that a direct object
must follow; when he hears "desire" he knows that many constructions that
follow begin a new internal structure unit. Accordingly, listeners establish segmentation following noun-phrase complement verbs. (By the time the listener
reaches the following noun-phrase [position 2], there is no further difference in
the potential internal structure organization of the sentence, so there is no subjective difference in click location for clicks in that location.)

Relations Between Clauses

The need for Strategy A follows from the fact that most sentences have more than one internal clause. Not only must the different clauses be segregated from each other, but the internal relation between the two clauses must be marked. There are two basic types of relations, coordinate ([23] *a*) and subordinate ([23] *b-d*). In coordinate constructions both clauses are structurally

(23)   *a* Wars are distasteful and politicians are always in favor
             of peace.
        b Wars are distasteful although *politicians are always in*
             favor of peace.
        c Wars *that are distasteful* are a source of political power.
        d Everybody wants *wars to be distasteful.*

and conceptually on the same level, while in subordinate constructions the subordinate clause is embedded within a higher, "main" clause; the main clause of such sentences expresses the primary content of the sentence, while subordinate clauses either modify that main content (as in [23] *b*), supplement it (as in [23] *c*), or express a presupposition underlying it (as in [23] *d*, "wars *can be* distasteful"). The clearest principle is that, *ceteris paribus*, the first N. . .V. . .(N) is taken to be the main clause (Strategy B).[2]

Strategy B: The first N. . .V. . .(N). . . clause (isolated by Strategy A)
               is the main clause, unless the verb is marked as subordinate.

In English, there are many specific morphemes that mark an initial verb as subordinate, and in such cases Strategy B does not apply. (c.f. Section III A below). However, various facts demonstrate the relative complexity of sentences in which the first verb is a subordinate verb. Consider first the sentences with a clause as subject ([8] *e*, [8] *f*). The less complex version is clearly (8) *e*, in which the subordinate verb ("left") is not the first verb in the sequence. In a general study of subjective preference, Bever and Weksel found that subjects indicate a stylistic preference for sentences in which the subordinate clause (marked by a conjunction) follows the main clause (for example, [24] *a* as opposed to [24] *b*).

(24)   *a* The dog bit the cat because the food was gone.
        b Because the food was gone, the dog bit the cat.

Clark and Clark (1968) found that sentences in which the subordinate clause occurs first are relatively hard to memorize.

---

[2] Note that such strategies capture generalizations which are not necessarily always true. That is, there are exceptions to every strategy — the validity of each strategy is that it holds for most of the cases.

These observations do not bear directly on perceptual complexity. In an independent perceptual experiment, Savin found that sentences in which the first verb is in a relative clause (such as [25] *a*) are more complex than sentences in which the first verb is the main-clause verb (as in [25] *b*). In Savin's experiment,

(25)   *a* The boy who likes the girl hit the man.
         b The boy hit the man who likes the girl.

more random words are recalled when preceding sentences like (25)*a* than (25)*b*.

Strategy B accounts for actual mistakes made in other comprehension experiments as well as accounting for the relative complexity of sentences in which the first verb is not the main verb. For example, Blumenthal (1967*a*) examined the nature of errors which subjects make in attempting immediate recall of center-embedded sentences ([47] *a*). His conclusion was that the main strategy that subjects use is to assume that the first three nouns are a compound subject and that the three verbs are a compound action (as in [16] *b*). That is, they impose a general "subject-verb" schema onto what they hear.

(26)   *a* The man the girl the boy met believed laughed.
         b *The man the girl and the boy met believed and laughed.

In immediate comprehension I found that subjects cannot avoid assuming that an apparent Noun-Verb-Noun ("NVN") sequence corresponds to a clause even when they are given explicit experience and training that this interpretation is incorrect. Subjects reported immediate paraphrases of center-embedded sentences with apparent NVN sequences (for example, underlined in [27] *a*).

(27)   *a* The editor *authors the newspaper* hired liked laughed.
         b The editor the authors newspapers hired liked laughed.

Even after eight trials (with different sentences) the subjects understood the sentences with this property less well than the sentences without it (for example, [27] *b*). That is, the "NVN" sequence in (27) *a* is so compelling that it may be described as a "linguistic illusion" which training cannot readily overcome.

Functional Labeling Strategies. Not only must listeners isolate internal structure clauses and assign their relations to each other, listeners must also assign the internal structural relations which bind the constituent phrases in each internal sentence. To do this, listeners use a set of labeling strategies that draw on semantic information, probabilistic structural features and knowledge of the potential structure underlying specific lexical items.

Semantic Strategies. A basic strategy for functional assignment is to combine the lexical items in the most plausible way. That is, we use Strategy C whenever possible to assign the correct internal relations within a potential unit independent of syntactic structure. For example, the three lexical items "man,"

> *Strategy C:* Constituents are functionally related internally according to semantic constraints.

"eats," and "cookie" are internally related, as in "The man eats the cookie." If Strategy B applies independently of the actual syntactic structure, we might expect that sentence in which the semantic relations are unique are relatively easy. Schlesinger (1966) supported this prediction by showing that center-embedded sentences are easier to comprehend when the semantic subject-verb-objects are semantically constrained. That is, (28) *a* is easier than (28) *b*. Clark and Clark (1968) demonstrated that if the superficial order of a complex

(28)   *a* the question the girl the lion bit answered was complex
        b the lion the dog the monkey chased bit died

sentence reflects the actual order of described events, then the sentence is relatively easy to retain. That is, (29) *a* and *b* are easier than (29) *c* and *d*.

(29)   *a* he spoke before he left
        b after he spoke he left
        c he left after he spoke
        d before he left he spoke

There is some evidence that the presence of unique semantic constraints allows syntactic factors to be bypassed entirely. For example, Slobin (1966) found that the passive construction is no more difficult to verify than the active sentence when the semantic relations are unique. That is, (30) *a* is no harder to verify than (30) *b*, while (30) *c* is harder than (30) *d*.

(30)   *a* the cookie was eaten by the dog
        b the dog ate the cookie
        c the horse was followed by the cow
        d the cow followed the horse

This finding was extended by Turner and Rommetveit (1967). They showed that children (even in the first grade) respond correctly to a sentence like (30) *c* only 50% of the time when they have to choose a picture appropriate to the sentence. Even at age four, however, they respond correctly to semantically-constrained sentences like (30) *a*.

In an ingenious experiment, Mehler and Carey (1968) collected further evidence that subjects may process meaning simultaneously with the processing of syntactic structure. They presented subjects with appropriate and inappropriate pictures following a single sentence; the task of the subjects was to indicate whether the picture was appropriate for the sentence. Two kinds of superficially similar sentences were used, progressive tense (31) *a*, and the participial construction (31) *b*. They found that the latencies (that is, response times) were relatively high for inappropriate pictures, and relatively high for the participial construction, which was assumed to have a relative complex syntactic structure.

(31) *a* they are fixing benches
      b they are performing monkeys

On this basis one would expect the following order of latencies (in order of increasing time to decide about the picture):

Construction	Picture	Predicted	Observed
PROGRESSIVE	appropriate	fastest	fastest
PROGRESSIVE	inappropriate	intermediate	all. . .
PARTICIPLE	appropriate	intermediate	the. . .
PARTICIPLE	inappropriate	slowest	same.

However, they found that whether a sentence had the more complex syntax *or* the picture was inappropriate, or both, the reaction time was delayed the same amount. This suggests that subjects process meaning and structure *simultaneously* rather than in sequence; either a relatively complex structure or a complex meaning can add decision time, but since they are processed in parallel, the presence of both a complex structure and a complex meaning does not add any extra time.

Semantic Strategies – Conclusion

The preceding experiments demonstrate that the most likely semantic organization among a group of phrases can guide the interpretation of sentences, independently of and in parallel with perceptual processing of the syntactic structure. The semantic constraints utilized in the previous experiments were necessarily removed from any natural context, so the effects of generic probability (that is, men usually eat cookies, as opposed to the reverse; if one event precedes another we tend to talk about the first event first and in the main clause; and so on). In the actual application of language, specific contexts must provide far stronger immediate constraints and basis for prediction of the most likely meaning of a sentence independent of its form. Thus, most normal perceptual processing of sentences is probably carried out with little regard to actual sequence or structure; rather, the basic relational functions (actor-action-object-modifier) are assigned on the basis of temporary ("contingent") and generic ("constant") semantic probabilities. Strategy C is clearly another process in which the knowledge of linguistically defined syntactic structure is not utilized actively in actual perception. Rather, as in the case of perceptual segmentation, listeners depend heavily on their knowledge of the properties of individual words and groups of words.

Sequential Labeling Strategies

However, we are capable of understanding sentences in which there are no differential semantic probabilities. Accordingly, a complete account of the mechanisms of speech perception must also include the capacity to analyze the structural relations within a sentence from pure sequential and syntactic information. There is a primary functional labeling strategy, based on the apparent order of the lexical items in a sentence, which applies in the absence of specific semantic information.

> *Strategy D:* Any *Noun-Verb-Noun* (NVN) sequence within a potential internal unit in the surface structure corresponds to *"actor-action-object."*

There is some recent experimental evidence that demonstrates the presence of this labeling strategy. The primary finding is that the passive construction is more complex to comprehend than the active (in the absence of semantic constraints, see above). For example, Slobin (1966) found that children verify pictures corresponding to active sentences more quickly than pictures corresponding to passive sentences. Also McMahon (1963) (replicated by Gough, 1966) found that generically true (32)*a,b* or false (32) *c, d* passives are harder to verify than the corresponding actives. Finally, Savin and Perchonock (1965) showed that the number of unrelated words that can be recalled immediately following a passive sentence is smaller than the number recalled if the test words follow an active sentence.

(32)   *a*   5 precedes 13
            b   13 is preceded by 5
            c   13 precedes 5
            d   5 is preceded by 13

The passive construction specifically reverses the assumptions in Strategy D, which is the presumed explanation for the perceptual difficulty of the passive. Of course, the fact that the passive construction is relatively complex perceptually might also be due to its increased length, and to its increased transformational complexity. However, the facts pointed out above show that transformational complexity is itself not a *general* explanation of perceptual complexity (cf. pp. 284 ff.).

Only the explanation in terms of the violation of Strategy D is consistent with the following experiments.

In the picture-verification experiment by Mehler and Carey discussed above, it was found that the progressive form is significantly easier to understand than the superficially identical participial construction; the participial construction fails to preserve the *NVN=actor-action-object* property in its surface structure.

Recall that in both the experiment by Blumenthal and by me (see page above), subjects' errors involved the assumption that the first noun or series of nouns in an apparent N...V...N...sequence is not only the grammatical subject in the external structure but also the actor in the internal structure. That is, listeners impose the "actor-action (object)" organization on what they hear as part of the basis for segmentation of clauses.

Bever and Mehler (1968) found another example of this constructive tendency in an immediate recall experiment referred to above — a sentence they just heard to maximally conform to an "NVN" sequence. For example, in (33) *a* the *NVN* sequence is maintained, while in (33) *b* it is interrupted:

(33)   *a* Quickly *the waiter sent the order* back.
        b The waiter quickly sent back the order.

In immediate recall, 87% of the syntactic order errors were from stimulus sentences like (33) *b* to sentences like (33) *a* rather than the reverse.

Lexical Ordering Strategy — Conclusion

These different experimental results converge on one common explanation: any NVN sequence in the surface structure is assumed to correspond directly to *actor-action-object* in the underlying structure. Like the semantic strategies, this process may reflect a statistical preponderance in actual utterances — although little is known about the actual frequencies of construction types at the moment.

Particular Lexical Strategies

However, there must be other strategies that supplement sensitivity to surface order and semantic constraints, since we can understand sentences which are not uniquely constrained semantically and which do not maintain the particular "canonical" order of the internal structure in the surface structure implied by Strategy D. Recent experimental work has brought out the fact that there is a heterogeneous set of strategies attached to specific lexical items, primarily function words and verbs.

It is a linguistic truism that inflectional endings and function words can represent the internal structure relations directly in the external structure of sentences. For example, the difference in functional labeling of the nouns in (34) *a, b,* and *c* depends entirely on the change in the preposition.

(34)   *a* the laughing at the hunters was impolite
          b the laughing of the hunters was impolite
          c the laughing near the hunters was impolite

          a John rode with Mary
          b John rode to Mary
          c John rode by Mary

A recent series of experiments indicates that listeners utilize the intersection of the potential internal structures which adjacent lexical items can have to guide sentence perception. Fodor and Garrett (1967) showed that center-embedded sentences with relative pronouns included ([35] *a*) are simpler to paraphrase than the same sentences without the relative pronouns ([35] *b*).

(35)   *a* the boy who the man who the girl likes saw laughed
          b the boy the man the girl likes saw laughed

They interpreted this as due to this perceptual strategy based on the use of the relative pronoun "who": N_1 *wh* N_2 *corresponds to* N_2 *verb* N_1 *in the underlying structure.* However, again the following theory of perceptual complexity would make the same factual predictions: "more transformations = more psychological complexity." In sentence (35) *b* a pronoun deletion transformation has applied to transform it from (35) *a.* Consequently, several additional studies have been used to increase the evidence for the argument that listeners project deep structure organization directly from the possible internal constituent structure/external structure combinations associated with the particular lexical items.

A series of experiments has shown that sentences with verbs that take complements (such as "see") have more psychological complexity than simple transitive verbs (for example, "hit") even when the complement verbs are used transitively. This finding supports the contention that perceptual processing is guided by the potential internal role that each lexical item *could* play. Thus complement verbs involve more complexity even when they are employed as simple transitive verbs. Fodor, Garrett, and Bever (1968) showed that center-embedded sentences are harder to paraphrase when they contain a complement verb ([36] *a*) than when they have a transitive verb in the same position ([36] *b*). (Both visual and auditory presentation were used.)

(36)   *a* the box the man the child *saw* carried was empty
          b the box the man the child *hit* carried was empty

The preceding experiments involve sentences with two center embeddings — which are inordinately difficult constructions in any case. Fodor, Garrett, and Bever also found that the anagram solution for sentences presented in a scrambled order is harder and less accurate if the sentence has a complement verb ([37] *a*) than a simple transitive verb ([37] *b*). (Subjects were presented with a randomized array of words on cards and asked to make a sentence out of them.)

(37)   *a* The man whom the child *saw* carried the box.
        b The man whom the child *hit* carried the box.

The results of these last two experiments might be due to non-structural differences between pure transitive verbs (for example, "hit") and complement verbs (for example, "see") rather than the fact that complement verbs have more potential internal structures; for example, the complement verbs we used characteristically require animate subjects, while the pure transitive verbs do not require animate subjects. To test directly the hypothesis that the relevant independent variable was the number of potential internal structures a verb can have, I compared the results for complement verbs that can take several kinds of complements with those that can take only one complement.

(38)   *a* John liked it that we slept a lot.
        b John liked to kick the bottle.
        c John liked Bill to win the race.
        d John saw that we slept a lot.
        e *John saw to kick the bottle.
        f John saw Bill to be a fool.
        g John decided that we should sleep a lot.
        h John decided to kick the bottle.
        i *John decided Bill to be a fool.
        j John remarked that we slept a lot.
        k *John remarked to kick the bottle.
        l *John remarked Bill to be a fool.

Each complement verb used in the two experiments was classified according to whether it takes three kinds of complements, two or one. For example, (38) *a–l* show that "like" can have three kinds of complements, while "see" and "decide" have two and "remark" has only one. An analysis of the data in both experiments shows that complement verbs with three possible complements are more complex than verbs with only one or two complements. (See Table 9.1a, b.)

I have presented the strategies of segmentation, semantic labeling, and sequential labeling separately for purposes of exposition. It is obvious that the operation of one of the strategies can simultaneously aid the operation of another strategy. In actual perception the strategies combine simultaneously

The Cognitive Basis For Linguistic Structures

TABLE 9.1a. Mean Relative Number of Subject-Verb-Object Triples Correctly Recovered per Sentence for Auditory Presentation Relative to Corresponding Transitive Verbs (Analyzed from data in Fodor, Garrett, and Bever, Table 1)

Number of potential complements/verb	1	2
Number of cases	4	8
Relative Number of SVO triples recovered	.89	.25

TABLE 9.1b. Relative Number of Errors in Visual Presentation (From Fodor, Garrett, and Bever, Table 2)

Number of potential complements/verb	1	2	3
Number of cases	5	15	9
Relative number of errors	.2	1.2	2.0

to isolate potential internal *actor-action-object. . . modifier* sentence units and to assign correctly the functional relations within those units. It seems reasonable to suggest that semantic cues are dominant, since structural factors (such as the reversal of the canonical actor-action-object order in passive sentences) do not affect psychological complexity when the semantic relations are unique, (according to Slabin). The structural strategies, in turn, project segmentation and internal structural labeling on the basis of general sequential properties of actual sequences (for example, "NVN" in the surface structure corresponds to underlying subject-verb-object, or "SVO"), or on the basis of the particular internal/external structural potential of individual lexical items.

The strategies used in speech perception to discover internal structures from external sequences are distinct both from basic linguistic capacities and from the system of intuitions which are described by a grammar. As in the case of the perceptual strategies of numerical judgments, it is not clear whether these linguistic strategies are derived by passive induction over actual experience or whether they are due to autonomous internal developments. In either case it is clear that the perceptual strategies accord closely with experience, particularly Strategies B, C and D. Furthermore, the deployment of the knowledge of specific lexical internal/external potentialities in perception could not come about without an accumulation of experiences of the lexical potentialities. In this sense the strategies constitute a form of behavioral inductions over actual speech behavior. Thus, just as in the judgments of numerosity, speech behavior can also be described in terms of three aspects: basic capacities, behavioral inductions, and epistemological systems. Of course, in adult speech behavior these three systems are ordinarily merged together; the presence of the behavioral strategies is brought out in experimental conditions such as those reviewed above; our primitive linguistic capacity (for example, for reference) appears directly in our speech production, while the structural intuitions relevant for linguistic analysis appear only in our conscious epistomological considerations of sentences.

B. The Development of Perceptual Strategies of Speech in the Child

As in the case of numerical judgments, the child appears to pass through different phases in which his linguistic behavior is successively dominated by each one of the three kinds of cognitive functioning. Consider first the expression of the basic linguistic capacities at age 2 years. It has been traditionally recognized (cf. MacCarthy, 1956) that children of this age have the basic capacity to recognize (and often to say) the names of some objects and actions – that is, the capacity for *reference* is already developed, although not widely extended. (Of course it is not clear whether they understand the arbitrary nature of the acoustic-referential relations or whether they believe that the names of objects and actions are intrinsic and indivisible from the objects and actions themselves.)

A more abstract linguistic notion is the capacity to recognize explicitly the concept of predication as exemplified in the appreciation of the difference between subject-action and action-object relations. Recently we have tested this capacity in young children with a task in which they are requested to act out simple active sentences with toy animals ([39] *a, b*).

(39)   *a*   The cow kisses the horse
           b   The alligator chases the tiger

The results of our first experiment in which each child received a total of six sentences of different kinds are presented in Fig. 2.[3] Even the children in our youngest age group did extremely well on the simple active sentences. The significance of this simple result (obvious to any parent) is that even the very young child distinguishes the basic functional relations internal to sentences. Furthermore, he appears to be able to distinguish different syntactic construction types, as opposed simply to interpreting the first noun of *any* type of sentence as the actor and the last noun as the object. The evidence for this is that while children from 2.0 to 3.0 act out simple active sentences 95 percent correctly, they also do far better than 5 percent on simple passives like (40) *a, b*. (See Fig. 3 for the performance on passives.) If children at this age always took the first noun as

---

[3]The responses include cases in which the child refused to act out the sentence, but chose the correct alternative acted out for him by the experimenter. They do not include cases in which the child refused to act out any sentences at all himself. The number of such cases was less than 15% at all ages, and did not materially change the results. See Bever *et al.* (in preparation) for a general discussion of the methodology and results of these experiments.

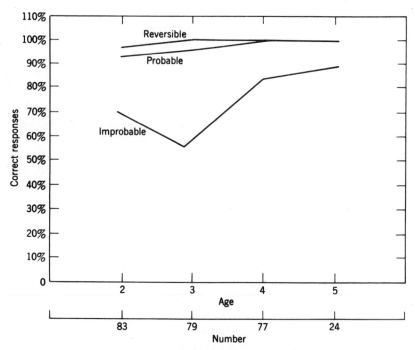

Figure 2. The proportion by age of correct responses to reversible active sentences like 39 (*a*), probable active sentences like (42) *a,* and improbable active sentences like (42) *b;* each child received only one active sentence of each kind.

(40)   *a*   the horse is kissed by the cow
            b   the tiger is chased by the alligator

the actor then they would systematically do as poorly on passives as they do well on actives. Since they perform almost randomly on passives, we must conclude that they can at least distinguish sentences they can understand from sentences they cannot understand. Thus, the basic linguistic capacity evidenced by the two-year-old child includes the notion of reference for objects and actions, the notion of basic functional internal relations, and at least a primitive notion of different sentence structures.

Beilin (forthcoming) has used the emergence of the capacity to recognize the relationship between the active and the passive construction as a measure of the development of the child's capacity to produce linguistic intuitions. (I should emphasize that while the facts are due to Beilin, the interpretation is not necessarily his.) Beilin shows that the child does not appear capable of appreciating the regularity of the relationship between active and passive sentences until about age seven to eight, which is also the age at which the child is alleged to have

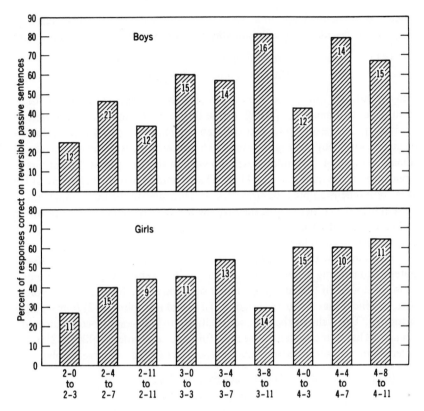

Figure 3. The proportion by age and sex of correct responses to reversible passive sentences [e.g., (40) *a*]. Each child received only one reversible passive sentence. (The numbers in each bar indicate the number of children interviewed at that age. The data is broken down by four-month age groups for purposes of the discussion below.)

developed the integer concept. Indeed, it is support for my claim that the adult form of linguistic and numerical epistomology constitutes the same type of cognitive phenomenon that Beilin finds a correlation between the child's ability to deal correctly with numerical transformations (e.g., recognizing that changing the array in (2) *a* to that of (2) *b* doesn't change the number of circles in any of the rows) with the ability to deal correctly with sentential transformations (as exemplified by the relation of the active and the passive).

As in the case of the development of the child's capacity to make judgements of relative numerosity, the linguistic behavior between the ages of 2 and 6 displays a period of relative dependence on perceptual generalizations. Consider first the early appearance of the basis for Strategy B, that the first N...V...(N)

sequence is the main clause. In a recent study we have asked young children to
act out sentences like (41) *a*. Presumably because of memory limitations, children

(41)   *a*   *The cow that jumped* walked away.
             b   The cow jumped and walked away.

often act out only one of the two clauses of such sentences. Which clause they
act out gives us a measure of which clause they consider the most important when
they hear it. Our results show that children between 1½ and 2½ who perform
poorly on acting out both actions in (41) *b* act out only the first action (the subordinate verb) in (41) *a*; children who do well on sentences in (41) *b* act out the
second action (the main verb in (41) *a*. That is, children at the beginning of language comprehension pick the first 'N. . .V' sequence on the most important part
of a sentence — in other words, they follow Strategy B completely; more advanced
children learn to discriminate the main verb from the subordinate verb and consider the main verb to be the most important action.

Consider now the development of the basis for a semantic strategy like
Strategy C, involving probabilistic constraints. We examined the development of
this in the course of the same experiment outlined above by including simple
active sentences that either followed (42) *a* or did not follow (42) *b* probabilistic
constraints. Fig. 4 shows the relative sensitivity to the semantic constraints at
each age. (That is, the percent correct performance on sentences like [42] *b* sub-
tracted from the percent correct on sentences like (42) *a* — a large number

(42)   *a*   The mother pats the dog.
             b   The dog pats the mother.

indicates a high dependence on semantic constraints.) Fig. 4 shows that this dependence undergoes a marked increase during the third year. These results were
found initially with only two sentences of each type, but have been replicated in
a second experiment with five sentences of each type (Fig. 5). These experiments
show that the two-year-old child is relatively unaffected by semantic probabilities.
The implication of this is to invalidate any theory of early language development
that assumes that the young child depends on contextual knowledge of the world
to tell him what sentences mean, independent of their structure.

It is obvious why the very young child cannot make use of contextual probabilities: he does not have enough relevant experience to know what the probabilities are. For example, the young child may know the meaning of the word
"pat" but may not have heard it enough, or done it enough, to know that usually
people pat dogs and not the reverse. Thus, it is not until the third year of life that
the kind of contextual probabilities that provide the basis for Strategy C in adult
perception develop as guides for sentence comprehension.

Shortly after this development the child goes through a phase in which he
depends relatively heavily on something like Strategy D for the comprehension

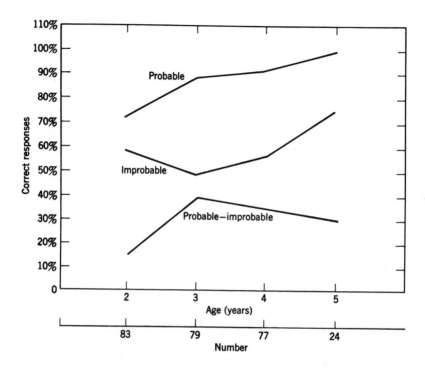

Figure 4. The proportion by age of correct responses to probable and improbable sentences, in which each child received one sentence of each kind (roughly half the children at each age received one probable and one improbable active sentence and roughly half received one probable and one improbable passive sentence). The bottom line represents for each age the difference in correct responses between the probable and improbable sentences, and thus is a measure of the children's dependence on probability as an aid to correct performance.

of sentences that do not have semantic constraints. This is brought out by his performance on acting out passive sentences like those in (40)*a* (see Fig. 3). The most important feature of these results is the steady increase in performance until age 3.8 for girls and 4.0 for boys, when there is a sharp (temporary) drop in performance. These results were obtained with only four sentences (of which each child acted out only one), so a larger experiment was run (again by a different experimenter and in a different city) in which twelve reversible passive sentences were used (of which each child acted out three). The results for the passive sentences in this group are presented in Fig. 6. Again the same brief decrease appears at the same ages (although in these materials, the decrease starts at the same time for boys and girls, but lasts to a later age in boys than in girls). Finally, in a separate experiment, we have studied the performance of the child on cleft-sentence

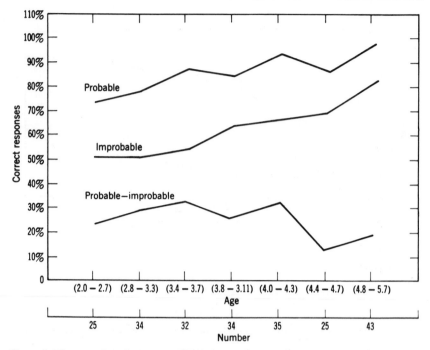

Figure 5. The same data display as in Fig. 4, except from a different experiment with different children in which each child received three probable sentences and three improbable sentences (balanced within each age group so that the same number of actives and passives of each kind were responded to).

constructions that can reverse the subject-object relation without reversing subject verb order, as in (43) *a, b*.

(43)   *a*   It's the cow that kisses the horse (actor first)
        b   It's the horse that the cow kisses (object first)

Fig. 7 presents the tendency to perform correctly on sentences like (43) *b*. Again, the same decrease in performance appears at about age four.

While any one of these results alone might not be convincing, the constant reappearance of the effect across different experiments with different materials indicates the reliability of the phenomenon. Since each experiment averages across large numbers of children, it is not clear whether the period of the decrease in performance is due to the active development of a perceptual strategy like D or simply to the failure to apply the earlier capacity to understand passives. Of course in both girls and boys in the experiment in Figure 3, the performance on passives is worse than random at the critical age that indicates an *active* tendency to use a strategy like D. Similarly, when the reversible passive sentences in

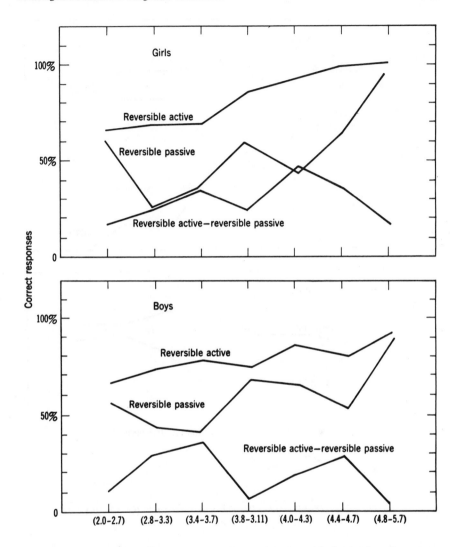

Figure 6. The proportion of correct performance by age and sex to reversible active and passive sentences in which each child acted out three sentences of each kind. The bottom line in each graph represents the difference between the performance on actives and passives, and thus is a measure of the children's dependence on the "actor-action-object" order as an aid to correct performance.

the larger experiment are looked at by overall difficulty (as measured by overall success during the first three years), the performance on each of the sentences goes below 50 percent (although at slightly different times). Only

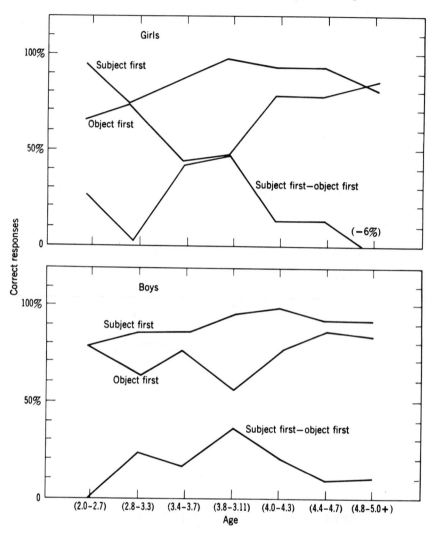

Figure 7. The same kind of data display as in Fig. 6, except for responses by different children to reversible cleft sentences with subject first (analogous to actives in Fig. 6) (e.g., [43] *a*), and object first (analogous to passives) (e.g., [43] *b*), in which each subject received three sentences of each kind .

longitudinal research can resolve the question as to whether all children pass through a phase of over-generalizing Strategy D or of simply losing their earlier competence and lapsing into random behavior on those semantically reversible sentences that do not conform to the SVO pattern. However, the fact that we obtain decrease to below 50 percent even when averaging across children, suggests strongly that all individual children pass through periods of actively applying Strategy D, to misinterpret those sentences in which the first noun is the object rather than the actor.

In any event, we have been able to explore in language the way in which the child may display relative dependence on basic mechanisms, perceptual generalizations, and systematic intuitions as he grows up. This is further support for the distinction between these separable aspects of language behavior that are integrated in adult capacity.

The Enumeration of Possible Perceptual Strategies

It is an open question as to how the child acquires Strategies B, C, and D. It could be argued that the strategies are formed in response to natural probabilities in the actual speech that the child experiences; in actual speech, sentences may tend to place subordinate clauses second (Strategy B); sentences do usually conform to some sort of contextual constraint (Strategy C); and the active actor-action-object order probably predominates in what mothers say to children (Strategy D). Thus, one could argue that these perceptual strategies are formed by the child as inductions over his experience, as opposed to being due to internal cognitive developments independent of specific experience. However, just as in the case of the acquisition of the strategy of assuming that a relatively large array has a relatively large number of components, one must be prepared to explain *why* it is the case that the perceptual strategies B, C, and D are the ones that the child recognizes as fruitful rather than the many other generalizations are equally justified by his experience. Thus, even an empiricist view of the acquisition of such perceptual generalizations must include a nativist component that selects certain possible generalizations and rejects others.

I have suggested that the child may extract particular perceptual strategies by selective induction over his early linguistic experience; different topics, different speakers and different situations justify different perceptual strategies (or at least different relative importance of the strategies). Thus, part of what a child learns when he adapts to the "linguistic style" of a situation is a particular configuration of the perceptual strategies which the language used in that situation justifies. Since the number of potential strategies (like the number of sublanguages and of sentences) is infinite, the child must have both a characterization of the set of possible perceptual strategies as well as a routine for the extraction of such strategies from his particular linguistic experience. Analogously, a recognition routine must have *a priori* limits on the kinds of recurrent information it treats as relevant for the formation of perceptual strategies, and a system for the distillation of that information into particular strategies.

All we can do at the moment is to define the problem of the specification of possible perceptual strategies. It is clear that probabilistic information about the internal structure and internal/external structure pair is the basis for certain psychological strategies that are developed. But it is not clear that all perceptual strategies are based on experience in this way, nor is it clear which additional linguistic structures are manipulated by strategies. That is, just as the general study of linguistics seeks to define language universals in terms of the basic structures and universal constraints on possible rules, the study of speech perception must be stated in terms of the basic form of the perceptual mechanism and universal constraints on possible perceptual strategies. Just as certain linguistic structures may be "innate" and some learned, certain perceptual strategies may be basic to all perceptual processes, and some derived from linguistic experience.

III. THE INFLUENCE OF THE CHILD'S PERCEPTUAL SYSTEM ON LINGUISTIC STRUCTURE AND LINGUISTIC BEHAVIOR IN THE ADULT

A grammar provides the basis for the prediction of new possible sentences from the ones that have already been uttered and heard. That is, the system of grammatical rules that relate internal and external structure is the finite basis for the *acquisition* of linguistic creativity. While the grammatical rules make possible the extrapolation of new sentences from old ones, the system of behavioral strategies make more efficient the *perception* and *production* of sentences.

The preceding sections have demonstrated the independence of the perceptual and grammatical systems for relating internal and external structures of sentences. These systems can manifest themselves as independent systems in the adult and are learned at least partially independently in the young child. However, there is one obvious connection between the two systems in the child: the child will learn the grammar for those sentences which he can understand (at least partially). Conversely, the child will have difficulty in learning the putative grammatical structure underlying sentences that he has difficulty in understanding. Thus, the child's system of speech perception constrains what he can understand and consequently restricts the kinds of grammar he can learn. To put this another way: the child will learn those grammatical structures most easily which are most consistent with his perceptual system – in those cases in which the grammar offers alternative structures the child will tend to learn only those that are perceptually simple.

In brief then, the child is simultaneously acquiring two kinds of linguistic systems that can modify each other. It is clear that the structures allowed by the grammar of a language restricts the kinds of perceptual strategies that are learned.

Obviously it is rare that strategies are acquired for the perception of sentences that are not learnable structures. However, it is also rare that rules are acquired which produce sentences that are impossible to understand. Thus, we can expect that certain aspects of sentence structure reflect the perceptual constraints placed on it by the child as he learns the structure and by the adult as he uses the structure. The following sections present examples of syntactic rules which are acquired in response to perceptual strategies.

SOME SYSTEMS OF ADULT LANGUAGE STRUCTURE AND BEHAVIOR DETERMINED BY PERCEPTION

A. Some Syntactic Rules

1. The Integrity of Main Clauses in External Structure. Consider the perceptual strategies A and B. These combine to form the perception of an initial "N. . . V. . .(N)" sequence as comprising the main independent clause of the sentence. I presented evidence above showing that the very young child's habits of speech perception are dominated by such a strategy; in those sentences with more than one clause, the first "N. . .V. . .(N)" sequence is taken by the young child as the most important clause. Certain facts of adult English syntactic structure appear to accommodate this perceptual strategy; for example, R. Kirk (personal communication) has observed that a subordinate clause verb that precedes its main verb is generally marked as subordinate by the end of its verb phrase. The most obvious device is the subordinate clause conjunction, as in (44). In each case the first verb is marked by the subordinate conjunction as subordinate.

(44)   a *Although* the research was secret the liberated files revealed that it concerned the metabolization of sauce Bearnaise.

   b *Because* the demands were non-negotiable nobody wanted any.

   c *If* the system corrupts itself the thing to do is to take it over.

   d *While* this conference was not attended by any Americans of African antecedence, that fact was obviously an accident.

Subordinate conjunctions are specific lexical items that accommodate to Strategy B by acting as specific markers of those cases in which a subordinate clause occurs before its main clause. There are also certain syntactic verb systems that appear to have formed in response to Strategy B: restrictions on the "syntactically" allowed deletion of words that mark functional relations among clauses. The sentences in (45) and (46) exemplify a heterogeneous set of grammatical restrictions on the stylistic deletion of "that" or "the fact" in initial position.

(45)   *a* The fact that the door was discovered to be unlocked amazed the tenants.

        b That the door was discovered to be unlocked amazed the tenants.

        c The fact the door was discovered to be unlocked amazed the tenants.

        d *The door was discovered to be unlocked amazed the tenants.

        e The door was discovered to be unlocked and that amazed the tenants.

For example, (45) *a* can be reduced to (45) *b* or (45) *c* by deletion of one of the initial noun phrases, but not to (45) *d*, in which *both* noun phrases are deleted. The cases in (46) show that, so long as some noun that marks the first clause as a nominalization is in initial position before the clause "the door. . .," both "that"

(46)   *a* The discovery of the fact that the door was unlocked amazed the tenants.

        b The discovery that the door was unlocked amazed the tenants.

        c The discovery the door was unlocked amazed the tenants.

and "the fact" may be deleted. Stated in this way, the facts in (45) and (46) exemplify a constraint on internal/external structure relations that requires initial subordinate verbs to be uniquely marked. Notice in (45) *e* that Strategies A and B do not apply if the sentence has more than one clause so long as the first clause is an independent clause (in the traditional grammarian's sense of "independent"). The facts in (46) show that this constraint does not apply to the deletion of "complementizers" when they do not precede an initial noun.

Perceptual strategy B also predicts certain facts about the deletion of relative pronouns on subject nouns. Consider the grammatical facts in (47). It would

(47)   *a* The man who/that came to buy the giraffe forgot his money.

        b *The man came to buy the giraffe forgot his money.

c   The senator who was in the saddle shot from the hip.

d   *The senator was in the saddle shot from the hip.

e   The senator in the saddle shot from the hip.

f   The monkey who was running after the bus slipped
on a banana.

g   *The monkey was running after the bus slipped on
a banana.

h   The monkey running after the bus slipped on a banana.

i   The monkey who was scared by the dog slipped on
a banana.

j   The monkey scared by the dog slipped on a banana.

k   The acid that was dissolved in the water became
colorless.

l   ? The acid dissolved in the water became colorless.

appear from (47) *a* and (47) *b* that there is a general syntactic restriction of the deletion of relative pronouns modifying initial nouns. This restriction follows from Strategy B, since the deletion of the relative pronoun would make the relative clause verb appear incorrectly to be a main verb of an independent clause. However, there are certain cases in which Strategy B predicts that the relative pronoun can be deleted. For example, the deletion of only the pronoun in (47) *c* to produce (47) *d* is blocked, but if the verb "was" is optionally deleted as well, then the pronoun must be deleted to produce (47) *e*. Strategy B allows this, since the subordinate clause verb "was" is already deleted.

In certain cases the relative pronoun can be deleted even in the presence of a following verb. Thus, (47) *h* can be derived from (47) *f* even though the verb form "running" directly follows the noun phrase "the man." However, the suffix "-ing" at the end of the verb marks it independently as a subordinate clause verb.

In a small number of cases of relative pronoun deletion, the form of the verb suffixes do not uniquely determine the verb as subordinate. Thus, (47) *j* can be derived from (47) *i*, even though the past participle verb form "scared" is homonymous with the past form of the verb (that is, to produce the apparent clause "the man scared somebody. . . "). However, the following participle, "by," marks the verb "scared" as not having a direct object in the external structure and therefore as being subordinate. Similarly, in (47) *l* the preposition "in" marks the verb "dissolved" as not having a following direct object in the external structure, and therefore either as intransitive or as a subordinate verb. Thus, Kirk's observation can be elaborated into a principle for the relations between the

internal clause relations from their external form; it is clear that this principle accommodates to the perceptual Strategy B on the one hand and that it constrains the form of the syntactic rules that relate the internal and external structures on the other hand.

Kirk's Claim: If the first noun phrase is followed by a verb not marked as a subordinate verb, by a preceding subordinate conjunction, by inflection (such as *ing*), or by an immediately following word (such as "by" in [48] *j* and "in" in [48] *d*), then the verb is a main verb of an independent clause (of which the noun phrase is the external surface structure subject).

This principle predicts that certain sentences are unacceptable in which the subordinate verb suffixes are homonymous with main verb suffixes. For example, (48) *a* is not acceptable although it is related to (48) *b*, in the same way as (48) *c* is to (48) *d*. The difficulty of (48) *a* is due to the fact that the verb "race" can

(48)		
	a	? The horse raced past the barn fell.
	b	The horse that was raced past the barn fell.
	c	The horse sent past the barn fell.
	d	The horse that was sent past the barn fell.
	e	The horse stumbled past the barn and fell.

occur as an intransitive or as a transitive (unlike "stumble" [pure intransitive]), as in [48] *e* or "send" [pure transitive] as in [48] *c, d*. In (48) *a* this facilitates the incorrect assumption that "horse" is the subject of "raced" as a main verb. Notice that, if Kirk's claim were always true, (48) *a* should be *ungrammatical* as opposed to merely unacceptable, since it also violates Kirk's claim. However, to block formally constructions like (48) *a* with verbs that can act both transitively and intransitively, all constructions with pure transitives (like [48] *c*) and pure intransitives (like [48] *e*) would be blocked in a grammar. The alternative is to restrict selectively deletion of "that (was)" to subordinate clauses with verbs that are not potentially phonologically homonymous with intransitive forms. Such a restriction is not only difficult to state, but is also inadequate. Consider the relative acceptability of (49) *a* over (49) *b* and (49) *c* over (49) *d*. For each of these pairs in the less acceptable sentence the "NP...VP" sequence created by deleting "that was" between the NP and VP, is relatively likely as an independent "subject-verb" sentence (italicized in the examples). That is, *any* feature of an initial

(49)		
	a	*The light airplane pushed past the barn* crashed into the post.
	b	*The pushing bulldozer pushed past the barn* crashed into the post.
	c	*The door slammed by the storm* splintered.
	d	*The door slammed during the storm* splintered.

NP—VP sequence that makes it appear relatively plausible to the listener as a sentence interferes with perception if the *NP—VP* is not actually a main clause.

Thus Strategy A and B are not offered as grammatical rules but as constraints to which otherwise optional rules may respond when the speaker/listener's knowledge of individual exceptions does not make them irrelevant.

There are some principles that are implicit to strategy which explain certain other syntactic phenomena of English.

In an "N. . .V" sequence in which "V" is appropriately inflected, "N" is the (external structure) subject of "V," unless some preceding noun is so marked.

An initial "N" is the external subject of the first appearing "V" (unless blocked for a particular verb by strategy B).

This explains the fact that the restrictions on relative pronoun deletion also apply to relative clauses in object position. Thus (50) *b* cannot result from (50) *a* in modern English, although (50) *d* is an acceptable variant of (50) *c*.

(50)   *a*   I ate the apple pie that was yummy.

        b   *I ate the apple pie was yummy.

        c   I saluted the apple pie that my mom made.

        d   I saluted the apple pie my mom made.

        e   The flag that was waving above *mom's apple pie*
               was groovy.

        f   The flag waving above *mom's apple pie was groovy.*

Notice that in (50) *e, f,* Strategy B has marked "the flag" as the subject of the first verb after "wave" so the apparent "NVN" sequence (underlined) is allowed (although of course it may cause perceptual difficulties).[4]

2. Syntactic Restrictions on Pronominalization. The structure of coreferential pronominalization is another example in which general perceptual principles appear to constrain formal grammatical structures. Indeed, some authors have recently questioned whether pronominalization is a syntactic phenomenon at all, since all attempts to provide a complete account in syntactic terms have failed up to now. However, certain general constraints are statable within syntax. First, whenever two nouns with the same reference appear in one clause, one of them must be transformed into a pronoun. Thus we cannot say (51) *a* unless there are two distinct "George's" in mind; rather, we must say (51) *b*:

---

[2] Principles like these must apply recursively as exemplified by sentences like "Max couldn't believe that the flag waving above mom's apple pie was groovy," in which the principle applies to the embedded sequence after "Max couldn't believe that. . ." Note that sentences like 50 (*b*) could occur in Old English, presumably because the main object (". . . .pie") was often inflected, in the accusative, making its confusion as a subject impossible.

(51)   *a*   ?George spoke to George.
              b   George spoke to himself.

In (51) *b* the first instance of "George" is said to "govern" the pronominalization of the second instance. It is immediately clear that the "government" of pronominalization always proceeds from *left to right* within clauses. Consequently, the second instance of "George" in (51) *a* cannot govern the first. If it did, the ungrammatical sentence (51) *c* would result (on the interpretation that "he" and "George" are coreferential):

(51)   *c*   *He spoke to George.

(Note that sentence [51] *c* can be grammatical if "he" and "George" are different people, but not if they are intended to be the same person.)

This *left-right* constraint on pronominalization also obtains in certain sentences with a main ("independent") clause and a subordinate ("dependent") clause, for example, (52) *a* must be transformed to (52) *b*:

(52)   *a*   ?George was late although Mary spoke to George.
              b   George was late although Mary spoke to him.

As above, pronominalization cannot proceed right to left; thus, (52) *c* is not a correct version of (52) *b*:

(52)   *c*   *He was late although Mary spoke to George.

However, pronominalization can proceed right to left if the main clause is to the right of the subordinate clause. In (52) *a* the "George" on the right can govern pronominalization of the "George" on the left (to yield [53] *b*), as well as the reverse (to yield [53] *c*).

(53)   *a*   Although Mary spoke to George, George was late.
              b   Although Mary spoke to him, George was late.
              c   Although Mary spoke to George, he was late.

In general, the only cases in which the left-right constraint can be violated are those in which the governed noun is in a clause subordinate to the governing noun (Langacker 1969, Ross 1967b). Thus, there are two independent constraints on the government of pronominalization: either it proceeds from left to right (to yield [51] *b*, [52] *b*, [53] *c*), or from main clause to subordinate clause (as in [52] *b*, [53] *b*). At least one of the constraints must be met; if *neither* is met, an incorrect sentence like (52) *c* can result from (52) *a*.

Such a complex system appears at first to be an example of a "pure" linguistic law. However, there is an intuitively clear general principle of all experience which could underlie such complex linguistic constraints. First, for one object to "stand for" another, like a pronoun for a noun, a connection must already be established between them. For example, a picture of a leaf cannot be used to re-present a tree unless the viewer already knows the connection. Analogously, in (51) *c* above, "he" cannot refer to "George," since the listener does not yet know who "he" is. The constraint that allows a superordinate clause noun to govern the pronominalization of a subordinate clause noun may also be interpreted as a linguistic reflection of an obvious regularity of experience: presentation of a whole includes a presentation of its subordinate part, but not vice-versa. For ex-ample, a picture of a tree also presents a leaf to view since it includes a leaf, but a picture of a leaf does not present a tree (without prior knowledge of the con-nection, as above). Analogously, a pronoun can appear, even preceding its govern-ing noun, if it is explicitly marked as in a subordinate part of the sentence. Since every sentence has at least one main clause, the listener can predict that a pronoun in a subordinate clause *will* be governed by a main-clause noun. But a pronoun in an initial main clause does not necessarily have a following subordinate-clause governing noun, since there may be no subordinate clause at all. (Recall Kirk's observation that subordinate clauses in English are always identifiable as such by the end of the verb phrase.)

To put it another way, the general perceptual principle is:

A symbol "S1" can stand for "S2" if (a) the prior connection is known or (b) there is an indication that a connection is about to be established.

The constraints on pronominalization would conform to this principle. (It should be noted that more recent linguistic investigations [Lakoff (in press)] have brought out some counter-examples to the proposals by Langacker and Ross for the syntactic treatment of pronominalization. Further research is necessary to see if further psychological considerations could account for the new examples.)

There are many considerations that show that many of the restrictions on coreferentiality are perceptual as opposed to structural, in any case. Consider first a clearly ungrammatical sequence (54 *a*):

(54)   *a* *John the hit Bill.
               b *John the hit ball.

No manipulation of the semantic constraints (as in [54] *b*), or of the way in which the sentence is pronounced, or at the gestures accompanying its utterance, can affect its unacceptability. This is characteristic of sequences that are unaccept-able on syntactic grounds — semantic or behavioral changes do not reduce their unacceptability.

However, semantic manipulations do affect the acceptability of certain sentences with coreferential pronouns, which indicates that pronominalization constraints are not purely syntactic. Consider (55) *a* and (55) *b*, in which the

(55)   *a*   *The shovel* broke the rake *it* fell on.
              b   The shovel *it* was below broke *the rake.*

underlined nouns and pronouns are coreferential. While each of these sentences
is acceptable, they cannot combine as in (56) *a* or (56) *b-d*. Notice that the unacceptability of (56) *a* is not directly due to the difficulty of grasping the content;
even after careful consideration of the content as clarified in (55) *a, b,* (56) *a* is

(56)   *a*   *The shovel$_1$ it$_2$ was below broke the *rake$_2$ it$_1$* fell on.
              b   *The shovel that was above it broke the rake it fell on.
              c   *The shovel it was below broke the rake that fell on it.
              d   *The shovel that was above it broke the rake that fell on it.

still nearly incomprehensible. Furthermore, (56) *a* is not unacceptable because
of the actual syntactic relations; consider the acceptability of (57) *a* and (57) *b*,
which have the same syntactic structure as that in (56) *a*, without having two
coreferential relations that cross each other from one clause to the other.

(57)   *a*   The shovel I was below broke the rake it fell on.
              b   The shovel it was below broke the rake I fell on.

Thus, the unacceptability of (56) *a-d* appears to be due to a restriction on having
two referential relations crossing over each other. However, if the relations between the nouns and verbs are uniquely determined semantically, coreference
relations can cross over between clauses, as in (58) (that is, it is semantically

(58)   The box it rolled out of scratched the ball it had
              contained.

predictable that *the box had contained the ball* and *the ball rolled out of the
box.*)

         Coreference also can occur over between clauses without unique semantic
constraints so long as the pronouns differ superficially. For example, (59) *a*
and (59) *b* can combine into (60) *a*, a perfectly acceptable sentence.

(59)   *a*   The boy deserved the girl he kissed.
              b   The boy she pleased deserved the girl.

(60)   *a*   The boy she pleased deserved the girl he kissed.
              b   The boy that wanted her deserved the girl he kissed.
              c   The boy she pleased deserved the girl that kissed him.
              d   The boy that wanted her deserved the girl that
                     kissed him.

         The conclusion from these facts is clear: so long as the referential rela-
tions are kept distinct from each other, by general semantic restrictions or by

unique referential possibilities of the pronouns, coreferential relations may cross each other; that is, the unacceptability of the sentences in (56) are *not* due to a syntactic restriction, but to a behavioral one.

Certain examples bring out even more clearly the effect of nonstructural behavioral variables on the acceptability of sequences with coreferential pronouns. Thus, (61) *a* and (61) *b* are unacceptable while (61) *c* and (61) *d* are acceptable,

(61)   *a*   *He and he liked the cannabis juice.
         b   *Him and him liked the cannabis juice.
         c   Her and him liked the cannabis juice.
         d   She and he liked the cannabis juice.
         e   ? He and him liked the cannabis juice.

since the two pronouns obviously refer to different people because of the difference in sex. In fact, (61) *e* is almost acceptable even with pronouns of the same sex; the difference in the external form of the pronoun is sufficient to make the sentence acceptable. The dependence of such pronominalization restrictions on nonstructural variables is brought out even more markedly by special execution of (61) *a, b*; these sentences are completely acceptable when spoken with accompanying gestures, first pointing to one (male) person and then another.

Thus, many of the factors that govern pronominalization are clearly the linguistic reflection of behavioral constraints on symbols that "stand for" other symbols; those syntactic mechanisms that are involved in the description of pronominalization clearly are grammatical responses to such behavioral constraints.

3. Syntactic Restrictions on Prenominal Adjective Ordering. The previous two examples of the effect of general psychological principles on structure would appear to be extremely general, if not universal; they both bear on the relation between subordinate and superordinate clauses, which is itself a putatively universal structural distinction. Certain perceptual strategies are language-specific, in that they depend on particular properties of a language which themselves are not universal. Consider, for example, the strategies involved in the immediate perceptual segregation of major phrases. The implication of perceptual strategies like A and B is that understanding a sentence involves a marking of the internal relations between the phrases in each clause. This itself assumes that the phrases themselves have been (or are being simultaneously) isolated from each other. It is easy to see the importance of such segregation. For example, in (62) *a*, the perceptual segregation of words in the verb must end (and begin) with "called," while in (62) *b* it must include the participle "up." Or in (62) *c* the subject noun phrase must end with the word *"snow,"* while in (62) *d* it must end with the following word *"catches."* If such perceptual segmentation into major phrases is not achieved, the internal relations themselves cannot be assigned. Of course, in many

(62)   *a* I called up the not very well painted stairs.

            b I called up the not very well painted Indian.

            c The powerful snow catches the travelers.

            d The powerful snow catches saved the travelers.

instances the semantic relations and unique lexical classifications in English can themselves determine the segmentation. Thus, there is no doubt (even temporarily) about the segmentation of the verb in (63) *a*, or the first noun phrase in (63) *b*. Furthermore, in many instances, stress and intonation patterns can

(63)   *a* I called from the not very well liked stairs.

            b The powerful snow barriers saved the travelers.

provide the necessary clues. (Consider the relatively high stress on "up" in (62) *a* or on "catches" in [62] *c*.)

In English the presence of certain function words at the beginning of a phrase can uniquely determine what kind of phrase it is, and therefore what to look for at its termination. For example, the determiners "the, a, some one, many," and the like, all signify the beginning of a noun phrase. A putative perceptual strategy (E) could be based on this fact:

Strategy E: "determiner . . . " begins a noun phrase.

Consider sentence (64) *a*. This principle leads a listener to expect a noun terminating the noun phrase begun by "the"; in (64) *a*, the form class possibilities of "pencil" and "fell" uniquely determine the interpretation that the noun phrase is "the ball" and that "fell" is the verb. In addition, there are certain classes

(64)   *a* The pencil fell.

            b The pencils fell.

            c The pencil (that) $\begin{matrix} \text{Sam} \\ \text{the boy} \end{matrix}$ found fell.

            d The nice pencil fell.

            e The plastic pencil fell.

of morphemes and words that uniquely identify the boundary of a head noun phrase; in (64) *b*, the plural morpheme "s" (given that a noun doesn't follow it), and in (64) *c*, the function word "that" or the proper noun "Sam" or the determiner "the," all signal that the immediately preceding noun was the head noun of its noun phrase. That is, there is a perceptual strategy (E').

Strategy E':   The first noun after "Determiner . . ." (Or the first
                     noun with a following morpheme that marks the
                     beginning of a new noun phrase.) is the head noun,
                     which terminates the noun phrase (independent of
                     nouns in relative clause).

Strategy E' operates correctly in cases like (64) *d*, where an adjective intervenes between the determiner and the noun. However, since the adjective "nice" is not a noun, Strategy E' does not establish the segmentation of the noun phrase until the noun "pencil" is heard. Strategy E' would operate incorrectly in cases like (64) *e*, in which one of the prenominal modifiers is itself lexically marked as a noun. Since "plastic" is the first noun after "the," Strategy E' would establish the following segmentation to sentence (64) *e*:

(65)   (The plastic)$_{np}$ (pencil)$_{np}$ · · · ·

which is incorrect. To block this kind of premature NP segmentation, the strategy E' must be restated so that it does not establish segmentation of a noun phrase until there is a word that is relatively less nounlike.[5]

> *Strategy E'''*:   After "determiner . . . ." the boundary of the head noun phrase is marked by (1) a set of morpheme classes that signal the end of a noun phrase (such as "s") or immediately subsequent morphemes that signify the beginning of a new noun phrase (such as "the," proper nouns) or a relative clause (such as "that") and (2) a subsequent lexical item that is less uniquely a noun.

E''' yields the correct segmentation for (64) *e* (and indeed covers most of the cases in [64]). However, it is not clear whether principle E''' extends the noun phrase as long as possible, or whether it establishes segmentation at the earliest possible point. If the former is true, then (66) *a* should be more complex than (66) *b*; in (66) *a* the word "marks" would be incorrectly included within the noun phrase because, while it is a verb, it is homophonous with a noun (as in [66] *b*).

(66)   *a*   The plastic pencil marks easily.
        b   The plastic pencil marks were ugly.
        c   The plastic rose fell.
        d   The plastic rose and fell.

On the other hand, if principle E''' applies at the first possible point, then (66) *c* should be more complex perceptually than (66) *d*; the word "rose" would *not* be included within the noun phrase, because, while it is a noun, it is homonomous with a verb (as in [66] *d*). Future experimentation is necessary to decide this question. In any case, the problems raised by the sequences in (66) are usually resolved by normal intonation and stress patterns.

[5] I am indebted to M. Halle and I. Grinder for suggestions on this problem.

However, nuances of stress do not resolve the segmentation problem exemplified in (64) *e*, so Strategy E" is required for the segmentation of noun phrases with prenominal modifiers. This strategy appears to act as a constraint on the external order of prenominal modifiers that might otherwise be freely ordered. Consider the constraints on the order of adjective classes exemplified in (67).

(67)   *a*   The red plastic box . . . .
            b   *The plastic red box . . . .
            c   The large red box . . . .
            d   *The red large box . . . .
            e   The large plastic box . . . .
            f   *The plastic large box . . . .
            g   The large red plastic box . . . .
            h   *The plastic red large box . . . .

Notice first that any two prenominal adjective sequence is acceptable if the first adjective is given contrastive stress. (For example, in [67] *b*, the phrase would have to be in a contrasting context like "not the metal red box, but the *plastic* red box . . . ."). However, with neutral stress the order of prenominal adjectives is constrained. Several recent theories (Vendler [1967], Martin [1968]) state that adjectives are ordered according to the extent to which an adjective is related lexically to a noun (Vendler), or to which it refers to a "substantive, concrete" quality of an object (Martin); the more "nounlike" an adjective is (on either of these two measures), the closer to the noun it must be. Thus, for example, following Vendler, we can argue that a substance adjective like "plastic" is more like a noun than a color adjective like "red," in the sense that it occurs in more kinds of constructions as a noun than does "red" (see [68]); similarly, color adjectives like "red" occur in more constructions as nouns than do size adjectives like "large" (see [69]). Martin has recently suggested a more semantic basis for a scale of "nounlikeness" of adjectives; substance words ("plastic") refer to the concrete "inner" structure of the noun they modify; color words ("red") refer to the exterior of the object they modify; and size words ("large") refer to qualities of the objects they refer to which must be assessed by the speaker relative to other objects of that type.[6]

(68)   *a*   Red is a color; redness is nice.
            b   Plastic is a substance; plasticity is nice.
            c   *That is made out of red.
            d   That is made out of plastic.

[6]I have summarized the arguments of Vendler and Martin in vastly abbreviated form. The reader should consult their original work on this problem.

e *The red broke.
f   The plastic broke.
g ? Reds are of variable quality.
h   Plastics are of variable quality.

(69)   *a*   Red is my favorite color.
         b *Large is my favorite size.
         c   He splattered some red on me.
         d *He splattered some large on me.
         e   Red and blue and green are colors.
         f ? Large and enormous and tiny are sizes.

Whichever metric of "nounlikeness" is used, the syntactic constraints on prenominal adjective ordering principle is expressed the same way: *in a series of prenominal adjectives, the more nounlike adjectives are ordered to be closer to the head noun they all modify.* The perceptual strategy for the segmentation of noun phrases developed in Strategy E" can explain this otherwise strange grammatical constraint. If more nounlike adjectives preceded less nounlike adjectives, then Strategy E" would produce premature segmentation. For example, principle 2 of E" would incorrectly segment the phrase in (67) *b* as shown in (70) as appeared to the correct segmentation of (67) *a* as in (71). This follows from the fact that "red" is less nounlike than "plastic." Thus, sequences that violate

(70)   (The plastic)$_{np}$ (red pencil)$_{np}$

(71)   (The red plastic pencil)$_{np}$

the general constraint on noncontrastive prenominal adjective order are incorrectly segmented by Strategy E".[7]

If the above arguments are correct, then the restriction on prenominal adjective ordering is an example of the effect of perceptual strategies on "grammatical" structure. I suggested above that perceptual strategies affect grammatical structures in those cases in which the child acquires the strategies before he acquires certain grammatical structures; grammatical structures acquired after he learns the strategies will be affected by them. Suppose that the child acquired Strategy E" before acquiring the ability to process more than one prenominal adjective at a time; this strategy could be expected to constrain the preferred

---

[7] Notice that a *general* "semantic" account of adjective ordering like Martin's is incorrect. If adjectives are postposed, then the order is free, as in *I like my pencils red and plastic* or *I like my pencils plastic and red.* That is, the ordering constraint only applies to *prenominal* ordering. Furthermore, prenominal comparative order is free, as in "I never saw a redder larger box". This is presumably due to the fact that the comparative suffix "–er" wants every adjective as equally nonnounlike.

adjective order that he eventually acquires — given that adjective order is otherwise syntactically free (which is indicated by the fact that, with contrastive stress,
any order of two adjectives is possible — see above). Recently we have tested this
view of the ontogenesis of prenominal adjective constraints with children between
two and five years of age. We present the child with phrases like those in (67),
some of which follow the adult constraints (such as [72]) and some of which do
not (such as [73]), and ask him to say back to us what we say (see Bever and
Epstein [forthcoming] for details). The crucial result is that younger children

(72)   The large plastic pencil fell from the table.

(73)   The plastic large pencil fell from the table.

perform better than do older children on the repetition of sequences that do not
follow the ordering constraints: the age at which the child's performance deteri-
orates on this task is just the age at which our other research shows him to be
acquiring strategies for speech perception. This is consistent with our proposal
that the constraints on prenominal adjective ordering are basically due to perceptual strategies.

        The details of a strategy like E" are obviously language-specific, since there
are many languages without explicit determiners, or without prenominal adjectives.
However, it is also clear that Strategy E" is a special instance of an extremely general principle of perceptual grouping (Principle F). This principle articulates the
fact that perceptual segmentation tends to be established only at points in a stimulus where a discontinuity of relations ("R_i") is perceived (but not at all such
points).

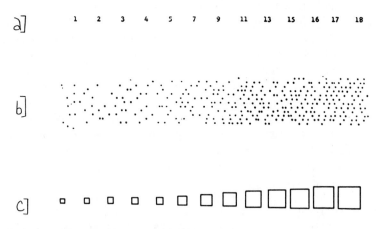

Figure 8. Examples of different kinds of perceptual segmentation. In each case there are two
main segments with an intermediate transition.

Principle F: In an ordered array of adjacent items. . .XYZ. . . , if XR_iY is the same as YR_iZ, then the array is grouped together. If YR_iZ is different from XR_iY, then the stimulus is segmented (XY) Z.

Consider first the application of Principle F to nonlinguistic stimuli. If asked to segment the sequence of numbers in Fig. 8a into groups, there would clearly be two main groups, 1-5 and 13-18, separated by a transition 5-13. The first and third segments are grouped by unit increases, and the middle transition segment by increases of 2.[8] Similarly, Fig. 8b and Fig. 8c are each made up perceptually of two segments with a transition fig. 8b. The first and third groups are ordered by slightly increasing density, while the middle group is transitional between them. In Fig. 8c the first and third segments are ordered by slightly increasing size, while the middle segment is ordered by radically increasing size. Notice that cases like Fig. 8c are special instances of contours. A visual edge is defined according to Principle F as a point at which R_i between two adjacent points differs from R_{i-1}.

The constraint on prenominal adjective endings in a sequence of adjectives is that the second must be more "nounlike" than the first. That is, in a sequence of prenominal adjectives, "$Adj_1 R_i Adj_2 R_j Adj_3 \ldots$," both R_i and R_j are the relation "less nounlike than."

Consider now the application of Principle F to the segmentation of cases that are directly analogous to the prenominal adjective ordering constraints within noun phrases (Fig. 9). The natural segmentation in each of these cases is following the fifth segment, and at no point preceding it. (In Fig. 9 the nounlikeness of the adjectives corresponds to the largeness of the numbers in Fig. 9a, the size of the figures in Fig. 9b, and the intensity of the shading in Fig. 9c.) Suppose that the sequential visual and numerical relations were analogous to a sequence that violates the adjective ordering constraints, as in Fig. 10. While a perceptual boundary following the fifth segment remains (just as in the case of the linguistic sequence), there is some uncertainty as to an additional boundary following the second segment in each array. It is exactly this perceptual uncertainty as to perceptual grouping that I have claimed is the basis of the ordering constraints on prenominal adjectives.

Every specific strategy of speech perception is a special case of a general principle of perception, at least in the sense that no general perceptual laws may be violated by a language-specific strategy. Thus, the fact that Strategy E" is a

[8]Notice that it is ambiguous to which group "5" and "13" belong uniquely. This is again a special case of the question as to whether segmentation is established at the earliest or latest possible point in a sequence. See above.

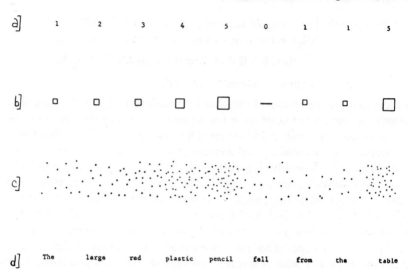

Figure 9. Examples of the perceptual segmentation corresponding to correct adjective orderings. In each case the first major segment terminates after the fifth item.

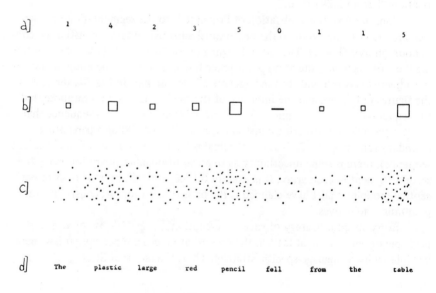

Figure 10. Examples of the perceptual segmentation corresponding to incorrect adjective orderings. In each case the first major segment terminates after the second item.

linguistic reflection of Principle F is not an *explanation* of Strategy E"; rather, it is simply a classification of the linguistic strategy in terms of the general principles that it utilizes.

B. The Reflection in Sentential Perceptual Complexity of Universal Perceptual Restrictions

During the course of this discussion I have emphasized the ways in which linguists depend on intuitions about sentences as the basic source for data that must be described by a grammar. The demonstration of the tripartite nature of speech behavior articulates the possibility that such intuitions about sentences also are of three basic kinds. For example, it is perfectly clear that the unacceptability of (74) *a* is due to the violation of the basic linguistic property of reference, while (74) *b* lacks an action. These sequences may be said to be unacceptable as sentences due to violations of basic (universal) linguistic properties. In contrast with this type of violation, the sequences in (75) are unacceptable as sentences due to violations of the rules governing the specific syntactic rules of English.

(74)   *a*   *Please pass me the bruck.
         b   *Tom, Dick and Harry.

(75)   *a*   *I hoped it for you to win the loot.
         b   *The group are better than you think.

That is, these sequences violate the surface level systematic properties of English. (Notice that the sequences in [74] and [75] could all be uttered and understood in ordinary speech.)

I pointed out above that the primitive basic capacities on the one hand and sophisticated epistemological systems are both easier to isolate in adult behavior than the perceptual system. Accordingly, the unacceptability of a sequence that is due to the failure to meet some basic property of all sentences (such as [74]) is easy to distinguish from unacceptability due to the failure to maintain properties specific to the particular language (75). However, sequences that are unacceptable due to the violation of perceptual strategies are relatively hard to identify. Thus, it is not immediately clear whether the ungrammaticality of sentence (76) *a* is due to linguistic properties of English or due to the mechanisms of speech perception. At first blush it might appear that sentences like (76) *a* should not be generated by a grammar of English, since they are not immediately acceptable; however, it is possible to argue that there is a near-continuous scale of acceptability between (76) *a* and (76) *j* in which the independent variable is the complexity of the sequence that separates the verb ("call") and the particle ("up"). Thus, it is plausible to argue that the apparent unacceptability of (76) *a* is due to the length of the phrase intervening between the verb and its particle. That is, (76) *a* is classified as acceptable syntactically, but complex perceptually, because of the load it places on immediate memory of the material between the verb and its particle. (Notice that the acceptability of [76*k*] shows that the

(76)   *a*   *John called the not very well liked but quite pretty girl on the next block where Jack has lived for years up.

       b   *John called the not very well liked but quite pretty girl who lives on the next block where Jack lived up.

       c   ? John called the not very well liked but quite pretty girl who lives on the next block up.

       d   ? John called the not very well liked but quite pretty girl who lives on the block up.

       e   John called the not very well liked but quite pretty girl up.

       f   John called the very well liked and quite pretty girl up.

       g   John called the well liked and quite pretty girl up.

       h   John called the pretty girl up.

       i   John called the girl up.

       j   John called up the girl.

       k   John called up the girl who is not very well liked but quite pretty and who lives on the next block where Jack has lived for years.

unacceptability of [76] *a* is not due to the length of the sentence per se, but to the length of the sequence interrupting the verb and its associated particle.)

Sequences that Interrupt Each Other — Save the Hardest for Last

To generate the acceptable sequences ([76] *h-k*), the formal grammar must also generate the less acceptable sequences ([76] *a-g*). That is, there is no natural way in which (76) *a-g* can be blocked by a grammar that also generates (76) *h-k*. However, there is a general perceptual rule (Principle G) which can be used to explain the unacceptability of (76) *a* on behavioral grounds, and thus explain why it is simultaneously grammatical and unacceptable.

Principle G: Sequences with constituents in which each subconstituent contributes information to the internal structure of the constituent are complex in proportion to the complexity of an intervening subsequence.

Notice that immediate memory may be exhausted either by the length of an intervening sequence *or* by the perceptual complexity of that sequence. Thus, (77) *a* is more acceptable than the equally long (76) *a*, while (77) *b* is less acceptable than the equally long (76) *g*. There are various other linguistic phenomena

(77)   *a*   John called Jane, Mary, Marsha, Sally, Joan, Mellisa, Erica, Felicia, Irma, Urania, Galacia and all the other girls in his class up.

       b   John called girls seen by the sailor he met up.

covered by Principle G. Recently Ross (1968) has suggested that there is a general constraint on postposition in English which orders "heavier," or more complex, noun phrases toward the end of a sentence. For example, (78) *a* is more acceptable than (78) *b*; (78) *c* is more acceptable than (78) *d*; and so forth. These cases are all characterized by the sequence "... Verb X Y ..." where X and Y both

(78)   *a*   John called up the girl in the white dress.

       b   John called the girl in the white dress up.

       c   John showed the girl the book that I liked a lot.

       d   John showed the book that I liked a lot to the girl.

have some unique internal relation to the verb (such as "particle, direct object, indirect object"). Ross's relative complexity constraint may be viewed as a special extension of Principle G. Consider the sequence "... Verb X Y ...," in which Y is less complex than X and both X and Y are related to the verb in the internal structure (that is, X and Y are dominated by VP). Suppose the complexity of the Verb-X relation taken independently is assigned a value of "x" and Y is assigned a value of "y" where $y < x$. Then the complexity of the relations (taken separately) in a sequence "V X Y" is the quantity $(x + y)$; assume that the interaction with short term memory is defined as a factor "m" which is proportional to the complexity of what must be remembered. The overall complexity (including the ordering) of "... Verb X Y ..." in which X must be held in memory would be $(x + y + m x)$ and of "Verb Y X" would be $(x + y + m y)$. Since by assumption $y < x$, the complexity of "V X Y" is greater than that of "V Y X." That is, in those cases in which the syntax provides free ordering between X and Y, the preferred order is one that places the more complex noun phrase so that it does not interrupt the relation between the verb and the less complex noun phrase; this ordering yields the simplest overall complexity of the sequence.

    This principle also accounts for the relative acceptability of post-verb ordering. The basic rule is that more complex adverbs are ordered towards the end of the sentence. Thus, (79) *a* is more acceptable than (79) *b*, while (79) *c*

(79)   *a*   John walked briskly in a slightly more northerly direction.

> *b* John walked in a slightly more northerly direction
>   briskly.
>
> *c* John walked north at a slightly brisker pace.
>
> *d* John walked at a slightly brisker pace north.

is more acceptable than (79) *d*. (The intuitive basis for the constraints on adverb order is far weaker than on adjective order.) Principle F would explain these facts, since in (79) *a* and 79 (*b*) the more complex adverbial phrase comes after the less complex phrase, while both modify the verb.[9]

Principle F also accounts for certain stylistic preferences that indicate that the more complex of two modifiers appears later in a sequence of two. For example, (a) is preferred over (b) in the pairs of examples below:[10]

> (80)   PRENOMINAL CONJOINED ADJECTIVES
>   OF THE SAME CLASS
>
> *a* The steel and artificially strengthened fibre plastic
>   tube broke.

---

[9] In (79) the adverb category (such as direction or manner) are held constant so the ordering constraints are not due to constraints on the order of adverb categories. The fact that relatively complex adverb phrases are always displaced towards the end of the clause allows us to investigate category restrictions on adverb order, by holding complexity constant and equal between any pair of adverbs. Such comparisons indicate that the canonical postverb adverbial order is DIRECTION MANNER PLACE DURATION FREQUENCY TIME PURPOSE. Thus (a) is correct, while (b) is not. Or to give an example with all categories,

> (a)   John walked north fast.
> (b)   John walked fast north.

(c) is correct and (d) is appalling. The reader is invited to test my intuitions pair by pair.

> (c)   Georgeala Cough rode *north fast in the park briefly*
>   *often yesterday for fun.*
> (d)   Georgeala Cough rode *for fun yesterday often briefly*
>   *in the park fast north.*

The source for these constraints is unclear to me at the moment, although it does appear that the direction and manner adverbs modify the verbs while the rest are sentence modifiers. Furthermore, the order Place... Purpose appears to be in the direction of increasing abstractness, and (consequently) of increasing psychological complexity. If this observation is true then principle D can account for these ordering constraints as well. The relatively complex adverb is ordered relatively late. To test the reality of the constraints themselves, M. Garrett and I played sentences like (a) and (b) to subjects with an accompanying task (click location) to increase errors. We found that subjects tend strongly to reverse adverbs sequences that violate the canonical order stated above.

[10] I am indebted to G. Miller for suggesting some of these examples.

b ? The artificially strengthened fibre plastic and steel
tube broke.

CONJOINED PREDICATE NOMINALS

a The machine is bulky and incredibly hard to operate
without the appearance of at least one malfunction.

b ? The machine is incredibly hard to operate without
the appearance of at least one malfunction and bulky.

POSTPOSITION OF COMPLEMENT SUBJECT
(when the object is not complex)

a It amazed Bill that John left early in the morning
to catch the train.

b ? The fact that John left early in the morning to catch
the train amazed Bill.

CONJOINED SENTENCES

a It rained while the dog barked at his master's voice
mysteriously coming out of a big black funnel.

b ? The dog barked at his master's voice mysteriously
coming out of a big black funnel while it rained.

Sequences With Two Simultaneous Functions – Three's a Crowd

Unfortunately it is not the case that the perceptual source of the relative
unacceptability of a syntactically allowed sequence is always so easily identified
and precisely described. Consider (81) *a*, a so-called "double embedding." It must
be generated formally by a contemporary linguistic grammar that also generates
(81) *b*. It is not possible to restrict the number of embedded subordinate clauses
to one, because of sentences like (81) *c*, which have two embeddings, but are perfectly acceptable. Indeed, since the internal structures of (81) *a*, (81) *c*, and
(81) *d* are identical and only (81) *a* is unacceptable, no restriction on the form
of internal structures themselves can account for the unacceptability of doubly
embedded sentences. Rather, it is a function of the way in which the internal
relations are presented in the external structure. Fodor and Garrett (1968) suggest
that it is the density of the number of internal structure sentence units per word
in the external structure that exceeds some critical threshold ("density" = 3/12
for [81] *a*; "density" = 3/14 for [81] *c*). This proposal is intriguing since it
would suggest that at least one dimension of perceptual complexity is quanti-
fiable. However, the proposal is incorrect. The density of internal structures
per word is even higher in (81) *d*, but (81) *d* is entirely comprehensible and

acceptable. Thus, the complexity of center-embedded sentences cannot be easily explained away by appeal to any obvious perceptual principle. This creates a dilemma — either we must accept the current form of generative grammar as incorrect, since it cannot avoid generating center embedded sentences in a natural way, or we must appeal to an unspecified perceptual strategy to account for its difficulty.

(81)   *a* The dog the cat the fox was chasing was scratching was yelping.

       b The dog the cat was scratching was yelping.

       c The fox was chasing the cat that was scratching the dog that was yelping.

       d The fox was chasing the cat scratching the yelping dog.

Chomsky and Miller (1963) have attempted to define such a perceptual principle. They argue that any perceptual principle may not interrupt its own operation more than once. In the case of a sentence like (81) *b* (represented schematically in [82] *b*) the perceptual assignment of the "actor"-action relation to the first noun and last verb is interrupted by the same assignment to the second noun and first verb. In (81) *a* (represented in [82] *a*), the perceptual assignment of actor-action to the first noun and last verb is interrupted by the assignment of the same relation to the second noun and the second verb, which is in turn interrupted by the assignment of the same function to the last noun and the first verb. (Upper lines in [82] represent subject-verb relations. Lower lines represent verb-object relations.)

(82)   *a*

       b

It is intuitively clear that a self-interrupting operation is more complex than one which does not interrupt itself. However, it is not theoretically motivated that one interruption be acceptable (as in [81] *b*) and two interruptions be entirely unacceptable (as in [81] *a*).

It is possible to subsume the relative unacceptability of double embedded sentences under a general perceptual principle (H), which simultaneously accounts for the perceptual difficulty of a superficially heterogeneous number of types of sentences.

Principle H: A stimulus may not be perceived as simultaneously having two positions on the same classificatory dimension.

Principle H states that unavoidable fact that a stimulus cannot be perceived in two incompatible ways at the same time. This principle combines with the view of speech perception as a function of direct mapping of external sequences onto internal structures to predict the difficulty of any sequence in which a phrase has a "double function" with respect to such a mapping operation. Before applying Principle H to explain the difficulty of center-embedded sentences, consider first some well-known facts.

Miller and Selfridge (1950) found that sequences with low-order probability approximations to English were difficult to perceive; for example, a sequence like (83) is more difficult than (84).

(83)   he went to the newspaper is in deep   (2nd-order approximation)

(84)   then go ahead and do it if possible   (7th-order approximation)

(A "2nd-order approximation" is generated by giving a subject two words [such as "he went"] and asking him to produce the next word of a sentence ["to"]; the next subject is given the last two words of the sequence ["went to"] and produces the next word ["the"]. A "seventh-order approximation" is generated by giving each subject the last seven words of the sequence each time.) The relative ease of perceiving sentences as they increase in order of approximation was taken by Miller and others as evidence for the organizing role of syntactic structure at levels higher than a single word. For example, in sequence (84) the words form a sentence, while in (83) they do not. However, this does not explain the exact psychological nature of the difficulty of low orders of approximation. In fact, if forming a sentence makes word strings easy, it might be predicted that sequence (83) should be psychologically simpler, since it simultaneously forms *two* sentences (as in [85] and [86]).

(85)   he went *to the newspaper*

(86)   *the newspaper* is in deep

The real basis of the psychological difficulty is clear: the underlined portion of the sequence is vital to each sentence − that is, it has a "double function." There is a general cognitive restriction that results in psychological complexity whenever such double functions appear. As a visual example, consider the representation of the two squares on the left when they are adjacent. The line labelled "y" is simultaneously shared by the right and left squares. As a result, Fig. 11 is generally perceived as a divided rectangle rather than as two adjacent squares. Often such double functions in vision can produce "impossible" figures from the combination of two possible figures, such as Fig. 12.

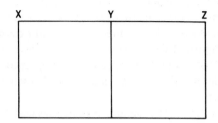

Figure 11. Figure most easily seen as a rectangle with one division at "y," rather than two squares joined at "y."

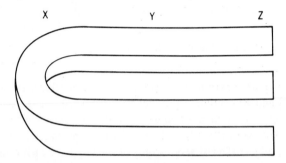

Figure 12. Figure that is "impossible" because of the combination of two- and three-dimensional projections at point "y."

The general psychological principle that governs these visual examples is a special case of Principle H: in a closed system, a component of a stimulus cannot serve two opposite functions at the same time. That is, in Fig. 11 line y cannot both end one square *and* begin another; or in Fig. 12 the segment labelled "y" cannot both end one kind of figure (the three-dimensional "u" opening right in the segments labelled x-y) *and* begin the other (the three poles in the segments labelled y-z).

There is a related explanation for the psychological difficulty of "center-embedded" sentences. Phillips and Miller (1966) noticed that part of the complexity of center-embedding may be due to the fact that in a sentence like (81) *a*, the second noun is the subject of one clause and the object of another (see [82]). If understanding a sentence involves labeling each word for its logical function in the underlying structure, then the second noun in (81) *a* could be interpreted as having a "double function" with respect to a strategy that maps external noun sequences onto internal structures, in which the first noun is the object of a verb of which the second noun is the subject. With respect to the preceding noun, it is an object with respect to the following noun. The general double-function hypothesis for perception following from Principle H is this:

> *Principle I:* In a sequence of constituents x, y, z, if x has an internal relation R_i to y and y has the same internal relation to z, and x, y, and z are superficially identical, then the stimulus is relatively complex, due to y's double function in the perceptual strategy, S_i.

$$S_i : x\ y \longrightarrow x\ R_i\ y$$
$$s_i$$

Notice that the prediction of the perceptual difficulty of center-embedded sentences from Principle I depends on the existence of strategies for the direct perception of the internal structure relations from the external sequence, which define the relations (R_i) that adjacent phrases bear to each other. One relevant strategy is presented in Strategy J.

> *Strategy J:* In .... NP_1 NP_2(VP).... sequence in the external structure, NP_1 is the internal object of an internal structure sentence unit of which NP_2 is the subject.

Of course, Strategy J (like A, B, and C) is not *always* true, as in (87), but it is

(87)   *The boy the girl* was seen by is here.

probably true of external sequences most of the time. The same is true of Strategy K.[11]

> *Strategy K:* In .... V_1 V_2 .... (in which the verbs are finite), V_2 corresponds to the main verb of a sentence with V_1 as the subordinate verb.

The relations assumed by Strategies J and K combine to make single embedded sentences like (81) *b* quite simple to perceive. But the same strategies make doubly-embedded sentences difficult because of Principle I. With respect to the internal relation set up by Strategy J, NP_2 is simultaneously the left hand and right hand member of a strategy in double embeddings, while V_2 is simultaneously the right and left hand member of Strategy K. Notice that the superficial identity of the three NP's and V's in an embedded sentence increases the

---

[11]Note that it is not crucial to this explanation that Strategies J and K exist independently — only that the external/internal relations they describe are utilized as listeners hear sentences which justify those strategies (such as [81] *a*).

difficulty since it makes the relation between the first and second and second and third constituent *absolutely* identical. Thus, if N_2 or V_2 differ superficially from their surrounding phrases, sentences like (81) should become easier. I have not tested this, but it seems to me that (88), in which N_2 and V_2 do differ superficially from their adjacent constituents, is relatively comprehensible (compared with [81] *a*).

(88)   The dog the destruction the wild fox produced was
            scaring will run away fast.

There are other kinds of examples in language explained by the double-function Principle I. Consider the complexity of the sentences in (89):

(89)   *a*   They did x̃ot want me nŏt to promise nŏt to help them.

        b   They did not want me to promise not to help them.

        c   John is nŏt nŏt available for nŏ charge at all.

        d   John is not available for no charge at all.

(89) *a* and (89) *c* are examples of triple negation, which has often been recognized as extremely complex, if acceptable at all. Like the embedded sentences (81) *a*, *b*, sentences with two negation markers are perfectly comprehensible and acceptable (as in [89] *b*, *d*). Principle I applies to predict both the difficulty of sentences with three negations and the relative ease of sentences with two negative markers. Consider the perceptual strategy L, which defines the perceptual operation signalled by a negative marker. Strategy L operates to place the second "not" in the above sentences as both the scope of the first negation and, simultaneously, the operator on the third negation.

> *Strategy L:* Negation markers (not, un, and the like) apply the operation of semantic negation to their syntactically defined scope.

According to Principle I, any sequence with such a double perceptual function is perceptually complex.

This principle also explains the difficulty of many co-called "left-branching" structures. Recently Yngve (   ) has proposed that phrases with a left-branching external hierarchical organization (such as [90] *a*) are harder to produce and understand than phrases with a right-branching organization (such as [90] *b*). According to this view (elaborated by Johnson, 1965) "left-branching" involves greater load on temporary memory than does "right-branching." This is allegedly due to the number of hierarchical phrase structure "commitments" for the rest of the sentence that are made by the words in a left-branching structure. For example, the word "very" in (90) *a* "commits" the talker to an adjectival phrase modifying a noun, while the word "the" in (90) *b* makes no such commitment. Presumably structures involving more commitments are harder to produce, because they require a greater memory load, to ensure that commitments made earlier in a sentence are fulfilled. This model of speech processing is intended to account for the relative difficulty of sentences like (90) *c* as compared with (90) *d*:

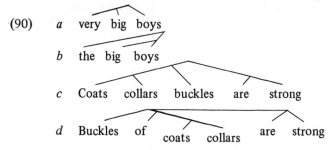

(90) *a* very big boys

   b the big boys

   c Coats collars buckles are strong

   d Buckles of coats collars are strong

This proposal is coherent as a model of complexity in speech production. But for speech perception it appears that one could argue that left-branching structures should be *simpler* to understand if there is any effect at all, just because the increased number of structural "commitments" that the speaker makes early in a sentence should make it easier (that is, more redundant) for the listener to predict the latter part of the sentence. Thus, even on formal grounds it is not clear that the amount of left-branching in a sentence should correspond to its perceptual complexity. Furthermore, there are many convincing counter examples. For example, consider the perceptual simplicity of the highly left-branching sentence in (91) *a*:

(91) *a* After a quite severe appendicitis attack the not very well dressed man fell over.
   b Buckles of collars of coats are strong.

Thus, left-branching as such cannot be used to predict or explain perceptual complexity. Principle I, however, does account for the perceptual complexity of the cases that appeared to support the left-branching hypothesis (90) *c*. Sentences (90) *c* and (91) *b* are predicted to be relatively more difficult than the other sentences in (90) and (91) because of the double function of at least one phrase. (Note that [90] *c* becomes immediately comprehensible if the word "coats" is changed to "fur" as in [92] *a*, and that [91] *b* becomes comprehensible if the word "collars" is changed to "containers", as in [92] *b*).

(92) *a* Fur collars' buckles' are strong.
   b Buckles of containers of coats are strong.

That is, while the superficial appearance and phrase structures in (92) *a, b* are identical with the incomprehensible sentences (90) *c, d*, Principle I does not apply to them because the internal relations between the three phrases now differ — the phrase in the middle is not both the left and right hand member of the same external/internal perceptual mapping because of the changes in the internal relations.

Principle I also predicts previously unexplored classes of perceptual complexity that are intuitively of the same sort as the previous examples. Consider the sentences in (93). In each case there is a phrase (indicated by "y") that is related to a previous phrase in the same way that it relates to a following phrase, and in each case, the sentences are extremely difficult to understand if they are acceptable at all. As in the cases of double embedding, triple negation, and "left-branching," the complexity of these sentences is a function of the presence

$$\text{(93)} \quad a \quad \text{They were tired of discussing } \underset{x}{} \text{ considering } \underset{y}{} \text{ producing } \underset{z}{} \text{ toys.}$$

(93) *a* They were tired of discussing considering producing toys.
                                      x y z

b They were tired of the discussion of the consideration
                                  x y

     z
of the production of toys.

of three superficially identical phrases in which the second phrase is modified by the first phrase in the same way in which it modifies the third phrase. Consider the relative perceptual ease of these sentences if only two phrases occur:

(94) *a* They were tired of discussing producing toys.
       b They were tired of the discussion of the production
             of toys.

The sentences in (93) also become much easier to understand if the internal relations among the three critical phrases are varied:

(95) *a* They were tired of discussing ceiling producing toys.
                                     x y z

b They were tired of the discussion of the evolution of the
                                  x y

     z
production of toys.

(Note that in [95] *a*, y is the internal structure object of z, while x and y are not directly related. In [95] *b*, y is the action carried out by z, but the object of x). Finally, the sentences in (93) become perceptually simpler if the superficial form of the critical phrases is varied, even while the internal relations are held constant:

(96) *a* They were tired of discussing the consideration of
             producing toys.
       b They were tired of the discussion of considering the
             production of toys.

In brief, I have tried to show that if speech perception is viewed (at least in part) as a direct mapping of external sequences onto internal structures, then the tautology in Principle H predicts the principle in Principle I, which in turn predicts the relative perceptual complexity of double embedding, triple negatives, and left-branching sentences among others. Thus, such sentences may be generated as syntactically (and semantically) acceptable, but be hard to understand nevertheless.[12]

THREE CONCLUSIONS

These discussions of the role of language behavior in determining language "structure" lead to several modifications of current views of the study of language. First, we must reassess the distinction between "knowledge" of a language and its "actual use," which places emphasis on the independent primariness of "abstract linguistic knowledge." Second, we must consider whether the acquisition of language systems is best interpreted in terms of the primary acquisition of a series of grammatically-defined rules or in terms of the development of the psychological systems underlying perception and memory. Finally, the demonstration that the structural and behavioral systems of language are often special expressions of cognitive universals should expand our conception of the innate components of language acquisition; we now must focus on the problem of how the different innate components are linked together in the course of language learning and how the learned aspects are incorporated in adult language behavior.

1. The Distinction Between Linguistic Competence and Performance in the Adult

The goal of a model of speech perception is to specify how we discover the internal structures of sentences from their external form. The review of

---

[12] Notice that the notion of "double function" in Principle I does not refer to all cases in which a given word may both be a subject and an object in the internal structure. That is, it is not clear that sentence (a) is more complex perceptually than sentence (b), even though "boy" in (a) is both a subject and an object, while in (b) it is only a subject.

    (a)   the boy that the girl likes hit the man.
    (b)   the boy that likes the girl hit the man.

Principle I says nothing about such cases. The "double function" under discussion is assigned by perceptual strategies that map external onto internal structures, not by internal-structure functions themselves; that is, if a word with a double function bears the same internal relation (other than conjunction) to the preceding and following word.

experimental work in the first part of this discussion was devoted to explorations of the role of speech perception in the structures isolated in "linguistic" investigations. The conclusion drawn from these studies was that behavioral processes manipulate linguistically-defined structures but do not mirror or directly simulate the grammatical processes that relate those structures within a grammar. Such a conclusion invalidates any model for speech recognition that attempts to directly incorporate grammatical rules as an isolable component of the recognition processes.

The first attempts to integrate transformational grammar with speech behavior were largely concerned with the "psychological reality" of the grammatical rules proposed by linguists (reviewed in Miller, 1962; Miller and McNeill, 1969). Many psychologists viewed transformational grammar as a novel and radical challenge to their experimental skill. They were particularly unwilling to accept the concept of an "abstract" underlying structure because the current psychological theory could not account for its existence. Thus, the conflict between "behaviorism" and "mentalism" reappeared in discussions of language behavior and motivated many experiments.

One product of this conflict has been the artificial distinction between "linguistic theory" on the one hand and "speech behavior" on the other. Linguists defended themselves against the accumulation of inexplicable psychological facts about speech by invoking the distinction between what we know and what we do. According to this view, "psycholinguistics" was a logical adjunct to "linguistics," on the following formula:

(97)   abstract grammar + "performance principles" = actual
        speech behavior

Grammar was taken to be an idealized account of our knowledge. The psychologists' problem appeared to be to find general performance principles that would describe how that ideal grammar is used in behavior.

At first it appeared that many of the processes and structures postulated in transformational grammar would provide direct accounts of behavior. For example, Miller and McKean (1964) found that the time to match pairs of sentences with the same internal structure is a function of the transformations that differentiate their external structures; this result appeared to justify the claim that "one linguistically defined transformation corresponds to one psychological operation." Further research at first appeared to back up this simple competence-performance equation, but more recent research (reviewed on p. 284 ff above) shows that this is incorrect. In point of fact, grammatically-defined *structures* may be reflected in speech behavior, but not grammatically-defined *processes*. Thus we seem to be in a dilemma: how can we account for the psychological validity of linguistically-defined structures without taking into account the linguistic processes that define those structures and their interrelations?

This dilemma is actually an illusion created by the artificiality of the distinction between "competence" and "performance" in grammatical analysis. A real grammar does not, in fact, describe an abstract linguistic world, but rather a set of intuitions about "grammaticality" held by native speakers. For example, the transformational grammarian appeals to an intuition shared by most of us about our language when he claims that he will consider only facts that pertain to complete sentences. We all agree roughly on what a sentence is, and, no doubt, we could define psychological tests that would identify most sentences most of the time. However, even if the agreement on what is (or is not) a sentence were much weaker than it is, the point would remain the same; the linguist uses an introspective behavioral criterion to choose among his intuitions about a language. He assumes that some of the structural distinctions inherent in a grammar are *consistently* reflected in his intuitions about sentencehood, structural relations, ambiguities, and so on. He uses these consistent reflections in his own behavior to decide what data about the language he must describe.

However, even if our linguistic intuitions are consistent, there is no reason to believe that they are *direct* behavioral reflections of linguistic knowledge. The behavior of having linguistic intuitions may introduce its own properties; that is, there is no guarantee that a linguistic grammar itself is either a *direct* or an *ideal* representation of the linguistic structure. I have emphasized that the discovery of the linguistically pertinent data that the grammar describes is itself a poorly understood psychological process. Therefore, a grammar is *not* necessarily a unique, basic "nonpsychological" representation of linguistic structure; it is merely the most direct and available of all behavioral reflections of grammatical structure.

In short, for the past ten years we have taken the psychology of linguistic intuitions for granted and have used those intuitions as data relevant to the construction of a universal linguistic grammar. Our apparent problem has been to put grammar and psychology back together again. We are finding that it is impossible to do this *directly* according to the simple equation in (97). Instead we find that we have developed two formulae for the interaction of ideal grammar and speech behavior in grammatical analysis:

(98) *a* ideal grammar + behavioral principles of having "linguistic intuitions" = "linguistic data" (such as the facts in [4])

b "linguistic data" + formal grammatical universals = "generative grammar"

Thus, to take linguistic grammar itself as the "basic" structure would be to make the same mistake as does the physicist who takes the parallelogram of forces as the "basic" concept of mechanical systems. The parallelogram of forces is itself derived from a special case of more general physical principles; it has its specific properties due to the specific nature of its application to slow-moving bodies on planes. Similarly, a linguistic grammar may have formal properties that reflect the study of selected subparts of speech behavior (for example, having intuitions about sentences), but which are not reflected in *any* other kind of speech behavior. Other kinds of speech behavior may bring out additional aspects of the structure of language, and they undoubtedly have laws of their own independent of the structure of language, but all the formalizations of systematic speech behavior including grammar must exemplify at least part of the actual linguistic structure.[13]

This conclusion is in conflict with many recent claims about the relationship of a linguistic grammar and behavior. For example, the common view has been expressed in the following quotations from a recent conference (Lyons and Wales, 1966).

> A theory of linguistic knowledge attempts to account for our "intuitions" concerning the language . . . (A theory of performance) is a theory of how, given a certain linguistic competence we actually put it to use, realize it, express it. (Wales and Marshall, pp. 29-30)

> If language were a game, "competence" would be the rules of the game, while the actions of its players would constitute performance. (Blumenthal, p. 81)

> A search for an analysis of the connection between the way the structural description is specified by the grammar and the way it is "specified" by speakers and hearers. . . is one way of formulating the psycholinguistic problem; the abstract nature of this connection between grammar and recognition is (to be) emphasized. . . the problem (is) which aspects of the structural description are relevant to explanations of particular performance tasks. (Garrett, in the discussion of Fodor and Garrett, p. 175)

These authors agree that there is a linguistic grammar that accounts for our basic linguistic intuitions of sequence acceptability, structural relations, and so forth. It is the psychologists' problem to explore the "behavioral" relevance of the structures internal to a grammar.

I have argued that a proper understanding of the behavioral and phenomenological nature of "basic linguistic intuitions" forces us to reject the claim that a linguistic grammar is in any sense internal to such linguistic performances as talking and listening. To quote Jonkheere (p. 86 in the same volume):

---

[13] Note that to take one external capacity as the underlying structure for another is to make the same mistake as do those linguists and psychologists who argue that one actual sentence form (for example, "the active") is central to other sentence forms (for example, "the passive").

It does not necessarily follow that the characterization of the rules a person is following in some form of rule-conforming behavior has to go into the explanation of how
he follows these rules or performs behavior in conformity with them.

The relationship between linguistic grammar based on intuition and that
based on the description of other kinds of explicit language performance may
not just be "abstract" (as maintained by Fodor and Garrett) but may be *nonexist-*
ent in some cases. First, apparently "linguistic" intuitions about the relative acceptability of sequences may themselves be functions of one of the systems of
speech behavior (for instance, perception) rather than of the system of structurally relevant intuitions. Second, the behavior of producing linguistically relevant
intuitions may introduce some properties which are *sui generis* and which appear
in *no* other kind of language behavior.

In this paper I have considered examples of the first kind, in which perceptual mechanisms underlie what initially appear to be idiosyncratic syntactic rules
and examples in which the unacceptability of "grammatical" utterances is due
to perceptual mechanisms. An example of grammatical structures relevant only
to intuitions may be the linguistically-defined transformations, since they do not
themselves play a direct role in sentence perception. If they also play no role in
speech production they will remain an example of grammatical mechanisms which
are relevant *only* to the behavior of having intuitions about sentences.

Once we accept the possibility that ongoing speech behavior does not utilize
a linguistic grammar, it is no surprise that the mechanisms inherent to ongoing
speech behavior do not manifest transformations or any operations directly based
on them. An explanation of why producing conscious intuitions about potential
sentences elicits transformations that are not utilized in other aspects of speech
behavior awaits a full theory of the phenomenology of linguistic intuitions. However, there are some aspects of such intuitions that provide an initially plausible
basis for the importance of transformations in linguistic grammars based on those
intuitions. The set of intuitions about sentences that are unique to modern transformational grammarians are not intuitions of sequence acceptability, but intuitions of structural relations among sentences. For example, the fact that active
and passive constructions are felt to share the same basic grammatical relations
and are sensed as somehow corresponding to one another is taken as a motivation
for describing both as instances of a common internal structure. If the only goal
of grammar were to generate acceptable sequences, the motive for generating both
active and passive as special instances of the same structure, differentiated by only
one rule, would be much less strong. Furthermore, even most cases of acceptability judgements involve judgements about *potential* sentences, in which one is
asked to extrapolate his linguistic knowledge onto imagined situations, which
often stimulates the linguist-informant to aid his "grammaticality" judgement
about a particular sequence by thinking of other sequences to which it is closely

related. Thus the formal description of a language using transformations depends on intuitions that are irrelevant to most ongoing speech behavior but that emphasize transformational relations between sentences.

What is the Science of Linguistics a Science of? Linguistic intuitions do not necessarily directly reflect the structure of a language, yet such intuitions are the basic data the linguist uses to verify his grammar. This fact could raise serious doubts as to whether linguistic science is about anything at all, since the nature of the source of its data is so obscure. However, this obscurity is characteristic of every exploration of human behavior. Rather than rejecting linguistic study, we should pursue the course typical of most psychological sciences; give up the belief in an "absolute" intuition about sentences and study the laws of the intuitional process itself.

This course of action has been fruitful in other areas of psychology. Consider the subjectivity of astronomical star-transit judgements, which according to Boring was one of the first problems to arise in the context of what we know today as psychology. For a time, astronomers believed in the "absolute" constancy of their judgement of the instant at which a star crossed a certain reference point. However it was noticed that different observers produced different judgements, so each pair of astronomers were related by a "personal equation," which specified the relative delay in their judgments. Ultimately it was observed that even an individual's judgement delay was not constant, and would vary from situation to situation.

These observations could have been used to justify rejection of any facts based on personal reaction time, and indeed astronomers turned to other timing techniques as soon as they became available. However, the study of reaction time itself became one of the main areas of experimental psychology. Given that reaction times are not absolute or free of the context in which they occur, psychologists have explored systematically the interaction between reaction time and its context.

The effect of stimulus context on absolute judgement of the stimulus has become a part of almost every branch of psychology. One of the most basic laws governing the interaction between stimuli is the *law of contrast* — for example, the well-known phenomenon of feeling that the ocean is cold on a hot day, while the same ocean at the same temperature feels warm on a cool day. That is, one's "absolute" judgement of a stimulus can be exaggerated by the difference between the stimulus and its context. This influence by contrast clearly can occur in "intuitions" about grammaticality. For example, (99) *b* preceded by (99) *a* may be judged ungrammatical, but contrasted with (99) *c* it will probably be judged as grammatical.

(99) a   Who must telephone her?
      b   Who need telephone her?
      c   Who want telephone her?

That is, not only are there several reasons for the unacceptability of sequences, but even the notion of structural grammaticality is itself subject to contextual contrast.

Often the nature of contextual influences on absolute judgements is less clear than in cases of contrast. For example, it is well known that the perception of an unsaturated spot of color is greatly influenced by its surroundings. Thus, surrounded by a yellow background, a pale green spot may appear blue, while the same green spot appears deep green if it is surrounded by red. These differences in judgement are quite stable, in the sense that even with conscious instruction about the nature of the situation, the perception of the colors is still influenced by the surrounding context in the same way.

Cases like this cannot be described as mere "contrast" effects; in what *a priori* sense does red contrast more directly with green than yellow does? Human observers themselves *contribute* this notion of contrast even in the absence of obvious physical parameters to be contrasted (unlike the case of the influence of hot or cold on the perception of lukewarm, in which the differences and contrasts have an "objective" contrasting measure). In the case of color perception, it is in the nature of our visual system to contrast red and green in one dimension and blue and yellow in another dimension.

It is quite likely that similar situations obtain between sentences, in which judgements of the grammaticality of one sentence are affected by the other sentences among which it is placed, even when the other sentences do not appear to contrast with the stimulus sentence in as direct a manner as in (99). This proposal is subject to demonstration. E.g. Take all the example sentences from several linguistic articles (excluding those sets that contrast directly as in [99]) and present them to subjects either in their original sequence, taken separately from each article, or entirely shuffled from all the articles. Subjects must simply indicate which sentences they think the original articles assumed to be grammatical and which were labeled ungrammatical. It would not be surprising if subjects should replicate the judgements of the original articles much more consistently when presented with the examples in their original order than when presented with all the sentences from the different articles in some random order. If this is true, the experiment will demonstrate that the judgements of "absolute" grammaticality are illusory and that a science of the influence of context on acceptability judgements is as necessary in linguistic research as in every other area of psychology.

Such a criticism does not invalidate linguistics, even without reform. Many intuitions about sentences appear to be strong enough to resist contextual effects, and we can expect that these intuitions will remain constant even when we have

developed an understanding of the intuitional process (for example, the relationship
between actives and passives, the fact that "John hit the ball" is a sentence of
English, and the like). However, recent trends in linguistic research have placed
increasing dependence on relatively subtle intuitions (cf. Lakoff 1968, Kiparsky
and Kiparsky 1969, Ross 1967a, MacCawley 1969) whose psychological status is
extremely unclear. Since there are many sources for intuitional judgements other
than grammaticality, and since grammaticality judgements themselves can be in
fluenced by context, subtle intuitions are not be trusted until we understand the
nature of their interaction with factors that are irrelevant to grammaticality. If
we depend too much on such intuitions without exploring their nature, linguistic
research will perpetuate the defects of introspective mentalism as well as its virtues.

2. The Acquisition of Grammar

Ideally, a model of language learning should specify how the child discovers
the systematic relations between internal and external structures of language used
in talking, listening and predicting potential sentences in his language. This review of language learning has explored the effects of the system of listening (and
presumably talking) in the young child on the system of predicting potential sentences in the adult. The existence of this interaction shows that it is not the case
that the predictive grammar is learned independently of the use of language; rather,
it is learned in the course of its use.

However, many recent studies have been devoted to exploring the child's
acquisition of language in terms of his acquisition of rules allegedly independent
of their use. A standard methodology is to observe the child's utterances at a
given stage and to then write a "miniature grammar" for his utterances; language
development is then described as an ordered series of such "grammars".

There are several methodological difficulties with such a program. First,
adult grammars are based on a variety of linguistic *intuitions* about sentences, not
actual utterances. The "grammar" for what an adult actually says (and what he
understands) would undoubtedly look quite different from the grammar that accounts for his intuitions about sentences *in vitro*. Thus, while a description of
the maturation of the child's productive (or perceptual) system for language is
interesting, it does not bear directly on his acquisition of a system of linguistic
knowledge. Second, any finite set of linguistic data about specific sequences
justifies an infinitude of grammars. Which grammar is used to generate a particular
corpus of data depends on intuitions *about* the acceptable sequences (like the
notion of relations between sentences) as well as *a priori* decisions by the linguist
as to what theoretical form a grammar must have, and what kinds of intuitions
are relevant to his description. Since young children do not present us with their

intuitions *about* sentences and intersentential relations, we cannot narrow the range of possible grammars implied by any finite set of their utterances. Furthermore, we cannot use preconceived notions about the form of grammar underlying a child's utterances (such as the assumption that it is initially nontransformational), because this would prejudge the sort of fact that we are trying to ascertain by collecting his utterances in the first place.

Suppose, however, that these difficulties with writing grammars for utterances of preschoolers were somehow overcome by finding a way of eliciting "linguistically relevant" intuitions from young children. One would then be able to study the development of the systems for predicting potential sentences. At each point in the child's development one would still have to examine the structure of his other systems of language behavior to assess their interaction with his allegedly "linguistic" intuitions. Thus, like an adult, a child may reject a particular sequence as ungrammatical simply because he cannot understand it. Of course the situation would be more complex than for an adult, even in the study of a child who could articulate his "linguistic" intuitions, since his perceptual and productive systems for language behavior would themselves be evolving and presumably would interact with each other and with the system of predicting new sentences from old.

Suppose, however, that one solved these problems as well, and were able to distinguish the effects on intuitions due to the different aspects of speech behavior. One then might predict that language structure emerges as some function of transformational rules. The most obvious prediction in this vein would be that the more grammatical rules a subgrammar of English has, the later it is acquired. Furthermore, if one holds the view that the grammar of one's linguistic knowledge is reflected directly in such behaviors as speech production and perception, then one would predict that sentences involving more transformations are processed relatively poorly by young children.

Brown and Hanlon have made exactly these assumptions and this prediction for the acquisition of language, rule-by-rule. They examined the relative frequency of various constructions whose linguistic analysis involves different numbers of transformations (see Chapter 1 in this volume). They conclude that almost all of their predictions based on relative numbers of transformations are confirmed. However, their results also confirm the hypothesis that sentences in which a relatively large amount of material must be recovered from the deep structure are relatively difficult.

First, three of their predictions involve the relative simplicity of declarative sentences compared to negatives or questions. They argue that this is due to the fact that the affirmatives have one less transformation in their derivation. However, *any* theory of speech processing must take into account the psychological primacy of the positive form of utterance, quite independently of the number of syntactic operations involved.

Even if one granted Brown and Hanlon these three cases, there are nine cases that involve specific deletion of internal structure material (for example, the truncated question form as compared with the question). Finally, the remaining predictions involve the negative question construction, which turns out to be relatively difficult for children. Brown and Hanlon argue that this relative difficulty is due to the fact that an extra transformation (negative) is involved. However, there are various linguistic and behavioral arguments that negative questions also involve the deletion of an entire sentence from their internal structure. That is, "didn't the girl hit the dog" has an internal structure more nearly corresponding to "*the girl hit the dog* didn't the girl hit the dog," from which the (italicized) sentence has been deleted by an optional transformation. As behavioral evidence for this proposal (which is the only relevant kind of evidence to compare with Brown and Hanlon's explicitly behavioral data) consider the fact that negative questions are ordinarily taken to be assertions (for example, the above sentence asserts that the questioner believes that the girl *did* hit the dog). (cf. Bever 1967, reported in Mehler and Bever, in press).

Thus Brown and Hanlon's results are equivocal concerning the possibility of predicting the effect of the number of formal transformations on the complexity of a syntactic construction type for children; their data could be explained equally well by a view of sentence complexity according to which the more internal structure material that is implicit in the external structure, the harder the sentence, since the child must contribute more information to the sentence himself.

This chapter has concentrated on the interactions between "linguistic" structures and perceptual mechanisms in the child and adult, although it is clear that mechanisms for *learning* a language affect the eventual structure of a language even more dramatically than do the perceptual systems. I have said little about the effects of general principles of learning on linguistic structure because I do not know anything about how language (or anything else) is learned, while I do have some initial understanding of the mechanisms of perception. There is no doubt, however, that as we understand more about the learning of language, we will be able to account for even more of the structures that we find in our adult ability to have intuitions about potential sentences.

The claim that languages are learned via a series of subgrammars of the adult language remains to be demonstrated. However, there are certain nongrammatical behavioral variables that we know to affect the learning of language, even though we do not yet understand the learning process itself. The most obvious behavioral constraint on language acquisition is the development of memory in the young child. The child's immediate and long-term memory must constrain his language ability in vocabulary size, utterance length, and amount of material in the external structure of sentences deleted from their internal structure. The fact that the child starts out with a small vocabulary and short utterances is well-attested. The recent research by Brown and Hanlon demonstrates further that the child also has some difficulty with constructions that depend on active reconstruction of deleted internal structure.

3. The Unity of Universals of Language and Thought in the Mind

Recent discussions of language and linguistic theory have emphasized the extent to which the capacity for language is innate in human beings. The formal articulation of innate language structures is contained in the *universal grammar,* which represents all of the formal characteristics and constraints that a grammar for a particular language must reflect. For example, the putative universal grammar states that every language has an internal structure, an external structure, and a set of transformations that map the first onto the second; that there are distinct categories for "noun" and "verb"; and so on. Chomsky (1965) suggested that we must distinguish between *formal* and *substantive* universals. Formal universals describe the *types* of rules that are possible (for example, that there are transformations), while substantive universals describe the universally available stock of terms used in languages (for example, that noun and verb are possible syntactic categories). Many substantive linguistic universals appear to be derivable from more general psychological universals. For example, the universality of the noun/verb distinction in language might be explained as the linguistic reflection of the general cognitive distinction between objects and relations between objects (cf. Chomsky 1965, p. 28). Thus the concept of "noun" would not have to be taken as a linguistic universal in itself but merely as the linguistic expression of such a cognitive universal. The formal universals are also susceptible to immediate explanation as special instances of general cognitive structures. For example, one could argue that there are transformational systems in other areas of behavior; e.g., the systematic set of transformations involved in interpreting a three-dimensional object from a two-dimensional projection of the object.[14]

This paper has explained the way in which behavioral systems affect all linguistic structures. There are many instances in which the "grammatical" structure of adult linguistic intuitions about potential sentences is influenced by the mechanisms of language perception and learning. The isolation of such cases suggests

---

[14]For a clear example of a formal universal that reflects general cognitive structures, consider Chomsky's proposal that it is a formal linguistic universal that ". . . proper names . . . must designate objects meeting a condition of spatiotemporal contiguity, and that the same is true of other names designating objects" (1965, p. 29). Surely one could argue that the same principle applies to the visual apprehension of objects, independent of their name.

that there are universal constraints on the form of grammars which are not inherent to the statement of universal grammar itself, but rather to the way in which grammar is learned and the use to which it is put. One general example of this sort is a universal constraint on the amount of ambiguity of internal structural relations in sentences. Many languages represent the internal relations by the order of the words in the external structure and a few selected function words (as does English). Other languages allow relatively free ordering but have a rich system of inflections (such as Russian); some languages have both ways of representing the internal relations to some extent. However, languages that have neither and languages that have both systems to a great extent appear to be very infrequent (if they exist at all). The relevant constraint appears to be that a language may not have *too much ambiguity of the internal relations* in the external forms of sentences. This condition is difficult to state formally as part of the universal grammar because it cannot be phrased equivocally — that is, all languages have *some* internal-structure ambiguity, so a universal grammar cannot rule out such ambiguous derivations entirely. On the other hand, the frequency of such ambiguities must be restricted. Such a restriction can be interpreted as coming about as a natural function of the fact that a language in which every sentence had an indeterminate internal structure (except from context) would not be learned by children. However, such a restriction is not a part of universal grammar but a statement about the universals of language learning.

One might be tempted to conclude from such investigations as these that our problem is now to "subtract out" general cognitive structures from linguistic structures in order to isolate the "pure" linguistic universals, as depicted in (100).

(100)   (Apparent Linguistic Universals) − (Cognitive Universals)
         = Real Linguistic Universals

Indeed the arguments in this chapter might be taken as demonstrations that there is not as much innate structure to language as we had thought, if the "universal grammar" is stripped of those aspects that draw on other psychological systems (cf. McNeill, in press, for considerations of just this possibility).

However, such an enterprise fails to take into consideration the fact that the influences of language and cognition are mutual; one cannot consider one without the other. The isolation of cognitive mechanisms that are utilized in language does not explain them away as linguistic structures any more than the fact that we can name abstract concepts explains how we come to have such concepts. The discovery that certain aspects of language are based on mechanisms of perception, learning and cognition provides us with a new puzzle about how they become integrated in human communicative behavior.

BIBLIOGRAPHY

Berko, Jean. The child's learning of English morphology. *Word,* 1958, 150-177.

Beth, E. W., and Piaget, J. *Mathematical Epistomology and Psychology,* Dordrecht, Holland: Reidel, 1966.

Bever, T. G., Fodor, J. A., and Weksel, W. On the acquisition of syntax: A critique of "contextual generalizations." *Psychological Review,* 1965, 72, 467-482.

Bever, T. G., Fodor, J. A., and Weksel, W. Is linguistics empirical? *Psychological Review,* 1965, 72, 493-500.

Bever, T. G., Fodor, J. A., Garrett, M., and Mehler, J. Transformational operations and stimulus complexity. Unpublished, M.I.T., 1966.

Bever, T. G., and Mehler, J. The coding hypothesis and short-term memory. Unpublished, M.I.T., 1966.

Bever, T. G. In Harvard Center for Cognitive Studies Report, 1967.

Bever, T. G. Associations to stimulus-response theories of language. *Verbal Behavior and General Behavior Theory,* 1968, 478-494.

Bever, T. G. Specification and utilization of a transformational grammar (final report). Contract No. AF 19 (628)–5127 awarded to Warren J. Plath, International Business Machines Corporation, 1968.

Bever, T. G., Fodor, J. A., and Garrett, M. The psychological segmentation of speech, delivered at International Congress of Psychology, Moscow, 1966.

Bever, T. G., Lackner, J., and Kirk, R. The underlying structure sentence is the primary unit of speech perception. *Perception and Psychophysics.* Vol. 5, pp. 225-234, 1969.

Bever, T. G., Lackner, J., and Stolz, W. Transitional probability is not a general mechanism for the segmentation of speech. *Journal of Experimental Psychology,* Vol. 79, No. 3, 1969.

Bever, T. G., Mehler, J., and Epstein, J. What children do in spite of what they know, *Science* 1968, 162, 921-924.

Bever, T. G., Mehler, J., Valian, V., Epstein, J., and Morrissey, H. Linguistic capacity of young children (in preparation).

Bierwisch, M. Some semantic universals of German adjectivals. *Foundation of Language,* 1967, 3, 1-36.

Blumenthal, A. L., and Boakes, R. Prompted recall of sentences. *Journal of Verbal Learning and Verbal Behavior,* 1967, 6, 674-676.

Boyd, J., and Thorne, J. P. The deep grammar of modal verbs. *Journal of Linguistics* (in press).

Braine, M. D. S. The ontogeny of English phrase structure: the first phase. *Language,* 1963, 39, 1-13.

Brown, R. W. *Social Psychology.* New York: Free Press, 1965.

Brown, R. W. The development of Wh questions in child speech. *Journal of Verbal Learning and Verbal Behavior,* 1968, 7, 279-290.

Brown, R. W., and Bellugi, Ursula. Three processes in the child's acquisition of syntax. *Harvard Educational Review,* 1964, 34, 133-151.

Brown, R. W., and Bellugi, Ursula. Three processes in the child's acquisition of syntax, in Lenneberg, E. (Ed.), *New Directions in the Study of Language,* Cambridge, Mass.: M.I.T. Press, 1964.

Brown, R. W., and Fraser, C. The acquisition of syntax. In Bellugi, Ursula, and Brown, R. W. (Eds.). *The Acquisition of Language.* (Monographs of the Society for Research in Child Development, 92). Lafayette, Ind.: Purdue University, 1964, Vol. 29, No. 1, pp. 43-79.

Burt, C. The development of reasoning in school children. *Journal of Experimental Pedagogy,* 1919, 5, 68-77, 121-127.

Campbell, R. N., and Wales, R. J. On syntactic and semantic aspects of comparatives (forthcoming).

Charlip, Remy. *Where is everybody?* New York: Scholastic Book Services, 1957.

Chomsky, N. Transformational analysis. Unpublished doctoral dissertation, University of Pennsylvania, Philadelphia, 1955.

Chomsky, N. *Syntactic Structures.* (Janua Linguarum 4). The Hague: Mouton & Co., 1957.

Chomsky, N. Explanatory models in linguistics. In Nagel, E., Suppes, P., and Tarski, A. (Eds.). *Logic, Methodology, and Philosophy of Science.* Stanford: Stanford University Press, 1962.

Chomsky, N. Formal properties of grammars. In Luce, R. D., Bush, R. R., and Galanter, E. (Eds.). *Handbook of Mathematical Psychology,* Vol. II. New York: John Wiley & Sons, 1963.

Chomsky, N. *Current Issues in Linguistic Theory* (Janua Linguarum 38). The Hague: Mouton & Co., 1964.

Chomsky, N. *Aspects of the Theory of Syntax.* Cambridge, Mass.: M.I.T. Press, 1965.

Chomsky, N. *Cartesian Linguistics.* New York: Harper & Row, 1966.

Chomsky, N. The formal nature of language. In Lenneberg, E. H. *Biological Foundations of Language.* New York: John Wiley & Sons, 1967a.

Chomsky, N. The general properties of language. In Darley, F. L. (Ed.). *Brain Mechanisms Underlying Speech and Language.* (Proceedings of the Princeton Conference on Brain Mechanisms Underlying Speech and Language, 1965). New York: Grune and Stratton, 1967b.

Chomsky, N., and Halle, M. *The Sound Pattern of English.* New York: Harper & Row, 1968.

Chomsky, N., and Miller, G. A. Introduction to the formal analysis of natural languages. In Luce, R. D., Bush, R. R., and Galanter, E. (Eds.). *Handbook of Mathematical Psychology,* Vol. II: Ch. 11. New York: John Wiley & Sons, 1963.

Clark, H. H. Some structural properties of simple active and passive sentences. *Journal of Verbal Learning and Verbal Behavior,* 1965, 4, 365-370.

Clark, H. H. Linguistic processes in deductive reasoning. *Psychological Review,* in press, a.

Clark, H. H. The influence of language in solving three-term series problems. *Journal of Experimental Psychology,* in press, b.

Clark, H. H., and Card, S. K. The role of semantics in remembering comparative sentences. *Journal of Experimental Psychology,* in press.

Clark, H. H., and Clark, Eve V. Semantic distinctions and memory for complex sentences. *Quarterly Journal of Experimental Psychology,* 1968, **20,** 129-138.

Clark, H. H., and Stafford, R. A. Memory for semantic features in the verb. *Journal of Experimental Psychology,* in press.

Closs, E. Diachronic syntax and generative grammar. *Language,* 1965, **41,** 402-415.

Cromer, R. The development of temporal reference during the acquisition of language. Unpublished Ph.D. dissertation, Harvard University, 1968.

Doherty, P., and Schwartz, A. The syntax of the compared adjective in English. *Language,* 1967, **43,** 903-936.

Donaldson, M. *A Study of Children's Thinking.* London: Tavistock, 1963.

Donaldson, M. Prepared comment on paper by D. McNeill. In *Psycho-linguistics Papers,* J. Lyons and R. J. Wales (Eds.). Edinburgh: Edinburgh University Press, 1966.

Donaldson, M., and Balfour, G. Less is more: a study of language comprehension in children. *British Journal of Psychology* (in press).

Drach, K. The language of the parent: a pilot study. in *Language, Society and the Child,* Working Paper #13, Language Behavior Research Laboratory, University of California, Berkeley, 1968.

Duthie, J. A further study of overlap error in three-term series problems. In Donaldson, M. *A Study of Children's Thinking.* London: Tavistock, 1963.

Ervin, S. M. Imitation and Structural Change in Children's Language. In Lenneberg, E. H. (Ed.). *New Directions in the Study of Language.* Cambridge, Mass.: M.I.T. Press, 1964.

Farnham-Diggory, S., and Bermon, M. Verbal compensation, cognitive synthesis, and conservation. *Merrill-Palmer Quarterly of Behavior and Development,* 1968, **14,** 215-227.

Fillmore, C. J. The Case for case. In Bach, E., and Harms, R. T. (Eds.). *Universals in Linguistic Theory.* New York: Holt, Rinehart and Winston, 1968.

Firbas, J. Thoughts on the communicative function of the verb in English, German, and Czech. *Brno Studies in English,* 1959, **1,** 39-68.

Firbas, J. From comparative word-order studies, *Brno Studies in English,* 1964, **4,** 111-126.

Fodor, J., and Bever, T. The psychological reality of linguistic segments, *Journal of Verbal Learning and Verbal Behavior,* 1965, **4** (5), 414-421.

Fodor, J. A., and Garrett, M. Some reflections on competence and performance. In J. Lyons and R. J. Wales (Eds.). *Psycholinguistic Papers: The Proceedings of the 1966 Edinburgh Conference,* 1966, Edinburgh: Edinburgh University Press.

Fodor, J. A., and Garrett, M. Some syntactic determinants of sentential complexity. *Perception and Psychophysics,* 1967, **2,** 289-296.

Fodor, J., and Garrett, M. Some syntactic determinants of sentential complexity. *Perception and Psychophysics,* 1968, **4,** 304-306.

Fodor, J. A., Garrett, M., and Bever, T. G. Some syntactic determinants of complexity II; verb structure. *Perception and Psychophysics* 3, June 1968.

356 The Cognitive Basis For Linguistic Structures

Fodor, J. A., Jenkins, J., and Saporta, S. Some tests on implications from transformational grammar. Unpublished, Center for Advanced Study, Palo Alto, California.

Foss, D. J., Bever, T. G., and Silver, M. The comprehension and verification of ambiguous sentences. *Perception and Psychophysics,* 1968, 4, 304-306.

Fraser, C., Bellugi, Ursula, and Brown, R. W. Control of grammar in imitation, comprehension, and production. *Journal of Verbal Learning and Verbal Behavior,* 1963, 2, 121-135.

Garrett, M., Bever, T. G., and Fodor, J. A. The active use of grammar in speech perception. *Perception and Psychophysics,* 1966, 1, 30-2.

Gough, P. B. The verification of sentences. The effects of delay of evidence and sentence length. *Journal of Verbal Learning and Verbal Behavior,* 1966, 5, 492-496.

Greenberg, J. H. Some universals of grammar with particular reference to the order of meaningful elements. In Greenberg, J. H. (Ed.). *Universals of Language,* Cambridge, Mass.: M.I.T. Press, 1961.

Greenberg, J. H. *Language Universals.* The Hague: Mouton, 1966.

Grice, H. P. Utterer's meaning, sentence-meaning, and word-meaning. *Foundations of Language,* 1968, 4, 225-242.

Grunig, B. Les théories transformationnelles. *La Linguistique,* 1965, 2, 1-24; 1966, 1, 31-101.

Halle, M. Phonology in generative grammar. *Word,* 1962, 18, 54-72; reprinted in Fodor, J. A. and Katz, J. J. (Eds.). *The Structure of Language: Readings in the Philosophy of Language.* Englewood Cliffs, New Jersey: Prentice-Hall, 1964.

Halle, M., and Stevens, K. N. *Speech recognition: a model and a program for research,* reprinted in Katz, J. and Fodor, J., *The Structure of Language,* Prentice-Hall, New Jersey, 1964.

Halliday, M. A. K. Notes on transitivity and theme in English, part 2. *Journal of Linguistics,* 1967, 3, 199-244.

Harris, Z. S. *Methods in Structural Linguistics.* Chicago: University of Chicago, 1951.

Harris, Z. S. Distributional structure. *Word,* 1954, 10, 146-162.

Harris, Z. S. From phoneme to morpheme. *Language,* 1955, 31, 190-222.

Harris, Z. S. Co-occurrence and transformation in linguistic structure. *Language,* 1957, 33, 283-340.

Harris, Z. S. Co-occurrence and transformation in linguistic structure, reprinted in Fodor, J. and Katz, J. (Eds.), *The Structure of Language,* New Jersey: Prentice-Hall, 1964.

Harris, Z. S. Transformational Theory, *Language,* 1965, 41, 363-401.

Harris, Z. S. *Mathematical Structures of Language.* (Interscience Tracts in Pure and Applied, Mathematics, 21). New York: John Wiley & Sons, 1968.

Harwood, F. W. Quantitative study of the speech of Australian children. *Language and Speech,* 1959, 2, 236-271.

Hiż, H. Congrammaticality, batteries of transformation, and grammatical categories. In Jakobson, R. (Ed.). *Proceedings of Symposia in Applied Mathematics,* XII. Providence: American Mathematical Society, 1961.

Hiž, H. The role of paraphrase in grammar. In C. I. J. M. Stuart (Ed.). *Monograph Series on Languages and Linguistics 17*. Washington: Georgetown University, 1964.

Hockett, C. F. Age-grading and linguistic continuity. *Language,* 1950, 26, 449-457.

Huddleston, R. D. More on the English comparative. *Journal of Linguistics,* 1967, 3, 91-102.

Jakobson, R. Implications of language Universals for linguistics. In Greenberg, J. H. (Ed.). *Universals of Language,* Cambridge, Mass.: M.I.T. 1961.

Jakobson, R., Fant, G., and Halle, M. *Preliminaries to Speech Analysis.* Cambridge, Mass.: M.I.T. Press, 1963.

Jesperson, O. *The Philosophy of Grammar.* London: Allen and Unwin, 1924.

Jesperson, O. *Essentials of English Grammar.* University, Ala.: University of Alabama, 1966. (Original edition, 1933).

Johnson, N. F. The psychological reality of phrase-structure rules. *Journal of Verbal Learning and Verbal Behavior,* 1965, 4, 469-475.

Johnson-Laird, P. N. The choice of the passive voice in a communicative task. *British Journal of Psychology,* 1968, 59, 7-15.

Katz, J. J. Mentalism in linguistics. *Language,* 1964, 40, 124-137.

Katz, J. J., and Fodor, J. A. The structure of a semantic theory. In Fodor, J. A. and Katz, J. J. (Eds.). *The Structure of Language.* Englewood Cliffs, N. J.: Prentice-Hall, 1964.

Katz, J. J., and Postal, P. M. *An Integrated Theory of Linguistic Descriptions.* (Research Monograph 26). Cambridge, Mass.: M.I.T. Press, 1964.

Kiparsky, P., and Kiparsky, C. Fact. To appear in Jakobovits and Steinberg (Eds.), *Semantics.* New York: Holt, Rinehart and Winston (1969).

Klima, E. S. Negation in English. In Fodor, J. A. and Katz, J. J. (Eds.). *The Structure of Language.* Englewood Cliffs, N.J.: Prentice-Hall, 1964.

Kobashigawa, B. Repetitions in a mother's speech to her child. *Language, Society and the Child,* Working Paper # 13, Language Behavior Research Laboratory, University of California, Berkeley, 1968.

Kotarbinska, J. On ostensive definitions. *Philosophy of Science,* 1960, 27, 1-22.

Lakoff, G. On the nature of syntactic irregularity (doctoral dissertation, Indiana University). *Mathematical Linguistics and Automatic Translation Report* NSF-16. Cambridge, Mass.: The Computation Laboratory of Harvard University, 1965.

Lakoff, G. Instrumental adverbs and the concept of deep structure. *Foundations of Language,* 1968, 4, 4-29.

Lakoff, G., and Ross, J. R. A criterion for verb phrase constituency. In Kuno, S. (Ed.). *Mathematical Linguistics and Automatic Translation Report* NSF-17. Cambridge, Mass.: The Computation Laboratory of Harvard University, 1966.

Langacker, R. The chain of command. In Reibel and Schone, *Studies in the Structure of English.* Englewood Cliffs, N.J.: Prentice-Hall, in press.

Lees, R. B. Grammatical analysis of the English comparative construction. *Word,* 1961, 17, 171-185.

Lenneberg, E. H. Cognition in ethnolinguistics. *Language,* 1953, 29, 463-471.

Lenneberg, E. H. *Biological Foundations of Language.* New York: John Wiley & Sons, 1967.

Lieberman, P. On the acoustic basis of the perception of intonation by linguists. *Word,* 1965, 21, 40-55.

Lieberman, P. *Intonation, Perception, and Language.* Cambridge, Mass.: M.I.T. Press, 1967.

Lyons, J. *Structural Semantics.* Oxford: Blackwell, 1963 (Publications of the Philological Society, XX).

Lyons, J. *Introduction to Theoretical Linguistics.* Cambridge, Mass.: Cambridge University Press, 1968.

Lyons, J., and Wales, R. J. (Eds.). *Psycholinguistics Papers.* Edinburgh: Edinburgh University Press, 1966.

Machmahon, L. E. *Grammatical Analysis as Part of Understanding a Sentence.* Cambridge, Mass.: Harvard University doctoral dissertation, 1963.

Malkiel, Y. Diachronic hypercharacterization in romance. *Archivum Linguisticum,* 1957, 9, 79-113; 1958, 10, 1-30.

Martin, J. E. A study of the determinants of preferred adjective order in English. Unpublished doctoral dissertation, University of Illinois, 1968.

Matthews, G. H. Analysis by synthesis of natural languages. *Proceedings of the International Congress on Machine Translation and Applied Language Analysis.* London: H.M.S.O., 1962.

McCarthy, D. Language Development in Children, in L. Carmichael (Ed.), *Manual of Child Psychology.* New York: John Wiley and Sons, 1954, pp. 492-630.

MacCawley, J. The role of semantics in a grammar. In Bach, E., and Harms, R., *Universals in Linguistic Theory.* New York: Holt, Rinehart and Winston, pp. 125-170, 1969.

MacCawley, J. The Annotated Respective. Unpublished paper, 1968.

MacCawley, J. D. Concerning the base component of a transformational grammar. *Foundations of Language,* 1968, 4, 243-269.

McKay, D. G. To end ambiguous sentences. *Perception and Psychophysics,* 1966, 1, 426-436.

McLay, H., and Osgood, C. E. Hesitation phenomena in spontaneous English speech. *Word,* 1959, 1, 19-44.

McNeill, D. The creation of language, in Lenneberg, E. (Ed.), *New Directions in the Study of Language,* Cambridge, Mass.: M.I.T. Press, 1964.

McNeill, D. Developmental psycholinguistics. In Smith, F. and Miller, G. A. (Eds.). *The Genesis of Language.* Cambridge, Mass.: M.I.T. Press, 1966.

McNeill, D. The development of language. In Mussen, P. A. (Ed.), *Carmichael's Manual of Child Psychology* (in press).

Mehler, J. Some effects of grammatical transformations on the recall of English sentences. *Journal of Verbal Learning and Verbal Behavior,* 1963, 2, 346-351.

Mehler, J., and Bever, T. G. Quantification, conservation and nativism (reply). *Science,* 1968, 162, 979-981.

Mehler, J., and Bever, T. G. Sentences can be memorized in terms of their underlying structures. In Bever, T. G. and Weksel W. (Eds.), *The Structure and Psychology of Language.* Holt, Rinehart and Winston (in press).

Mehler, J., and Bever, T. G. The study of competence in cognitive psychology. International Journal of Psychology, 1968, 3, 4, 273-280.

Mehler, J., and Carey, P. The Interaction of veracity and syntax in the processing of sentences. *Perception and Psychophysics,* 1968, 3, 109-111.

Miller, G. A. The magical number seven, plus or minus two, *Psychological Review,* 1956, 63, 81-97.

Miller, G. A. Some psychological studies of grammar. *American Psychologist,* 1962, 17, 748-762.

Miller, G. A., and Chomsky, N. Finitary models of language users. In Luce, R. D., Bush, R. R., and Galanter, E. (Eds.). *Handbook of Mathematical Psychology,* Vol. II. New York: John Wiley & Sons, 1963.

Miller, G. A., and Isard, S. Some perceptual consequences of linguistic rules. *Journal of Verbal Learning and Verbal Behavior,* 1963, 2, 217-228.

Miller, G. A., and McKean, K. A chronometric study of some relations between sentences. *Quarterly Journal of Experimental Psychology,* 1964, 16, 297-308.

Miller, G. A., and McNeill, David. *Handbook of Sociology.* Chapter 26, "Psycholinguistics," 1969.

Miller, G. A., McKean, K., and Slobin, D. The exploration of transformations by sentence matching. In Miller, G. A. Some psychological studies of grammar. *American Psychologist,* 1962, 17, 748-762.

Miller, G. A., and Selfridge, J. Verbal context and the recall of meaningful material. *American Journal of Psychology,* 1951, 63, 176-185.

Mossé, F. *A Handbook of Middle English,* tr. J. A. Walker. Baltimore: The Johns Hopkins Press, 1952.

Neisser, J. *Cognitive Psychology.* New York: Appleton-Century-Crofts, 1957.

Osgood, C. E. Effects of motivational states upon decoding and encoding. In Osgood, C. E. and Sebeok, T. A. (Eds.). *Psycholinguistics,* Bloomington: Indiana University, 1954, 2nd edition 1965.

Osgood, C. E., and Sebeok, T. A. *Psycholinguistics: A Survey of Theory and Research Problems.* Bloomington, Ind.: Indiana University Press, 1965, pp. 55-56.

Peirce, C. S. *Collected Papers, Vol. III.* Hartshorne, C. and Weiss, P. (Eds.). Cambridge, Mass.: Harvard University Press, 1933.

Penelhum, T. Personal identity. In *Encyclopedia of Philosophy,* Vol. 6. Paul Edwards (Ed.). New York: MacMillan & Free Press, 1967.

Pfuderer, Carol. Some suggestions for a syntactic characterization of babytalk style. *Language, Society and the Child,* Working Paper #13, Language Behavior Research Laboratory, University of California, Berkeley, 1968.

Phillips, J., and Miller, G. A. Harvard Center for Cognitive Studies Report, 1966.

Piaget, J. Une forme verbale de la comparaison chez l'enfant. *Archives de Psychologie,* 1921, 18, 141-172.

Piaget, J. *Judgment and Reasoning in the Child.* London: Kegan Paul, 1928.

Postal, P. M. On So-Called "Pronouns" in English. In Dinneen, F. P. (Ed.). *Monograph Series on Languages and Linguistics 19.* Washington: Georgetown University, 1966*a.*

Postal, P. M. A note on "understood transitively." *International Journal of American Linguistics,* 1966*b,* **32,** 90-93.

Quine, W. van O. *From a Logical Point of View.* Cambridge, Mass.: Harvard University Press, 1953.

Reichenbach, H. *Elements of Symbolic Logic.* New York: Free Press, 1947.

Reitman, W. R. *Cognition and Thought: An Information Processing Approach.* New York: Wiley, 1965.

Ross, J. R. Relativization in extraposed clauses. In Kuno, S. (Ed.). *Mathematical Linguistics and Automatic Translation Report* NSF-17. Cambridge: The Computation Laboratory of Harvard University, 1966.

Ross, J. R. Constraints on variables in syntax. Doctoral dissertation (dittoed), M.I.T., Cambridge, 1967.

Ross, J. R. *Universal constraints on variables.* Unpublished dissertation, M.I.T., 1968.

Ross, J. R. *Auxiliaries as Main Verbs.* Cambridge, Mass.: M.I.T., 1967*a* (mimeographed preliminary version).

Ross, J. R. On the cyclic nature of English pronominalization, in *To Honor Roman Jakobson.* The Hague: Mouton & Co., 1967*b.*

Sapir, E. *Language.* New York: Harcourt, Brace & World, 1921.

Sapir, E. Grading: a study in semantics. *Philosophy of Science,* 1944, **11,** 93-116.

Sapir, E. The psychological reality of phonemes. In Mandelbaum, D. (Ed.). *Selected Writings of Edward Sapir,* California: University of California Press, 1949.

Savin, H., and Perchonock, Ellen. Grammatical structure and the immediate recall of English sentences. *Journal of Verbal Learning and Verbal Behavior,* 1965, **4,** 348-353.

Schlesinger, I. "The Influence of Sentence Structure on the Reading Process," U.S. Office of Naval Research Tech. Rept. 24, 1966.

Shipley, E. F., Smith, C. S., and Gleitman, L. R. *A Study in the Acquisition of Language: Free Responses to Commands.* (Technical Report VIII). Philadelphia: Eastern Pennsylvania Psychiatric Institute, n.d. [1967].

Siegel, S. *Nonparametric Statistics for the Behavioral Sciences.* New York: McGraw-Hill, 1956.

Sinclair-de-Zwart, H. *Acquisition du langage et developpement de la pensée.* Paris: Dunod, 1967.

Skinner, B. F. *Science and Human Behavior.* New York: Macmillan, 1953.

Slobin, D. I. Grammatical transformations in childhood and adulthood. Unpublished doctoral dissertation, Harvard University, 1963.

Slobin, D. I. Grammatical transformations and sentence comprehension in child and adulthood. *Journal of Verbal Learning and Verbal Behavior,* 1966, **5,** 219-227.

Slobin, D. I. Recall of full and truncated passive sentences in connected discourse, 1967.

Slobin, D. I. Questions of language development in cross-cultural perspective. Forthcoming in *Proceedings of the Conference on Language Learning in Cross-cultural Perspective,* Michigan State University, 1968.

Slobin, D. I. Recall of full and truncated passive sentences in connected discourse. *Journal of Verbal Learning and Verbal Behavior,* 1968, 7, 876-881.

Slobin, D. I., and Welsh, C. *Elicited imitation as a research tool in developmental psycholinguistics.* Language Behavior Research Laboratory, Working Paper # 10, University of California, Berkeley, 1968.

Smith, C. S. A class of complex modifiers. *Language,* 1961, 37, 342-365.

Smith, C. S. A class of complex modifiers in English. *Language,* 1961, 41, 37-58.

Smith, C. S. A study of the syntactic knowledge of young children, in Bever, T. and Weksel, W. (Eds.), *Studies in Psycholinguistics* (in press), 1969.

Stene, A. The Animate gender in modern colloquial English. *Norsk Tidsskrift for Sprogvidenskap,* 1934, 7, 350-355.

Sutherland, N. S. Discussion of Fodor, J. and Garrett, M. Some reflections on competence and performance. In Lyons, J. and Wales, R. J. (Eds.), *Psycholinguistics Papers.* Edinburgh: Edinburgh University Press, 1966.

Svartvik, J. *On Voice in the English Verb.* The Hague: Mouton and Co., 1966.

Tarski, A. *Introduction to Logic and to the Methodology of the Deductive Sciences.* New York: Oxford University Press, 1965.

Thorne, J. On hearing sentences, in Lyons, J. (Ed.), *Psycholinguistics Papers,* Edinburgh: University of Edinburgh Press, 1966.

Turner, E. A., and Rommetveit, R. The Acquisition of sentence voice and reversibility. *Child Development,* 1967a, 38, 649-660.

Turner, E. A., and Rommetveit, R. Experimental manipulation of the production of active and passive voice in children. *Language and Speech,* 1967b, 10, 169-180.

Turner, E. A., and Rommetveit, R. Focus of attention in recall of active and passive sentences. *Journal of Verbal Learning and Verbal Behavior,* 1968, 7, 543-548.

Valdman, A. Review of Guiraud, P. *Le francais populaire. Language,* 1968, 44, 123-127.

Vendler, Z. *Adjectives and Nominalizations.* The Hague: Mouton, 1968.

Vendler, Z. The transformational grammar of English adjectives. Transformations and discourse analysis papers, University of Pennsylvania, 1963.

Vlastos, G. Degrees of reality in Plato. In *New Essays on Plato and Aristotle.* Renford Bambrough (Ed.). London: Routledge and Kegan-Paul, 1965.

Vygotsky, L. *Thought and Language.* Translated by Hanfmann, E. and Vakar, G., Massachusetts: M.I.T. Press, 1962.

Wales, R. J., and Campbell, R. N. The ontogenesis of comparison. Forthcoming.

Watt, W. C. English locative sentences. Paper given at the Forty-second Annual Meeting, Linguistic Society of America, 1967. Abstract in *Handbook* of the Meeting, p. 62.

Watt, W. C. English Reduplication. *Journal of English Linguistics,* 1968a, 2, 96-129.

Watt, W. C. Habitability. *American Documentation,* 1968*b*, 19, 338-351.

Watt, W. C. On two hypotheses concerning psycholinguistics. In this volume, 1969.

Watt, W. C. Linguistic recoverability. Forthcoming.

Weir, R. H. *Language in the crib.* The Hague: Mouton & Co., 1962.

Weir, R. H. Some questions on the child's learning of phonology. In Smith, F. and Miller, G. A. (Eds.). *The Genesis of Language,* Cambridge: M.I.T. Press, 1966.

Whorf, B. L. Some verbal categories of Hopi. In Carroll, J. B. (Ed.). *Language thought and reality: Selected writings of Benjamin Lee Whorf.* Cambridge, Mass.: M.I.T. Press, 1956.

Yugvie, V.

Zipf, G. K. *Human Behavior and the Principle of Least Effort.* Cambridge, Mass.: Addison-Wesley, 1949.

Author Index

Bach, E., *214, 264, 353, 356*
Balfour, G., 242, 251, *264, 353*
Bambrough, R., *359*
Bellugi, U., *106, 132*, 180, 202, 206, *214–215*, 234, 248, 250, *264, 352, 354*
Berko, J., 78, *106, 351*
Bermon, M., 272, *276, 353*
Beth, E.W., 262, *264, 351*
Bever, T.G., 7, *9*, 109–120, *132–133*, 165, *215*, 277ff, *351–357, 359*
Bierwisch, M., 252, *264*, 268, *276, 351*
Blumenthal, A.L., 293, *351*
Boakes, R., *351*
Boyd, J., 263, *264, 351*
Braine, M.D.S., 78, *106, 351*
Brown, R., 5, *9*, 10ff, 54–56, 61, 71, 78, 80, 83, *106, 132*, 180, 202, 206–207, *214–215*, 234, 248, 250, *264*, 284, 348–349, *351–352, 354*
Burt, C., 272, *276, 352*
Bush, R.R., *214, 216, 352, 357*

Campbell, R.N., 240, 255–256, *264–265*, 352
Card, S.K., 267, *276, 353*
Carey, P., 294, 297, *357*
Carmichael, L., *356*
Carroll, J.B., *360*
Charlip, R., *106, 352*
Chomsky, N., 3, 8, *9*, 13, 20, *53*, 60–62, 65–66, *76*, 78, *106*, 110, *132*, 135–137, 139–143, 153, 156–158, 160, 162, 167, 172, 177, 179, 187, 190, 195–196, 198–199, 202, 207, 211, *214, 216*, 227, *232*, 236, *264*, 269, *276*, 332, 349, *352, 357*

Clark, E.V., 65, *76*, 175, *214*, 292, 294, *353*
Clark, H.H., 1, 65, 73, *76*, 142, 175, *214*, 219ff, 267ff, *276*, 292, 294, *352, 353*
Closs, E., 70, *76, 353*
Cromer, R., 92, *106, 353*

Darley, F.L., *214*
Dinneen, F.P., *216, 358*
Doherty, P., 269, *276, 353*
Donaldson, M., 1, 233ff, *264*, 267, 271, *276, 353*
Drach, K., *106, 353*
Duthie, J., *276, 353*

Edwards, P., *264*
Epstein, J., *280, 351*
Ervin, S.M., *353*
Ervin-Tripp, S., 78ff, 115, *132*, 211, *214*

Fant, G., 227, *232, 355*
Farnham-Diggory, S., 272, *276, 353*
Fillmore, C.J., 141, *214*, 262, *264, 353*
Firbas, J., 73, *76, 214, 353*
Fodor, J.A., 4–5, 7–8, *9*, 10–11, *53*, 57, 66, *76*, 109–110, *132*, 136, 142–143, 145, 147–150, 154–155, 166–168, 189, *214–215*, 284, 287–288, 298–300, 331, 342–343, 351, *353–355, 359*
Foss, D.J., 165, *215*
Fraser, C., *106, 132*, 180, 202, *214, 352, 354*

Galanter, E., *214, 216, 352, 357*

363

364

Normalization, 121–124
Notional, 126, 129
Numerosity, 282, 300, 303

Old English, 69
Order of, acquisition, 32
  emergence, 13, 36, 38–40, 51
Output sentence, 2

p-Inclusion, 190–191, 199, 201
  maximal, 192
  strong, 193
Parroting, 192–193, 197, 199
Perceptual, grouping, 324
  segmentation, 319
Performance, 13, 108, 116, 209,
  262–263, 341–343
  ambiguity, 148
  mechanism, 5, 137–139
Phoneme, 222
  distribution of, 227
Phrase marker, 2, 5
Phrase structure, grammars, 5, 230
  rules, 3, 13
Pragmatic interpretation, 79
Prepassive passivization, 181
Primary linguistic, data, 111
  input, 111, 117
Pronominalization, 315–317, 319
Proximity hypothesis, 66
Pseudotruncates, 185
Punishment, 45
Puzzle-solving, 151–152

Quasi-holophrase, 191–193, 197, 199
Questions, "How," 90–91, 94–95
  locative, 96
  tag, 14–15, 17, 24–29, 32, 34,
  38–39, 41–42, 49, 51, 58–59
  temporal, 92
  truncated, 13–16
  "What," 91, 93, 96, 102
  "When," 90, 94–95

"Where," 95
"Who," 89
"Why," 90–91, 94, 96
"Will," 101

Recognition theories, 227
Recognizing Questions, 80
Recoverability, 158–159
Reference, 220–221
  mechanisms, 220
Reinforcements, 221
  negative, 45
  positive, 44
Relational logic, 233
Relational Terms, 233ff, 267
  different, 236–238, 240, 242,
  247–250, 254, 262
  less, 236, 242–248, 250–251, 256
  more, 236, 242–248, 250–251,
  256, 262
  same, 236–238, 240, 242, 247–
  250, 254, 262
Relative numerosity, 280
Repetitions, 115, 118, 125, 128
Replaying the stimulus, 115
Response perseveration, 95
Reversible passives, 151
Rewrite rules, 2

Science of Linguistics, 344
Segmentation, 219, 224–226, 229–
  231, 286–287, 289, 291, 296,
  320–326
  markers, 221–222, 227
Semantic information, 127, 129
Semantic interpretation, 79, 103
  of questions, 81
Sentence length, 10, 36, 38
Sequiturs, 42–43
Simplex sentences, 61
Simplicity/frequency correlation, 74
Sound spectrographs, 219
Spontaneous speech, 113, 122, 125

369